In recent years, the effects of economic op[...] have fuelled growing dissatisfaction with [...] led to new forms of political populism [...] political resentment created by globaliza[tion ....... in politi]cs was evident in the decision by UK voters to leave the EU in June 2016, the November 2016 election of Donald Trump to the presidency of the United States, as well as the rise of populist movements on left and right throughout much of Europe. To many voters, the economy appears to be broken. Conventional politics is failing. Parties of the left and centre-left have struggled to forge a convincing response to this new phase of globalization in the aftermath of the 2008 crisis. This book examines the challenges that the new era of globalization poses for progressive parties and movements across the world. It brings together leading thinkers and experts including Andrew Gamble, Jeffry Frieden and Vivien Schmidt to debate the structural causes and political consequences of this new wave of globalization.

**In the series:**

*After the Third Way: The Future of Social Democracy in Europe*
Edited by Olaf Cramme and Patrick Diamond
ISBN: 978 1 84885 992 0 (HB); 978 1 84885 993 7 (PB)

*Europe's Immigration Challenge: Reconciling Work, Welfare and Mobility*
Edited by Elena Jurado and Grete Brochmann
ISBN: 978 1 78076 225 8 (HB); 978 1 78076 226 5 (PB)

*Left Without a Future? Social Justice in Anxious Times*
Anthony Painter
ISBN: 978 1 78076 660 7 (HB); 978 1 78076 661 4 (PB)

*Progressive Politics after the Crash: Governing from the Left*
Edited by Olaf Cramme, Patrick Diamond and Michael McTernan
ISBN: 978 1 78076 763 5 (HB); 978 1 78076 764 2 (PB)

*Governing Britain: Power, Politics and the Prime Minister*
Patrick Diamond
ISBN: 978 1 78076 581 5 (HB); 978 1 78076 582 2 (PB)

*The Europe Dilemma: Britain and the Drama of EU Integration*
Roger Liddle
ISBN: 978 1 78076 222 7 (HB); 978 1 78076 223 4 (PB)

*The Predistribution Agenda: Tackling Inequality and Supporting Sustainable Growth*
Edited by Claudia Chwalisz and Patrick Diamond
ISBN: 978 1 78453 440 0 (HB); 978 1 78453 441 7 (PB)

*The Crisis of Globalization: Democracy, Capitalism and Inequality in the Twenty-First Century*
Edited by Patrick Diamond
ISBN: 978 1 78831 515 9 (HB); 978 1 78831 516 6 (PB)

Edited by Patrick Diamond

# the crisis of globalization
## Democracy, Capitalism and Inequality in the Twenty-First Century

I.B.TAURIS
LONDON • NEW YORK • OXFORD • NEW DELHI • SYDNEY

I.B. TAURIS
Bloomsbury Publishing Plc
50 Bedford Square, London, WC1B 3DP, UK
1385 Broadway, New York, NY 10018, USA

BLOOMSBURY, I.B. TAURIS and the I.B. Tauris logo are trademarks of Bloomsbury Publishing Plc

First published in Great Britain 2019
Reprinted 2019

Copyright Editorial Selection © 2019 Policy Network

Copyright Individual Chapters © 2019 Lorenza Antonucci, Patrick Diamond, Jeffry Frieden, Andrew Gamble, Jane Gingrich, Anton Hemerijck, Robin Huguenot-Noel, Roger Liddle, Silvia Merler, Manuel de la Rocha, Patricia Rodi, Vivien A. Schmidt, Dimitris Tsarouhas, Loukas Tsoukalis, Frank Vandenbroucke

Patrick Diamon has asserted his right under the Copyright, Designs and Patents Act, 1988, to be identified as Editor of this work.

All rights reserved. No part of this publication may be reproduced or transmitted in any form or by any means, electronic or mechanical, including photocopying, recording, or any information storage or retrieval system, without prior permission in writing from the publishers.

Bloomsbury Publishing Plc does not have any control over, or responsibility for, any third-party websites referred to or in this book. All internet addresses given in this book were correct at the time of going to press. The author and publisher regret any inconvenience caused if addresses have changed or sites have ceased to exist, but can accept no responsibility for any such changes.

A catalogue record for this book is available from the British Library.

A catalog record for this book is available from the Library of Congress.

ISBN: HB: 978-1-7883-1515-9
PB: 978-1-7883-1516-6
ePDF: 978-1-7883-1629-3
eBook: 978-1-7883-1628-6

Typeset by Riverside Publishing Solutions, Salisbury SP4 6NQ
Printed and bound in Great Britain

To find out more about our authors and books visit www.bloomsbury.com and sign up for our newsletters.

# Contents

*Contributors* — vii
*List of Figures* — ix
*Preface* — x

**Introduction**
  The Great Globalization Disruption: Democracy, Capitalism and Inequality in the Industrialized World
  **Patrick Diamond** — 1

**Part I  Taking Stock – the Rise of the New Populism**

1. Globalization and the New Populism
   **Andrew Gamble** — 27

2. The Backlash Against Globalization and the Future of the International Economic Order
   **Jeffry Frieden** — 43

3. Populist Political Communication Going Mainstream? The Influence of Populist Parties on Centre-Left Parties in Western Europe
   **Patricia Rodi** — 53

4. Europeans and Globalization: Does the EU Square the Circle?
   **Silvia Merler** — 73

5. How can Social Democratic Parties in Government Deal with the Consequences of Globalization?
   **Manuel de la Rocha** — 91

**Part II  Brexit, Populism and the Future of the European Union**

6. Brexit and Globalization: Collateral Damage or an Accident Waiting to Happen?
   **Loukas Tsoukalis** — 109

7. The EU in Crises: Brexit, Populism and the Future of the Union
   **Dimitris Tsarouhas** — 127

| 8 | Brexit: A Consequence of Globalization or a Case of British Exceptionalism?<br>**Roger Liddle** | 145 |

**Part III What is to be Done? Domestic and International Policies to Deal with Globalization**

| 9 | Where Might the Next Generation of Progressive Ideas and Programmes Come From? Contemporary Discontents, Future Possibilities for Europe<br>**Vivien A. Schmidt** | 167 |
| 10 | Globalization as a Losing Game? Reforming Social Policies to Address the Malaise of Globalization's Losers<br>**Lorenza Antonucci** | 187 |
| 11 | Social Investment Beyond Lip-Service<br>**Anton Hemerijck and Robin Huguenot-Noel** | 207 |
| 12 | Addressing Global Inequality: Is the EU Part of the Equation?<br>**Frank Vandenbroucke** | 235 |
| 13 | Social Democracy in an Era of Automation and Globalization<br>**Jane Gingrich** | 259 |

**Postscript**   277
  **Patrick Diamond**

**Index**   282

# Contributors

**Lorenza Antonucci** is currently Research Fellow in the Department of Social Policy, University of Birmingham.

**Patrick Diamond** is Senior Lecturer in Public Policy, Queen Mary, University of London and Chair of Policy Network.

**Jeffry Frieden** is Professor of Government at Harvard University.

**Andrew Gamble** is Emeritus Professor of Politics at the University of Cambridge.

**Jane Gingrich** is Associate Professor of Comparative Political Economy at the University of Oxford.

**Anton Hemerijck** is Professor of Political Science, European University Institute, Florence and Centennial Professor of Social Policy, London School of Economics and Political Science.

**Robin Huguenot-Noel** is a policy analyst at the European Policy Centre.

**Roger Liddle** is a Labour member of the House of the Lords.

**Silvia Merler** is Affiliate Fellow at the Bruegel thinktank in Brussels.

**Manuel de la Rocha** is an Economist and former Economic Adviser to the Spanish Socialist Party.

**Patricia Rodi** is a postgraduate researcher at Loughborough University.

**Vivien A. Schmidt** is the Jean Monnet Chair of European Integration and Professor of International Relations at the Pardee School of Global Studies at Boston University.

**Dimitris Tsarouhas** is Professor of Political Science in the Department of International Relations at Bilkent University, Turkey.

**Loukas Tsoukalis** is Jean Monnet Professor of European Organization, University of Athens and President, Hellenic Foundation for European and Foreign Policy (ELIAMEP).

**Frank Vandenbroucke** is Professor at the University of Amsterdam.

# List of Figures

| | | |
|---|---|---|
| **Figure 4.1** | European's perception of globalization | 74 |
| **Figure 4.2** | Demographics | 76 |
| **Figure 4.3** | Education | 77 |
| **Figure 4.4** | Education | 78 |
| **Figure 4.5a** | EFSI statistics | 83 |
| **Figure 4.5b** | EFSI statistics | 84 |
| **Figure 11.1** | Social protection spending vs. competitiveness | 212 |
| **Figure 11.2** | Unemployment 2017 | 212 |
| **Figure 11.3** | Participation rate | 213 |
| **Figure 11.4** | Female participation rate | 214 |
| **Figure 11.5** | Elderly participation rate | 215 |
| **Figure 11.6** | ALMP spending per unemployed | 216 |
| **Figure 11.7** | Employment rate by educational level | 216 |
| **Figure 11.8** | At-risk-of-poverty before and after taxes | 217 |
| **Figure 11.9** | Child income poverty rate | 219 |
| **Figure 11.10** | Public debt to GDP ratio 2017 | 219 |
| **Figure 11.11** | Social investment life-course multiplier effect | 220 |
| **Figure 13.1** | Public support for redistribution in five EU countries | 260 |
| **Figure 13.2** | EU relative employment loss in manufacturing 1991–2014 | 262 |
| **Figure 13.3** | GVA per capita across Europe's regions in 2014 | 263 |
| **Figure 13.4** | Income support programmes in major industrialized countries | 268 |

# List of Tables

| | | |
|---|---|---|
| **Table 4.1** | Allocation of European Fund for Strategic Investments | 81 |
| **Table 4.2** | Youth Guarantee across EU countries | 85 |

# Preface

This volume originates in the collaboration between Policy Network, the Foundation for European Progressive Studies (FEPS) and the Renner Institute. As international progressive thinktanks based in London, Brussels and Vienna, we have drawn together our respective networks to engage academics, policy experts and political practitioners from across Europe and the United States. We would like to extend thanks to all of the participants in the two-day Policy Network symposium on globalization and inequality held at St Catherine's College, Oxford in July 2017, in particular Dr Lorenza Antonucci, Professor Tim Bale, Professor Andrew Gamble, Professor Jeffry Frieden, Dr Jane Gingrich, Professor Anton Hemerijck, Silvia Merler, Manuel de la Rocha, Professor Vivien Schmidt, Professor Helen Thompson, Professor Dimitris Tsarouhas, Professor Loukas Tsoukalis, Professor Frank Vandenbroucke and Professor Helen Wallace.

We are very grateful to Josh Newlove and the Policy Network team for all of their support in preparing this volume. Finally, we would like to thank Dr Ernst Stetter and Dr Ania Skrzypek for their rewarding partnership, and for the financial support of FEPS without which this volume would not have been possible.

# The Great Globalization Disruption: Democracy, Capitalism and Inequality in the Industrialized World

Patrick Diamond

In recent years, globalization has entered a new phase driven by structural shocks from financial crises to the undermining of representative democracy. This is an age of upheaval and disorder epitomized by the rise of Donald Trump to the presidency of the United States, Great Britain's unanticipated departure from the European Union (EU), and the rapid growth of populist parties in the established democracies of Europe, as well as in the Southern and Eastern periphery. We are living in a new world which makes us, in Margaret Mead's evocative phrase, 'immigrants in our own land' (cited in Hall 2015: 255). The 'great globalization disruption' relates to the ongoing integration of capital, labour and product markets alongside structural economic and technological change. Economics and politics are pulling in opposite directions. The logic of market liberalism demands greater openness, free trade and deregulation to sustain global growth and expansion. Yet the politics of Western democracies implore greater national protectionism, using the nation-state to defend citizens from market forces that have little respect for established political bargains and solidarities. The social contract that sustains liberal democracy is under strain.

This volume asks what challenges the 'great globalization disruption' will pose for progressive social democratic and liberal politics across Europe and the United States. The first section of the chapter examines the background to the 'great disruption', in particular the breakdown of the post-1945 social contract. The chapter then outlines the central themes and core argument of the volume. One of the most remarkable features of the 2008 crisis has been the muted ideological response, particularly on the left. Neo-liberalism has dominated politics for so long it has become almost impossible to envisage credible governing alternatives. The book seeks to understand the new era by bringing together contributions from leading thinkers and scholars who debate the structural causes and political consequences of the 'great globalization disruption'. The collection aims to forge a compelling response that reunites the imperatives of economic integration, democratic legitimacy and national sovereignty with the goal of a fairer, more equal society, as a generation of progressive leaders achieved so skilfully in the aftermath of World War II.

The debate about globalization is often confused because established scholars are not always clear what they mean by 'globalization'. In conventional accounts, globalization refers to the integration of capital, product and labour markets across the borders of national politics. Anthony Mcgrew (2010: 16) defines globalization as, 'a long-term historical process that denotes the growing intensity of worldwide interconnectedness: in short, a "shrinking world"'. Numerous political controversies are blamed on globalization including the fragmentation of welfare states, the collapse of social democracy, and the growth of popular opposition to immigration. The term has become so ubiquitous that it is used to explain virtually any shift in state-society relations. Writers from the US economist Stephen D. King to *The Financial Times* commentator Martin Wolf predicted the end of globalization. Yet the pace and scale of global integration has scarcely diminished. Since the early 1990s, trade and foreign direct investment flows have increased from 0.9 to 3.2 per cent of global GDP (OECD 2017: 3).

The expansion of the global economy, trade liberalization, and the shift in the relative power of states – with China rapidly ascending and the west declining – have been felt most acutely in the destruction of industrial and manufacturing employment. During the first decade of the twenty-first century, the UK and the United States, having suffered a major deindustrialization 'shock' in the 1980s, both experienced a further dramatic decline in manufacturing, a consequence of China joining the World Trade Organization (WTO), and the accession countries of Central and Eastern Europe entering the European single market (Gamble 2016). Blue-collar industrial workers, once the backbone of the Western economies, were rapidly displaced. The sense of anger and grievance, especially among working class communities, was palpable. Two other factors compounded the impact of deindustrialization on the politics of Western democracies.

The first factor is a general rise in volatility. Instability has increased because financialization and the contagion effects of financial crises have intensified the impact of shocks across the international system. The advance of globalization continued against the backdrop of the 2008 crisis and its aftermath. Western economies have been caught in a 'deflationary trap'; interest rates are held at historically low levels, as central banks are compelled to print money through 'Quantitative Easing' (QE) to inject liquidity into the economy (Gamble 2016). The conundrum for policy-makers is that the policies of QE and bank 'bail-outs' designed to support aggregate demand have advantaged existing owners of assets, to the detriment of wage earners. The inequalities created by the neo-liberal policy consensus of the last three decades including weaker collective bargaining, deregulated labour markets, cuts to personal and corporate taxation, and reduced social security entitlements have fuelled the rise of social and economic inequality. The policy response to the 2008 crisis has exacerbated the root causes of inequality.

Nor are the long-term prospects for the global economy especially favourable. Despite some initial 'green shoots', we are living in a climate of deflation and 'secular stagnation' where growth rates are languishing or even declining. While the 2008 crash destroyed a significant chunk of productive capacity, particularly in countries such as Britain and the United States where the economy is heavily weighted towards financial services, sluggishness in Western countries is the consequence of the fundamental shift in economic power from west to east. There has been much interest in developments such as 're-shoring', where productivity improvements made possible by digital technologies have led to manufacturing capacity returning to industrialized countries. Nevertheless, manufacturing is less important to the world economy as a whole, while future growth is likely to be driven by the expansion of services, particularly in retail, hospitality, health, education, domestic services, personal care, and so on. In this climate it becomes harder to raise productivity and employment; services are, 'inherently less conducive to productivity growth' since they are 'sheltered' from international trade and less likely to benefit from technological innovation (Iversen and Wren 1998: 512). Meanwhile, manufacturing is contracting in the emerging market countries, and the prospects for long-term global growth appear weak (Rodrik 2012; Gamble 2016).

Moreover, while there has been a modest upswing in the global economy, it is not easy to see where the next phase of sustainable growth will come from. There is little indication of any imminent return to the multilateral world order once under-written by the United States, which is now being undermined by the 'America First' rhetoric of the Trump Administration. The global system since 1945, and especially since 1989 in the aftermath of the collapse of the Berlin wall, relied predominantly on US leadership. But today, open markets and free trade are less acceptable to key sections of the American electorate given their association with economic restructuring and industrial dislocation, which is linked to off-shoring, falling real wages and job losses. The global governance regime of regulations and rules is less stable with greater fragmentation occurring across the regions of the world economy, as national governments attempt to exert greater influence (Rodrik 2012). Neither the United States nor China is able to exercise unqualified global leadership. Against this backdrop, the period of stagnation since the late 2000s promises to make the 'next phase' of globalization in the industrialized countries even more politically unsettling.

A second factor compounding the political impact of deindustrialization has been the claim of neo-liberals that nations can prosper only by liberalising their economies and societies. This has led to striking cutbacks in the protective role of the state. In the liberal market regimes such as the UK and the United States during the inter-war years, and even more acutely during the 'neo-liberal' era since the late 1970s, domestic political action was restrained in the name of limited government to allow capital and labour to flow more freely throughout the global economy. During this period there was a move towards floating exchange rates, personal and corporate taxation was cut dramatically, and expansionary fiscal policy was largely jettisoned even in times of economic distress, while structural reforms were imposed to free up labour and product markets (Rodrik 2012). Economic openness and market liberalism were believed to be mutually intertwined.

The effect of these policy changes over the last 40 years has been to make economics and politics across the industrialized nations into unnatural bedfellows. According to the logic of neo-liberalism, economic imperatives must prevail over democratic institutions and political decision-making, creating a backlash among disgruntled citizens while explaining the rise in support for populist and challenger forces. Not surprisingly, the process of globalization as well as advancements in technology that pose a threat to jobs and living standards have led to growing dissatisfaction with political outcomes in Western democracies. The fundamental issue with globalization and trade is not that politically potent coalitions of 'winners' and 'losers' suddenly emerge. As the Harvard economist Dani Rodrik emphasizes, there have always been winners and losers in capitalist economies; market forces lead to patterns of 'creative destruction' while technological advancements in domestic markets generate rapid changes in employment alongside rising inequalities in wages and relative living standards. The burning political issue in recent decades has been that the liberalization of trade and economic openness are perceived to produce increasingly *unfair* results; capital, goods and labour move rapidly across borders with little respect for national political sovereignty; globalization is thus believed to erode domestic political norms, to undermine democratic bargaining, and to threaten long-standing social contracts (Rodrik 2012).

Established parties have struggled to respond to rising dissatisfaction following the breakdown of the social contract. For decades, the prevailing ideology of neo-liberalism emphasized the limited role of governments. Insurgent 'authoritarian populist' parties have sought to exploit rising economic and political discontent. These parties are 'authoritarian' in three distinct senses: firstly, they exploit voters' desire for security in the face of disorder relating to terrorism, crime and loss of stable employment; secondly, these parties urge 'conformity' to established social norms and moral values; thirdly, populist leaders demand 'obedience' to those who offer an image of strong group identity and a coherent sense of loyalty and protection (Norris and Inglehart 2018: 10–11). That vision is based on grievances, including an oversimplified version of reality that harks back to a bygone era which may, or may not, have ever actually existed (Hall 2013).

As a consequence, the next phase of 'knowledge-driven' globalization is likely to create new dividing-lines that undermine established party systems, while allowing 'challenger parties' to break into the electoral marketplace. The traditional cleavages in European democracies are being replaced by new divisions centred on educational achievement. The ability to access the labour market and to secure a high-wage job in a competitive global economy is now heavily dependent on access to higher education. The fulfilment of the liberal ideal of meritocracy might be considered cause for celebration, but the repercussions are troubling. More fundamentally, the rise of the global elite convinces those who have done well out of globalization that their rewards have been earned, so they owe few obligations to the rest of society (Hall, 2015).

The tectonic shifts in politics that resulted were symptomized by the knife-edge decision of UK voters to leave the EU in June 2016; the November 2016 election of Donald Trump to the presidency of the United States; the defeat of Matteo Renzi's proposals to change the Italian constitution in a referendum; and the rise of electoral support for populist forces of the left and right throughout Europe. There is a growing sense that the democratic consent for transnational governance, free trade and liberalization is eroding, as politics almost everywhere is deemed to be in a state of unprecedented upheaval. Few established parties have a coherent strategy for breaking out of the impasse.

The root cause of the malaise is that since the financial crisis and Great Recession in the aftermath of the 2008 meltdown, global capitalism no longer appears capable of generating broadly shared prosperity. The ten years since 2008 have witnessed the slowest and most anaemic recovery in the history of Western capitalism. The International Monetary Fund (IMF) revealed the persistent weakness of global productivity in goods and services, particularly in Europe which has been adversely affected by an unprecedented debt crisis (Arias and Wen 2015). Serious recessions usually have long-term 'scarring' effects. The 2008 crash altered the regional and sectoral composition of globalization, strengthening emerging market countries relative to the advanced economies. This shift will have serious repercussions for the future legitimacy of global capitalism. If the next phase of globalization and the anticipated 'great disruption' lead to an acceleration of economic influence to the east, given that economic crises often produce a 'rebalancing of power' between states, the domestic political consent for openness in the industrialized economies is likely to be further eroded.

The legitimacy of globalization is diminishing because, for many voters, the economy appears broken and politics is palpably failing them. Wages and living standards have been falling for 30 years in the face of declining productivity and the long-term shift in bargaining-power from labour to capital. In the context of globalization, workers may have benefited from gaining access to cheaper consumer goods, but the benefits have been outweighed by the persistent decline of real wages. According to the Organization for Economic Co-operation and Development (OECD), the proportion of national income allocated to wages has fallen in almost all of the industrialized nations since the 1970s (OECD 2012). Economic insecurity is rising, fuelling popular discontent with public bureaucracy and representative democracy, particularly at the EU level (Hall 2013). The 'blue collar' working-class has become contemptuous of the political establishment, which increases the salience of attacks on technocratic expertise and privilege, adding ballast to populist voices and sentiments. The new divide in European politics is between those who live in places that are connected to new sources of global growth, and those who reside outside the zones of economic expansion; dynamic urban, cosmopolitan centres are increasingly divorced from suburban towns and rural communities where more conservative and socially authoritarian values prevail (Jennings and Stoker 2017). Geographical polarization is heightened by the rise of the 'intangible economy' which creates more socially disruptive forms of inequality (Haskell and Westlake 2017). As a consequence, the central pillars of representative democracy are under unprecedented attack.

## The 'Trilemma' of Globalization

This chapter maintains that we need to better understand why 'the great globalization disruption' is posing acute problems for democratic politics. Dani Rodrik argued that the three fundamental goals of post-war liberal democratic societies – global economic integration, national sovereignty, and political democracy – are becoming detached from one another. There is a fierce political reaction against globalization leading to demands for protective action that safeguards worker's livelihoods within the nation-state. Liberal democracy is under unprecedented assault. The backlash against free trade and open markets undermined the legitimacy of liberal political economy, and the associated ideas of Western liberalism centred on freedom and prosperity. More worryingly, liberal political institutions lost credibility and trust amid declining popular faith in democratic politics. The progressive tradition that linked the reforming radicalism of Franklin Roosevelt and Clement Attlee with the contemporary third way of Bill Clinton and Tony Blair lies in tatters. Clinton and Blair's refusal to confront the polarising forces of unfettered global capitalism is one of many reasons for the contemporary obsolescence of the progressive tradition. We are thus living in a 'post-liberal' age.

The political climate of turmoil and the eclipsing of liberalism have evidently thrown the post-war project of European integration into doubt. Rodrik claims the launch of the euro and European monetary integration are problematic for member-states; it is questionable whether the eurozone can survive in the long-term. The single currency requires nation-states to surrender economic sovereignty to institutions such as the European Central Bank in Frankfurt that have no democratic mandate. Deregulation associated with the single market has been even more politically disruptive since liberalization 'redistributes resources across sectors and social groups so profoundly that it creates deep distributive dilemmas to which there is no technocratic solution' (Hall 2013: 439). The consolidation of the European market leads to growing inequality within and between member-states. Yet because the EU is not a fully constituted polity, there are relatively few instruments in place to produce a fairer distribution of the gains from growth. The EU's impotence is an important explanation for rising political discontent, including the decision of UK citizens to vote narrowly to leave the EU in 2016.

This volume's purpose is to address the most important debates about the relationship between politics and economics during the next phase of globalization. The authors assess the impact of globalization and deindustrialization on both Brexit and the US Presidential results. They consider the extent to which deindustrialization and globalization are responsible for inflicting the political shocks of Brexit and the Trump presidency. Was Brexit merely a reaction by the so-called 'losers' of globalization against austerity and market restructuring? What are the implications of Brexit for other EU member-states and the long-term prospects of the Union? What are the similarities between the Brexit 'shock' and the Trump victory, and how is this akin to political turbulence in other parts of the Western world? The introductory chapter takes stock of the debates underlying the political and economic shockwaves of recent times.

## Globalization and the Post-War Social Contract

Despite a wave of contemporary interest, there is nothing especially 'new' or innovative about the internationalization or globalization of Western economies. Globalization has been underway since the early twentieth century, as Keynes observed. More importantly, globalization has gone through many cycles and periods of reversal. Economic integration was undermined by two world wars, alongside the sporadic return to protectionism among national elites that occurred in Britain following the abandonment of the Gold Standard in 1931 (Gamble 2016). After 1945, there was a managed process of global integration where exposure to free trade was counter-balanced by rights of economic and social citizenship that were enshrined in institutions such as the welfare state, giving global capitalism 'a human face'. By the late 1990s, globalization was in the ascendency. There was euphoria about the potential of economic integration and technological change to drive unending growth, epitomized by the rapid expansion of the Internet. The rationale was that states which did not liberalize their economies to become the beneficiaries of market-led globalization would stagnate, falling behind in the global race, becoming the victims of relative decline.

Much of the jubilation about globalization's potential that characterized the two decades prior to the 2008 financial crisis has waned. The evidence is that globalization has entered a protracted phase of instability which has seen lower growth accompanied by economic and technological disruption. The situation results not merely from the integration of the global economy, but related structural changes that include: the impact of technological change, digitization and automation; the long-term effects of climate change for sustainability and competitiveness; the rise of economic and social inequality; the impact of changing demography and the ageing society. New technologies have been significant in shaping the reaction against economic and industrial change. The reaction is not merely to do with automation or 'robots' destroying industrial and service sector jobs. The diffusion of Information and Communication Technology (ICT) has made the world immeasurably better connected, but the effects are not always benign. ICT created the infrastructure for the complex financial trading that led to the 2008 crash. Moreover, financialization and globalization were important factors in sweeping away barriers to the free movement of capital. They led to the erosion of the tax state's legitimacy, epitomized by the growth of large-scale tax avoidance captured in the 'Panama' and 'Paradise' papers in 2016–17, which weakened the social contract that has underpinned modern capitalism since World War II (CNBC 2017). These political forces combine with the integration of capital, product and labour markets to shape a new era labelled 'the great globalization disruption'. The long-term consequences are far from predictable. As the legitimacy of markets and representative democracy has been undermined, economics and politics have moved in opposite directions.

The consequence of the erosion of basic democratic bargains is to widen the divide between the so-called 'winners' and 'losers' of globalization, exacerbating inequalities and provoking a collapse of confidence in economic and political elites. Of course, there is no straightforward division between globalization's 'winners' and globalization's 'losers'. The apparent split between 'cosmopolitan' and 'communitarian' voters is one-dimensional (Goodhart 2017). Scholars such as Mike Savage and Fiona Devine have charted a markedly diverse and variegated class structure. In Britain, a structural divide can be observed within the working-class between older working-class voters who inhabit declining industrial towns, and the 'new working-class' employed in precarious service sector jobs with few adequate sources of income maintenance or social protection (Jennings and Stoker 2017). The advanced capitalist countries have witnessed the growth of precarious employment including 'zero hours' contracts, freelancing, enforced consultancy contracts, outsourcing, and the associated 'opportunities' of the so-called 'gig economy'. As a consequence, employment rates have remained relatively stable, but there has been persistent downward pressure on real wages. Falling tax revenues have added to the structural pressures on the financing of welfare states. These changes have fuelled the rise of discontent among the new working-class, whose members increasingly see politics as providing few solutions to the problems they endure.

## Progressive Movements and Forces

Liberalism, the doctrine that emphasizes freedom and democracy which defined mainstream Western political thought throughout the twentieth century, has atrophied as the political forces of the democratic left have struggled to forge a convincing response to the new phase of globalization. Social democratic leaders in Western Europe and the United States memorably embraced globalization in the 1990s with remarkably few caveats or qualifications. If the world was witnessing the 'end of history', as was famously proclaimed by Francis Fukuyama, and the experiments in economic planning in the Soviet Union had ended disastrously, there was little alternative but to embrace global capitalism. The core assumption of progressive politics in the 1990s was that there was now a consensus about the goal of combining a 'dynamic' open economy with active government to ameliorate social injustice. It was widely believed that Western societies had learned to embrace globalized capitalism, albeit modified capitalism 'with a human face'. This worldview mirrored the debates of the 1960s about 'the end of ideology' popularized by the American sociologist, Daniel Bell. Bell insisted that the only issues for debate in the United States were essentially technocratic, since Western capitalism was universally accepted as the most superior model of political and social organization. Then as now, such judgements proved to be premature. The survival of liberal globalized capitalism in Western countries cannot be taken for granted.

The centre-left argument 20 years ago was that government investment in education would improve the supply of human capital, ensuring a 'social minimum' that enabled everyone to benefit from global integration. Today, that spirit of optimism has been upended. It is evident that globalization is working less well for those on low to middle-incomes. The rise of globalization is associated with, 'the stagnation of the well-being of many in the lower half of the income distribution in a number of OECD countries' (OECD 2017: 3). Many citizens are in work but wages are stagnating and only government subsidies in the form of tax credits and state benefits make employment viable. The social status of work has declined, particularly in the low-waged service sectors, amid concerns about the erosion of dignity, the associated growth of worker surveillance in call-centres and production plants, and the insidious rise of precarious employment. Many workers no long feel that centre-left parties are willing to protect them from the adversities of market capitalism, and their emotional connection with progressive movements has inevitably been strained. The long-term consequence is a crisis of confidence in mainstream social democracy.

## Chapters

### Section I: Taking Stock – the Rise of the New Populism

The first section of the book sets the scene by addressing what is currently meant in political and scholarly discourse by 'globalization' and 'populism'. The chapters then consider the impact of these forces on the societies and economies of the advanced capitalist states.

In a synoptic opening chapter on 'Globalization and the New Populism', **Andrew Gamble** considers the factors that produced the dramatic rise in electoral support for populism. Relative economic decline has been an important factor in the development of democratic discontent and declining political legitimacy across the Western world. The crisis first struck almost a decade ago, yet despite the efforts of policy-makers to bail-out the financial sector and support the economy through Quantitative Easing (QE), few countries have been able to escape the spiral of low growth, falling productivity and stagnating living standards – Canada and Australia standing apart as notable exceptions. The mood of popular disillusionment with global capitalism has been exploited by 'anti-system' parties such as the Alternative for Germany (AfD), the Italian Five Star movement, and the People's Party in Denmark who share a deep antagonism to the EU, immigration and economic openness. Trump's victory in the 2016 presidential election is perhaps the most puzzling manifestation of the populist surge and voter disaffection. Trump's arrival in the White House and his mantra of 'Making America Great Again' threatens to unravel the liberal world order. The problem for global capitalism is not simply that globalization creates 'losers' and new political dividing lines that populist forces can exploit. Globalization has encouraged the ascendency of economic and political elites who have paid less and less attention to the price that domestic electorates are prepared to pay for integration into the international economy. As a consequence, the social contract that made economic integration acceptable to the mass of working people has been undermined.

Yet as Gamble writes, 'The causes of the new populism are much more deep-rooted than just a reaction to the austerity after the financial crash'. The populist 'backlash' has been driven by antipathy towards liberalized international economies, marked not only by rising economic inequalities, but the decline of traditional industries, the disappearance of class structures and of moral norms that are centred on solidarity and community, and growing resentment against the wealthy who appear to owe no allegiance to any particular country or group of citizens. The politicization of national identity occurred as a reaction against the spread of a virulent strain of rootless, itinerant, even immoral global capitalism. The 2008 crash was thus the catalyst for populist movements to exploit a wide array of cultural as well as economic and political grievances.

In his chapter on 'The Backlash Against Globalization', **Jeffry Frieden** takes up the theme of the relationship between the economy, cultural change and political instability. He observes that recent events, notably the UK's decision to withdraw from the EU and the election of Trump to the US Presidency, alongside the emergence of increasingly successful populist parties, called into question the sustainability of the international economic order that emerged from the Bretton Woods agreement. Trump's programme is focused on undermining the international system by eschewing free trade, pulling out of accords such as the Paris agreement on climate change, and questioning America's long-term support for the North Atlantic Treaty Organization (NATO). Over the next decade, the author foresees the fragmentation of trade, investment and finance into separate regions of the world economy. In this vision, the barriers between regional trading blocs are likely to grow, while the economic processes of globalization may be halted.

It appears that, 'The political revolution of 2016 has already set in motion processes that may be impossible to reverse', as US governments are more willing to engage in trade conflicts and protectionism to appease their domestic electorates. Frieden contends that the 'mechanisms' in place to support those most 'harmed by globalization' are inadequate; states have struggled to shield citizens from social and economic aftershocks. Progressive movements across countries need to identify programmes that prepare young people for the next phase of 'knowledge-based globalization', while 'protecting' older voters who have struggled to adapt as, 'a compelling alternative to populism and economic nationalism'.

In defining the nature of populism in the advanced economies, **Patricia Rodi** addresses the question of whether populist appeals are filtering into the policy programmes of 'mainstream' parties in Western Europe, focusing on styles of political communication and rhetoric. She draws on the work of Cas Mudde to define populism as a 'thin-centred ideology' which considers society, 'to be ultimately separated into two homogenous and antagonistic groups, "the pure people" versus "the corrupt elite", [arguing] that politics should be an expression of the general will of the people'. Centre-left parties struggle to resist the populist tide as the transformation of capitalism over the last three decades undermined traditional social democratic institutions and policies.

Rodi then traces the influence of political populism on social democratic parties in two Northern European countries, namely Britain and Sweden. She finds that the British Labour party, when confronted by the growing threat of the UK Independence Party (UKIP) and three successive election defeats, has been increasingly influenced by the rhetoric of populism, especially in portraying their opponents, as 'corrupt and unresponsive to the people'. Such effects were less marked among the Swedish social democrats who have been in power since 2014, despite the presence of an increasingly successful radical right party. The chapter maintains that to undermine the populist threat, social democrats have to engage citizens by adopting 'language and policies' that matter to voters, where necessary anchored in the politics of solidarity and class.

Drawing on a wide range of empirical data, **Silvia Merler** examines the attitude among European citizens to the impact of globalization. The EU was intended to be the 'filter' that ensured the goals of economic growth, democratic legitimacy and social cohesion remained compatible and mutually reinforcing, despite economic integration. 'Managed globalization', which has been the centrepiece of the EU's approach since the 1950s, eschewed 'old-style' protectionism and state interventionism while rejecting the deregulatory liberalism of the free market. Not surprisingly, the 2008 crisis has eroded confidence in the global economy among all sections of society. Yet the author finds there are inevitably divergent attitudes. Women and older people are increasingly sceptical of economic integration, as are those living in towns and rural areas. Citizens in periphery countries in the eurozone were more apprehensive than citizens in the core Western European states.

Merler finds that in member-states where national economic performance relative to other EU countries is weak, not surprisingly there are growing doubts about economic integration. Similarly, Will Jennings and Gerry Stoker (2017) claim that UK voters living in places that have experienced relative economic decline were more likely to vote to leave the EU. Thus, Merler argues that political change is driven by economic and industrial adjustment, not merely by culture or values. After the 2008 crisis, EU institutions were guided by neo-liberal ideas that appeared oblivious to, or uninterested in, the social and economic repercussions of structural change and austerity for ordinary voters. The chapter argues EU policy-makers should promote structural convergence across the Union. Initiatives such as the 'EU Invest Plan' and the 'Youth Guarantee' are important, but bolder proposals are needed to reverse the populist tide.

**Manuel de la Rocha** focuses on the impact of the 2008 financial crisis on social democracy in the Southern European countries most afflicted by fiscal austerity. The centre-left in Italy, Greece and Spain similarly embarked on the third way approach pioneered by Tony Blair in the UK and Gerhard Schroeder in Germany. The third way eschewed the traditional critique of free markets associated with social democracy and embraced globalization, financialization, and the internationalization of economies. In so doing, however, centre-left parties neglected their core constituency of working people. These voters feared that they would be displaced by technological change, remained anxious about the downward pressure on wages and living standards, and worried that the welfare state was no longer an adequate shelter for 'the new hard times'.

De la Rocha contends that by vacating the political space traditionally colonized by social democrats, centre-left parties allowed populist forces in European politics to displace them. These populist movements ostensibly offer security and protection in a world of change. To restore their electoral and political strength, social democratic parties have to offer a convincing critique of markets, and be prepared to update and modernize the proudest achievement of post-war social democracy in Europe – the national welfare states vital to sheltering citizens from the unpredictable effects of globalization. At the same time, it is important to be aware of the limits of pursuing social democracy in one country. Many of the challenges thrown-up by globalization can only be addressed by national governments working together, particularly through the auspices of the EU. De la Rocha emphasizes that the answer is to reform, not abandon the European project.

## Section II: Brexit, Populism and the Future of the European Union

The second section of the book addresses the UK citizenry's decision to exit the EU in June 2016 by a narrow majority.

**Loukas Tsoukalis** analyses the drivers of the UK's negative verdict on 40 years of EU membership. The roots of Britain's discomfort with the

European project lie deep; they did not arise only in the last decade as a response to the backlash against globalization. As Tsoukalis states, Britain's view of Europe is captured in Winston Churchill's famous declaration: 'We are with Europe but not of it. We are linked but not comprised. We are interested and associated, but not absorbed.' When Britain joined the European Economic Community (the forerunner to the EU) in the early 1970s, the UK quickly exercised influence over trade, budgetary arrangements, financial services, regulation, enlargement, as well as foreign and security policy. But the British political class remained ambivalent about European integration. Even an ostensibly pro-European Prime Minister such as Tony Blair was unable to unify the country behind the European project. The Labour Government's decision to allow the free movement of workers from the accession countries into the UK without a transition period, and its alleged indifference to the impact of global markets on livelihoods and living standards among British workers, fanned the flames of Euroscepticism prior to the 2016 referendum.

What exactly drove the Brexit decision is unclear. As Tsoukalis emphasizes, the result was less the revolt of the so-called 'left behinds' than 'an unholy alliance between members of golf clubs in the English countryside and the "sans culottes" of globalization in the decaying heartlands of British manufacturing industry'. Rather, Tsoukalis argues, the liberalization of the British economy over the preceding three decades created new dividing lines in British politics between 'nationalists' and 'cosmopolitans', and between 'social conservatives' and 'liberals' which destabilized the established party system. Europe itself has experienced a succession of crises over the last ten years, and at times, the EU looked like 'an ungovernable post-modern empire' which hardly endeared the project to the UK electorate. Nonetheless, the political cohesion of Europe is likely to persist for the foreseeable future.

In his chapter on 'The EU in Crises', **Dimitris Tsarouhas** examines how the issue of Brexit was propelled to the top of the UK's political agenda. The chapter contends that Brexit is 'the symptom, not the cause' of the EU's current malaise. The EU faces multiple crises, notably sovereign debt, mass migration, Russian military adventurism, and the rise of populism and Euroscepticism. It would be naïve to assume that the victory of pro-European forces encompassed in Emmanuel Macron's presidential victory in France means populism in Europe has been defeated. The EU is continuing to suffer the aftershocks of the financial and fiscal crises of 2008 despite a superficial improvement in economic performance, with citizens on the periphery of the eurozone hit hardest.

The coherence of the EU has been further eroded by the advance of political populism and the growth of 'increasingly authoritarian tendencies' in Eastern Europe, particularly in Hungry and Poland. The root causes of the migration and refugee crises that struck Europe have not abated given the ongoing political and human security catastrophes in the Middle East. The future stability of the EU will be secured only where there is a willingness to enact bold reforms that entrench a robust pillar of social rights promoting convergence between member-states and solidarity between citizens.

The final chapter in this section by **Roger Liddle** provides a further perspective on the Brexit crisis, seen as the defining event in contemporary British politics. Liddle claims that the socio-economic drivers of insecurity that led UK voters to vote to leave the EU can also be found elsewhere in Europe. The labour market has been hollowed out while low-skilled, non-unionized employment in the service sector has increased. There is a growing risk that the low-skilled with few formal educational qualifications will be permanently marginalized. Meanwhile, trade unions and collective pay bargaining are in long-term decline, and gender inequalities have persisted, which exposes increasing numbers of families and individuals to the risk of poverty. The weakness of the EU as a political actor meant there has been no effective response to the social and economic grievances commonly associated with the rise of globalization.

The chapter contends the watershed decision of British voters to leave the EU in 2016 was not inevitable. The campaign for Britain to remain an EU member led by senior Conservative Ministers (with the Labour party largely absent from the debate) was ineffective. The campaign made a series of exaggerated claims about the impact of Britain's departure on the living-standards of British voters, who were encouraged to disregard the advice of experts. Nor did advocates of Remain effectively confront the central issue in the British debate about Europe, namely immigration. Too many voters believed UK governments were powerless to act given the principle of free movement, which they felt was widely abused and out of control in the aftermath of the Europe-wide refugee crisis. At the same time, the issue of Britain's relationship with Europe has been unresolved for four decades. Both the Conservatives and the Labour party have historically been divided on membership, and were unable to reconcile themselves to a European future. Ironically, the 'Global Britain' vision of Brexit supporters is for the UK to be even *more* exposed to globalization, operating as a deregulated, free market 'mid-Atlantic tax haven', trading freely with the rest of the world.

## Section III: What is to be Done? Domestic and International Policies to Deal with Globalization

The third section of the book assesses the efficacy of the policy response to political polarization and rising inequality in the face of the 'Great Globalization Disruption'.

The chapters ask what policy options are available to progressive policy-makers at the domestic and international level in dealing with the disruptive effects of globalization, as well as the long-term fall-out from the crisis. What can we learn from successes and failures so far? How damaging has fiscal austerity been to support for incumbent progressive governments? Was a 'quasi-Keynesian' strategy feasible after 2008 given the mounting debt crisis? How should nation-states negotiate the dilemma of whether to raise barriers that limit access to global markets and weaken growth; should they accept the removal of national regulations which promote prosperity, but in turn compromise their policy autonomy, exposing citizens to greater insecurity?

Martin Wolf argues if democratic legitimacy for globalization is to be restored, 'economic policy must be orientated towards promoting the interests of the many, not the few … the marriage of liberal democracy with capitalism needs some nurturing' (Wolf 2016). The question remains how far policy-makers can prevent insular nationalism and liberal globalization from colliding through effective governance and activist public policies? How should progressive forces in Europe and the United States respond to the dilemmas raised by the 'next phase' of globalization? How should democratic left parties relate to more polarized and anxious electorates? How do centre-left parties campaign in an environment where faith in technocratic expertise has been undermined? Where might the next generation of social democratic governing ideas and programmes come from? These questions are addressed painstakingly by each contributor.

**Vivien A. Schmidt** highlights that most EU member-states have struggled to produce a convincing response to recent crises against the backdrop of declining legitimacy at the supranational and nation-state level. Populists have adeptly exploited the current malaise. Progressive voices sound less confident in the face of rising inequality, against the anger of the 'left behind', and amidst the growth of the new politics of socio-cultural identity. Contemporary discontents are, at root, the consequence of political ideas that enlarged inequality and insecurity. Market liberalism promoted an ethic of 'individualism' and the 'limited state' which perceptibly undermined protection against economic and social risks. Social liberalism then promoted political and social values derived from cosmopolitanism and multiculturalism that prompted a 'cultural backlash' among certain voters, leading to a marked rise in incivility and political mistrust. At the EU level, the policy mix of ordo-liberal fiscal orthodoxy and austerity alongside neo-liberal structural reforms led to the rise of youth unemployment, the decline of productivity, and reduced economic growth in many eurozone economies. All of these forces have electoral salience and political currency, as citizens are exposed to new insecurities and feel increasingly disengaged from the democratic process.

Schmidt emphasizes that in this climate, progressive ideas come not only from governing elites, but a wide array of 'ideational agents', including social movements, advocacy coalitions of civil society actors and policy-makers, policy entrepreneurs, and the 'epistemic communities' of economists and political thinkers – who come together to construct new ideas. The chapter reflects that historically, progressive agendas were not fully formed when a bold leader such as Franklin Roosevelt came to office in the 1930s. It took time for the battle of ideas to be won, and for ideas to be translated into actionable proposals. The chapter insists that to counter the 'populist upsurge', progressives must focus their energies on the 'in-betweens' who have neither benefited from the 'boom at the top' enjoyed by the wealthy, nor the programmes that provide 'welfare for the bottom'. Above all, leaders must convey ideas in 'uplifting ways', offering attractive visions of the future, an alternative to the siren voices of populism.

**Lorenza Antonucci** takes up the challenge by contesting the widely held assumption that the populations of advanced capitalist states can be neatly divided into globalization 'winners' and globalization 'losers'. She attests that a large section of Western societies has been adversely affected by growing precariousness and mounting inequality in the distribution of material incomes. Today, not only are the former industrial working-class who inhabit the relatively low growth regions of national economies vulnerable to periods of economic marginalization and income stagnation, but highly educated younger workers face similar challenges. Policy strategies that rely on narrow tools of human capital investment – notably the expansion of higher education – alongside the increasing residualization of the welfare state and the growth of means-testing, have thus far proved ineffective in tackling the root causes of precarity.

Antonucci proposes a three-pronged framework for action at the national and European level. Firstly, there is the need to rekindle the universalism of welfare states by introducing a basic income guarantee for targeted sections of the population, especially young people most at risk of growing precariousness. Secondly, labour market protection must be updated to address the challenges of today's society, for example reconciling paid employment and caring responsibilities for men and women of working age. Thirdly, national reforms ought to be accompanied by the revitalization of EU social policies, using devices such as the European Semester and benchmarking to promote convergence in social standards. These reforms allow national governments and EU actors to mount a concerted offensive against rising inequality in the face of continuing fiscal and budgetary constraints.

In a subsequent chapter, **Anton Hemerijck** and **Robin Huguenot-Noel** make the case for a radical approach to European social investment. The social investment strategy was conceived by the Swedish sociologist, Gosta Esping-Andersen. Esping-Andersen rejected the neo-liberal axiom that public expenditure is detrimental to economic efficiency, and criticized the dominant welfare state model that prevailed in much of Western Europe, 'the male-breadwinner, pension-heavy and insider-biased welfare provision', which led to 'stagnant employment and long-term unemployment, in-work poverty, labour market exclusion, family instability, high dependency ratios and below-replacement fertility rates'. The aim of social policy was to smooth transition-points in the 'work-family life-course'. The authors report that spending on social investment across EU member states has been cut in the aftermath of the 2008 crisis, despite the fact lower spending does not lead to any discernible improvement in economic performance. The highest spending countries in Europe, notably Sweden, Finland, the Netherlands and Austria are among the strongest growth economies. The authors claim major criticisms of the social investment paradigm in the academic literature, in particular the assertion that social investment does not have any discernible impact on employment and that spending disproportionately benefits the middle class, have been over-stated.

The ambition of the social investment approach was to entrench a common strategy for the development of the European social model and welfare systems across member-states. Hemerijck and Huguenot-Noel argue that the strategic failing of centre-left parties over the last 20 years has been their reluctance to lay claim to the social investment agenda, which has been seized by Christian Democratic, Liberal and Green parties who claimed credit for the expansion of childcare provision and active labour market policies to the detriment of social democracy. To succeed in the future, centre-left parties should stop treating social investment as a strategy suited to periods of economic prosperity and embrace the potential of social investment as a 'counter-cyclical' measure during hard times of crisis and recession, 'when social needs are most acute'. The chapter articulates a vision of 'capacitating' social justice influenced by Amartya Sen's view of 'capabilities' where citizens are equipped with the means to lead flourishing lives.

**Frank Vandenbroucke** continues this line of inquiry examining the interface between Europeanization, globalization, and inequality, all concepts conflated in mainstream literature and commentary. He argues that different states have markedly divergent experiences of globalization; as a consequence, there are noticeable differences in patterns of economic inequality across countries. Vandenbroucke confronts deterministic accounts that imply EU member-states are moving ineluctably towards market liberalization and rising inequality. The challenge for EU countries is to embed social cohesion in state and society, mobilising 'a variety of policy instruments' to safeguard national welfare states.

The strategic priorities highlighted in Vandenbroucke's chapter include investment in education to narrow the disparities in human capital, as well as advancing the notion of a 'European Social Union' that ensures those moving across borders are economically active and 'earn' access to social benefits. The author contends that nationality should determine which member-state is 'first and foremost responsible' for each citizen's welfare; national institutions and policies need to be allowed to function effectively in order to tackle the underlying drivers of inequality.

Finally, **Jane Gringrich's** chapter restates an important paradox; why, given the support in public attitudes surveys for classically 'left' positions on economic policy, do social democratic parties not perform better? The author reveals the electoral environment confronting centre-left parties has become less hospitable in the face of rapidly changing class structures and political realignments, as well as structural pressures in advanced market economies that mainstream politicians and parties are struggling to confront. Social democrats have been accused of neglecting their main political constituency among the organized working-class. The strategy of investment in higher education and the human capital of the highly skilled does precious little to help former industrial workers who feel marginalized by economic change. Across the developed economies, the subjective status of 'non-college' educated men has been in decline (Hall 2015). Particular regions have been hard-hit by the scale and pace of industrial degeneration over the last four decades.

Gringrich examines how social democratic governments in Europe have responded to structural change, and presents an 'Anglo-approach', a

'Continental path', and a Scandinavian model. Gingrich demonstrates that the Nordic countries have been able to entrench egalitarian labour markets through long-term investment in skills, alongside workplace agreements between employers and trade unions. The chapter emphasizes centre-left parties are not doomed to lose elections while there is significant demand among voters for 'left policies'. Recent history tells us that rather than looking for the most technically efficient options such as earned income tax credits or measures that drive behavioural change in the welfare state, social democrats have to think about the visibility and political impact of their policies to secure the long-term allegiance of voters.

## Conclusion

An effective and credible response to globalization requires a political vision that does not jettison the individualism which is inherent to modern societies, but cultivates new forms of collectivism and solidarity. This chapter's contention is that to reshape the 'great globalization disruption', it will be necessary to reawaken the tradition of 'liberal egalitarianism' which has come under sustained attack from the reactionary forces of populism. Liberal egalitarianism necessitates a commitment to greater equality and social cohesion tempered by the belief in economic openness and liberty rooted in aversion to bureaucratic statism.

Despite its association with rootless cosmopolitanism, the progressive tradition has resonance that goes well beyond the urban enclaves of metropolitan liberalism with connections stretching back to the radical and rumbustious working-class political and social movements of the late nineteenth and early twentieth centuries. The radical liberal socialism of this period elaborated by disparate figures from Leonard Hobhouse in Britain to Eduard Bernstein in Germany constituted a powerful attack on the prevailing ethic of the limited state, reductionist individualism, and laissez-faire doctrines. Moreover, the distinction between 'negative' and 'positive' liberty in political discourse legitimized the role of active government, laying the foundations for the progressive social reforms at the turn of the century in Germany, the United States and the UK.

In the immediate aftermath of World War II, universal welfare states emerged accompanied by the Keynesian method of macro-economic demand management that sought to eliminate the damaging cycles of boom and slump. The socialist tradition was an important influence on radical liberal egalitarianism, although socialists were reluctant to confront the critique of state bureaucracies and central planning that emerged in the wake of the failed experiment in the Soviet Union. Liberal egalitarianism posited that markets had to be reconciled with social justice through the active role of government.

During the final decades of the twentieth century, liberal egalitarians explored how to utilize the capacities of the state to increase equality of opportunity while strengthening human self-fulfilment. Under the influence of American scholars, notably John Rawls, egalitarians in Europe shaped strategies to achieve distributive justice, although this led to a critique from Michael Sandel and the communitarian left. The criticisms of liberal egalitarianism highlight the importance of relationships at the heart of the 'moral' economy, insisting that economic life cannot be judged by the utilitarian calculus of profit and loss alone (Rogan 2017). The work of Amartya Sen has been crucial in emphasising the central importance of personal freedom and the need for involvement by the state to ensure that citizens are equipped with the 'capabilities' to lead rich and meaningful lives. More practically, the next generation of liberal egalitarian thinking has to abandon the 'growth first, distribute later' strategy of the last three decades of economic and social policy, actively intervening in markets to promote more equal outcomes while strengthening the bargaining power and economic agency of workers.

The radical egalitarian tradition should be re-discovered by progressives as they confront a more closely integrated international economic system driven by the next phase of globalization, digitization and technological disruption. There has to be a balance between an open, integrated economy and a dynamic nation-state that retains the scope for domestic action to maintain the allegiance of voters (Rodrik 2012). Liberal egalitarianism seeks to forge more equal societies underpinned by universal civil, political and social rights. The ambition is to guarantee the economic and social inclusion of all citizens in order to fulfil the aims of progressive politics as defined by the Polish philosopher, Leszek Kołakowski (1982: 11): 'An obstinate will to erode by inches the conditions which produce avoidable suffering, oppression, hunger, wars, racial and national hatred, insatiable greed and vindictive envy'.

## References

Arias, Maria A. and Wen, Yi. 'Recovery from the Great Recession has varied around the world', *Federal Reserve Bank of St Louis* (October 2015). Available at https://www.stlouisfed.org/publications/regional-economist/october-2015/recovery-from-the-great-recession-has-varied-around-the-world (Accessed 21 February 2018).

CNBC 'Tax avoidance is a "legacy issue," OECD's Angel Gurria says', *CNBC* (November 2017). Available at https://www.cnbc.com/2017/11/06/tax-avoidance-is-a-legacy-issue-oecds-angel-gurria-says.html (Accessed 14 February 2018).

Gamble, A. *Crisis Without End: The Unravelling of Western Prosperity* (Basingstoke, Palgrave Macmillan 2016).

Goodhart, D. *The Road to Somewhere: The Populist Revolt and the Future of Politics* (London, C. Hurst & Co. 2017).

Hacker, J. 'The Promise of predistribution'. In Diamond, P. and Chwalisz, C. (eds) *The Predistribution Agenda: Tackling Inequality and Supporting Sustainable Growth* (London, I.B.Tauris 2015) pp. xxi–1.

Haidt, J. 'When and why nationalism beats globalism'. *The American Interest* 12(1) (2016).

Hall, P. 'The future of the welfare state'. In Diamond, P. and Chwalisz, C. (eds) *The Predistribution Agenda: Tackling Inequality and Supporting Sustainable Growth* (London, I.B.Tauris 2015) pp. 241–53.

Hall, P. 'Democracy in the European Union: The problem of political capacity'. In Armingeon, K. (ed.) *Staatstatigkeiten, Parteien und Demokratie* (Berlin, Verlag fur Sozialwissenschaften 2013) pp. 429–41.

Haskell, J. and Westlake, S. *Capitalism Without Capital: The Rise of the Intangible Economy* (Princeton, Princeton University Press 2017).

Iversen, T. and Wren, A. 'Equality, employment and budgetary restraint: The trilemma of the service economy'. *World Politics* 50(1) (1998) pp. 507–46.

Jennings, W. and Stoker, G. 'Tilting towards the communitarian axis: Political change in England and the 2017 General Election'. *The Political Quarterly* 88(3) (2017) pp. 359–79.

Kolakowski, L. *Main Currents of Marxism* (Oxford, Oxford University Press 1982).

Mcgrew, A. 'Globalization and global politics'. In Baylis, J. Smith, S. and Owens, P. (eds) *The Globalization of World Politics: An Introduction to International Relations* (Oxford, Oxford University Press 2010) pp. 14–31.

Norris, P. and Inglehart, R. *Cultural Backlash: Trump, Brexit, and the Rise of Authoritarian Populism* (Cambridge, Cambridge University Press 2018).

OECD: Meeting of the OECD Council at Ministerial Level, Key Issues Paper (June 2017). Available at https://www.oecd.org/mcm/documents/C-MIN-2017-2-EN.pdf (Accessed 21 February 2018).

OECD Employment Outlook, Chapter 3, (October 2012). Available at http://www.oecd.org/els/emp/EMO%202012%20Eng_Chapter%203.pdf (Accessed 22 February 2018).

Rodrik, D. *The Globalization Paradox: Why Global Markets, States and Democracy Can't Co-Exist* (Oxford, Oxford University Press 2012).

Rogan, T. *The Moral Economists: R.H. Tawney, Karl Polanyi, E.P. Thompson, and the Critique of Capitalism* (Princeton: Princeton University Press 2017).

Wolf, Martin. 'Can global capitalism and liberal democracy survive?' *The Irish Times* (August 2016). Available at https://www.irishtimes.com/business/economy/martin-wolf-can-global-capitalism-and-liberal-democracy-survive-1.2774359 (Accessed 6 February 2018) https://www.google.co.uk/?client=safari&channel=ipad_bm&gws_rd=cr&dcr=0&ei=ORKdWuKVNKmYgAaGjZbICw (Accessed 2nd March 2018) https://www.google.co.uk/?client=safari&channel=ipad_bm&gws_rd=cr&dcr=0&ei=MCGPWoHrFpPXgQa2-JSwBw (Accessed 21st February 2018) https://www.google.co.uk/?client=safari&channel=ipad_bm&gws_rd=cr&dcr=0&ei=4CqPWo38IOzNgAaJmp-4Bg (Accessed 17 February 2018).

# Part I

**Taking Stock – the Rise of the New Populism**

CHAPTER 1

# Globalization and the New Populism

Andrew Gamble

In the last ten years there has been a marked rise in various forms of populism in Western democracies. The question is, why? One explanation is that it is the result of globalization, which has benefited some but not others, causing a backlash among the losers, who now seek to turn back globalization or obstruct its progress. The rise of the new populism is seen to be drawing its strength from those left behind by globalization, particularly the white working class in former heavy manufacturing districts. In this chapter I will examine this argument and its plausibility. One of the difficulties in pinpointing the argument is the vagueness of terms like 'populism' and 'globalization', and the loose way they are used in political discourse. We will address our understanding of these terms before going on to explore the links between them, in particular the theory of the globalization paradox put forward by Dani Rodrik (Rodrik 2011). Attention will be paid throughout to political context: Globalization means different things in different periods and so does populism. They are not single uniform phenomena, rather there are many 'globalizations' and many 'populisms' (Berger and Huntington 2002; Canovan 1981; Mudde and Kaltwasser 2017; Muller 2016).

A crucial context for understanding the contemporary interrelationship between these terms is the financial crash of 2008 and its aftermath of relative economic failure. We are still in a period defined by the 2008 financial crash. At the end of 2017, it was already nine years since the financial crash itself, and more than ten years since the start of the 2007 credit crunch. Swift and decisive action by governments on both sides of the Atlantic in 2008 prevented a financial meltdown, but it came at a heavy cost. There was a sharp recession and a very slow recovery, characterized by sluggish growth, stagnant or depressed living standards, and low productivity (Gamble 2016). The failure of Western economies to rebound from the 2009 recession as they had from every previous recession since 1945 perplexed policy-makers, especially since interest rates remained close to zero, the central banks supported banks liquidity with quantitative easing, and private companies had mountains of cash available for investment.

In the second half of 2017 and the start of 2018 the growth prospects of the international economy began to improve. The IMF expected all leading economies, with the exception of the UK, to expand faster in 2018. Stock markets responded by reaching all time highs in the hope that the generalized recovery the world had been waiting for since 2009 was, at last, materialising. The tax cuts announced by the Trump administration were predicted to add a further stimulus to the world economy, even as they pushed the US deficit towards £1 trillion, and the overall debt to $20 trillion, 104 per cent of GDP. Many observers were still cautious about whether a corner had finally been turned. Anxieties about the future of the international economy continued to be voiced. The Bank of International Settlements, and some of its former officials, have drawn attention to the huge debts which still exist in the system and which threaten to explode should the authorities start to raise interest rates to the kind of levels needed for financial health. The flood of money which had been injected into the international economy since 2008 meant that many new forms of shadow banking had emerged, posing grave financial risks if interest rates started rising sharply. Yet interest rates needed to rise sharply to give the financial authorities sufficient room to lower rates again in order to deal with the next downturn. If there is another financial crash and associated economic recession while interest rates are still very low, and QE has not been unwound, then the international economy risks widespread debt defaults and a plunge into a far more serious recession than that of 2008. Central banks have run out of tools to avoid such an outcome (Evans-Pritchard 2018).

There are more optimistic views about the immediate prospects for the international economy, but there is general agreement that the structural problems highlighted in 2008 and the period which followed have not yet been solved. The issues of new governance arrangements for the international economy to reflect the shifting balance of power, the obstacles to raising growth rates and productivity and to finding profitable investment outlets, the mountain of debt – public and private – which still hang over the international economy, and the erosion of legitimacy and trust in those governing it, were all mostly unresolved in 2018. There was still a political impasse, and it was unclear what political forces could break the logjam. The ability of government to just about manage meant that although incumbents were frequently ousted, they were replaced by other incumbents, sometimes centre-left but mostly centre-right, who continued the broad international consensus on appropriate policy priorities and policy instruments. Many governments adopted austerity programmes in the expectation that shifting the burden of adjustment on to public services and private households would facilitate a strong recovery. But the austerity programmes dragged on endlessly without stimulating recovery or eliminating the deficit or the accumulated public debt which, in many countries including the United States and the UK, continued to rise. Some of the deepest austerity was experienced in the eurozone, because of its sovereign debt crisis in 2010–12. It was temporarily solved by the European Central Bank finding its way to act as other Central Banks and beginning its own programme of quantitative easing (QE). It is against this background of national economies, still functioning but failing to bounce back, that the rise of populism needs to be understood.

## Populism

Populism is not a very precise term, at least in the way it is often used in media and political discourse. It has been ascribed to parties of both the right and the left, as well as to individual politicians. The term is vague because there is an inherently 'populist' element to modern democracies. Politicians gain power by making pitches to the people for their support. The legitimacy of modern democracy depends on their ability to appeal to voters' values, their identities or their material interests, and often all three. All democratic politics is 'populist' in this sense, but to be characterized as a populist party or politician requires additional criteria to be met. Populists are distinct from other politicians because they are anti-system and anti-establishment. They typically counterpose 'the people' to 'the elite', and blame the elite for all the problems, suffering and oppression of the people. Elites are corrupt, they do not listen, they are insulated from the people, and no longer represent their concerns or their interests. Such populist discourses flourish in authoritarian regimes, often covertly. But they are also an inherent feature of democracies. Populist parties in democracies are natural parties of opposition, sometimes permanent opposition. Problems arise if they win office. As anti-system parties they are dedicated to overthrowing or at least radically overhauling the system, displacing the existing elites and remaking the state and its relationship to the people. They are not expected by their followers to become part of the elite itself as soon as they win power. If they are not absorbed by the existing elite and the 'deep state' they must become the new establishment, which generally means moving in an authoritarian direction, restricting democracy, as in Turkey, Poland and Hungary.

Many of the populisms which have attracted attention in the last decade, such as the Front National in France, are not newcomers. They are long-established anti-system parties which have benefited from the political conditions since the financial crash and increased their support, although so far without managing a breakthrough. Other parties, such as the AfD in Germany or the Five Star movement in Italy are new parties which have grown very rapidly. Other parties will not work with them, which means they will find it hard to enter government unless they can win a majority on their own, but in the case of Italy, at least, it is no longer unthinkable that this could happen. In some of Europe's new democracies, such as Poland and Hungary, national populist parties have won power and are threatening the fragile institutions of liberal democracy, particularly the rule of law and human rights, which were established after the collapse of communist rule. In other democracies, such as Austria, national populist parties have entered government as a coalition partner. There is now a national populist presence in the politics of almost every Western democracy, including Sweden and the Netherlands. Almost all these parties are on the right. There are very few left populist parties, apart from Syriza in Greece and Podemos in Spain. What unites the national populist parties is their opposition to the EU and to globalization. Many advocate referendums to pull their countries out of the euro and out of the EU altogether. Brexit has many admirers on the national populist right in Europe, none on the centre right. The European elite is seen as a unified bloc which has taken away national sovereignty and undermined national identity. The peoples of Europe have to escape its yoke.

The politics of many European democracies are being remade by the advance of national populism, but its most dramatic recent manifestations have come in two of the oldest and traditionally most secure Western democracies – Britain and the United States. In Britain, the populist UK Independence Party campaigned successfully for a referendum on Britain's membership of the EU, and then was part of the Leave Coalition that delivered a narrow vote for Brexit in the referendum on 23 June 2016. UKIP managed to do so without ever having more than two MPs in the Westminster Parliament (both of them defections from the Conservatives), even though it won four million votes in 2015 and had achieved significant representation in the European Parliament. Being on the winning side of the Brexit vote did not benefit UKIP: The party has been consumed by in-fighting, losing most of its votes and its Westminster representation in the general election in 2017. But despite this, the result of the referendum was a signal victory for the populist anti-system politics which was at the core of UKIP's appeal. It was predictable that no sooner had the vote been won than the party quickly turned to warning that the vote would be betrayed. The elites would cheat the people of what they had voted for. The populists had won the vote but it was still Establishment Conservatives, most of whom had voted Remain, who dominated the government and parliament. More than two thirds of MPs had voted for Remain. It was an even higher percentage for members of the House of Lords.

There was a different situation in the United States, where an outsider, Donald Trump, first won the Republican nomination (although he was doubtfully a Republican and in the past had funded the Democrats) and then went on to defeat Hillary Clinton in the electoral college in the presidential campaign of 2016. Trump was not a professional politician. He was a property developer and a TV reality show host. He drew support from populist groups like the Tea Party and the far right fringe of US politics, and built a campaign around outlandish populist claims (about his opponents) and populist commitments (such as building a wall on the southern border to keep out Mexican immigrants). His tactic was always to pitch himself and the people against Washington and the elites. Washington was the swamp which had to be drained. In many ways this was an old trope in US politics; the importance of state politics in the United States meant that generations of politicians had run against Washington, but Trump took it to a new level.

Having won power on an economic nationalist, anti-immigrant, anti-globalization platform, the question became how far he would seek to deliver it. Would he really attempt to drain the swamp, and change the principles, the procedures and the personnel of US Government? At the beginning he had radicals on his staff like Steve Bannon, who wanted to do exactly that. But Trump also surrounded himself with representatives of the US military and the US financial and business elites, as well as by the Republican party political elite. The policies he enacted in his first year were mostly through administrative orders, aimed in particular at scrapping government regulation of business. His one big legislative achievement was his tax package, crafted by Republicans and passed at the end of 2017, and which disproportionately favoured the wealthy elite, including Trump himself, but which was sold as benefiting the American middle class. Trump disengaged the United States from the rest of the world as much as he could, cancelling US involvement in the Trans-Pacific Partnership (TPP) and the Paris agreement on climate change, but he was more cautious in delivering on his promises to fight a trade war with China or to pull out of the WTO or NATO.

The victory of Donald Trump in 2016 was the most important breakthrough made by national populists in the ten years following the financial crash. To win the presidency in the most powerful state in the international order, by threatening to overturn many of the institutions and principles which had built and sustained this order since 1945, was a shock. If it could happen in the United States it could happen anywhere, and even if it was not repeated elsewhere, the victory of populists in the United States could start to unravel the networks, alliances and institutions which had maintained and deepened international cooperation. Trump's long-standing economic nationalism (Laderman and Simms 2017) and his crude America First slogan, an echo of the America First movement of the 1930s which sympathized with Hitler and opposed entering the war on the side of the democracies, alarmed many of its allies, who had been used to the United States pursuing its own interests, but not at the same time disengaging from active leadership of the international order.

It is unclear at the moment whether the Trump phenomenon is a passing spasm which will soon be forgotten under a more traditional president, or whether it betokens a lasting shift in international politics. If the United States continues to be openly contemptuous of many of the institutions which it worked so hard to establish to project US power and influence, and actively disengages from them, the international order might rather quickly unravel as other nations take the opportunity to carve out their own spheres of interest. A return to a world of trade wars, currency wars, and stronger borders to deter immigration would be the likely consequence. Such an outcome is not inevitable but it has become a possibility, especially since the financial crash and the increasing strength of national populism in so many countries. Steve Bannon has referred to national populism as the 'global tea party' (Bannon 2014, as cited by Feder 2016), Its leaders in the United States and Europe have established strong networks to share ideas, drawing inspiration and comfort from each other's successes. Anti-globalization, anti-European integration, and anti-immigration were common themes which drew them together.

## Globalization

Much of the populism that has been so evident in the last nine years, and in particular the political earthquakes of Brexit and the election of Donald Trump, are strongly associated with the hard economic times of the period since the financial crash. But if this populism is only the product of austerity, it might then be expected to decline sharply if and when the international economy finally recovers. Many observers, however, doubt this. As already indicated, some of the populist movements are new, but others are of long standing. Just as the causes of the financial crisis have been traced to much deeper structural problems in the Western political economy, so the populist eruptions have also come to be seen in a much longer perspective. Their causes are sought not just in the years since the financial crash but in the two decades preceding the crash, which saw huge changes in the way both the international market order and national economies were structured. These changes are ascribed to processes of globalization and to the adoption of neo-liberal doctrines as the ruling common sense.

How far is globalization itself responsible for the rise of national populism and increasing political polarization that has taken place in so many Western democracies in the last ten years? The meaning of 'globalization' has been sharply contested since the term came into general use in the 1990s. Globalization was not an event but a process, and it is a process which is hardly new. Capitalist globalization has lasted at least as long as the international capitalist economy itself. This modern world system, as Wallerstein termed it, began in the fifteenth and sixteenth centuries in Europe. In these five centuries the strength of globalising forces has waxed and waned. At times it has been very intense as in the second half of the nineteenth century, at other times, as in the middle decades of the twentieth century, much less so. The revival in the strength of globalising forces in the 1980s, 1990s and early 2000s was extremely marked, but some of its proponents got carried away and began to speak of the creation of a borderless world, or the end of the nation-state (Ohmae 1995, 1999). This hyper globalization was always a fantasy and rightly criticized (Held et al. 1999; Hirst and Thompson 1996). There is not one but many globalizations. Globalization needs to be broken down into the diverse set of processes which increase the flow of goods, people, and capital, making the international economy ever more interconnected. As in previous periods of globalization there was a deployment of new technologies, this time associated above all with the IT revolution, which permitted a further shrinking of distance in the international economy and a further increase in mobility. In rapid periods of globalization everything speeds up.

The big shifts which drove globalization in the 1990s were firstly the end of the Cold War and the breakup of the Soviet bloc, but secondly, and of much greater significance, the entry of China, India and other rising powers into full participation in international trade. The tantalising prospect of the international economy becoming One World again hovered through the 1990s, the first time since the nineteenth century that it had seemed realistic, and in that earlier period it was severely restricted by the existence of the European colonial empires. The phenomenal growth of the Asian economies caused a great shift in the way production was organized, with Western multinationals taking advance of the efficiency and low costs of Chinese factories to outsource much of their manufacturing to China and other Asian economies, building extremely complex and elaborate production chains in the process. This new division of labour in the international economy gave a huge boost to world output and to world trade, as well as removing inflationary pressure from the Western economies. It was the major factor in the upswing in the 1990s and early 2000s, which brought prosperity and steady growth to the Western economies, and dramatic transformations in some of the poorest and most highly populated states. A measure of the transformation that was under way is the UN estimate in 2001 that for the first time the world now had more of its population living in cities than on the land. It also indicated how much further there was to go before every part of the world economy was developed and integrated.

The other side of this globalization was that though it brought great wealth to the financial and industrial elites in the Western economies, it also meant further de-industrialization for them, the loss of domestic manufacturing capacity and jobs. Many of those displaced found new jobs but often more precarious, with lower pay and lower status. This pattern was repeated in many countries; only a few escaped it. It created a mass of discontented and alienated citizens, a new 'precariat', those unable or unwilling to adapt to the new economy, which increasingly demanded adaptability, reskilling, flexibility, mobility. The new economy created a widespread resentment among those left behind, which was easily directed at the cosmopolitan global elites who were so much at ease with globalization and were so obviously the beneficiaries of it. Globalization created great benefits, but they were very unevenly distributed. There were clear winners and losers, and new dividing lines in politics as a result. In the Anglo-Saxon countries the particular form which globalization took led to a dramatic increase in inequality, with huge gains going to the richest 1 per cent. Inequality had not been so marked in Europe and the United States since before World War I (Piketty 2014). The contrast between the spoils of globalization's winners and the losses of the losers was stark, and fuelled further resentment. The hugely inflated bonuses which bankers pocketed, and the extravagant lifestyles they funded, became symbols of the era, and more targets for populist rage.

This is the argument as to how globalization fed populism. The political elites became detached from large numbers of their citizens, and no longer represented or understood them. Instead their primary loyalties came to be to the international networks of the proliferating international organizations and institutions which provided global governance for an increasingly complex world. These developments have led to the globalization paradox analysed by Dani Rodrik. The world system as Immanuel Wallerstein conceived it always contained a tension between the drive for ever greater economic integration of markets and production, and the fragmentation of political authority among a number of competing states. This is the tension Rodrik explores in relation to the latest phase of globalization. The increasing interdependence of the international economy exists alongside the desire of individual countries to retain and exercise their own sovereignty, and also the need for them, as democracies, to retain the support of their citizens. Rodrik suggested this creates a trilemma. It is possible to achieve any two of the three – increasing economic interdependence, national sovereignty and democratic legitimacy, but not all three at once. In the first combination – economic interdependence and national sovereignty – authoritarian governments use their power to pursue economic interdependence and sacrifice democracy. In the second combination – economic interdependence and democratic legitimacy – national sovereignty and nation-states wither away to be replaced by a cosmopolitan government. In the third combination – national sovereignty and democratic legitimacy – governments stay close to the wishes and interests of their citizens, and take steps to limit or even reverse economic interdependence.

Of these three alternatives there are examples of the first and the third, much less of the second. The EU was originally conceived by some of its architects as a regional prototype for the third, but in practice although it has developed some supranational elements, it remains very much an association of nation-states, and much discussion, particularly of the handling of the eurozone crisis has focused on whether the EU has become an example of the first type, creating a form of government supported by the national governments which insulates policy-making from democratic control, and which promotes greater interdependence and the giving up of sovereignty. The dilemma for global elites is that they are committed to the twin principles of a liberal international order and democratic national government. These were founding principles for the international order after 1945. But the question has always been, if there is a clash between these two principles which takes precedence? In the first three decades of the liberal international order, great attention was paid to what was acceptable to democratic electorates in each nation, and as a result national governments were accorded a great deal of autonomy and often the United States made concessions in order to make it easier for states to stay within the Western alliance and be fully contributing members of the international order. The United States was so much the dominant power that it could afford to do this, and although this never stopped the United States from pursuing its own interests, or from overthrowing governments it perceived were a threat to them, it was often prepared to make concessions to its democratic allies because of the overriding need to maintain the cohesion of the 'West' against the Soviet bloc. Cold war security considerations meant that its core allies (which came to include Germany and Japan) were generally treated sympathetically.

This began to change in the 1970s because the United States could no longer afford to bear the costs of the fixed exchange rate system that had been agreed at Bretton Woods. In cutting loose and floating the dollar, it both removed one of the main barriers to inflation, which was gathering pace, and signalled the determination of the United States to give greater priority to its own needs and interests. The international system was gradually reshaped to fit these changed priorities, and it led to a new set of policies and instruments for managing the international economy which became the framework within which all Western states had to work, some more eagerly than others. The doctrines of neo-liberalism were important in shaping the new regime which emerged. They included the monetarism of Milton Friedman and the supply-side economics of Arthur Laffer. Many of the new ideas became policy orthodoxy by the end of the 1980s for the leading international institutions like the IMF and the World Bank, and were dubbed the Washington consensus. This was a package of policies including privatization, deregulation, low taxes, flexible labour markets, weak trade unions and low public spending which was imposed on countries which got into economic difficulties and required loans to bail them out, and also on developing countries, as a condition for aid and restructuring of their debt.

This was also the policy package which became associated with globalization. The promotion of free markets around the world, and therefore the acceleration of flows of capital, goods, services and money became the hallmarks of this phase of the development of a new liberal international order, which after the collapse of communism in Europe now extended into all corners of the world, with very few countries remaining outside. The governance of this new international order was much more complex than in the past because of the degree of cooperation, the number of players, and the scale of the challenges, many of which such as mass immigration, terrorism, climate change and nuclear proliferation were recognized as inherently transnational. One response was the proliferation of international organizations and NGOs to facilitate the management of these problems and secure greater cooperation between states (Slaughter 2009). To some it seemed that a global polity and a global civil society were in the making to go alongside the global economy.

What was sometimes overlooked was the need to embed the new transnational institutions in the national democracies. This was often not done because it was difficult to do. Some of the new members of the international order were not democracies and did not accept liberal principles. In the democracies it was often hard to engage citizens with the complexities of international rule-making. It was easier to focus on the international networks rather than the national ones. In these ways the various global elites gradually became more similar to one another and more detached from the citizens from whom ultimately they derived their legitimacy and their authority.

Rodrik believes there is no easy solution to his trilemma. He regards cosmopolitan government rooted in a global demos as unattainable. He is opposed to economic interdependence being sustained by authoritarian politics. His preference is therefore for national sovereignty which is legitimated through democracy. This is also the demand of most of the new national populists. They are opposed to globalization and the global elites it has spawned, and they want to take back control of borders, money and laws. They want to bring back production which has been outsourced and give priority to the national economy and the communities which depend upon it. If this means becoming much more closed to the outside world and retreating from existing levels of economic and political interdependence and cooperation, and accepting a lower standard of living, that is a choice many of them are prepared to make. The vitality of the democracy and the ability of the majority opinion to be reflected in the policy of a sovereign government is what counts. This is heard particularly on the right but also on the left of politics. It was, for example, the basis of Tony Benn's argument in the 1980s in the British Labour party against Britain remaining a member of the European Community, and against NATO. Benn still considered himself a committed internationalist, but it was an internationalism based on cooperation between independent sovereign socialist nations, not an internationalism based on trade and security.

Most of the global elite do not want to see the liberal international order undermined, believing that although it is highly imperfect, it is the best available solution to maintaining openness, cooperation and peace. But the more thoughtful members of the elite agree with Rodrik that globalization and neo-liberalism have gone too far. The existing model no longer works, and there needs to be substantial change if the liberal international order is not gradually to unravel. The hyper globalization which led to the financial crash, Rodrik argues, needs to be replaced by a smart globalization, which recognizes the important role played by governments in regulating markets, compensating losers and curbing excesses. This means a politics which starts to recognize that many citizens do not benefit from greater openness and are hostile to many of the changes it forces upon them. Martin Wolf has argued that an open liberal international order is still the ideal, the current difficulties of the international economy and the backlash against globalization mean that it needs to be given a lower priority than looking after citizens and ensuring that they do not become so disaffected that they start supporting much more radical parties and movements which want, like Steve Bannon, to tear down the whole edifice of the liberal international order (Wolf 2018a, 2018b).

This would imply trying to resurrect the earlier compact which underpinned post-war reconstruction and the creation of the liberal international order under US leadership. This compact was founded on governments delivering employment, social security, health care, and education for all their citizens. These became defined as the entitlements of democratic citizenship, the addition of social rights to civil and political rights. Such states earned their legitimacy by being responsive to what their citizens wanted and delivering it. When they failed to deliver what voters wanted, they could lose office. The model is a beguiling one. It worked imperfectly, but it did capture something that helps account for the stability of many of the Western democracies, some of them quite new or reborn after the defeat of fascism. Western democracies, by a number of indicators, worked better for their citizens and were closer to them in the immediate post-war decades than more recently. Part of the explanation comes down to the impact of globalization and the gradual transfer of more and more decision-making and authority to bodies over which citizens had no direct control. If political elites had remained trusted, this might not have mattered. But every Western democracy has seen a decline of trust in both the competence and the integrity of elected representatives. In these conditions, populism thrives.

## Conclusion: Embedded Populism?

If the new populism has risen during the recession, will it therefore fade away once the recession ends and growth resumes? This is a comforting thought, but may be too optimistic, both because the prospects of a sustained recovery are still very uncertain, and also because the causes of the new populism are much more deep-rooted than just a reaction to austerity after the financial crash. Thirty years of globalization and widening inequality have led to resentment against the rich, but also a deep alienation from society and the way it has become organized. The erosion of traditional class identities tied to heavy industry and working class communities has weakened the base of traditional centre-left parties, and this has been exploited by the new populist parties. The centre-left parties cannot regain these voters simply by promising a return of prosperity, since they have become so closely identified with younger professional cosmopolitan voters who are at home in the global economy and the opportunities and autonomy it brings.

The key issue which has focused resentment against globalization and the EU has been immigration. Free movement of goods, services, capital and persons were the foundations of the EU single market, and they were also the implicit basis of the global markets which boomed in the 1990s. The UK was a strong supporter both of the European single market and also of the opening of world markets associated with globalization. The successful UK growth model of the 1990s was built on the export of services, particularly financial services, and flexible labour markets which encouraged the development of a low wage economy and the recruitment of large numbers of migrant workers. This reached its peak in the early 2000s, when the UK chose not to impose restrictions on the ability of new EU member states to seek work in Britain. At the same time, immigration from non-EU countries was also rising, so that by the time of the financial crash, immigration was running at over 300,000 a year. Despite the promise of the Conservatives to reduce this figure to the tens of thousands, they signally failed to do so. Many Conservatives blamed the EU for this failure, but that was only part of the story, since EU migrants only made up half of the total. The other half came from outside the EU.

Hostility to the scale and pace of immigration was one of the major factors leading to support for Brexit. The failure of national governments to control immigration was seen by many citizens as symptomatic of the politics of globalization. It benefited those in the networks of globalization and penalized those who had to compete with immigrants for jobs, housing and access to public services. There was some overt racism as well, but the main factor was the widespread feeling that communities and neighbourhoods were being changed in ways which a majority of their inhabitants did not understand and did not want. Centre-left parties in the UK and in many other European countries found themselves on the wrong side of this argument as far as many of their traditional supporters were concerned. The levels of immigration into the EU also became high during the recession years: what might have been easy to manage while economies were still growing became difficult when unemployment was high and living standards stagnant. Yet one of the consequences of globalization has been to make the riches of the West ever more visible and desirable to citizens of poor countries in Africa, Asia and Latin America. Most of the rich countries have seen their birth rates decline to the point where some of them are facing actual population decline. Encouraging immigration of young, healthy, energetic and resourceful people is one solution, but nothing has done more to fuel the growth of the populist parties, who are able to blame immigration on the liberal global cosmopolitan elites with their selfish concern for their own privileges, insulated from the rest of the society in which they live. Trump and many other populist leaders seized on that issue, and Trump crystallized all the frustration of his base in calling for a wall on the Mexican border. Support for the wall was highest in those states furthest removed from it, and the value of a wall in actually stopping illegal immigration was doubtful, but that did not matter. What mattered was the symbolism of closing a border and making people feel more secure, and no longer overrun. The wall affirmed the identity of US citizens, and remains a powerful rallying call for Trump's base.

National populism should not, therefore, be seen as an aberration or some kind of malign affliction. It has a deep connection to the way in which the international political economy has been organized over the last three decades, which have transformed the prospects for so many citizens and communities, and not always positively. For a long time this revolt looked to be containable, but the political and economic impasse since the financial crash has provided fertile ground for populism to thrive, drawing on a range of cultural as well as economic grievances. It may not achieve its goals. Its successes breed a counter-response, but it has already reshaped politics and put a question mark over how durable a liberal, open international order will prove to be (Zielonka 2018).

## References

Berger, Peter and Huntington, Samuel. *Many Globalizations: Cultural Diversity in the Modern World* (Oxford, Oxford University Press 2002).

Canovan, Margaret. *Populism* (New York, Harcourt Brace 1981).

Evans-Pritchard, Ambrose. 'World finance now more dangerous than in 2008, warns central bank guru', *The Telegraph* (22 January 2018). Available at http://www.telegraph.co.uk/business/2018/01/22/world-finance-now-dangerous-2008-warns-central-bank-guru/ (Accessed 16 July 2018).

Feder, J. Lester. 'This is how Steve Bannon sees the entire world', *Buzzfeed* (16 November 2016). Available at https://www.buzzfeed.com/lesterfeder/this-is-how-steve-bannon-sees-the-entire-world (Accessed 16 July 2018).

Gamble, Andrew. *Crisis Without End? The Unravelling of Western Prosperity* (London, Palgrave-Macmillan 2016).

Held, David; McGrew, Anthony; Goldblatt, David and Perraton, Jonathan. *Global Transformations* (Cambridge, Polity 1999).

Hirst, Paul and Thompson, Grahame. *Globalization in Question* (Cambridge, Polity 1996).

Laderman, Charlie and Simms, Brendan. *Donald Trump: The Making of a World View* (London, I.B.Tauris 2017).

Mudde, Cas and Kaltwasser, Cristobal. *Populism: A Very Short Introduction* (New York, Oxford University Press 2017).

Muller, Jan-Werner. *What is Populism?* (Philadelphia, University of Pennsylvania Press 2016).

Ohmae, Kenichi. *The Borderless World: Power and Strategy in the Interlinked Economy* (New York, Harper Business 1999).

Ohmae, Kenichi. *The End of the Nation-state* (London, Harper Collins 1995).

Piketty, Thomas. *Capital in the 21$^{st}$ Century* (Cambridge, MA, Belknap Press 2014).

Rodrik, Dani. *The Globalization Paradox* (Oxford, Oxford University Press 2011).

Slaughter, Anne-Marie. *A New World Order* (Princeton, Princeton University Press 2009).

Wolf, Martin 'Davos 2018: the liberal international order is sick' *The Financial Times* (2018). Available at https://www.ft.com/content/c45acec8-fd35-11e7-9b32-d7d59aace167 (Accessed 27 June 2018).

Wolf, Martin. 'Counter-Revolution by Jan Zielonka – project backlash', *The Financial Times* (2018). Available at https://www.ft.com/content/e4290c10-069f-11e8-9650-9c0ad2d7c5b5 (Accessed 27 June 2018).

Zielonka, Jan. *Counter Revolution: Liberal Europe in Retreat* (Oxford, Oxford University Press 2018).

CHAPTER 2

# The Backlash Against Globalization and the Future of the International Economic Order

Jeffry Frieden

Political events of the past few years have called into question the future of an integrated international economy. Brexit, the election of Donald Trump, the rise of parties of the right and left that are sceptical about economic integration – whether at the global or European level – have all challenged the previously common assumption that globalization had become the natural and normal state of international economic affairs.

In reality, scholars and other analysts have been discussing a globalization backlash for some 20 years; what has changed is that we now have some idea of what it looks like. For the future of the world economy, the election of Donald Trump is by far the most important result of this backlash. The United States has been the unquestioned leader of the international economic order since it managed its creation at Bretton Woods in 1944, and President Trump has been explicit about his intention to remake that order. Although there are obstacles to his goals, the fact that he is the chief executive of the world's most important economy means that his views will have a profound impact.

Whether hostility to international economic integration continues to grow or not, the wheels are already in motion to remake fundamentally the global economy's ordering principles. Given the shift in the American government's orientation, other nations' governments have incentives to work out alternative arrangements not so reliant upon American leadership. If current trends persist, and the United States continues to abandon its traditional leadership role, the world is likely to be far more fragmented among regional trading areas. Barriers between these areas and the United States (and its closest trading partners) are likely to grow. Fragmentation in trade relations is likely to lead to similar fragmentation in international finance and investment.

The continuation of current trends is not inevitable. However, the past five years have set in motion developments that will be difficult to slow and even more difficult to reverse. The future of the world economy is likely to be substantially different from its recent past.

## The World Economic Order: the Past 70 Years

The United States and its close allies constructed the contemporary international economy during and immediately after World War II. This economic order, which prevailed first throughout the capitalist world, then after 1989 in the entire world, was based on organizing principles that were similar to, and grew out of, the approach that had come to order advanced industrial societies domestically.

The central goal of the Bretton Woods Agreement was to oversee the gradual liberalization of international trade, investment, and finance after the disastrous experiences of economic nationalism and protectionism that had characterized the interwar period. However, the United States' construction of a new international economic order, in concert with its allies, incorporated an understanding that the political economies of the post-World War II industrialized world were profoundly different from those of the Victorian gold-standard era. Economic openness was eminently desirable, but it could not come at the expense of the social policies that had become standard in the advanced societies. Nor was it advisable to move too quickly in subjecting domestic industries to international trade competition, or in opening the current and capital accounts of countries that had recently experienced massive financial crises. So the Bretton Woods system was based on compromise. International economic integration would progress, but so would national commitments to counter-cyclical macroeconomic demand management and to the modern welfare state.[1]

Since World War II, the world economy has gradually, sometimes in fits and starts, become more open. In the 1950s and 1960s the process was largely restricted to the Western industrial economies, among which trade barriers came down, international investment grew, and international finance revived. The 1970s were a troubled decade of recessions, high unemployment, and high inflation, during which the desirability of an integrated global (capitalist) economy was often called into question. The issue was joined and decided over the course of the 1980s. The advanced industrial countries brought inflation down and continued their efforts to increase economic integration – including, most prominently, with substantial progress toward a single market and exchange-rate stability in the European Union (EU). In the aftermath of the debt crisis of the early and middle 1980s, most developing countries turned away from import substitution and toward export promotion, following the example of such countries as South Korea and Taiwan. Even more strikingly, China and Vietnam also chose to join the capitalist world economy, with market-oriented reforms and their own versions of export promotion. Especially important was the collapse of central planning in the Soviet Union and its allies, most of which joined the world economy – some of them eventually joining the EU.

The 1990s were the height of a certain 'globalization euphoria.' Dozens of developing and former Communist countries had joined the world economy, many of them were demoncratising, the Cold War was over, and world economic growth was healthy. For the first few years of the new century, globalization and economic expansion continued and even accelerated, turning into a boom and eventually a bubble. The bubble burst with a vengeance in 2007, leading to the longest and deepest global recession since the 1930s. Recovery was slow, but it did come. However, by 2010 it was clear that there was increasing scepticism about the desirability of globalization. Within a few years, the change in the prevailing winds had become a storm.

## The Globalization Backlash

The United States is by far the most important locus of this backlash against globalization, given America's size and centrality to international economics and politics. There are certainly other countries in which similar trends are at work: Brexit in the UK and right-wing populism in Central and Eastern Europe are prominent examples. However, given this essay's focus on the trend's implications for the world economy, I concentrate on developments in the United States.

While the American public was favourably inclined toward globalization in the 1990s, after about 2000 public opinion surveys began demonstrating a growing scepticism about, even hostility toward, international economic integration. The Great Financial Crisis of 2007–9 excited and deepened this scepticism. In its wake, the Tea Party movement in the Republican Party burst onto the scene. Although its principles were never entirely clear, the Tea Party movement rejected Republican moderates and showed disdain for presidential candidate Mitt Romney's association with traditional elites.

Hostility to elites, from both the right and the left, became a direct attack on economic internationalism during the presidential election campaign of 2016. Donald Trump was explicit in his antagonism to foreign trade, investment, and immigration, while Bernie Sanders evinced analogous scepticism about international trade and investment in the Democratic primaries. This was the first time since the 1930s that both major parties had candidates for the presidential nomination who were openly hostile to economic integration, and that any major party had an actual nominee with similar views. The victory of Donald Trump in the 2016 presidential election marked the victory of an economic nationalism that had long been far from the mainstream of American politics. Trump and his supporters expressed hostility to internationalist big business, to big finance, to the international economy more generally, to immigrants, and to many traditional foreign-policy commitments.

As candidate, Donald Trump promised much more restrictive trade policies. The threats included 35–45 per cent tariffs on Chinese imports, an across-the-board border tax of 20 per cent sanctions on China for alleged currency manipulation, and a 15 per cent tax on outward foreign investment. These may have only been threats – and they have certainly not been implemented – but the broader meaning of the campaign should not be lost. Trump's position was a massive deviation from the traditional Republican position, which for 70 years has been more or less committed to open trade and investment. Indeed, for some 40 years the Democrats have been far more protectionist than the Republicans; that relationship has clearly reversed. The Trump administration is unquestionably the most openly protectionist administration in modern history; and its victory seems to presage a major turn for the Republican Party away from economic internationalism and toward something much closer to the Republican position of the early twentieth century, the years of Republican protectionism and isolationism.

There are clear economic roots to the support for President Trump's America First attitudes toward the international economy. American public opinion tends to associate international trade and investment with job insecurity and job losses. Many Americans also associate globalization with increasing income inequality, especially with the outsized growth in the income and wealth of the top 10 per cent or 1 per cent of American society – the financial, corporate and professional elite that has benefited enormously from their global ties, while leaving the middle and working classes behind.

Discontent has been building for a long time in important parts of the country, especially the mid-Western industrial belt. The region's problems started in the late 1960s and accelerated through the 1970s and 1980s, as a phalanx of developing countries embarked on export drives. The process should be seen as affecting *communities* more than disconnected individuals. American manufacturing is concentrated in the Midwest and parts of the South, and is particularly important to some towns and small cities in these regions. Many of these entered in a sort of downward spiral starting with trade and investment-related pressures on local manufacturing. Factory closings increased unemployment and underemployment, lowering wages and labour force participation. Local economic problems reduced local-government tax revenue, so that local public services deteriorated (Feler and Senses [2017] carefully discuss and document these indirect community-level effects). As the community's economic base eroded there were devastating *social* effects, including a rise in alcoholism, opioid abuse and suicidality (Pierce and Schott 2017).

These trends have had a clear political impact. Increased trade, in particular with China, has caused some regions to lose jobs and see reduced wages.[2] The political effects are multifarious. Affected regions are more politically polarized (Autor et al. 2016a). Their legislators tend to vote in more protectionist directions (Feigenbaum and Hall 2015). They were more likely to swing their votes toward Donald Trump in the 2016 presidential election (Autor et al. 2016b; see also Jensen et al. 2017).

There are undoubtedly non-material sources of America's new populism, including cultural bias and ethnic prejudice. Similarly, the economic trends the country has experienced are at least as much due to skill-biased technological change as they are to globalization. Nonetheless, globalization is a clear policy target, and economic nationalism is popular at least in part because it seems to help Americans at the expense of foreigners.

The central point is that the current direction of American international economic policy is not an aberration, and not a passing fancy. To be sure, supporters of protectionism and economic nationalism in the Trump Administration face several obstacles. Some segments of the Republican Party, and of the business community that has typically been a crucial supporter of the party, are likely to be deeply concerned if the Administration follows through on its rhetorical dismissal of the value of multilateralism, international economic cooperation, and openness to international trade and investment. The electorate may well turn against President Trump and his new-model Republican Party. Nonetheless, the 2016 election was a watershed in modern American politics. It signalled the rejection of the current international economic order by large segments of the public. So far, there has been no generally popular response, either from within the Republican

Party or from the Democratic Party. The domestic politics of international economic policy in the United States has changed fundamentally.

## Implications for the International Economy

It has to be taken as given that American foreign economic policy will continue its current direction at least through 2020, and perhaps beyond. Of course, trends in other parts of the world are also relevant to thinking about the future of the global economic order. However, in the light of American international economic predominance for the past 75 years, virtually any projection into the future has to start with expectations about the position of the United States.

We assume, as discussed above, that domestic political trends in the United States mean that American foreign economic policy will continue to move away from its post-World War II commitment to economic integration, multilateralism, and international economic cooperation. In this context, other countries and regions have no choice but to attempt to adjust to a new reality.

From Brussels to Brasilia to Beijing, foresighted policy-makers have to think about how they can best move forward given the potential course of American foreign economic policy. Their most straightforward concern is to carve out alternatives to policies that had previously assumed American engagement in, and leadership of, attempts at international economic collaboration. This will place a premium upon developing economic relations that navigate the troubled shoals of American foreign economic policy and its difficult domestic politics.

In trade, we can expect that governments everywhere will search for more bilateral trade agreements with partners other than the United States. The recent Canada–European Union trade agreement, well underway long before 2016, is nonetheless an example of the sort of arrangement to be expected. The member states of the Southern Common Market in South America (Mercosur) have already expressed strong interest in a similar arrangement with the EU, and such expressions of interest will undoubtedly proliferate.

Countries outside North America are likely to redouble efforts at regional integration. The logic of economic integration suggests that, failing multilateral progress, governments will seek to strengthen trade relations with countries with which they have traditionally close ties, or with which geography and economic structure suggest strong complementarities.

The Chinese government has redoubled the efforts it began in 2013 with the 'Belt and Road Initiative' to stimulate trade and investment within Asia, assisted by the activities of the new Asian Infrastructure Investment Bank. And the Chinese are likely to be even more heavily committed to working in Africa to develop both markets and sources of supply of primary products.

Elsewhere in Asia, the eleven remaining members of the Trans-Pacific Partnership, rebranded as the Comprehensive and Progressive Agreement for Trans-Pacific Partnership, are moving forward with their efforts at regional cooperation. It may be that, with the United States no longer involved, the members of a reinvigorated TPP could be open to some involvement on the part of China. Certainly countries like Australia, Vietnam, South Korea and Japan both want closer ties with their Asian and trans-Pacific partners, and the possibility of a mild counter-balance to Chinese influence.

(3) The EU, in addition to strengthening its economic interactions with Canada and, perhaps, Mercosur, has reasons to continue to build its economic bonds with the former European colonies in Africa and Asia. The EU's naturally close ties to the Middle East and North Africa are likely to be improved and enhanced by the Trump Administration's alienation of many governments in the region. It is also likely that the EU will find it both desirable, and eventually easier, to build closer economic links to Russia and its Eurasian allies. It is unclear how this connects with Chinese attempts to tie Central Asia more closely to its economic powerhouse, but there may be little to stand in the way of a more tightly integrated Eurasia, stretching from Ireland to Japan (with the position of the UK uncertain).

(4) Latin America finds itself in a difficult position, given its geography and traditional economic connections to North America. Nonetheless, as mentioned, the major economies of South America are already seeking closer ties to the EU; even Mexico seems to be looking for a counter-weight to the United States.

While at this point these are just speculations about the future, there is little question that the edifice of the international economic order is being transformed. Given the difficulties of multilateral trade negotiations within the World Trade Organization (WTO), there were already indications of a regionalization of trade and investment; this is likely to accelerate. At the institutional level, the Trump Administration seems intent on undermining the authority of the WTO, especially its Disputes Settlement Mechanism, which it regards as an infringement on American sovereignty. If this attempt were to be successful, and the WTO's monitoring and enforcement functions were impeded – at least with regards to American trade – we would expect the result to be a further dampening of trade with the United States, and the greater likelihood that American trade concerns would lead to unilateral measures – and, presumably, retaliation from the targets.

One important implication of this is that even if political developments in the United States begin to change the course chosen by the Trump Administration, the political revolution of 2016 has already set in motion processes that may be difficult or impossible to reverse. It is probably the case that we are witnessing the transformation of America's role in the international trading order toward greater unilateral action, and a greater reliance upon bilateral ties, with increased levels of trade protection and more trade conflicts with other countries. Elsewhere, we are likely to see a growing regionalization of international trade and investment, as countries outside North America attempt to shield themselves from the impact of the new American stance.

## What Might be Done?

What one thinks of these prospects is, of course, a purely normative question. I, for one, do not regard them as innocuous. International economic integration has been extraordinarily beneficial, especially to developing countries. Its undesirable distributional effects can be handled in such a way as to alleviate some of the suffering that globalization can cause, and has caused. Indeed, many countries have been more successful than the United States in addressing the issues that international trade and investment raise about the domestic distribution of income.

It is, nonetheless, clear that in the United States – and in many other countries – mechanisms to compensate those harmed by globalization have been insufficient. Individuals and, most important, communities that have seen their quality of life deteriorate for decades, and that have at least some reason to blame at least some of the deterioration on globalization, are right to expect that their governments take responsibility for helping to cushion the blow. Virtually no country's government has come up with a fully satisfactory and comprehensive response to the economic and social impact of globalization – and the result has been a backlash that is now calling the very structure of the world economy into question.

Existing political parties and institutions appear to offer few alternatives to populist demands. It is easy to see that the populist policies will not be successful in the long run – and probably not even in the short run – but this is not cause for celebration: the popular response to populist failures may well be to move in even more extreme directions.

Over the coming years, political parties, politicians, and political activists who believe in both progressive social policies and an open world economy face a major challenge. They need to provide effective, politically feasible proposals for policies that address the socio-economic effects of globalization. These include ways of broadening the positive impact of international economic activities to include much more of the population. This will have to involve preparing more young people for the economic demands of the modern world economy; and protecting, retraining, or compensating older people who have not yet been able to adapt.

The policies necessary to provide a compelling alternative to populism and economic nationalism are difficult to define, and even more difficult to achieve politically. However, there is little doubt that the industrialized world faces a decade of serious clashes over the way forward in the domestic and international political economies.

## Notes

1. Ruggie (1982) is the classic statement of this compromise, which he called 'embedded liberalism.' For a summary of the interwar collapse and the reconstruction efforts at Bretton et al. (2006, Chapters 6–11).
2. Most of the studies investigating the relationship use some variant of the China Shock instrument first developed in Autor et al. (2013). While I am not familiar with studies on the analogous distributional implications of the integration of capital markets, there are a few on the impact of foreign direct investment ('offshoring'); see especially Owen and Johnston (2017).

## References

Autor, David H.; Dorn, David; and Hanson, Gordon H. 'The China Syndrome: Local labour market effects of import competition in the United States', *American Economic Review* 103(6) (2013) pp. 2121–68.

Autor, David H.; Dorn, David; Hanson, Gordon; and Majlesi, Kaveh. 'Importing Political Polarization? The Electoral Consequences of Rising Trade Exposure' (Working paper 2016).

Autor, David; Dorn, David; Hanson, Gordon; and Majlesi, Kaveh. 'A Note on the Effect of Rising Trade Exposure on the 2016 Presidential Election' (Working paper November 2016).

Feigenbaum, James and Hall, Andrew. 'How legislators respond to localized economic shocks: Evidence from Chinese import competition', *Journal of Politics* 77(4) (2015).

Feler, Leo and Senses, Mine Z.. 'Trade shocks and the provision of local public goods', *American Economic Journal: Economic Policy* 9(4) (2017) pp. 101–43.

Frieden, Jeffry. *Global Capitalism: Its Fall and Rise in the Twentieth Century* (New York, W W Norton 2006).

Jensen, J.; Bradford, Quinn, Dennis; and Weymouth, Stephen, 'Winners and losers in international trade: The effects on U.S. Presidential voting', *International Organization* 71(3) (Summer) (2017) pp. 423–57.

Owen, Erica and Johnston, Noel P. 'Occupation and the political economy of trade: Job routineness, offshorability, and protectionist sentiment', *International Organization* 71(4) (Fall) (2017) pp. 665–99.

Pierce, Justin and Schott, Peter. 'Trade Liberalization and Mortality: Evidence from U.S. Counties' (Working paper October 2017).

Ruggie, John G. 'International regimes, transactions, and change: Embedded liberalism in the post-war economic order', *International Organization*, 36 (Spring 1982).

CHAPTER 3

# Populist Political Communication Going Mainstream? The Influence of Populist Parties on Centre-Left Parties in Western Europe

Patricia Rodi

## Introduction

Populism is a hotly debated topic, and is perceived by politicians and academics alike as a great threat to Western democracies. Jean-Claude Juncker, the President of the European Commission (2014–), warned that the European Union is in a battle with 'galloping populism' (Charter 2016) while Martin Schulz, the erstwhile president of the European Parliament (2012–17), declared that 'Unscrupulous populists, who have no solutions to offer, are taking advantage of the situation to prey on the fears of ordinary people' (Banks 2016). In the media, journalists argued populism is 'a real threat to mainstream democracy' (Painter 2013).

There is an alleged 'populist zeitgeist' emerging across Europe (Mudde 2004), where politicians of right and left, on the fringes and in the mainstream, from Jeremy Corbyn to Nigel Farage and Donald Trump to Bernie Sanders, have adopted and imitated populist forms of expression and communication. However, the extent to which populist methods and practices have been adopted by mainstream parties varies widely. Some contributors identify only a minimal effect on mainstream parties' political programmes (see Rooduijn et al. 2014), while others have shown – largely by anecdote – that a handful of mainstream politicians have actively adopted populist means of communication and action since the 1990s (Mudde 2004; Hawkins 2009).

The present chapter investigates populist political communication and its potential impact on centre-left parties, with specific focus on adaptation by centre-left parties to the distinct communicative characteristics of populism. This is necessary, not only in the light of recent populist backlashes in many Western democracies against mainstream governments and given political and economic developments since 2008, but because centre-left parties have been dominant within Western European political systems since World War II (Keating and McCronne 2013). There is, as such, a need to give attention to the possible reasons and consequences of such 'populist contamination', and to further explore whether these centre-left parties have become more populist in their communication activities. As populism remains a widely-debated topic, it is essential that the term is handled with care and precision. As such, the chapter will focus on pinpointing the main characteristics of populist political communication, and provide a straightforward guide to identify where it does occur.

The contribution compares the British Labour Party and the Swedish Social Democratic Party and examines the potential contagion of populist political communication in these cases. These two parties are of particular interest due to the countries' different forms of democracy. For example, it has been argued that majoritarian democracies provide fertile ground for populism (cf. Stanyer et al. 2017; Rooduijn et al. 2014). In view of this relationship I anticipate that different forms of democratic models – as seen in the UK's majoritarian and Sweden's consensual forms of government – can condition whether or not the mainstream centre-left will incorporate populist means of communication.

The chapter proceeds by discussing the emergence of populist parties in Western Europe and the effects this has on centre-left parties. The subsequent section provides an introduction to populism in a communicative context and pinpoints the distinct characteristics of populist political communication. Lastly, the chapter explores whether populist political communication now appears in the communication channels and messages of the dominant centre-left mainstream parties in Sweden and the UK, before drawing conclusions regarding the wider implications of these findings.

## Centre-Left Parties and Populism in Western Europe

On the face of it, social democratic parties have experienced falling support in countries across Europe. Some have even argued that there is a 'crisis of social democracy' (Keating and McCrone 2013). Before moving on, let's briefly take stock of the position that was held by left-wing politics and political parties in recent decades.

The transformation of capitalism has undermined many social democratic ideas and practices. Specifically, the decline of the manual working class during the 1960s changed the class structure, and old class divisions became increasingly blurred (Oskarsson 2005; Keating and McCrone 2013). As a result, class as a determining factor in voter preferences was, by the late 1990s, in decline (Evans et al. 1999; Evans and Tilley 2012). Globalization, de-industrialization and growing inward-migration in Europe made way for the emergence of new political cleavages in relation to socio-cultural and religious issues. Such cleavages gained relevance in the context of party competition and party affiliation. New parties rejected the traditional class-based orientation of politics in the form of Green parties in the 1970s, followed by radical right parties in the 1980s and 1990s (Meguid 2008). In light of this, many political parties, especially those on the left, were faced with a shrinking core base of voters. This led some social democratic parties to re-think their electoral strategies and to develop new responses and programmes to 'catch' a wider voter base (Evans and Tilley 2012). The result was a shift towards the ideological centre and, in extreme cases, even towards the right (as seen with Tony Blair's New Labour). Some have argued that many social democratic parties gave up their fundamental scepticism about the free market (although to varying degrees), allowing socio-economic issues to give way to socio-cultural issues (cf. Mudde 2014; Kitshelt 1994). Others (see Mair 1995; Kitschelt and McGann 1995) felt that the lack of recognisable differences between traditional parties contributed to the growing division and remoteness that some electorates felt, and may even have increased the chances for populist parties to rise.

More recently however, growing migration has come to challenge the boundaries of welfare regimes in Europe that have often been tied to citizenship (Keating and McCrone 2013). Alongside the rising discontent with current politics and traditional parties, this has become a powerful tool for populist parties. These parties, as seen both on left and right, have capitalized on such sentiments, claiming, in the name of the people, to better understand and express the feelings of marginalization than the traditional established parties. The established parties are described as a cluster of self-interested elites who do not care about the people's wishes and interests (Mudde 2004). It is therefore not surprising that we have witnessed populist parties rallying under the slogan: *They do not represent us* (with respect to the traditional political parties), as seen by Podemos in Spain.

One of the most notable challengers to centre-left mainstream parties in Western Europe has come from the populist radical-right (Keating and McCrone 2013). These parties pose a particular danger with their appeal to those who feel threatened by a combination of foreign elites, European integration and globalization (Keating and McCrone 2013). Although the two political families are very different, they often compete for the working-class vote (Rydgren 2004). In fact, populist radical-right parties have made an impression with many voters due to their ability to communicate with the 'man on the street' (Betz 1994). Take UKIP's Nigel Farage, who casts himself as a 'man of the people'. Such an image stands in stark contrast to the leaders of the mainstream political parties in the UK, who are criticized, by Farage, of acting and speaking in a manner that is entirely detached from 'ordinary people'.

Others have noted that the increased presence and electoral successes of the populist radical right has had a contagious effect, driving mainstream parties to copy some of the policy positions of the populist radical right on immigration, multiculturalism and populism (Meguid 2008; Bale and van Spanje 2010; Green-Pedersen et al. 2008; Green-Pedersen and Krogsturp 2008; Rooduijn et al. 2014). As populism is not considered a coherent ideology, but a thin-centred-one, it is devoid of concrete and specific policy solutions (Mudde 2004). If populism is contagious, I suggest that we need to move away from policies, and focus on where populism is most likely to be manifested – in the written and oral communication of political parties and actors (Wirth et al. 2016; Aalberg et al. 2017). In fact, many experts have already presented evidence that mainstream political actors have adopted the communication strategies and practices of populist parties to address the competition from rival political projects (cf. Mudde 2004; Jagers and Walgrave 2007). Leaders of European mainstream centre-left parties such as Tony Blair, Steve Stevaert and Wouter Bos have all been identified as displaying populism in how they communicate (Mair 2002; Mudde 2004).

In light of this, one would expect that, if there is a contagion effect from the presence of populist parties, this should play a part in whether or not mainstream parties adopt populist political communications. When populist parties become successful there is a possibility that mainstream parties will react by trying to exclude populist actors from political power, but will include populist themes and ways of communicating (Mudde 2004; Rooduijn et al. 2014). As far as centre-left parties are concerned, there is no reason to believe such parties will remain entirely immune to the populist surge. In fact, all political parties regularly face decisions about strategy (Bale et al. 2010). Poor electoral performance and the increased presence of populist parties can therefore play a part in how political parties decide to strategically communicate to voters. Since political actors can shape and re-shape their communication more easily than policy positions, it seems reasonable to expect that if the mainstream parties believe that populism is the main driver for the populist parties' success, then they might be compelled to adopt degrees of such communication to fight off competition. Take the Brexit referendum. Some have argued that the former Prime Minister of the UK, David Cameron might never have called a referendum had it not been for the rise, and the perceived threat, of UKIP. In this regard, I anticipate that the stronger populist parties are in terms of electoral success,[1] the more likely the centre-left parties are to adopt degrees of populist communication. Likewise, as long as populist parties are relatively unsuccessful in electoral terms, mainstream centre-left parties would not be inclined to adopt populist forms of communication.

An additional factor that has been highlighted within the populist debate is the effect that different forms of democracy can have on the opportunities and limitations of populism (Mudde 2007). For example, majoritarian systems, as seen in the UK, pose particular difficulties for new parties to successfully enter the political arena. Due to such obstacles, new parties have a stronger incentive to initiate demands that will find a place in the programmes of the established parties. In a recent study, Rooduijn et al. (2014) found that countries including the UK were more prone to adopt programmatic populist claims than those with more consensual models such as Sweden. Since there are only two major parties in the UK, the mainstream parties were more likely to frame their competitors in terms of opposition versus government or 'us' versus 'them'. With this in mind, I posit that the UK Labour Party is more likely to adopt populist political communication than the Swedish SAP.

What, though, is the potential danger posed by populism? The main threat from a communication perspective is that populist politicians often present overly-simplified, black and white views, and take uncompromising stands which can lead to polarization in society. Another factor is that many contemporary actors have been classified as populist – from Jeremy Corbyn and Farage to Emmanuel Macron and Marine Le Pen. The consequence of classifying any politician as populist if they appear popular, controversial or if they step outside the 'norms' of politics, is that everyone ends up in the same 'populist pool'. It is therefore important to distinguish between different degrees of populism and between what specifically characterizes populist communication, so that we can more easily distinguish populism from placing an emphasis on national empowerment and nationalism.

## Into the Mainstream? Populism as a Form of Political Communication

To discuss the current impact of populism on the mainstream centre-left in Europe, it is important to provide a tighter definition of the concept of populism. The mark of populism is the separation of society into two homogenous and antagonistic warring camps: the 'good people' versus the 'corrupt elite'; populism claims to defend the unrestricted sovereignty of the people (Wirth et al. 2016; Mudde 2004).

Populism is described as a 'thin-centred ideology' in that it lacks few concrete policy-related solutions. It often rails against the political establishment, but does not necessarily specify what should replace it. It is therefore often the case, as mentioned previously, that populism in practice is usually found alongside 'thicker' left- or right-wing ideologies, such as nationalism or socialism (Midde 2004; Jagers and Walgrave 2007). Because of this, populism has a number of distinct communicative characteristics. For example, a left-wing party may employ means of populist communication by calling out the corrupt elite and by decrying the exploitation of employees, while the radical right often shifts attention to immigrants and the 'foreign' elite.

So how do we identify populist communication and what are the main characteristics? Firstly, let's turn our attention to 'the people'. At the core of populism lays a positive reference to the people. Although the people are described as an underdog against the elite, it always includes a positive image of a homogenous people. Populism frequently talks and justifies actions by identifying with and appealing to the people (Jagers and Walgrave 2007). The phrase 'the people' is a 'catch-all' concept used to connect with voters (Hawkins et al. 2012; Mudde 2004; Taggart 2000).

In opposition to the people are 'the elite'. The elite are separated from the people. Populists antagonize this relationship by arguing that the elite do not share the peoples' values and interests, and that they do not act on behalf of the people (Albertazzi and McDonnell 2008; Mudde 2004; Taggart 2000). A clear separation is therefore at work, distancing the 'us' (the people) from the common enemy established by 'them' (the dominant elite). The elite may sometimes be identified by the use of metonymy (alternate names) e.g. Brussels, Wall Street or the IMF (Jagers and Walgrave 2007; Wirth et al. 2016).

The antagonism between the two groups (the people vs. the elite) is crucial. Populism is essentially structured around these elements and it is only when they are combined with one another that they classify as populist. This is of crucial importance, since there is an overuse and misuse of the term populism. On the basis of this, there are a number of communicative characteristics of populism that stand out and can be summarized in the following way:

The first characteristic consists of *stressing the people's virtues*. This is connected to the importance and construction of the people (Mudde 2004; Jagers and Walgrave 2007). The people are perceived as obtaining the ability to solve problems and to make correct decisions. Populists try to appeal to the people by stressing their positive qualities and virtues, emphasising past achievements in particular (Albertazzi and McDonnell 2008).

Second, populism is based on two further core dimensions, namely: the empowerment of the people, and the betrayal of the people by the elite. These two elements are only possible if the people are perceived as homogeneous, having no internal differences, with common understandings, longings, feelings, wills and opinions (Jagers and Walgrave 2007; Taggart 2000). Hence, *describing the people as a homogenous entity* makes up the second communicative characteristic.

Third, populism also attempts to *unite with the people* by claiming to represent or embody the people. Paradoxically, many political actors who use populist political communication and rhetoric reject political representation, but at the same time, most of them are actually political representatives themselves (Taggart 2000). Actors who use populist communication must therefore be able to ensure they are perceived as of the people. By doing so, they communicate in a way that portrays them as acting in the name of the people.

The fourth characteristic concerns the idea of the people as the democratic sovereign. The idea is that the people should have sovereignty while the elite are portrayed as depriving the people of their rights (Mudde 2004). Political actors can communicate support for popular sovereignty either in a general sense by arguing for more power for the people, or in relation to institutional reforms, such as introducing direct democratic elements in the decision-making process.

For populists, the only cleavage that exists is the one between elites and the people. Attacks on the elite therefore lay the ground for the fifth communicative characteristic. This can be achieved through emphasising what I call 'elite negativity'. Elite negativity can take its expression by portraying the elite negatively, as being corrupt or unresponsive to the people (Mudde 2004). In its essence, displaying the elites in a negative light is about reinforcing the view that the elites do not represent the people but only themselves.

Lastly, the idea of popular sovereignty holds with the notion that the will of the people should be favoured over the preference of the elite. For populists, this can only be achieved by supporting the *limitation of elite power* in terms of decision-making, and by denying the elites power altogether, or by arguing for a replacement of the political class in the name of the people.

This chapter sets out two expectations that can potentially affect whether or not mainstream centre-left parties adopt populist political communication: firstly, the success of a populist party and secondly, the type of democratic system that prevails. The communicative characteristic, as identified above, will act as a tool to judge when centre-left parties adopt populist communication strategies. In doing so, the chapter will establish whether parties use populist communication more frequently.

## Labour, the Social Democrats and the Populist Contenders

This chapter focuses on two cases, the Swedish Social Democratic Party and the British Labour Party. The two parties offer an ideal testing ground, as the amount of populist influences and political systems differ markedly between these countries.

As far as the background of the two selected parties is concerned, Sweden was long described as the European exception (Demker 2012) in relation to populist influences. For years, populist parties were unsuccessful in Sweden. But the last decade saw a rise in the fortunes of political populism. During the 2010 general election, the populist radical right-wing party, the Sweden Democrats (SD) surpassed the four-percentage threshold necessary for entering parliament, and are today Sweden's third largest party.

For the UK, populism has only posed a relatively small oppositional threat to the mainstream parties. One reason is the nature of the two-party system and the limited chances this allows for populists and smaller parties to break onto the current electoral scene. However, the success of UKIP as seen in the 2014 European Parliamentary elections, where the party came first with 26.6 per cent of the vote, and in the 2015 general election where the party got 3.8 million votes (but only one seat), has led some to suggest there is a growing populist influence (both directly and in-directly) on British politics, which was seen most clearly in the context of the 2016 Brexit referendum (Stanyer et al. 2017).

To establish if populist political communication is used in the communication of the British Labour Party and Swedish Social Democratic Party, we have analysed[2] a total of 14 political party documents (manifestos[3] and speeches) from the period between 2006 and 2017. Election campaigns are of particular interest as they relate to an intensified and narrow time period of political communication: The adaptation of populist political communications can be expected to be higher than during ordinary political periods.

## Populist Political Communication going Mainstream?
### The British Labour Party 2010

During the 2010 general election, Labour made use of populist political communication through which they provoked the Conservative Party – framing the Tories as the political elite, and the Labour party as the true representatives of the people: '...the decisions they seek to make for our country would favour the privileged few over the many. They would isolate Britain...' (2010, 0:5). This was followed by: 'We speak for the ordinary people of this country who work hard, want their kids to do better than them, and worry about the economic, environmental and social challenges we face. We are on their side, it is their voice, needs and hopes...' (2010, 0:5). There is a clear elite negativity in evidence, in that Labour claim the elite are not acting on behalf of the people but of a select few at the top. In this framing, the Labour party are the ones who speak for the people (uniting with the people).

The speeches given by the then Labour leader, Gordon Brown, in 2010, contain a higher degree of populism than seen in the party's manifesto of that year. Brown repeatedly *unites with the people* by pledging: '...myself and my party to fighting each and every day for a fairer future for the people of Britain ... We will always put the British people first – before personal interest, our party interest, or any vested interest. We will renew this nation – not for our own benefit or the benefit of a narrow section or clique – but for all the people of this country we love. We are the people's party – and we are pledged to serve the people' (27 March 2010). Indeed, as stated in the manifesto, Brown emphasizes the interests of the people should be put before the interest of the elite.

An additional characteristic of populist communication is to claim *the popular will* (the communicative characteristic of a *homogenous entity*).

This is apparent in Brown's speeches where he stresses 'British values', describing the British people as having similar traits: 'For whenever *we* see injustice, *we* want to end it. Whenever *we* see suffering, *we* want to relieve it. Whenever *we* see unfairness, *we* want to rectify it. These are Britain's values and these are Labour values – not the values that spring from markets, but the values that spring from our hearts' (4 May 2010).

Moreover, Brown frequently uses a communication style that praises the achievements of the British People and simultaneously downplays both his own and other politicians' role: 'No – it is not our achievement – it is *your* achievement. And it's the achievement of *the people of Britain*' (4 May 2010).

Despite the minor electoral increase obtained by the populist radical right in the 2010 election (+0.9 per cent for UKIP and +1.2 per cent for the BNP) (Rooduijn et al. 2014), the communication channels of Labour are characterized by a high degree of populist political communication, specifically within public speeches by key figures. The 2010 general election resulted in a major loss of parliamentary seats for the Labour Party.

## 2015

In the run up to the 2015 general election, support for UKIP was predicted to grow significantly (YouGov 2015), which could potentially cause Labour to use more populist communication within their political platform. In fact, the 2015 manifesto and speeches, as expected, have a higher degree of populist political communication than 2010. Labour figures and Labour material repeatedly describe the people as homogenous, and present the people as sharing common attributes: 'The British people are known for tolerance, responsibility to others and for our belief in the value of hard work. We look confidently outward to the world. These are great British traditions' (2015: 8).

Similar to the 2010 manifesto, in 2015 the Conservatives were portrayed by Labour as representing the political elite, who conspired with the people at the top, at the expense of the people: 'We can continue with a Conservative plan based on the view that success comes only from a privileged few at the top. Or we can change direction, begin to return power to people and build an economy together in which everyone can contribute to a shared and enduring prosperity. We believe that Britain only succeeds when working families succeed' (2015: 9).

The speeches given by the 2015 Labour leader Ed Miliband were also characterized by higher degrees of populist communication. There is a strong emphasis on targeting the political elite (the Conservatives) and claiming they are self-interested, only looking after the people at the top (the rich and powerful) while neglecting working people. This reoccurs in statements such as: 'Because for too long, you have been told something that simply isn't true. That's what's good for the richest and most powerful is always good for the whole of our country. That as long as a few individuals and companies are OK, we can just wait for the wealth to trickle down to everyone else. With one rule for the few and another rule for the many' (13 April 2015) followed by: 'I am ready. Ready to put an end to the tired old idea that as long as we look after the rich and powerful we will all be OK. Ready to put into practice the truth that it is only when working people succeed, that Britain succeeds ... Because I believe the wealth, the success, the future of our country does not simply come from a few at the top. It comes from every working person' (13 April 2015). Miliband stressed the fundamental importance of working people, and of their importance for Britain and for the success of the country, while pressing an economic anti-establishment communication that targeted the rich. Miliband further criticized media tycoons, 'Rupert Murdoch', 'tax avoiders' and 'multinationals' stating: 'Who do you want standing up for you? The answer will never be David Cameron' (13 April 2015).

The characteristic of *uniting with the people* is apparent in most speeches, where Miliband stresses, on numerous occasions, the importance of '...giving power back to those to whom it really belongs: The British people' (13 April 2015). Evidently Labour increased its use of populist communication since 2010; this was more apparent in the speeches than the manifesto, however. Labour lost the general election, and secured only a minimal increase of +1.5 per cent in vote share compared to the previous election.

## 2017

The 2017 snap election was called by Conservative Prime Minister Theresa May, with the hope of securing a convincing majority which could bolster her position in the context of the Brexit negotiations. YouGov (2017) polling in advance of the vote indicated only 5 per cent support for UKIP – a significant decline since the 2015 election.

In light of this, the 2017 manifesto contains few populist references, in contrast to its 2015 predecessor. Regardless, Labour still portrayed the Conservatives as corrupt and unresponsive to the people, thus deploying *elite negativity* during the campaign. Such populist communication can be found in subsequent statements: '…the Conservatives' attempt to balance the books on the backs of the poorest' (2017: 56) and 'workers are being forced into self-employment by unscrupulous employers to avoid costs and their duties to workers' (2017: 51). There is reference to, 'This wasted potential is holding us all back', implicitly presuming some degree of *closeness* to the 'us' – the unspecified people – seeking to embody what the party and the people feel.

Similarly, speeches by key figures are also characterized by *elite negativity*. Jeremy Corbyn, Labour leader in 2017 said: '…a Tory party intent on managing the decline of our public services, a Tory party that cuts support and services to working people while cutting taxes for the very rich and for the biggest businesses … They (the Conservatives) won't reverse the tens of billions in tax giveaways to their wealthy friends but they will impose on working people another big dose of austerity' (Glasgow 2017).

## The Swedish Social Democratic Party 2006

For the 2006 general election, the SD obtained only 2.9 per cent of the national vote, and were unable to break the 4 per cent threshold necessarily for entering parliament. Nevertheless, the success that they experienced locally was identified as a parliamentary breakthrough. The 2006 election constituted a turning point in Swedish politics, as for the first time since 1994, a centre-right coalition government was elected to power.

In contrast to the British Labour Party, the Swedish Social Democratic Party rarely displays populist rhetoric within their communications. In fact, the 2006 manifesto contains no populist communicative characteristics at all. The 2006 Social Democratic leader, Göran Perssson, displayed minimal populist communication within his speeches. Notably though, Persson uses the word 'human beings' when addressing the voters and only on very rare occasions uses the phrase 'the Swedish people': 'The Swedish people gave a firm no! We do not want that type of politics and the opposition lost again' (Almedalen 2006).

Although negativity towards the opposition is apparent, direct criticism against a party or the 'Alliancen'[4] is rarely found. Notably, elite negativity is mostly directed towards conservative ideology (to which the opposition adheres) or policies regarding reducing taxes on income and capital, for example.

## 2010

Similarly to 2006, only a handful of statements within the 2010 manifesto can be characterized as populist. This is particularly interesting since the voting intentions for the SD were predicted to be 4.66 per cent.[5] During the election, the SD managed to break the threshold, entering parliament for the first time with 5.70 per cent of the national vote.

*Elite negativity* and *uniting with the people* can be found within the manifesto under the statement: 'We want to see a development towards a health care system that does not benefit those with the most money. Advantages for those who pay more should not be happening. We want to protect the taxpayer's money' (2010: 6).

Elite criticism is not very apparent throughout the manifesto. On the rare occasions the party do direct criticism it is mostly applied without pointing the finger at anyone in particular: 'We have tried the other way for four years now. Where the richest are gaining from lower taxes and borrowed money' – addressing the parties (coalition) in government.

Similar to its manifesto, the 2010 Social Democratic Party leader, Mona Sahlin, rarely uses populist communication in her speeches. The single occasion when she describes the people as homogenous, she does so by describing the people as having a common understanding and opinion: 'Equal societies are better societies. Not only for the worst off, but also for the best off. Equal societies are better to live in for everyone ... Such a society has the support of the Swedish people' (Almedalen 2010).

The general election resulted in a loss for the Social Democratic Party and a win for the centre-right block.

## 2014

Prior to the general election of 2014, there was a great debate amongst politicians, the media and the public, regarding the increased support for the SD. Polls prior to the election indicated +10.1 per cent voting intention for the SD, a major increase in support since the last election (Sifo 2014). However, this seemed to affect Social Democratic Party communication only minimally. Once again, the party displayed only a small element of populism within speeches and the party's manifesto.

The manifesto displays the populist characteristics of *elite negativity* and of the party seeking to *unite with the people*. This can be found in statements such as: 'Risk capitalists with short-term interests do not belong in the welfare state. The privatization of welfare activities that have been built up with taxpayers' money is a theft from Swedish taxpayers' (2014: 34).

Turning our attention to the speeches made by key figures, the 2014 Social Democratic leader, Stefan Löfven, uses rhetoric that attempts to *unite with the people* urging that: 'Sweden's voice will be heard in the whole world. We find strength in each other. And I long for the day when we can start realizing Sweden's potential, together' (Almedalen 2014).

Löfven *stresses the peoples' virtues* by demonstrating the positive attributes of the people: 'You make demands, but you also give a helping hand to others, because you know that you will receive a helping hand back. Together we help each other to succeed'. This was combined with *elite negativity* towards the current government perceived as acting in an unlawful manner: 'During eight years we've had a government that have put all their waking hours and all our new resources into reducing taxes. They have privatized … and outsourced our friends and families' (Almedalen 2014).

## Comparative Analysis

Comparatively, the British Labour Party displayed a higher degree of populist political communication than the Swedish Social Democratic Party. The chapter began with the assumption that the impact of populist challenger parties would prompt centre-left mainstream parties to adopt populist styles of communication. The analysis, however, suggests that the expectations are only partially borne out. While the presence of the populist radical-right has increased in Sweden, it appears that the Social Democratic Party displayed only minimal populist communication, despite both the predicted and actual success of the SD in elections and polls. Although it appears slightly higher in the party's communication from 2014, it remains an exception to the rule. One potential reason for the Swedish Social Democratic Party's lack of populist political communication could be that the success of the SD has only recently started to gain significance. It might be that we have not yet witnessed the potential mainstreaming of populist political communication into the SD.

The British Labour Party, on the other hand, displayed a greater degree of populist political communication when the presence of UKIP increased. Notably, in the run up to the 2015 election, voting intentions for UKIP were predicted to rise and it is specifically in this context that communications from Labour contain a high degree of populist communication. In fact, it does to some extent validate the claim that higher degrees of populist success can act as a contagion for mainstream parties to take on the communicative elements of populism.

In fact, Labour was more likely to frame their competitors in terms of 'us' versus 'them' and more frequently displayed elite negativity – blaming the Conservative party for society's woes – while deploying communications that sought to unite the party and the different leaders (Brown, Miliband and Corbyn, respectively) with 'the people'. Indeed, because it is harder for new parties to break into the electoral arena in majoritarian models such as the UK, populist parties have a stronger incentive to initiate demands that will be incorporated in the programmes of the existing parties. A Labour defeat coupled with the rise of UKIP acted as an incentive for the party to adopt more populist political communication to win back votes.

The Swedish Social Democratic Party, however, rarely reinforce any direct antagonism between the elite and the people. Instead, they appear to direct criticism towards policies that would be disadvantageous for the Swedish people (without using anything that anchors in the word 'the people'), even in speeches.

## Conclusion

This chapter has investigated populism, with a specific focus on the distinct communicative characteristics of populist parties, and considered the implications for centre-left mainstream parties in Western Europe, and how they communicate with voters. While populist communication is used to varying effect by the centre-left parties under consideration, the chapter has only scratched the surface. It does identify the fact that that the mainstream parties adopted populist means of communication on an ad-hoc basis, at different points when it was seen to fit specific circumstances. Interestingly, populist political communication, although used to a greater extent in the UK, is not that prominent. Take Jeremy Corbyn – a politician who has been labelled as 'the torchbearer of British populism' (Gray 2017) – who in fact only uses populist communication fleetingly. As a consequence, we clearly need to be more accurate and careful in who and what we label as 'populist'.

So how can centre-left mainstream parties counteract populism? One potential option is the cleaving of many social democratic parties to the centre. Instead of imitating populist discourses or trying to 'catch all', social democratic parties should focus on reclaiming their ideological appeal by focusing on class and solidarity. Another important point is that the alienation many citizens now feel towards politics and the establishment must be taken seriously. That is not to say that political actors should downplay complex issues, or they should use populist communication to counteract populist influences. Rather, mainstream centre-left politicians ought to engage with citizens in language that can be understood by the electorate, and addresses the issues that matter to people – reflecting true social democratic values.

## Notes

1. Gaining influence refers to electoral success and increasing poll results before new populist parties compete in an election.
2. All material has been analysed using a qualitative content analysis schema, built according to the populist political communicative characteristics as illustrated above.
3. All available positive cases of speeches during the GE periods in each country were collected. Thereafter three speeches from each GE period were selected at random. The research has included speeches from the party conferences – Almedalen week - in the Swedish case made by the party leaders during the GE period. The event is considered to be one of the most important forums in politics where representatives from the major political parties take turn to set out their agenda.
4. The Alliance is a centre-right political alliance in Sweden, consisting of the four centre-right political parties, Moderata samlingspartiet, Liberalerna (former Folkpartiet), Centerpartiet and Kristdemokraterna.
5. Results from Novus, United Minds, Skop, Sifo, Sentio Research and Novis (August 2010).

## References

Albertazzi, D., and McDonnell, D. 'Introduction: The sceptre and the spectre'. In Albertazzi, D and McDonnell, D (eds) *Twenty-first Century Populism: The spectre of Western European democracy* (Basingstoke, Palgrave 2008) pp. 1–11.

Bale, T., Green-Pedersen, C., Krouwel, A., Sitter, N. and Luther, K. *If You Can't Beat Them, Join Them? Explaining Social Democratic Responses to the Challenge from the Populist Radical Right in Western Political Studies* 58 (2010) pp. 410–26.

Banks, Martin. 'Martin Schulz lashes out at "unscrupulous populists"', *The Parliament Magazine* (6 May 2016). Available at https://www.theparliamentmagazine.eu/articles/news/martin-schulz-lashes-out-unscrupulous-populists (Accessed 26 June 2018).

Betz, H.-G. *Radical Right-Wing Populism in Western Europe* (Scholarly and Reference Division, St. Martin's Press 1994).

Brown, Gordon. 27 March, 2010 Speech on Election Pledges – http://www.ukpol.co.uk/gordon-brown-2010-speech-on-election-pledges/ (Accessed 26 June 2018).

Brown, Gordon. 4 May 2010 Speech – https://labourlist.org/2010/05/another-brilliant-brown-speech (Accessed 26 June 2018)/.
Charter, David. 'Juncker calls for more union to beat "galloping populism"', *The Times* (14 September 2016). Available at https://www.thetimes.co.uk/article/juncker-calls-for-more-union-to-beat-galloping-populism-prtgzntzz (Accessed 26 June 2018).
Corbyn, Jeremy. 28 May 2006, Speech Glasgow – http://www.edinburghlabournorthernandleith.org.uk/jeremy_corbyn_speech_glasgow_may_28th_2017 (Accessed 26 June 2018).
Demker, M. 'Scandinavian right-wing parties. Diversity more than convergence'. In Mammone, A. Godin, E and Jenkins, B. (eds) *Mapping the Extreme Right in Contemporary Europe from Local to Transnational* (London, Routledge 2012).
Evans, G. and Tilley, J. 'How parties shape class politics: Explaining the decline of the class basis of party support', *British Journal of Political Science* 42(1) (2012) pp. 137–61.
Evans, G., Heath, A. and Payne, C. 'Class: Labour as a catch-all party?' In Evans, G., Norris, P. (eds) *Critical Elections: British Parties and Voters in Long-term Perspective* (London, Sage 1999).
Fierke. K. and Jorgensen, K. *Constructing International Relations: The Next Generation* (Abingdon, Routledge, 2001).
Gray, Freddie. 'Corbyn copy: Why Jeremy and Trump are (almost) the same', *The Spectator* (17 June 2017). Available at https://www.spectator.co.uk/2017/06/corbyn-copy-why-jeremy-and-trump-are-almost-the-same/ (Accessed 26 June 2018).
Green-Pedersen, C. and Krogstrup, J. 'Immigration as a political issue in Denmark and Sweden', *European Journal of Political Research* 47 (2008) pp. 610–34.
Hawkins, K. A. (2009) 'Is Chavez populist? Measuring populist discourse in comparative perspective', *Comparative Political Studies* 42(8) (2009) pp. 1040–67.
Hawkins, K., Riding, S. and Mudde, C. 'Measuring Populist Attitudes' (CandM Working Paper No. 55) (2012).
Jagers, J. and Walgrave, S. 'Populism as political communication style: An empirical study of political parties' discourse in Belgium', *University of Antwerp, Belgium European Journal of Political Research* 46 (2007) pp. 319–45, doi: 10.1111/j.1475-6765.2006.00690.x.
Keatin, M. and McCrone, D. *The Crisis of Social Democracy in Europe* (Edinburgh, Edinburgh University Press, 2013).
Kitschelt, H. *The Transformation of European Social Democracy* (Cambridge, Cambridge University Press, 1994).
Lijphart, A. *Patterns of Democracy* (New Haven, Yale University Press, 1999).
Löfven, Stefan Tal Almedalen. 29 June 2014: https://www.socialdemokraterna.se/vart-parti/politiker/stefan-lofven/tal3/tal-2014/almedalen-2014/ (Accessed 26 June 2018).
Mair, P. 'Populist democracy vs. party democracy'. In Mény and Surel (eds) *Democracies and the Populist Challenge* (New York, Palgrave Macmllan, 2002).
Meguid, B. *Party Competition between Unequals: Strategies and Electoral Fortunes in Western Europe* (Cambridge, Cambridge University Press, 2008).

Mény, Y. and Surel, Y. 'The constitutive ambiguity of populism'. In Meny, Y. and Surel, Y. (eds) *Democracies and the Populist Challenge* (New York, Palgrave Macmillan, 2002) pp 1–21.

Miliband, Ed. 13 April 2015, Manifesto Speech – http://www.politics.co.uk/comment-analysis/2015/04/13/ed-miliband-manifesto-speech-in-full (Accessed 26 June 2018).

Moffitt, B. *The Globak Rise of Populism – Performance, Political Style, and Representation* (Stanford, Stanford University Press, 2016).

Mudde, C. *The Populist Zeitgeist. Government and Opposition* (Cambridge, Cambridge University Press, 2004) 39: pp. 541–63.

Mudde, C. *Populist Radical Right Parties in Europe* (Cambridge University Press, 2007).

Oskarson, M. 'Social structure and party choice'. In Jacques Thomassen (ed.) *The European Voter. A Comparative Study of Modern Democracies* (Oxford, Oxford University Press, 2005).

Painter, Anthony. 'The populist signal is getting louder – and mainstream politics is under threat' (22 March 2013) *The New Statesman*. Available at https://www.newstatesman.com/politics/2013/03/populist-signal-getting-louder-and-mainstream-politics-under-threat (Accessed 26 June 2018).

Perrson, G. 2 July 2006, Speech at Almedalen.

Rooduijn, M, de Lange, S and van der Brug, W. 'A populist Zeitgeist? Programmatic contagion by populist parties in Western Europe', *Party Politics* 20(4) (2014) pp. 563–75.

Rydgren, Jens. *The Populist Political Challenge* (New York, Berghahn Books, 2004).

Sahlin, Mona, Almedalen. 8 June 2010: http://www.svenskatal.se/20100708-mona-sahlin-almedalstal-2010/ (Accessed 26 June 2018).

Sifo. August 2014: https://www.kantarsifo.se/sites/default/files/reports/documents/valjarbarometern_augusti_2014_2.pdf (Accessed 26 June 2018).

Stanley, B. 'The thin ideology of populism', *Journal of Political Ideologies* 13(1) (2008) pp. 95–110.

Stanyer, J., Salagado, S. and Strömbäck, J. 'Populist actors as communicators or political actors as populist communicators: Cross-national findings and perspective'. In Reinemann, C., Aalberg, T., Esser, F., Strömbäck, J. and de Vreese, C. H. (eds) *Populist Political Communication in Europe* (Abingdon, Routledge 2017) pp. 353–64.

Taggart, P. *Populism* (Buckingham, Open University Press 2000).

Van Spanje. J. 'Contagious parties. Anti-immigration parties and their impact on other parties' immigration stances in contemporary Western Europe', *Party Politics* 16(5) (2010) p. 563.

Wirth, W., Esser, F., Wettstein, M., Engesser, S., Wirz, D., Schulz, A. and Schemer, C. 'The Appeal of Populist Ideas, Strategies and Styles: A theoretical model and research design for analyzing populist political communication' (Working Paper 88 2016).

YouGov: https://d25d2506sfb94s.cloudfront.net/cumulus_uploads/document/s57qaa3btf/YG-Archives-Pol-Trackers-Voting-Trends-with-UKIP-050515.pdf (Accessed 26 June 2018).

YouGov: https://d25d2506sfb94s.cloudfront.net/cumulus_uploads/document/1e3v2ys385/YG%20trackers%20-%20Voting%20Intention%20PUBLISHED.pdf (Accessed 26 June 2018).

YouGov: https://d25d2506sfb94s.cloudfront.net/cumulus_uploads/document/1e3v2ys385/YG%20trackers%20-%20Voting%20Intention%20PUBLISHED.pdf (Accessed 26 June 2018).

CHAPTER 4

# Europeans and Globalization: Does the EU Square the Circle?

Silvia Merler

## Introduction: Europe and Globalization

In recent years, few issues have been as controversial as globalization, or as politically salient. Overall, globalization is a complex phenomenon offering an opportunity for economic growth, but with potentially negative social implications that it is not straightforward to assess. This uncertainty is reflected in the difficulty of envisioning a response to the potentially negative consequences of globalization. Europeans' assessment of globalization as an opportunity for economic growth is mixed (Batsaikhan and Darvas, 2017). At the European Union (EU) level, 70 per cent of respondents to the Euro-barometer survey stated that they strongly or at least somewhat agreed with the idea that globalization could be an opportunity for economic growth. The proportion dropped by more than ten points during the crisis, and has recently bounced back, although with significant differences across countries (Figure 4.1).

There is no lack of literature suggesting the EU has an important role to play vis-à-vis globalization. Buti and Pichelmann (2017) argue the process of EU integration has traditionally been conceived as a way to square 'Dahrendorf's quandary'[1] between globalization as an opportunity for growth, social cohesion and political freedom, by allowing for catch-up economic growth and convergence while preserving Europe's social models. Wallace (2000) argues that the impact of globalization in Europe has to be read through an experience of 'Europeanization'. In Europe, efforts to manage cross-border connections are part of the historical experience and the geographical arrangement of the continent. This long history in turn produced a set of embedded features that shape European responses to cross-border connections. And the pattern of European responses exhibits certain specificities that make Europe as a region different from most other regions in the world. Europe has considerable capacity for collective engagement, but is diffusely managed depending on the issues being addressed.

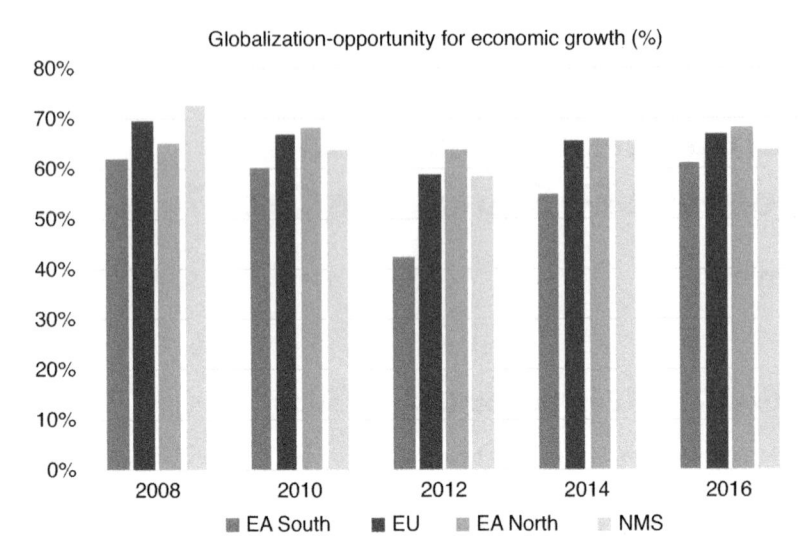

**FIGURE 4.1** European's perception of globalization.
*Source:* Eurobarometer (69.2; 73.4; 78.1; 82.3; 86.2).

Wallace sees hard cooperation as achievable on political economy issues, and claims that Europeanization is sufficiently deeply embedded to act as a filter for globalization. Jacoby and Meunier (2010) argue that the advocacy of managed globalization – an approach that is neither ad hoc deregulation nor old-style economic protectionism – has been a primary driver of major EU's policies in the past. Antoniades (2008) argues that economic globalization emerged in the EU as a debate on the nature and future of Europe. On the one hand, the EU was instrumental in bringing about the globalized post-Cold War economic order, by aggressively promoting the principles and policies upon which this economic order has been based. On the other hand, this proactive engagement was translated within the EU into a highly polarized and antagonistic public discourse that led to an identity crisis. After 2005, this discourse started to change due to the rise of flexicurity as a new way to think about Europe's place and orientation in the global political economy. Bini Smaghi (2007) argues that EU citizens believe globalization is influenced far more by the EU than by national governments, which creates a 'demand' for more 'Europe' in the globalization process – to which Europe does not seem to be responding. In the light of this long-standing debate and the recent economic crisis, understanding what is driving Europeans' economic assessment of globalization and what role they see for the EU can help to understand if the EU has been instrumental in squaring Dahrendorf's quandary. It is also important from a policy perspective, because it constitutes a valuable background against which to evaluate recent EU economic and social initiatives.

## Europeans' Attitudes towards Globalization

In this chapter, we investigate empirically how Europeans' economic assessment of globalization is influenced by specific socio-economic characteristics, and whether these have changed with the crisis. We also look at how Europeans' assessment of globalization is mediated through the conception that Europeans have of the role of the EU. To do so, we use two waves of opinion surveys (Eurobarometer) conducted regularly by the European Commission across all Member States – one wave before the crisis (2008) and one after (2013).[2] The two Eurobarometer waves that we selected include questions that ask respondents to state their degree of agreement on selected statements about globalization. One of the questions asks whether respondents agree that 'globalization is an opportunity for economic growth':[3]

> QUESTION (2008 wave): For each of the following statements, please tell me whether you strongly agree, somewhat agree, somewhat disagree or strongly disagree: 'Globalization is an opportunity for economic growth'
>
> 1. Strongly agree
> 2. Somewhat agree
> 3. Somewhat disagree
> 4. Strongly disagree
> 5. DK

We use this question to construct a binary dependent variable that equals 1 if a respondent strongly or somewhat agreed with the statement that globalization is an opportunity for economic growth and 0 otherwise. This variable allows us to gauge the extent to which Europeans share the view that globalization has economic benefits to offer, and estimate how different factors affect the probability that respondents will express a positive view of globalization.[4]

A first group of factors that we consider are characteristics of the respondents, such as their *age, gender, marital status*, what kind of *community* they live in (a rural area/village, a small city or a large city) and

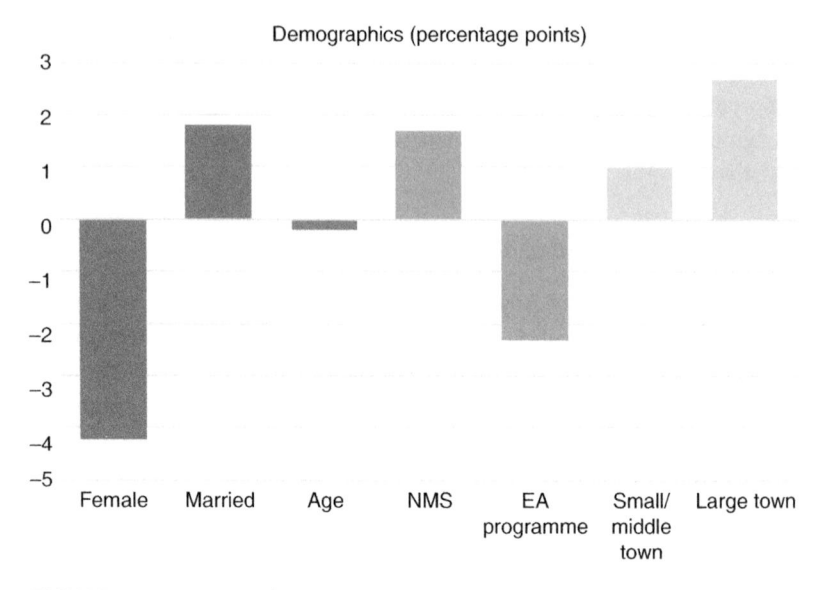

**FIGURE 4.2** Demographics.
*Source:* Own estimates based on Eurobarometer (69.2; 73.4; 78.1; 82.3; 86.2).

their level of *education*. We look at whether respondents are *unemployed* and whether they have experienced *economic hardship*.[5] A second group of variables aims at capturing the respondents' assessment of the national and European economic situation. In the two surveys that we use, interviewees were asked to state whether they considered the domestic situation of the economy or employment better or worse than the *average* in EU countries.[6] Lastly, the Eurobarometer asks respondents to state what the EU 'means to them personally', and reports the number of individuals who answer with specific terms, which we use to investigate how Europeans' view of the role of the EU is related to their perception of globalization.[7] We also include specific controls for individuals in new member states and euro area countries that have been subject to the EU/IMF adjustment programmes, to understand whether they systematically differ in their assessment of globalization from the rest of the EU (Figure 4.2).

Demographic characteristics appear strongly correlated with respondents' opinion about globalization as an opportunity for economic growth (Figure 4.2). Women appear more sceptical than men, as their probability of expressing a positive opinion is between 5.8 and 4.1 percentage points lower than for comparable men. Married individuals tend to hold a slightly more

Education (percentage points)

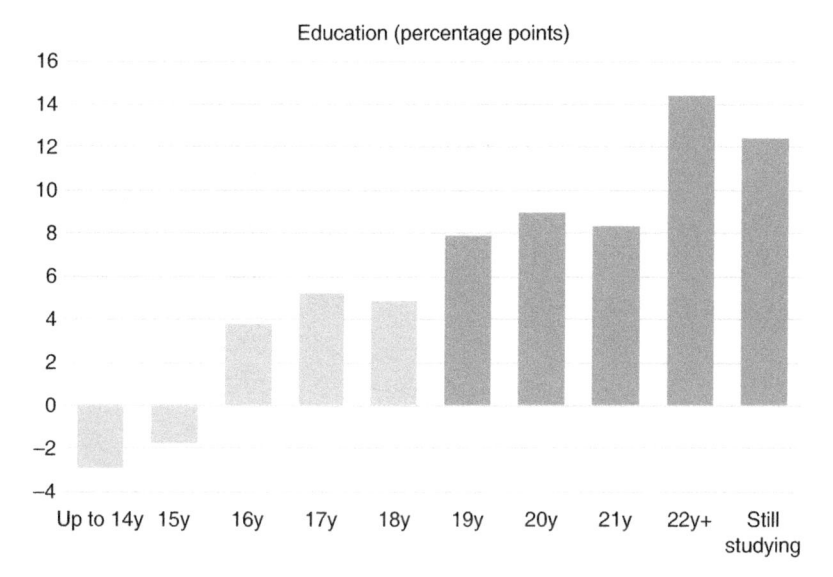

**FIGURE 4.3** Education.
*Source:* Own estimates based on Eurobarometer (69.2; 73.4; 78.1; 82.3; 86.2).

favourable opinion than comparable unmarried ones, and older respondents tend to be more sceptical, although the marginal effect is small. A negative time trend appears to exist between 2008 and 2013, suggesting that respondents' assessment of globalization as an opportunity for economic growth deteriorated over time, most likely capturing the effect of the global financial crisis and the euro crisis. There also seem to exist differences across countries, with respondents in New Member States being more positive, and respondents in EA countries that experienced an EU/IMF adjustment programme being more negative, than respondents in the rest of the EU. Respondents' views about globalization are unsurprisingly also influenced by the type of community they live in, which may be a proxy for the effect of exposure to a more (or less) cosmopolitan environment. Compared to respondents living in rural areas/villages, respondents living in large cities are consistently more likely to state that globalization is an opportunity for economic growth, while respondents living in small cities are still more positive than the rural group, but the effect is smaller (Figure 4.3).

Education is also an important factor whose effect seems to be non-linear. Respondents who left school when they were 14 years old are less likely to see globalization as an opportunity for economic growth

Economic and EU variables (percentage points)

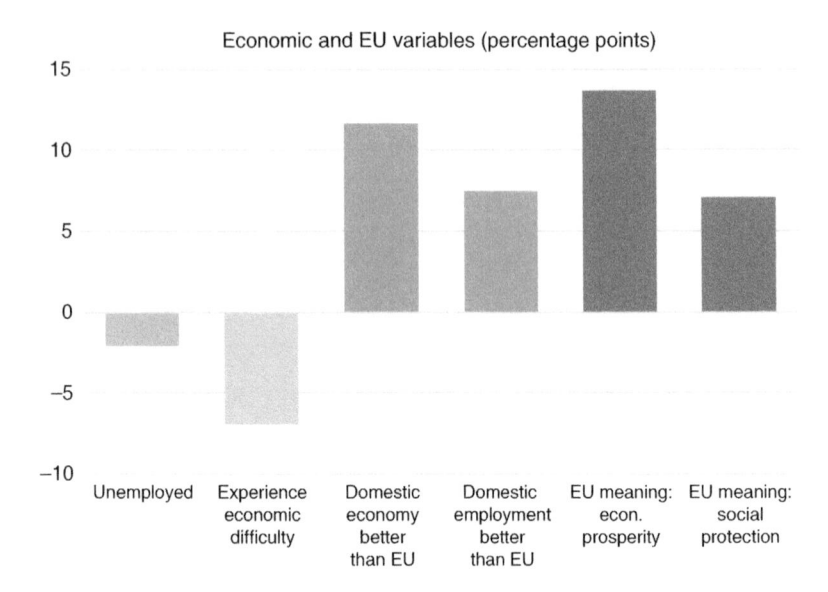

**FIGURE 4.4** Education.
Source: Own estimates based on Eurobarometer (69.2; 73.4; 78.1; 82.3; 86.2).

than respondents with no full-time education, although the result is not statistically significant. From 16 years on, every additional year of education is associated with an increase in the probability of holding a positive view about the economic opportunities of globalization, but the strongest effect by far is among people with very high educational levels (20, 21 and 22 years) and among respondents who are still studying, probably capturing the positive effect of respondents' younger age (Figure 4.3). Similar effects are found in Batsaikhan and Darvas (2017).

Respondents' personal economic situation is also strongly and significantly correlated with their likelihood of perceiving globalization as an opportunity for economic growth. Unemployed respondents are between 2 and 3.8 percentage points less likely to answer positively than people who are employed, all else being equal. Respondents who have experienced economic difficulties – difficulties paying bills – are between 5.5 and 10.8 percentage points less likely to see globalization as an opportunity for economic growth than people who did not experience the same economic hardship, all else being equal (Figure 4.4).

Coming to the role of the EU, the perception of the domestic economy's relative position with respect to the EU average is significant. Respondents who see the domestic economy as lagging behind the rest of the block are 10–12 percentage points less likely to see globalization as an opportunity for economic growth. Similarly, those who see the domestic employment situation as worse than the EU average are about 6.6–7.9 percentage points less likely to have a positive view of globalization. What the EU 'means' to respondents seem to matter for their view about the economic side of globalization. Those who see the EU as meaning 'economic prosperity' are nearly 14 percentage points more likely to see globalization as an opportunity for economic growth. The correlation is of 7–9 percentage points among those who see the EU as meaning 'social protection'. These findings are not exceptional within the literature (Edwards 2006). Looking at 17 developed and developing countries, 'values' are a powerful explanation for variations in public opinion; they have more explanatory power than evaluations of the economy or partisanship, and roughly the same explanatory power as skill levels. Balestrini (2014) finds that citizens' views of their country's direction, the state of democracy, and whether EU membership is beneficial explain their attitudes towards globalization to a greater extent than education.

## Policy Initiatives

The previous section highlighted some important features relating to Europeans' perceptions of globalization. First, an individual's economic situation (whether they are unemployed or experience difficulties paying bills) is an important factor, but national relative position in the EU seems to matter even more: people who see their country doing worse than the EU average in economic or employment terms are more sceptical in their assessment of globalization. Moreover, the perception of the EU's role is very important: respondents to whom the EU 'means' economic prosperity and social protection are more likely to see globalization as an opportunity for economic growth. Since the financial and euro crisis, EU institutions and economic policies have been called into question. The EU is often portrayed as the promoter of a neo-liberal paradigm, blind to the social implications of its economic prescriptions. The need for change was acknowledged by the European Commission's president, Jean-Claude Juncker, who, in his opening statement before the European Parliament plenary session, stressed the need to reverse the high rate of youth unemployment, poverty and loss of confidence in the European project. Buti and Pichelmann (2017) rightly point out that EU institutions and policies are prone to populist attack not only from this economic angle, but also from the perspective of identity, expressed as fear of European 'homogenization'. They argue that the EU faces a difficult trade-off between more involvement in distributional issues, as the economic view of populism would prescribe, and less involvement in member-states' affairs as the 'identitarian' view would imply. The EU created a European Globalization Adjustment Fund (EGF) in 2007 to co-fund policies to help workers negatively affected by globalization find new jobs. Claeys and Sapir (2018) provide an evaluation of the EGF and find the programme was politically high profile but its economic effectiveness is more difficult to evaluate – although estimates suggest only a small proportion of EU workers who lost their jobs because of globalization received EGF financing. More recent initiatives – such as the Juncker Investment Plan or the Youth Guarantee – can be read as an attempt to strike a balance between the perceived need for stronger EU involvement while avoiding 'intruding' into sensitive national competences.

## Investment Plan

The Investment Plan for Europe ('the Juncker Plan') consists of three objectives: (i) remove obstacles to investment; (ii) provide visibility and technical assistance to investment projects; and (iii) make smarter use of financial resources. These objectives are served by three pillars. First, the European Fund for Strategic Investments (EFSI), which provides an EU guarantee to mobilize private investment and where the European Commission works together with the European Investment Bank (EIB). Second, the European Investment Advisory Hub and the European Investment Project Portal provide technical assistance and visibility of investment opportunities. Third, improving the business environment by removing regulatory barriers to investment both nationally and at the EU level. As of 12 December 2017[8] based on approved projects, 81 per cent of the 315€ billion target had been reached. Table 4.1 shows the ranking of countries in terms of the expected triggered investment in percentage of GDP, as well as the total EFSI financing.

EFSI is not geographically earmarked and according to the December 2017 data, all EU countries had been reached. However, the EU15 received about 89 per cent of all EFSI funding, whereas the rest of the EU received only 11 per cent (excluding multi-country operations). An external evaluation by Ernst and Young (2016) reports that reasons mentioned for lower EFSI support in Central and Eastern Europe are the competition from the European

**TABLE 4.1** Allocation of European Fund for Strategic Investments

| Country | EFSI finance approved by EIB Group (€ million) | Set to trigger investment of (€ million) | Ranking (1–28): EFSI-triggered investment per € of GDP |
|---|---|---|---|
| Estonia | 112 | 803 | 1 |
| Greece | 1703 | 5753 | 2 |
| Bulgaria | 349 | 1575 | 3 |
| Portugal | 1898 | 5480 | 4 |
| Spain | 5572 | 31,875 | 5 |
| Finland | 1409 | 5590 | 6 |
| Latvia | 182 | 615 | 7 |
| Lithuania | 324 | 934 | 8 |
| Italy | 6572 | 3676 | 9 |
| Poland | 2515 | 8869 | 10 |
| France | 8697 | 39,592 | 11 |
| Croatia | 187 | 745 | 12 |
| Slovakia | 475 | 1247 | 13 |
| Ireland | 982 | 3990 | 14 |
| Czech Republic | 543 | 2484 | 15 |
| Belgium | 1261 | 5832 | 16 |
| Sweden | 1779 | 6314 | 17 |
| Slovenia | 59 | 490 | 18 |
| Netherlands | 2252 | 8091 | 19 |
| Hungary | 73 | 1241 | 20 |
| Austria | 931 | 2825 | 21 |
| United Kingdom | 2659 | 18,871 | 22 |
| Germany | 5091 | 21,987 | 23 |
| Romania | 327 | 1092 | 24 |
| Denmark | 531 | 1620 | 25 |
| Luxembourg | 89 | 284 | 26 |
| Cyprus | 45 | 81 | 27 |
| Malta | 11 | 34 | 28 |
| Multi-country | 4445 | 41,052 | . |

Source: European Commission.[9]

Structural and Investment Funds (ESIF), less capacity to develop large projects, less experience with Public Private Partnerships, a less developed Venture Capital market, and the small size of projects (Figure 4.5A and 4.5B).

One positive aspect – especially in light of the results in the previous section – is the fact that three of the top five recipients in terms of total investment as a percentage of GDP are countries that experienced EU/IMF macroeconomic adjustment programmes during the crisis (Greece, Portugal and Spain). In terms of sectors, energy and research-development-innovation have the largest number of projects, but investment in energy-related projects is by far the largest sector. There are also numerous multi-sector projects, which receive a sizable share of investment. The key question is whether the projects financed through EFSI are really additional that is, projects that would never be financed otherwise. On this, there are some sceptical views. Claeys and Leandro (2016) look at similarity of EFSI and regular EIB projects and find only one out of 55 projects for which no similar EIB standard project exits. Ernst and Young (2016) find that respondents to surveys and interviews indicated that some of the financed projects could have been financed without EFSI support, meaning that these investments could be interpreted as not being fully additional (although the perception is not homogeneous).

## Youth Guarantee

The rise of youth unemployment has certainly been one of the most visible effects of the euro crisis. The Youth Guarantee is a commitment by Member States to ensure all those under the age of 25 years receive a good quality offer of employment, continued education, apprenticeship or a traineeship within four months of leaving formal education or becoming unemployed. The Youth Employment Initiative (YEI) is one of the financial instruments launched to support the guarantee, and provides support to young people living in regions where youth unemployment was higher than 25 per cent in 2012 – it was subsequently topped up in 2017 for regions with youth unemployment higher than 25 per cent in 2016. The total budget of the Youth Employment Initiative is €8.8 billion for 2014–20 – increased in 2017 from an initial €6.4 billion. Youth unemployment has been going down since 2015, but the key question is how much this is due to cyclical factors, as opposed to policy action. The most recently available country-level data on the implementation of the Youth Guarantee (as of 2015) are reported in Table 4.2. Coverage – i.e. the percentage of young people not in education, employment

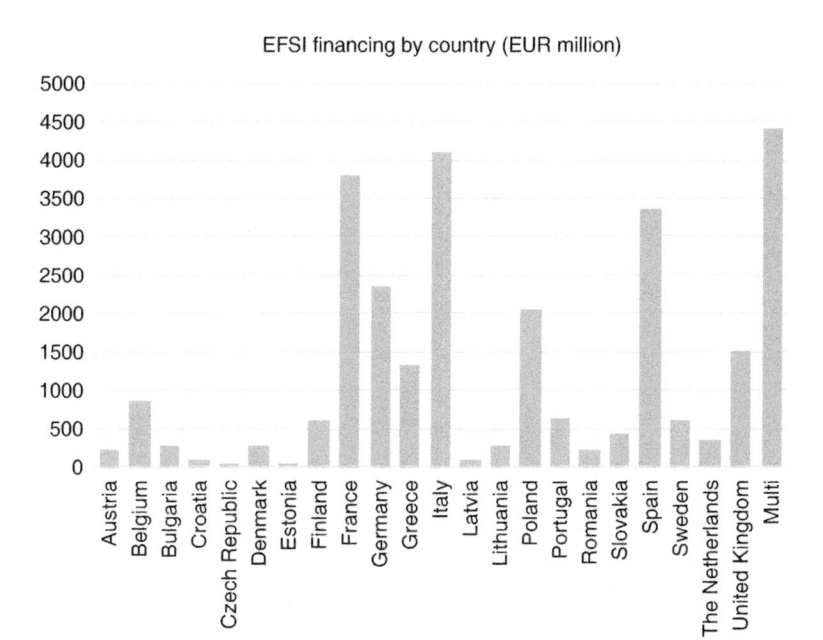

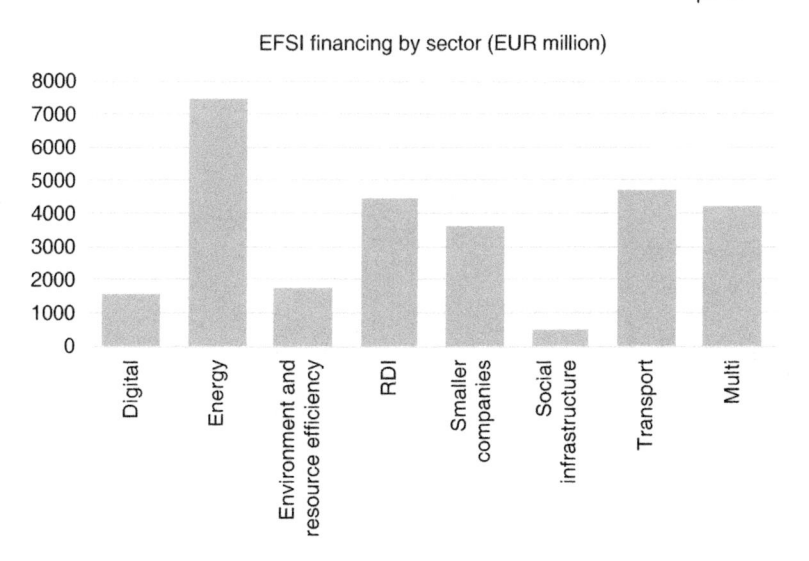

**FIGURE 4.5A** EFSI statistics.

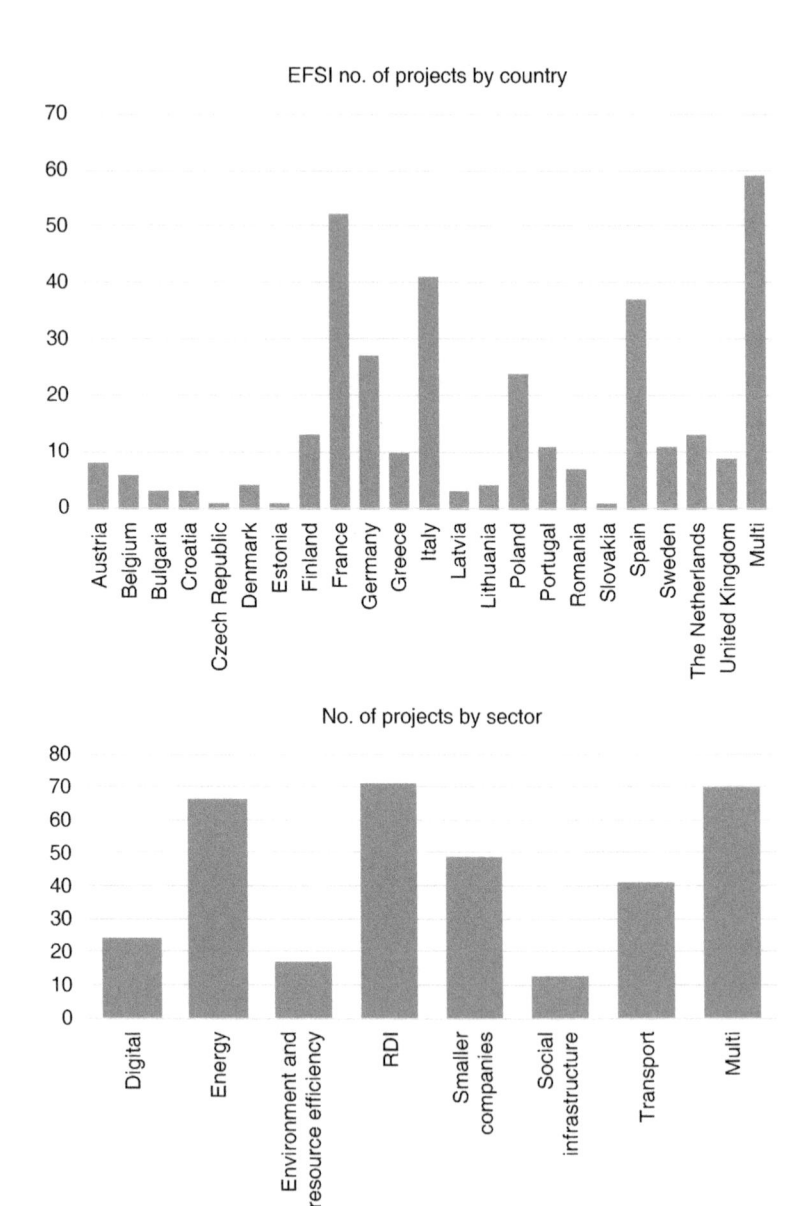

**FIGURE 4.5B** EFSI statistics.
*Note:* Including approved and signed projects; amounts for some projects are not disclosed.

**TABLE 4.2**  Youth Guarantee across EU countries

|  | 2015 results |  |  | 2015 statistics |  |
|---|---|---|---|---|---|
|  | Coverage | Implementation | Outcome | NEET rate | Youth un. rate |
| **Hungary** | 3% | 94% | 30% | 17% | 17% |
| **Malta** | 6% | 74% | 69% | 13% | 12% |
| **Italy** | 11% | 73% | 64% | 27% | 40% |
| **Spain** | 11% | 74% | 38% | 21% | 48% |
| **Bulgaria** | 14% | 36% | 23% | 23% | 22% |
| **Romania** | 17% | 48% | 20% | 21% | 22% |
| **Cyprus** | 20% | 8% | 15% | 19% | 33% |
| **UK** | 20% | 22% | n.a. | 13% | 15% |
| **Estonia** | 23% | 55% | n.a | 13% | 13% |
| **Latvia** | 28% | 43% | 2% | 15% | 16% |
| **Luxembourg** | 31% | 34% | 61% | 8% | 17% |
| **Greece** | 34% | 24% | 41% | 27% | 50% |
| **Lithuania** | 45% | 43% | 46% | 13% | 16% |
| **Czech Republic** | 46% | 62% | n.a | 15% | 13% |
| **Netherlands** | 48% | 38% | n.a. | 8% | 11% |
| **Portugal** | 49% | 43% | 45% | 14% | 32% |
| **Slovenia** | 50% | 38% | n.a. | 13% | 16% |
| **Ireland** | 51% | 38% | 71% | 18% | 21% |
| **Slovakia** | 54% | 41% | 4% | 20% | 27% |
| **Sweden** | 56% | 43% | 47% | 7% | 20% |
| **Croatia** | 60% | 33% | 56% | 21% | 42% |
| **Germany** | 61% | 50% | n.a | 10% | 7% |
| **Denmark** | 63% | 75% | 50% | 8% | 11% |
| **Poland** | 63% | 43% | 14% | 16% | 21% |
| **Belgium** | 70% | 44% | 43% | 16% | 22% |
| **Finland** | 71% | 49% | n.a | 13% | 22% |
| **France** | 81% | 24% | n.a | 16% | 25% |
| **Austria** | 89% | 50% | 63% | 10% | 11% |

*Source:* EC's country fiches.

or training (NEET) – tends to be low (less than 50 per cent in 16 out of 28 countries) and implementation – i.e. the take-up of an offer within four months – is also below 50 per cent in 18 out of 28 countries. A special report of the European Court of Auditors, released in April 2017, looks in depth at Ireland, Spain, France, Croatia, Italy, Portugal and Slovakia and concludes that implementation is lagging behind. The ECA point out it seems not to be possible to address the whole NEET population with the resources available from the EU budget alone, and that the YEI gave very limited contributions to the achievement of the Youth Guarantee's objectives.

## Conclusion

Few issues have been as controversial and as politically salient in recent years as globalization. Opinions differ as to the link between globalization and inequality on one hand and growth on the other. Mirroring these differences, there is no more clarity on the policy side as to how the so-called 'losers' of globalization should be compensated. In Europe, there is a long-standing conception of EU integration as a way to square the circle between globalization, social cohesion and political freedom. Advocacy of managed globalization has been identified in the past as a primary driver of major EU policies. Since the financial and euro crisis, however, EU institutions and economic policies have been increasingly called into question. The EU is portrayed as the promoter of a neo-liberal paradigm, blind to the social implications of its economic prescriptions by Eurosceptic parties that often advocate forms of protectionism. The need for change was acknowledged by European Commission's President Jean-Claude Juncker who, in his opening statement before the European Parliament plenary session, stressed the need to reverse the high rate of youth unemployment, poverty and loss of confidence in the European project. The data analysed in this chapter highlights that economic factors, both at the individual and country level, are important to understand Europeans' economic assessment of globalization. Interestingly, individual economic indicators – such as personal unemployment or economic difficulties – matter, but they matter less than people's assessment of their countries' economic position vis-à-vis the EU average. This emphasizes one additional reason why fostering income convergence across the EU is important.

Whether this is still possible after the crisis of last decade is a legitimate question. But the rise of Euroscepticism that we have witnessed in national elections testifies to the importance of this objective. Besides economic factors, the perception of the EU as an avenue of economic prosperity and social protection is important, with people who associate the EU with these features displaying a more positive view of globalization as an opportunity for economic growth. This highlights the importance of EU action and it seems to have been acknowledged by EU policy-makers themselves, as mirrored in the Juncker Agenda. To date, however, the results of flagship initiatives are mixed. The European Globalization Fund seems to be improvable, potentially in terms of its scope, which could be enlarged beyond globalization to assist workers displaced by intra-EU trade and off-shoring that result from the working of the single market (see Claeys and Sapir 2018). While the EU investment plan is clearly advancing – although with mixed reviews when it comes to the additionality of the projects financed with EFSI funds – the Youth Guarantee seem to be far from achieving its targets. While these are steps in the right direction, the EU does not yet appear to have succeeded in squaring the Dahrendorf challenge, establishing itself as a successful mediator between its citizens and the challenges of globalization.

## Notes

1. Dahrendorf (1995) argued that to stay competitive in a growing world economy, countries would be obliged to adopt measures that could inflict irreparable damage on the cohesion of the respective civil societies, or to implement restrictions of civil liberties and of political participation.
2. Details about the survey are available at http://www.gesis.org/eurobarometer-data-service/survey-series/standard-special-eb/sampling-and-fieldwork/. The data was downloaded from GESIS' archives. We use wave EB 69.2 in 2008 and EB 79.3 in 2013. This is because while almost all waves of the survey include the basic attitudinal questions on globalization that we use to construct our dependent variable, only few waves include some of the questions that we rely on for constructing independent variables.
3. The answering options are worded slightly differently in the 2013 wave, where instead of 'strongly agree/disagree' the answer states 'totally agree/disagree' and instead of 'somewhat agree/disagree' we have 'tend to agree/disagree'. Overall, however, they are comparable.
4. By running a Logit model of our dependent variable on six incremental sets of independent variables. Our dataset is a pooled cross-section of 52,355 observations from Eurobarometer over two years (2008 and 2013).
5. This is defined as someone declaring that they experienced 'difficulties paying bills' either most of the times or from time to time.

6. We construct dummy variables equalling 1 for those who answered they saw the domestic situation as either 'much better' or 'somewhat better', which will help us capture the effect of perceived relative positioning within the EU.
7. We construct a dummy variable equal to 1 for those people who mentioned 'economic prosperity', another dummy equalling 1 for those who mentioned 'social protection' and a third dummy equal to 1 for those mentioning 'unemployment'. On top of these variables, we sometimes include country dummies, or area dummies identifying new member states and euro area countries that have been subject to the EU/IMF adjustment programmes.
8. See http://www.eib.org/efsi/efsi_dashboard_en.jpg.

## References

Antoniades, A. 'Social Europe and/or global Europe? Globalization and flexicurity as debates on the future of Europe', *Cambridge Review of International Affairs* 21(3) (2008).

Balestrini, P. P. 'Public opinion regarding globalization: The kernels of a "European Spring" of public discontent?' *Globalizations* 12(2) (2015) pp. 261–75.

Batsaikhan, U. and Z. Darvas. 'Europeans rediscover enthusiasm for globalization', *Bruegel blog* (2017).

Bhagwati, J. *In Defense of Globalization* (Oxford, Oxford University Press 2004).

Bini Smaghi, L. 'Globalization and public perceptions', Dinner speech by Lorenzo Bini Smaghi, Member of the Executive Board of the ECB at the joint meeting of the GEPA-GPA-GSPA (2007).

Bourguignon, F. *The Globalization of Inequality* (Princeton, Princeton University Press 2015).

Buti, M. and Pichelmann, K. 'European integration and populism: addressing Dahrendorf's quandary', LUISS Policy Brief (January 2017).

Claeys, G. and A. Sapir 'The European globalization adjustment fund: Easing the pain from trade?', Bruegel Policy Contribution, Issue 5 (2018).

Collier, P. *The Bottom Billion: Why the Poorest Countries are Failing and What Can Be Done About It* (Oxford, Oxford University Press 2007).

Dahrendorf, R. 'Economic Opportunity, Civil Society and Political Liberty', UNRISD Discussion Paper 58, Geneva (March 1995).

Dollar, D. 'Globalization, poverty, and inequality' in Weinstein (ed.) *Globalization: What's New?* (New York, Columbia University Press 2005) pp. 96–128.

Edwards, M. S. 'Public opinion regarding economic and cultural globalization: Evidence from a cross-national survey', *Review of International Political Economy* 13(4) (2006) pp. 587–608.

European Court of Auditors 'Special report No 5/2017: Youth unemployment – have EU policies made a difference?' (2017). Available on ECA's website at: https://www.eca.europa.eu/en/Pages/DocItem.aspx?did=41096 (Accessed 16 July 2018).

Ernst and Young. 'Ad-hoc audit of the application of the Regulation 2015/1017 (the EFSI Regulation)', Final report (14 November 2016). Available on the EC's website at: https://ec.europa.eu/commission/sites/beta-political/files/ey-report-on-efsi_en.pdf (Accessed 16 July 2018).

Jacoby, W. and S. Meunier. 'Europe and the management of globalization', *Journal of European Public Policy* 17(3), (2010) pp. 299-317.

Merler, S. *Convergence in Europe: arrested development?* (Council for European Studies, Columbia University, 14 July 2016). Available at https://ces.confex.com/ces/2017/webprogram/Paper16319.html (Accessed 20 July 2018).

Rajan, R. G. *Fault Lines: How Hidden Fractures Still Threaten the World Economy* (Princeton, Princeton University Press 2010).

Sapir, A. 'Globalization and the reform of European social models', *Journal of Common Market Studies* 44(2) (2006) pp. 369-90.

Wallace, H. 'Europeanization and globalization: Complementary or contradictory trends?' *New Political Economy* 5(3) (2000) pp. 369-82.

Weinstein (ed.) *Globalization: What's New?* (New York, Columbia University Press 2005).

CHAPTER 5

# How can Social Democratic Parties in Government Deal with the Consequences of Globalization?

Manuel de la Rocha

## Introduction: Social Democracy in Crisis

Social democracy emerged and became established in Europe during the 1950s and 1960s as a compromise between capitalism and the market. Workers accepted capitalism and the market system on the basis that the state should play an important role as a redistributive agent. This is how modern welfare states were born and strengthened in the years and decades following World War II, and social democracy enjoyed its golden age in this period. In the 1970s and 1980s, a conservative offensive began. Increasingly, many of neo-liberalism's precepts became more acceptable to social democrats, who found themselves on the defensive particularly after 1989 following the fall of communist regimes. As the leftist intellectual Karl Polanyi (1944) has written, 'Capitalism is governed by a double movement – a push for the liberalization of markets and a contrary pull in favour of regulating them in the interest of the social majority'. Since the 1980s, however, the pendulum has swung in favour of free markets which, fuelled by new technologies, launched rapid expansion and transformed the system into the global financial capitalism that currently prevails.

Around the same time, socialist and social democratic governments began to accommodate the ideas of the neo-liberal paradigm, partly due to the exhaustion of Keynesian-style policies that no longer met their desired objectives. The inherent goal of social democracy, which used to be the protection and advancement of the working class, was put aside, and priority was given to the regulation and control of capitalism for its own survival, especially after the fall of the Berlin Wall. All of this resulted in a progressive weakening of the ideological postulates of social democracy.

The only serious attempt to redefine and modernize social democratic principles was the so-called Third Way, which emerged in the mid-1990s when social democracy was facing a challenging moment, both historically and politically. The centre-left's capacity to adapt to globalization and to offer a robust alternative to neo-liberal supremacy was being seriously questioned. The Third Way, led by Tony Blair and Gerhard Schroeder, claimed not only to be an alternative to the dominant paradigm of neo-liberalism, but also to present something that was different to the old post-war socialism characterized by hierarchical state control of the key resources of the economy.

The Third Way willingly accepted the domination of markets and private property as the engines of innovation and wealth creation, although it did seek to temper its most harmful and unjust effects. Social democrats were criticized for being more concerned with maintaining the size and power of the state than with producing effective policies that addressed the stark problems for people arising from globalization. They argued in favour of the restructuring of public administration, giving enormous importance to the issue of efficiency, cost reduction and individual choice. Under these premises the privatization of public services, originally initiated by Conservative governments, was taken further by social democratic governments with the aim of reducing costs.

The greatest shortcoming of the theoretical writings and political programmes inspired by the Third Way relates to the implications for inequality and social justice. Although there was concern about rates of poverty and social exclusion, equality ceased to be a goal in itself, and few concrete solutions were found to address the problem of rising economic inequality. By placing so much emphasis on improvements in competitiveness and efficiency, the proponents of the Third Way ended up reducing the values of the left to mere principles of technocratic management, to the point where they became scarcely differentiated from neoliberal ideology. Thus, the Third Way failed in its attempt to transform and modernize social democracy, and to impose itself globally as the new way forward for the left. Even if we acknowledge certain positive elements in the theoretical content of Third Way thinking, in practical terms the policies that were executed by its main proponents were perceived by many as merely a moderate form of neo-liberalism, and did not appear to question or dispute some of the most harmful liberal tendencies, such as financial deregulation which led directly to the great economic crisis that unfolded in 2008 and which shook the foundations of the capitalist-globalized system in a way not seen since the crisis of 1929.

## The Great Recession and its Impact on Social Democratic Ideas and Ideology

The bankruptcy of the American investment bank, *Lehman Brothers*, in September of 2008 set off one of the biggest economic crises since the Great Depression. The severity of the crisis has revealed the weaknesses of an immensely unstable process of economic and financial globalization. As Wolfgang Streeck contends, the bursting of the real estate bubble which caused the collapse of Lehman Brothers was nothing more than, 'a manifestation of a basic underlying tension in the political-economic configuration of advanced-capitalist societies; a tension which makes disequilibrium and instability the rule rather than the exception'. The deregulation and liberalization of financial markets accelerated their integration and dominance over more productive forms of capitalism. This has reduced the stability of the international economic system and increased the frequency of financial crises.

In the context of globalization and neoliberal domination, the 2008 financial crash led to a severe economic crisis which had huge repercussions for the productive sectors, for workers and companies, and for labour markets. Perhaps most dangerous is the profound delegitimization of democratic politics which has occurred since then, due to the incapacity and the unwillingness of institutions to adopt measures which respond to the general interest of the public in the face of pressure from speculators and unfettered markets. Increasingly, markets are not only exempt from the regulation and control of public authorities, but in their attempt to maximize benefits without incurring risks, advocates of free markets try to dictate and impose – through false interests and subtle forms of power – measures of liberalization and continuous adjustment that obstruct the recovery of the productive economy, and make it impossible to maintain the welfare and social protection policies which are such a characteristic feature of social democracy.

However, the Great Recession has shattered many of the fallacies of neoliberal thought, such as the supposed efficiency of financial markets based on self-regulation, or the belief that economic cycles are a thing of the past. Markets can generate economic growth and wealth but without adequate control and regulation they become unstable and produce bubbles, in the financial sector, in real estate, with raw materials, and so on, that can burst causing crises, the consequences of which are enormously damaging.

Along with the growth of the financial sector, the other side of the evolution of capitalism manifests itself in the model of economic and social growth that has been driven forward by the neoliberal paradigm in Western economies, particularly in the United States. Since the beginning of the 1970s, practically the entire Western world has seen a discrepancy between improvements in productivity and wage increases, which suggests that income and wealth are increasingly concentrated in the hands of a few, while workers have witnessed their salary levels stagnate for decades. Some economists, most notably Thomas Piketty, have depicted this situation of an unprecedented rise in inequality as inherent to the capitalist system.

In addition, it has been shown that GDP growth is not enough to guarantee equitable and lasting progress. The predatory energy and resource-intensive growth model, that arises in the light of the deregulatory forces of the market is neither efficient, nor sustainable in the medium-term. It produces harmful side effects, such as climate change, which need to be urgently addressed.

Yet despite the apparent failure of neo-liberalism and the detrimental effects of the crisis on large sections of the population, socialist and social democratic parties have been unable to stem their electoral decline. What is more, in many countries it was mostly social democratic parties that were punished for the ostensible failures of the prevailing model, at least in an electoral sense, often losing votes to populist political offerings of the left and right.

In retrospect, it seems clear that in the early 1990s, social democracy put too much emphasis on the benefits of the form of globalization that was emerging at that time, which was believed to increase growth, wealth and overall prosperity in the world. Social democrats didn't spot, or at least underestimated, the negative impacts of globalization on a wide segment of society. They could not even imagine, let alone warn of, the instability and risks that it entailed, and that eventually led to the 2008 crisis.

The reality of globalization, unfortunately, turned out to be much more problematic. Global financial capitalism has become significantly more aggressive in the last three decades, and the 'losers' of globalization are far greater in number than originally envisaged. Among those losers are the long-term unemployed in developed countries (those who will not find a job again because their skills have become obsolete), young people – including graduates – who cannot find skilled work, those who have lagged behind in the digital revolution, and the workers whose employment sectors have disappeared.

The efforts to update the worn-out Keynes-Beveridge model to protect and promote social protection were too accommodating to the neoliberal system, and did not offer any real alternative. In the absence of a differentiated political project, social democracy offered merely palliatives that did not challenge the foundations of the prevailing economic orthodoxy.

## Consequences of the Social Democratic Decline

The ideological decline of European social democracy has inevitably affected the strength of its electoral support. The main leftist parties have gone from being the representatives of the electoral majority across Western Europe during the second half of the twentieth century, to a political force in evident decline during the first decades of the twenty-first century, especially since the beginning of the Great Recession in 2008. The electoral data reflects this evolution:

- From 1950 to the present-day, social democrats across Europe have lost an average of 12 per cent of the vote in national elections.
- The 'golden age' of social democracy is now seen to have been in the 1950–70 period, and since then, there has been a gradual and continuous erosion of centre-left support that coincides with a period of increasing globalization.
- Although social democracy has been losing votes since the 1950s, the decline has accelerated over the last decade.
- If the focus is on the post-crisis years, PSOE (Partido Socialista Obrero Español/Spanish Socialist Workers' Party) is the European socialist party that has suffered the biggest fall in support after the Greek PASOK (Πανελλήνιο Σοσιαλιστικό Κίνημα/Panhellenic Socialist Alliance). PASOK received 43.9 per cent of the votes in 2009 and only 7 per cent in 2015, while PSOE won the Spanish election in 2008 with 43.9 per cent and in 2018 is touching 20 per cent support in the opinion polls. Similarly, the German SPD (Sozialdemokratische Partei Deutschlands/Social Democratic Party of Germany) secured 20.5 per cent in the 2017 federal election – the worst result in the party's history during (see Estefanía 2016).

The decline of social democracy has led to important changes in the political landscape of almost all European countries. During the post-war period, European politics was dominated by competition between the centre-left and centre-right parties, generally through a large social democratic and a large conservative-Christian democratic party which offered real political alternatives, but that nonetheless agreed on the basic framework in which liberal capitalist democracy should operate. These parties were large enough to form majority governments, to set agendas, and to carry out their policies. The decline of social democracy overturned this state of affairs. In many European countries, most notably in Germany, this breakdown has made it more difficult to form stable governments, which leaves voters increasingly frustrated with traditional parties and institutions.

These developments have paved the way for the advent of populist parties on both sides of the political spectrum. On the far right, we have seen the emergence of parties with xenophobic and anti-democratic attitudes. But new populist parties of the extreme left have emerged as well, and in some cases are outperforming traditional social democratic forces, notably Podemos in Spain, Syriza in Greece, the Five Star Movement in Italy, and La France Insoumise of Jean-Luc Mélenchon in France. Populist parties of both the left and right have succeeded in attracting citizens who have historically supported moderate social democratic parties – such as industrial or low-skilled workers – by directly confronting the economic fears generated by globalization, and the associated cultural and technological change. Despite their differences, all of these parties tend to share a nationalist vision that rejects globalization and the political and economic elites that defend the status quo of global capitalism.

This situation is apparent in France with Marine Le Pen, and in Germany, where the right-wing populist party, AfD (Alternative for Germany/Alternative für Deutschland), promoted itself as the authentic 'alternative' to the economic and political elite. It seems clear that if social democrats fail to provide voters with relevant solutions to the challenges their societies are facing, the decline of the left will persist and populism will continue to grow. In the longer term, the entire liberal democratic system will be put at risk. The emergence of populism has also altered the electoral axis and the key dividing-lines of European politics, which can no longer be defined on the traditional divide between left and right. Now, there are at least two other dimensions of electoral politics that have to be taken into account:

The 'up-down' axis: This relates to the elites who allegedly represent the establishment as opposed to the citizens. The social democratic parties who dominated the political arena for decades are perceived to have become increasingly out-of-touch, having little empathy with the circumstances of the most disadvantaged groups whose situation has progressively worsened.

In these circumstances, it is easier to understand why the traditional leftist parties are seen as part of the elite.

The 'openness-nationalism' axis: here, those in favour of an open society, who endorse the integration of Europe in a more globalized world, are counter-posed against nationalists and protectionists from left to right who reject immigration, international trade, the EU, multinationals and everything associated with globalization.

Social democrats need to understand and better respond to the new political dividing-lines that are reshaping European democracies. This should be done by maintaining the best tradition of the left, by articulating progressive social values and by defending the role of the welfare state, while at the same time by embracing a reformist spirit; by paying attention to what happens in the local communities and coming closer to the most disadvantaged groups; and by distancing itself from elites, while defending a united Europe but a democratic Europe, that favours globalization and international trade, but only when it is done fairly. Upholding and advancing all of these values and principles together with sound policies is no easy task, and represents the great challenge that social democracy now faces if it wants to recover its relevance in the decades ahead.

## Searching for Solutions: The Difficulty of Defining a Social Democratic Electoral Offer

The crisis of social democracy is a crisis of Western European democracy itself, and of the idea that democratic systems can channel the goals and aspirations of a wide part of the population. There is a systemic problem in the present political and socio-economic model, which needs to be addressed. The consequences of the Great Recession have sown doubt in the system among the majority of voters. Citizens are increasingly aware that the instruments of democratic politics remain essentially national, and cannot confront challenges that are, by their nature, supranational or global in scope (from social dumping to tax evasion, as well as climate change, migration and terrorism).

In this context, centre-left parties must re-think their political strategies. If in the past social democracy was willing to accept the current capitalist system as part of a wider social contract, it is now clear that the contract is broken, which automatically calls the system into question. The capitalist model of the 1950s and 1960s is very different from the current system of financial capitalism which is increasingly globalized, predatory and destabilising, for which mild remedies and temporary fixes are not sufficient.

One of the great challenges for social democracy is how to identify its target voters given these changing circumstances. In the past, centre-left parties established themselves as the dominant force in industrialized societies that were much more homogeneous than they are today. Social democrats were the defenders of workers' interests against capital. At the time, there was a strong culture of class-based politics, as working people shared common interests and aspirations. However, the situation has now changed dramatically. The divide between the 'winners' and 'losers' of globalization in societies that are more heterogeneous has created an electoral dilemma for leftist parties.

A first obvious electoral divide is between 'insiders' and 'outsiders'. If social democratic electoral programmes target public sector workers, civil servants, retired citizens and the middle classes (the insiders), then temporary workers, immigrants, students, and the unemployed (the outsiders) risk ending up in the hands of populists from the left and right. On the other hand, if social democrats neglect the demands of the insiders, and those with decent jobs, who have been a natural source of support for social democratic parties, they will be tempted to vote for more centrist Macron-style parties that prioritize the stability of the existing social order (that social democrats helped to create, if should be said).

Furthermore, the dilemma of social democracy has been largely determined by the budgetary restrictions that have affected almost all EU countries for a decade. Improvements to major public services, such as to education, health and social services, are expected to benefit mainly the lower-income middle classes. However, in general, investments of this type require tax increases to cover the cost without dramatically increasing public deficits. And this is where the core of the problem lies for social democrats. The middle-class insiders who provide the bulk of the public finances are opposed to paying more taxes and punish those governments who impose higher taxes electorally. This leaves social democrats with few options to carry out transformative political programmes.

In addition, in most European countries there is a generational divide that leads to a dilemma for traditional left parties. In societies with ageing populations, public spending on pensions and healthcare tends to grow, which puts more pressure on those of working age who are typically the ones that have to pay the most.

Most surveys demonstrate that the biggest decline in votes for social democratic parties has occurred among young people who have suffered a marked decline in their material living standards. Those born in the 1980s (so-called 'millennials') are the first generation since the war to reach the age of 30 with lower real incomes than those born during the previous decade. The rise of generational inequality has accelerated since 2008, while social democracy has been unable to offer effective responses to the problems faced by young people.

## Laying out a New Social Democratic Agenda

By too often conforming to the neo-liberal agenda while failing to propose an alternative conceptual framework, social democrats have given the leftist populist parties a window of opportunity. They have managed to build an appealing narrative, rooted in certain concepts derived from the work of authors such as the Italian revolutionary and political philosopher Antonio Gramsci, the Argentine intellectual Ernesto Laclau, and other Latin American influences. The political discourse of the 'elites' versus 'the people' is intuitively attractive since it threatens to disrupt the status quo, while it also connects to the lived reality of millions of citizens – those at the bottom of society, the 'losers' of globalization, those who feel alienated, insecure and who no longer see social democratic parties as defenders of their interests.

This is why traditional left parties have to make their political language more robust. They must be more radical in their criticism of the capitalist system, and the privileges of corporate elites, while being clearly reformist in their deeds and overall line of action. Social democrats' strong defense of the policies and accomplishments of the past often makes them appear conservative, or too close to the privileged classes. For instance, a strong defense of the public sector must be coupled with an equally strong demand for quality and efficiency in the delivery of public services. Further, in modernising their political discourse, social democrats must recognize that the labour-capital dichotomy has lost much of its historical resonance in societies where a large number of citizens are self-employed, entrepreneurs, or small business owners. Likewise, the struggle for equality should not lead to a distortion of meritocracy that undermines the importance of effort and talent.

If social democrats are to restore their appeal to the majority of working people, they need to reconstruct their political discourse far beyond the mere denunciation of the negative effects of globalization. Rather, it has to be articulated within a conceptual framework that gives social democrats a clear direction and sense of priorities. The basis upon which social democracy ought to build its new project is the idea of a new social contract between capital and labour, between different generations, and between the public and private sectors. It is a contract based on social justice and shared prosperity, which allows us to overcome the enormous inequalities created by the capitalist system, exacerbated by globalization. The generation of wealth in any society is always a collective effort, so the question is how to allocate income fairly. More specifically, we must consider what are the best mechanisms for redistribution? It is these mechanisms (i.e. salaries, taxation, public spending, collective bargaining) that shape the effectiveness of welfare states, and it is the failure of these mechanisms that is the main cause of citizen unrest, especially among young people who feel that they do not have any future.

Ultimately, this means coming up with a very different approach to human progress and prosperity. For conservatives, it comes down to economic growth, with some degree of redistribution. For social democracy, prosperity and progress should be measured according to the advance of three key elements, namely: social justice; environmental sustainability; and the strengthening of democracy. There cannot be widespread prosperity and social cohesion if these elements are not present together, as they reinforce one another. These ideas encompass, but clearly surpass the traditional social democratic approach to class struggle. The notion of solidarity continues to be central but in a broader sense – solidarity between existing generations; solidarity with future generations to which we must leave a more habitable planet; solidarity with citizens of other countries and with immigrants; solidarity between countries; above all, solidarity with developing countries.

Translating this proposition into public policy would mean six categories of action:

Firstly, on predistribution policies, redistribution in welfare states has reached its limit. The Beveridge-Keynesian model of redistribution is no longer effective in reducing inequality, which makes it necessary to focus on the primary causes of inequality. The Nobel laureate in Economics, James Meade, a colleague of J.M. Keynes, defined predistribution as being based on the need to, 'radically reform markets and power relations in order to empower the working class, [by] transitioning from a democracy of private owners to a democracy in which the citizens own the system'. Predistribution seeks to promote market reforms that encourage a more equitable distribution of economic power *before* public redistribution takes place through taxes and public spending alongside mechanisms such as collective bargaining, education and training, market competition, public procurement, and public-private partnerships.

Secondly, on continuing the fight against inequality. This is not exclusive to income and wealth inequality but relates to all other kinds of inequality including based on gender, sexual orientation, race, disability, and immigration status.

Thirdly, regarding sustainability and climate change policies, there has to be a determined transition towards a new model of energy supply, transport mobility and the creation of smart cities.

Fourthly, progressives must work to deepen democracy. Representative democratic systems have shown worrying signs of instability and fracture. Democracy cannot mean simply voting every four or five years to elect a parliament. Deepening democracy requires the increased participation of civil society, the involvement of citizens in the internal operation of the system, and introducing new forms of political engagement.

Fifthly, policies around development co-operation and multilateralism must form part of a global development agenda. Progressives should argue for an increase in development aid to fulfill the commitments made in the past. They must also advocate for the strengthening of multilateral agencies, especially the United Nations, while at the same time demanding efficiency gains and results.

Sixthly, there should be more Europe, but also a different Europe. Many of the initiatives already mentioned can only be implemented effectively at the European level. Unfortunately, in the last decade the policies imposed by the EU have put financial and monetary stability ahead of social stability. This situation raises a key question about the future of social democracy, and whether it is possible to advance progressive, social democratic policies within the framework of a twenty-first-century European Union. The way that the EU is designed, in particular the eurozone, leaves little margin for individual policy at the national level. It is necessary for social democratic parties to take European politics, including elections for the European Parliament, much more seriously. Only if the current Conservative centre-right majority that dominates the main European institutions (the Commission, Council and European Parliament) is changed will it be possible to envisage a shift towards full employment and the reduction of inequality as the central objectives of EU and eurozone policies.

Obviously, the narrative and the story are important but must be accompanied by concrete measures and policies, especially in economic matters. The good news is that a genuine 'economic corpus' is developing full of solid policy proposals, with great intellectual strength that should serve as the basis for any modern social democratic economic programme.

## Modernization of the Welfare State

One aspect traditionally central to the political discourse of left parties has been the defence of the welfare state. Social democrats played a decisive role in the creation of welfare states more than 50 years ago, and must remain the strongest defenders of welfare provision. Yet, the world has evolved dramatically in recent decades. Economic and social change, driven in part by new technologies, trade, demographics and migration, now have a dramatic influence on the outcomes of public policies. The modernization of the welfare state must go beyond simply increasing spending and criticising austerity, and must focus much more on the quality and impact of public spending. In this sense, the reforms adopted by the Nordic countries can serve as a guide.

In the early 1990s, the Nordic states, in particular Sweden and Finland, faced serious economic crises, with low economic growth, unprecedented levels of unemployment and high deficits that had in part been caused by the increased level of public spending that was necessary to maintain their long-standing welfare state practices. National governments were compelled to introduce economic reforms whose primary goal was to revive economic growth, while ensuring the future viability of welfare states. Not all of these reforms were carried out by social democratic administrations, but they were not reversed when the centre-left regained power.

Firstly, the Nordic countries managed to reform their institutions and make their labour and product markets more competitive, not only by means of simple deregulation, but also via reforms that were aimed at increasing training, geographical mobility and work incentives. Much more emphasis was placed on active employment policies, on continuous training, on the employability of workers, and on gender equality. The case of Denmark stands out in this regard with its well-known 'flexicurity' model that combines a liberalized labour market with a powerful system of continuous training for workers financed in large part by the state.

Secondly, the reform process was accompanied by major adjustments in public spending. Since the 1990s enormous emphasis has been placed on the quality of spending, and on the prioritization of investment and expenditure in sectors that promote economic growth. In addition, rigorous budget evaluation and policy review systems were put in place, and absolute transparency in their use was promoted.

Many social programmes evolved from a system of universal benefits to a means-tested system that is dependent on the level of income. In the areas of education and health, reforms were carried out with the ultimate objective of improving the quality and efficiency of services and their outcomes. Supplying both sectors has remained the responsibility of the state, although not necessarily managed from the public sector. Co-payments in healthcare were introduced to reduce unnecessary spending. In Sweden, a major reform of the pension system was also carried out to maintain the basis of a pay-as-you-go model, encouraging greater labour-force participation and delaying retirement to ensure economic sustainability over time. Likewise, welfare provision has been decentralized, with greater responsibility given to individual municipalities and regions.

Thirdly, the state was re-orientated toward new technologies and innovation, by greatly increasing their investment in R&D, education and ICT innovation, which they have maintained even in periods of crisis.

The reforms carried out have been successful from an economic and fiscal perspective, especially in Sweden and Norway. Thus Nordic countries regained economic dynamism, and over the last two decades have enjoyed growth and productivity rates clearly above the European average. This was achieved while maintaining the lowest levels of unemployment and inequality, and the highest rates of active population in the EU.

A key aspect of this relatively successful Nordic social model lies in its capacity to continuously reform and adapt institutions and policies in the face of economic and demographic challenges, and especially its ability to maintain dynamism and innovation in the field of public policies.

Finally, it is worth highlighting a series of interesting proposals, inspired in part by the Nordic model, that make up the so-called 'social investment' approach throughout the life-course. This is about generating virtuous cycles which guarantee equal opportunities and increased investment in people throughout the course of their life, starting from early childhood. The social-investment framework focuses on improving their employability and productivity, which leads to greater potential growth and, therefore to higher tax revenues. Thus, the main priority of the social investment approach becomes advancing family policies understood in a broad sense, including the likes of: universal extension of early-age school, the extension of assistance for dependent citizens, the implementation of gender equality and anti-discrimination legislation that encourages the full integration of women and disabled citizens into the labour market.

## Reforming the Organization and Functioning of Social Democratic Parties

The final essential criteria for the recovery of social democratic parties is to do with internal reform and the selection of party leaders. For much of the twentieth century, leftists formed mass parties – not only in the sense of their garnering wide electoral support, but also because of the large number of members who lined their ranks and who actively participated in the organic life of the party. Over time this has changed and party membership has been reduced to a tiny percentage of voters, and is often characterized by a very high average age. For large parts of the population, traditional parties, including social democratic parties, have transformed themselves into closed organizations, increasingly more distant from society, and dominated by clientelism and opportunism, instead of talent and merit. Leaders can often be regarded as having little regard for grassroots activists, who feel marginalized in the political decision-making process, and who ultimately end up leaving the party.

The populist parties are taking advantage of this situation. By embracing new technologies and social media, they have opened up and allowed millions of people to participate in the party's decision-making processes. Social democrats should draw lessons from the populist left parties and their mass mobilization strategies in order to attract new activists, including from among the liberal professionals, academics, students, small-scale entrepreneurs, and young people. It is necessary to consolidate the selection system through open primary elections in which members and sympathizers can participate so as to mobilize left-wing voters, sparking a conversation on the issues that really matter to people.

Finally, the personality of the candidates matters as well. The electoral result obtained by Jeremy Corbyn in the 2017 British elections teaches us about the importance of coherence. In a world dominated by uncertainty about the future, some values such as trust, honesty and authenticity are valued above others, like charisma, oratory or super leadership. Along with Corbyn, names such as the mayor of New York, Bill Di Blasio, the mayor of London, Sadiq Kahn, the new Spanish Prime Minister, Pedro Sánchez or the Swedish Prime Minister, Stefan Lofven, embody this type of profile of an authentic and close politician who can revive the social democracy.

## Conclusion

Social democracy was the ideology that played the most decisive role in shaping the European economic and social model created after World War II. At the time, Europe enjoyed almost three decades of continuous economic growth which benefited a large majority of the population, especially among the working class. Since the 1970s, the rise of neo-liberalism accelerated by the fall of communism led to a slow but deep decline in the fortunes of left parties. Although the financial crisis of 2008 exposed the deficiencies of the neo-liberal approach, social democracy failed to reap the rewards of a loss of confidence in markets. Social democratic parties have a lower share of the vote than for decades. Worse still, populist parties of left and right sought to capture traditional social democratic voters. This loss occurred because of ideological compromises made over the years in the face of neo-liberal ideas, sometimes executed by supposedly left-wing governments.

Updating the political discourse of social democracy means restoring the domination of democratic politics over market forces, while subordinating the latter to the collective interest. It is about recovering the spirit of reform by articulating an alternative economic model that goes beyond the technocratic management of capitalism and transcends national borders to create more democratic and just societies that temper the most negative aspects of globalization. Given the extent of financial globalization, progress and prosperity must go hand in hand with three fundamental concepts: social justice, environmental sustainability, and strong participatory democracy.

The renewal of the social democratic agenda also involves modernising the welfare state, improving efficiency and flexibility, decisively pursuing investment in growth and innovation, and equipping citizens, especially the most vulnerable, with capacities to face new challenges. Ultimately, it is about laying out an optimistic narrative for the future which embraces the spirit of progress, humanism and solidarity in the face of conservative individualism. It is a vision that should appeal to all classes and sections of society. In short, a political project framed by an idealistic spirit: the belief in a better, more decent and more just society for all.

## References

Berman, Sheri. 'The disastrous decline of the European centre-left'. *New York Times* (2 October 2017).

Berman, Sheri. *The Primacy of Politics: Social Democracy and the Making of Europe's Twentieth Century* (Cambridge, Cambridge University Press 2006).

Estefanía, Joaquín. '¿Quién será la cuarta socialdemocracia?' *Alternativas Económicas* 41 (2016).

Hemerijck, Anton. 'Taking social investment seriously for the Eurozone', *Intereconomics* (2016) pp 10–16.

Muñiz, Manuel (Coord). "Technological Change, Inequality and The Collapse of the Liberal Order', G20 Insights (April 2017).

Paramio, Ludolfo. 'La socialdemocracia maniatada: de los orígenes y la edad de oro a la trampa de la crisis de la eurozona', *Editorial Catarata* (2012).

PSOE. 'Ponencia Política aprobada tras el 39 Congreso Ordinario', Madrid (2017).

Streeck, Wolfgang. 'The crisis of democratic capitalism', *New Left Review* 71 (September–October 2011).

Vallespín Fernando and Bascuñan, Mariam M. '*Populismos*', Alianza Editorial (2017).

# Part II

## Brexit, Populism and the Future of the European Union

CHAPTER 6

# Brexit and Globalization: Collateral Damage or an Accident Waiting to Happen?

Loukas Tsoukalis

In a referendum held on 23 June 2016, with a relatively high turnout by the standards of recent years, a majority of the British people voted to leave the European Union (EU). It was 52 against 48 per cent in a country divided along many cross-cutting lines. Arguably the most important political decision taken in the British Isles since the end of the World War II, Brexit will have major implications for the economy, foreign policy as well as for domestic politics, possibly also for the unity of the UK.

The withdrawal of the UK will, of course, also constitute a big loss for the rest of the EU in what may appear as a never-ending series of crises. Following the crisis of the euro and the refugee crisis, one of the big countries has now decided to leave, thus marking a dramatic reversal of an unstoppable (so we thought) process of integration with the addition of ever more members and functions. Negotiating the terms of divorce is difficult enough. Negotiating the terms of a new relationship between the UK and the rest of the EU following Brexit will be even more difficult. After all, Brexit cannot change geography. The British Isles are tied in many different ways with the rest of the European continent and such ties can only be loosened at a high cost.

In this chapter, we shall begin by examining the troubled history of Britain's European relationship, a relationship that turned ever more problematic during the recent phase of globalization coinciding with a new push on the accelerator in European integration. Brexit did not come out of the blue, and we need to dig into history to understand why. We shall then proceed to examine the decision to hold the referendum, the nature and outcome of the renegotiation, the issues raised during the debate preceding the popular vote, and the real choice(s) facing British people. What were the dividing lines on the big question of Leave or Remain? Was Brexit really the result of a popular/populist revolt against globalization, a revolt that has challenged the established political order in many countries and brought Donald Trump to power in the United States? And what is the link, if any, between globalization and European integration? Is Brexit showing the way out for other countries, or is it likely to be a unique event? These are the main questions we shall attempt to address below.

## No Love Lost

If Britain had chosen to do so, it could have played a leading role in European integration from the very beginning and could have shaped the European model much closer to its own image. Luckily, it chose not to, ardent supporters of European unity would hasten to add now liberated from the constraints of political correctness. Britain joined late in what has always looked from its side like a business affair, based mostly on a narrow calculation of economic benefits and costs: an arranged marriage if you prefer, certainly not an affair of the heart.[1] There was little love at best, but also in crucial moments, real misunderstanding by British political leaders of the motives and intentions of their partners, notably those in the driving seat in European councils. Or, was it just lack of empathy?

In the words of Winston Churchill: 'We are with Europe but not of it. We are linked but not comprised. We are interested and associated, but not absorbed'.[2] In his famous Zurich speech, Churchill spoke in favour of the United States of Europe, but Britain was not meant to be part of it. Nothing much has really changed since then as far as many British citizens and their political leaders are concerned. Britain's political elite has always been divided on European integration and not terribly interested in it, with some notable exceptions (more so among intellectuals and academics). When the Conservatives led Britain into the Common Market, as European integration characteristically used to be referred to on that side of the Channel, Labour was against. And then roles were progressively reversed, ending up today with a strongly Eurosceptic Conservative party and a mildly pro-European (although with a vocal Eurosceptic minority) Labour party that usually prefers to talk as little as possible about Europe.[3]

All along, genuine Europhiles have remained a small, persecuted (!) minority within Britain's two big parties, the Liberal Democrats being the only consistent pro-European political force in the country, yet small. With a mostly Europhobic tabloid press owned by foreigners (not Europeans) and persistently low levels of public support for European integration (always among the lowest, if not the lowest, as registered in Eurobarometer surveys), and with even less interest in and knowledge of the European project, the latter has, understandably, never been treated as a vote winner by Britain's political class. If anything, it has been like a poisoned chalice[4] that has led several prominent British politicians to their premature political death. True, Britain was a late entrant to a club where the basic rules had already been set by others and it then had to fight successive battles in the name of reform to change the rules as regards the European budget, the common agricultural policy, and more. However, the problem goes much deeper: many British people and their political representatives simply do not consider themselves European,[5] and only a minority speak any European languages except for their own. Not surprisingly, they are not at all keen to transfer money and power to European institutions or share their destiny with foreigners on the continent of Europe.

However, as a member of the EU, Britain succeeded in playing a determining role in important areas of European policy, such as the internal market, trade, enlargement, as well as foreign and security policy. For years, it used to find allies among those who appreciated British pragmatism, liberal views, and a strongly pro-Atlantic policy, as well as among those who looked for a counterweight to France (or France and Germany together), and in countries outside the Union eager to become part of the European project. For the British, further enlargement had the added advantage that it would make deeper EU integration less likely.

Given its relative weight as a country that had run a huge empire until a few decades previously, the quality of its civil service, with the Foreign Office as the Rolls Royce leading the rest, Britain's influence in European affairs was hardly surprising, although usually not acknowledged by most of its politicians. Britain commanded respect, even from those who disagreed, and in turn respected the rules once adopted, unlike some of its continental partners for whom new legislation was just one more stage in the negotiation and obeying the rules a relative matter. The differences in political culture and legal traditions, not to mention institutional capacity in rule implementation and enforcement, were bound to cause more friction as integration deepened.

Britain was always on the liberal side in economic terms and keen on safeguarding the interests of the City of London as an international financial centre almost irrespective of the political colour of those who happened to be in power. It had a more global outlook than almost anybody else in Europe. But it also consistently tried to put its foot on the brakes and restrain the pro-integration zeal of its partners on different fronts, resorting to exceptions and opt-outs when everything else failed. This happened more and more as European integration shifted to higher gear from the early 1990s onwards. Exceptions and opt-outs in turn led to more isolation, thus preparing the ground for the grand exit.

## A Divided Country

Many Conservatives blamed Thatcher's demise in 1990 on a conspiracy of pro-Europeans inside the party and turned more Eurosceptic, while sterling's forced withdrawal from the European Exchange Rate Mechanism in 1992, when the international financier, George Soros, won his bet and some billions at the expense of the Bank of England, hurt British pride and British pockets. To make matters worse, France and Germany were at the time leading the way towards monetary union. This was certainly one big step too far for the British. Feeling unable to stop it, they finally opted out. The creation of economic and monetary union without Britain has been a major turning point in Britain's relations with the rest of the EU. Other opt-outs followed, notably from the passport-free Schengen area, large parts of justice and home affairs, and the Charter of Fundamental Rights. The British felt increasingly uncomfortable with the accelerating pace of integration in Europe and decided to distance themselves.

The arrival of New Labour, led by Tony Blair, the most European-minded prime minister since Edward Heath, did not fundamentally change the domestic scene. Despite constantly repeating his priority to keep Britain 'at the heart of Europe', Blair never invested much effort in trying to influence public opinion and tackle Euroscepticism head on, although, admittedly, this would have been a difficult task given the troubled history of Britain's relationship with the EU.[6]

If anything, the opposite happened, albeit unintentionally. Strategic decisions taken during the Blair era later became catalysts for Brexit. The New Labour governments embraced wholeheartedly globalization and deregulated markets on the assumption that the expected tide would help to lift all boats, while (to be fair to them) also emphasising the need to empower citizens to better take advantage of the opportunities created. It is now clear that New Labour grossly underestimated the unequal distribution of gains and losses arising from free and global markets, which laid the groundwork for the subsequent revolt of the losers. Income inequalities grew during the last 25 years or so.[7] On the other hand, the Blair governments decided not to take advantage of the long transitional period allowed by accession treaties for the free movement of workers after the big bang enlargement of the EU in 2004. This was based on the mistaken belief that relatively few citizens from the new members would take advantage of this freedom. In any case, immigration was supposed to be good for the British economy, hence for the country as a whole. The result was approximately one and a half million people who migrated from Central and Eastern Europe to the UK in the years that followed enlargement, and immigration became the most decisive factor for Brexit on referendum day. History sometimes plays strange games.

The bursting of the biggest international financial bubble since 1929 soon turned into an existential crisis for the euro. In many British eyes, Europe and the eurozone in particular were totally incapable of managing the crisis, stagnating economically yet integrating further, becoming more undemocratic in the process and run by Germans: a terrible combination indeed – and not far from the truth. British and US media, prominent economists and lesser mortals as well, predicted disaster and disintegration with a distinct element of *Schadenfreude*. However, they all underestimated, once again, the sense of commitment of Europe's political leaders to the common project (or perhaps more accurately, their collective instinct of survival).

Britain felt marginalized in a union where the euro was at the centre, and risked becoming the recipient of policies (and failures) decided elsewhere. And it became increasingly isolated. The fiscal compact treaty and the election of Jean-Claude Juncker as president of the European Commission are only two examples of how 'Perfidious Albion' had apparently lost its knack of forming alliances on the European continent. Isolation is often a self-fulfilling state of mind.[8]

Meanwhile, on the domestic front Euroscepticism was growing. The UK Independence Party (UKIP) on the ultra-nationalist right[9] succeeded in drawing support mostly from old age conservatives and nationalists but also from those who felt left behind during the big economic and social transformations of recent decades, including former Labour voters. It combined nostalgia for the past with a strong denunciation of European constraints on British sovereignty and a strong emphasis on immigration. UKIP succeeded in winning the largest number of votes at home in the European Parliament elections of 2014 and caused an earthquake in the British political system. Nigel Farage, the leader of UKIP, together with Marine Le Pen in France and politicians of the same kin in other countries, were mounting a frontal attack on the liberal political order and European institutions as well.

In the Conservative camp, an increasing number of MPs apparently decided that the most effective way of dealing with the mounting challenge from the right would be to adopt much of the vocabulary of their challenger. Under the leadership of David Cameron, the Conservative Party distanced itself further from the European political mainstream, while giving the distinct impression that he personally did not have much of an interest in what went on in Europe. In the words of the former president of the European Council, Herman Van Rompuy: 'How do you convince a room full of people, when you keep your hand on the door handle? How to encourage a friend to change, if your eyes are searching for your coat?'.[10] And while the Conservative party was shifting further to the right, in 2015 Labour elected a new leader, Jeremy Corbyn, from the far left of the party. In Britain's increasingly polarized politics, Europe did not easily fit in.

There are many different kinds of Britain:[11] a very international economy with a deregulated jobs market that attracts many people from the EU and beyond, with institutions and universities that are more open than anywhere else in Europe (speaking the lingua franca surely helps), a multi-ethnic and multicultural society, and London as the most global of cities, alongside New York. Yet, Britain (or, its greater part) is also an increasingly parochial country, with England withdrawing into a 'Little England' mentality, while Scotland diverges politically, is distinctly more pro-European and many Scots still think of divorce.

Britain is very much a divided country with large inequalities. It is certainly not unique in this respect, although more extreme than big countries such as Germany and arguably also France. Espousing globalization as an essentially neo-liberal agenda and with an emphasis on services and the financial sector in particular, Britain has ended up with more internal divisions and inequalities. Only a small minority of British politicians ever considered the European project as a means of collectively managing and taming globalization, a means of projecting a common model and defending common interests and values in a rapidly changing world where the relative weight of individual European countries, the UK included, is rapidly diminishing.

## Renegotiation and High Stakes

Under strong pressure from within his party, Prime Minister Cameron announced in his Bloomberg speech in January 2013 that he intended to ask, if re-elected, for a renegotiation of Britain's terms of membership of the EU on the basis of which he would later call an 'in' or 'out' referendum. A comprehensive review of EU competences and how they affect the UK had already been launched by the Foreign Secretary, intended to highlight the alleged over-centralization of powers in Brussels. It was a painstaking exercise and very comprehensive, as was to be expected from the British civil service. But having produced no spectacular results in political terms, the final report was quietly set aside.[12] After Cameron won an (unexpected) outright majority in the 2015 election, he proceeded to outline the UK's demands in the renegotiation. Thus, 40 years after the 1975 referendum, history was repeating itself: another renegotiation of the terms of membership for the UK, again for internal party reasons (this time it was the turn of the Conservatives), and with narrow terms of reference.

Cameron started by calling for a 'reformed' (and leaner) EU to suit British interests. But as the response from Brussels and the national capitals came loud and clear, he gradually scaled down the expectations. He wanted to be able to claim victory in the end and hence justify a decision to campaign for Britain to stay in. After all, the renegotiation was meant to be, at least in part, a public relations exercise for domestic (and mostly internal party) consumption. Harold Wilson had done more or less the same back in 1975.

There was very little time to renegotiate or simply address some of the fundamentals of Britain's membership of the EU and precious little interest from its partners to do so: they were hardly keen on adding more exceptions to an already long list and even less keen on making concessions to a British prime minister who had previously succeeded in alienating almost everybody in European councils. Last but not least, the negotiating power of the two sides was highly imbalanced, an unpleasant yet inescapable fact that so many Brexiters have refused to acknowledge before or after the referendum. Domestic politics in Britain was, once again, out of kilter with European politics. But while the renegotiation was bound to be limited in scope, the stakes at the referendum were much higher. Britain was thus taking a big gamble with the most important relationship it has with the rest of the world, namely the one with the big regional bloc in its immediate neighbourhood.

Britain wanted a less regulated and more competitive Europe, open to global economic forces. At the time, many among its EU partners were only too keen to concur, and it did not therefore prove too difficult to agree on an appropriate wording to that effect. The European Commission had already launched a campaign to reduce EU red tape. Of course, the beauty of economic regulation is in the eye of the beholder. In the EU, it has been the object of ever-lasting negotiations on many different fronts in an attempt to reconcile different histories, institutions and the specific interests of member countries. Free trade, sovereignty and democracy make an explosive mix.[13] In a globalising world economy, the EU has so far attempted, albeit with limited success, to reconcile all three at the regional level. Yet, for zealots within the Conservative party, it has always been difficult to accept that markets need rules and international rules need some form of joint management, hence also compromise.

Britain had decided back in the early 1990s to stay out of European monetary union for perfectly understandable economic and political reasons. But there was a price to pay for staying out, namely in terms of reduced influence in European affairs since membership of the eurozone also determined membership of the core group in the EU. During the euro crisis, Britain became marginalized and also got itself in a bind: rational people on the British side of the Channel could not really wish for the breakup of the eurozone knowing only too well that there was no way of insulating themselves from the negative consequences of a breakup; However, they should try to build fences to protect themselves as much as possible from the ongoing euro crisis and the decisions associated with it. This is precisely what Prime Minister Cameron (and his predecessors) tried to do, and he largely succeeded. He also tried to obtain formal guarantees for the City of London, but these were much more difficult, if not impossible, to obtain. The future of a large offshore centre in an increasingly regulated international financial environment and on the edge of a regional currency bloc is not entirely clear.

Britain wanted measures to reduce net migration from the rest of the EU and the welfare benefits associated with it, given the disproportionately large numbers arriving at its shores, only comparable to Germany within the Union. But it had to fight against the principle of inseparability of the four fundamental freedoms of the single market for goods, services, persons and capital. It was a principle elevated to a theological dogma in many European capitals. Had the other Europeans offered the British an effective emergency brake on intra-EU migration, the result of the referendum would in all likelihood have been different. Control of inward migration was to become the single most important issue in the referendum. But the rest of Europe was apparently not ready to pay the price to keep Britain in. In fact, most political leaders on the European continent had not even realized the danger until it was too late. Cameron at least won the right to restrict payments of in-work benefits and child support to immigrants from other EU countries, but it was not enough.

The British government also won an agreement that legislative proposals by the European Commission could be blocked in the future, if the majority (55 per cent) of national parliaments were opposed. And it obtained a formal exception to the 'ever closer union' objective enshrined in the preamble of the Treaty on European Union. This had been first introduced in the Maastricht version of the treaty back in 1992. 'Where is the beef?' the pragmatic British might have asked, but apparently pragmatism has its limits also in the UK.

However, behind anodyne phrases, behind flags, hymns, and all kinds of symbols, there has always been a wide gap between Britain and many of its European partners concerning the expectations that each has from European integration. While the British prime minister spoke of 'network Europe' and cooperation in a common market, the large majority of his partners already shared a common currency and took further steps in integration. Some even dared talk of political union, although federalist rhetoric had toned down, only to revive once again more recently. The gap is wide and goes far back in time. What had changed in the years preceding the Brexit referendum was the, reluctant or otherwise, readiness of the British to let others go ahead, if they wished, as long as their partners let the UK stay out of new integration projects. In other words, Britain had reconciled itself to a place on the outer periphery of European integration much before the referendum took place.

## Questions Not Asked and the Unholy Alliance

British people were asked to choose in the referendum between 'Leave' and 'Remain', following a renegotiation that did not and could not alter much the fundamentals of Britain's EU membership. Cameron obtained concessions from his European partners that could in no way be presented as a major change of the terms of Britain's EU membership, especially as regards immigration. And he thus failed to rally a significant number of prominent and less prominent members of his own party on the Remain camp. The Conservative rank and file was deeply divided during the campaign, even though the majority followed the leader, while Labour leadership was at best lukewarm in favour of Remain.[14]

Those who wanted to leave the EU raised, first and foremost, the spectre of uncontrolled immigration. They also stressed the need to regain control of national borders and legislation, and they exaggerated the budgetary costs of Britain's EU membership. On the other side, those who wanted to stay emphasized the likely negative effects of Brexit on the domestic economy; only a few dared praise the virtues of the common European project and Britain's part in it. Numbers were thrown at each other indiscriminately and many people resorted to fake news and fake statistics: Turkey's future EU accession, apparently unavoidable, would bring millions of new immigrants to British shores, while many economists who should have known better were only too ready to produce specific numbers in bleak scenarios for the British economy after an eventual Brexit. The debate often sank very low and truth suffered a great deal in a country that was deeply divided and in which political parties and politicians no longer enjoyed much respect, nor indeed did old venerable institutions, including the UK Treasury and the Bank of England, not to mention the IMF. The advice of world leaders, including President Obama, and all kinds of experts was not much listened to either. Demagogues had taken over.

The campaign leading to the Brexit referendum revealed big cracks in the British political system and British society in general. Something had gone badly wrong in previous years. Globalization and economic liberalization had produced big winners and many losers, while the ideological and policy convergence between the two main parties, the Conservatives and Labour, since the 1990s had left many of the losers unrepresented and with little trust for political parties and politicians.[15] And then came the bursting of the big bubble in 2007–8, which exposed the fallacy of the prevailing neo-liberal ideology. Saving the big banks with hundreds of billions of taxpayers' money was hardly consistent with economic liberalism. Years of austerity followed and incomes stagnated. But arguably the worst of all was that many people no longer felt they were in it together with the much better off. When a renowned economist, or indeed the Treasury, predicted a loss of GDP after Brexit, the instinctive response from many people was 'It's your GDP, not mine'.[16]

Pro-Europeans within the UK and the rest of the EU had laid their hopes in the conservative – with a small 'c' – instinct of the majority of voters. When it comes to the crunch, British people were expected to vote for the status quo rather than for an uncertain future, more out of fear of the unknown than out of love for what was on offer. The EU was surely not the object of love for most British people for reasons that often went far back in history, but at least this was the devil you know, so thought and hoped supporters of Remain. But it all depends on how you define (or better, perceive) the status quo. A key message, apparently successful, of the Leave campaign was that EU membership would lead to more (and even worse) change in the future, also less control in British hands.

Was Britain's membership of the EU the victim of collateral damage caused by economic and technological developments as well as political decisions that went far beyond the EU?[17] Was it, in other words, the victim of globalization on a neo-liberal agenda? I believe the answer is yes, but only partly so. In its more recent phase, European integration has become increasingly identified with globalization and liberalization. For those who consider rapid change and global competition as a threat, Europe is seen as part of the problem and not part of the solution. The rejection of the European constitutional treaty in the French and Dutch referendums in 2005 should have served as an early wake-up call, but alas, did not. The permissive consensus on which European integration had been based for so long was being eroded.[18]

In Britain, the problem was much worse because the reservoir of support for the European project had always been very shallow. Therefore, when things got really rough, as the big financial crisis and austerity followed on years of growing global competition, slow growth and rising inequalities, there was precious little support to draw from – and European institutions became a convenient scapegoat for popular discontent. Given the history of Britain's relationship with the EU, the increasing number of opt-outs and recent crises, Brexit was like an accident waiting to happen. Cameron made the fatal wrong turn of the wheel by calling the referendum and mishandling both the renegotiation and the campaign, yet under extenuating circumstances: the road was in a bad condition and so was the car.

The evidence suggests that those left behind in an era of rapid economic transformation turned in large numbers against EU membership in the referendum, because the EU was identified with immigrants, open borders and loss of control. However, the losers from economic change ended up in an unholy alliance with right wing nationalists, with people yearning for old imperial glories and others daydreaming about Britain as an offshore island ready to strike free trade deals with the rest of the world. As a seasoned observer of the European scene has so aptly described it,[19] it was an unholy alliance between members of golf clubs in the English countryside and the 'sans culottes' of globalization in the decaying heartlands of the British manufacturing industry.

Was it interests or values that brought such different people together in a broad-based alliance to vote for Brexit? The old dividing line between right and left was replaced by another one now, separating nationalists from cosmopolitans, social conservatives from liberals, those who try to resist change from others who see opportunities for themselves in rapid economic and technological transformation. Values overlap with interests, although of course not entirely. It was a combination of both that brought the unholy alliance together – and the fuzzier the terms of the alliance the better. Such alliances can win elections or referendums in times of political flux, but they are unable to deliver the goods once they have won. Within the alliance that won the British referendum, some talk of global Britain and free trade, while others yearn for protection.

The evidence from numerous exit polls, as well as from surveys and studies before and after the referendum, points to a deeply divided country along many different lines. The main parties were divided from MPs down to voters, although the respective majorities moved in opposite directions. According to the data available, 61 per cent of Conservative supporters voted for Leave and 61 per cent of Labour for Remain.[20] Under-25s voted overwhelmingly for Remain and over-65s for Leave. The correlation in terms of education was also very strong: the more educated, the more pro-European.

Class was bound to be an important factor. But it also correlated strongly with education, income and wealth. In Britain, and other countries as well, notably the United States, the white working class contains many of those who lose out as a result of economic change. Not surprisingly, it produced large majorities for Leave, while members of ethnic and religious minorities opted mostly for Remain, apparently on the belief that a European Britain provides safer guarantees for their rights. It may look odd at first sight that people of Pakistani or Caribbean origin seem to trust Brussels and the European legal order more than white Brits, but there is logic in it.

Metropolitan London, big cities and university towns opted for open borders and Europe, while the English countryside, towns with large numbers of immigrants and/or low incomes and high unemployment voted for Leave. Last but not least, a large majority of Scots and a smaller majority of Northern Irish voted Remain. Europe has become an important factor dividing the UK.

Was the popular decision for Brexit, albeit with a small majority, the result of the populist tsunami that has also hit other European countries,[21] not to mention the United States where it brought Donald Trump to power? If by populism we mean political movements or parties that fight against 'the system' by claiming the main division to be between 'the people' on the one side and corrupt or incompetent 'elites' on the other, while also offering simple solutions to extremely complicated problems, then surely there was a strong populist undertone in the Leave campaign, although led mostly by representatives of the privileged class. Yet, behind populism we usually find big political failures and accumulated popular frustration. Such movements do not grow out of nothing. And there were surely good reasons for many people to be unhappy, if not angry, with the old political order when the Brexit referendum took place.

The real choice facing British people in the referendum was between continuing on a special status or semi-detached membership of the EU with voting rights and opting for a new kind of relationship with the rest of the EU, a relationship to be negotiated, but with no voting rights. This choice had been shaped by the way Britain's EU membership had developed over the years, and it did not change much as a result of the renegotiation. It was more complicated and nuanced than the black or white choice of leave or remain offered to voters in the referendum. Of course, referendum questions need to be simple, but there is a price to pay for simplicity – and the latter can often be misleading.

Other important questions were also left hanging in the air and never properly addressed during the campaign. One has to do with the trade-off between sovereignty and interdependence. If in the name of sovereignty, people choose to do away with the constraints of EU membership, are they also ready to do away with the constraints emanating from European and global interdependence, and what is the economic price they are prepared to pay? Another question has to do with power: how much negotiating power does the UK really have in or out of the EU? On these questions, the gap between myth and reality remained large during the campaign. After the referendum, myths began to explode, a process that is likely to be long and will surely be traumatic.

## Who's Next?

We learned that the transition team of newly elected President Trump called European political leaders asking which countries would follow the UK on the way out, apparently convinced that Brexit was only the beginning of an unstoppable process of disintegration.[22] After all, Nigel Farage had been a trusted source of information on the UK and Europe for the incoming US President; hence no love lost for the European project in the new centres of power in Washington DC – and no deep knowledge either.

Europe had gone through a succession of crises with a cumulative effect morphing into an existential crisis for European integration: Brexit was the worst, no doubt, since the very beginning. The biggest international financial crisis since 1929 had threatened the very existence of the common currency, the euro, while the implosion of much of Europe's immediate neighbourhood had brought increasing numbers of refugees, immigrants and also terrorists to Europe. The EU did not have the institutions or policy instruments to deal with such crises, and it was deeply divided between and within countries. The resulting cost was very high in both economic and political terms.[23]

The crisis of the euro and the refugee crisis came on top of long-term underlying trends that had been gradually undermining the capacity of European institutions to deliver the goods. There was the problem of overstretch, the product of continuous expansion in terms of both membership and functions – a sure sign of success. At the same time, the centre of decision-making remained weak and so did the legitimacy base on which the whole thing rested. Another related to the prevailing economic conditions during the last 25 years or so, characterized by intensifying global competition, slow growth and widening inequalities within developed countries, thus making the EU the (innocent?) victim of collateral damage caused by globalization and much more.

At the worst moments of these crises, Europe looked like an ungovernable post-modern empire whose neighbourhood had caught fire. Anti-systemic parties and Euroscepticism grew in several countries, EU politics turned toxic and common decisions were too often beyond reach. It was in this context that the majority of British people voted for Brexit. And a few months later, came the election of President Trump. Was the anti-systemic (or populist) tsunami unstoppable?

Yet, in the worst moments of these crises, there were enough European political leaders (notably in Germany, France and the other founding members, plus a few others when lucky), who thought that the cost of European disintegration would be absolutely prohibitive – and they also knew they could still draw support from large numbers of citizens across Europe. Even when the EU looked at its most dysfunctional and unhappiness among members reached new depths, a few but key political leaders tried to keep the whole thing together. They did so not so much out of love but more out of fear of being left alone in a rapidly changing world where size matters, and also out of fear of the high cost of divorce. The best illustration of the above are the successive emergency decisions (not always the wisest) each time the eurozone reached the edge of the precipice, and also public opinion surveys that show consistent popular majority support for the common currency, even in the worst moments of the euro crisis.

## Conclusion

All countries in the EU are different, but the UK is more different than the rest. It is big enough to think it can make a difference, and there are enough Brits who believe, for reasons of history mostly, that they have a real alternative to being part of European integration. Future will tell who was right, although the price for knowing the correct answer may prove to be very high.

As for the rest of the EU, no country is expected to follow Britain on the way out, President Trump and others rest assured. Fear is indeed a strong unifying factor, but Europeans would be taking a huge risk if they were to rely on fear too much and for too long to keep the troops together. The European project needs to adjust to a rapidly changing environment within and outside the common borders. And there are rays of hope pointing in this direction. Adjustment will require, among other things, an agreement on a new special relationship with the UK: it will be a damage limitation exercise.

## Notes

1. Helen Wallace refers to a transactional approach, in Helen Wallace, 'JCMS Annual Review Lecture: In the name of Europe'.
2. The quotation is from an article penned by Churchill in the *Saturday Evening Post* on 15 February 1930.
3. Hugo Young tells very eloquently 'the story of fifty years in which Britain struggled to reconcile the past she could not forget with the future she could not avoid'. It is the story of Britain's troubled relationship with Europe. See Hugo Young, *The Blessed Plot: Britain and Europe from Churchill to Blair*. See also Roger Liddle, *The Europe Dilemma: Britain and the Drama of EU Integration* from the point of view of an engaged European in the Labour party.
4. 'Poisoned chalice' is the term used by Vernon Bogdanor in his Gresham lecture on 'The Growth of Euroscepticism' delivered in London on 20 May 2014, http://www.gresham.ac.uk/lectures-and-events/the-growth-of-euroscepticism.
5. The question of identity keeps cropping up in the British debate on relations with Europe, more than in any other country, for obvious reasons of history and geography. Garton Ash writes about Britain's multiple identities of which the European identity forms a part: Timothy Garton Ash, 'Is Britain European?', *International Affairs*, 77/1 (2001), 1–14.

6. Roger Liddle laments New Labour's failure 'to transform how the British feel in their guts about Europe' (Liddle, *The Europe Dilemma*, p. xxiii).
7. Inequalities have become again a respectable subject for economists and there has been a rapidly growing literature with a new wealth of data and insightful analyses of causes and effects. One of the best works is by a British author, Anthony Atkinson, *Inequality* (Cambridge, MA: Harvard University Press, 2015), especially pp. 82–109 dealing with the more recent period in the United States and the UK.
8. See also Loukas Tsoukalis, *In Defence of Europe: Can the European Project Be Saved?* especially pp. 135–45 from which I have drawn heavily for this chapter.
9. Robert Ford and Matthew Goodwin, *Revolt on the Right: Explaining Support for the Radical Right in Britain*.
10. In a speech he gave at the annual conference of Policy Network in the City of London on 28 February 2013, http://europa.eu/rapid/press-release_PRES-13-86. See also Anand Menon, 'Littler England: The United Kingdom's retreat from global leadership', *Foreign Affairs*, 94/6 (2015).
11. Helen Wallace, 'Does Britain need the European Union? Does the European Union need Britain?'
12. See Michael Emerson (ed.), *Britain's Future in Europe: Reform, Renegotiation, Repatriation Or Secession?*
13. Dani Rodrik, a Harvard economist, argues that countries today are faced with a trilemma consisting of global markets, sovereignty and democracy and they can only choose a combination of two out of three – unless they happen to be the hegemon, I would add. See Dani Rodrik, *The Globalization Paradox: Why Global Markets, States and Democracy Can't Coexist*.
14. Given the huge political importance of the referendum, the literature on the subject is already enormous and rapidly growing. Among the best sources, see Harold D. Clarke, Matthew Goodwin and Paul Whiteley, *Brexit: Why Britain Voted to Leave the European Union*; Geoffrey Evans and Anand Menon, *Brexit and British Politics*; Tim Shipman, *An All Out War: The Full Story of How Brexit Sank Britain's Political Class*; Helen Thompson, 'Inevitability and contingency: the political economy of Brexit', *The British Journal of Politics and International Relations*.
15. This is, of course, a more general problem that extends beyond the British Isles. See the seminal work by Peter Mair, *Ruling the Void: The Hollowing of Western Democracy*.
16. Evans and Menon, *Brexit and British Politics*, p. 62.
17. See, for example, Kevin H. O'Rourke, 'This backlash has been a long time coming', in *Brexit Beckons: Thinking Ahead by Leading Economists*.
18. Tsoukalis, *In Defence of Europe*, pp. 45–54.
19. I have borrowed this phrase from Iain Begg, professor at the London School of Economics.
20. Evans and Menon, *Brexit and British Politics*, p. 81.
21. See Cas Mudde, 'Europe's populist surge'.

22. This information was revealed by outgoing US Ambassador to the EU, Anthony Gardner, at his parting press conference and reported in the *Financial Times* (Alex Barker), 13 January 2017.
23. For a discussion of Europe's multiple crises and the long-term underlying trends, see Tsoukalis, *In Defence of Europe*.

## References

Bogdanor, Vernon. 'The Growth of Euroscepticism' (Gresham, London, 20 May 2014). Available at http://www.gresham.ac.uk/lectures-and-events/the-growth-of-euroscepticism (Accessed 18 July 2018).

Clarke, Harold D., Goodwin, Matthew and Whiteley, Paul. *Brexit: Why Britain Voted to Leave the European Union* (Cambridge, Cambridge University Press 2017).

Emerson, Michael (ed.). *Britain's Future in Europe: Reform, Renegotiation, Repatriation or Secession?* (London, Rowman & Littlefield 2015).

Evans, Geoffrey and Menon, Anand. *Brexit and British Politics* (Cambridge, Polity 2017).

Ford, Robert and Goodwin, Matthew. *Revolt on the Right: Explaining Support for the Radical Right in Britain* (London, Routledge 2014).

Garton Ash, Timothy. 'Is Britain European?' *International Affairs* 77(1) (2001) pp. 1–14.

Liddle, Roger. *The Europe Dilemma: Britain and the Drama of EU Integration* (London, I.B.Tauris/Policy Network 2014).

Mair, Peter. *Ruling the Void: The Hollowing of Western Democracy* (London, Verso 2013).

Mudde, Cas. 'Europe's populist surge', *Foreign Affairs* 95(6) (2016) pp. 25–30.

O'Rourke, Kevin H. 'This backlash has been a long time coming'. In Richard E. Baldwin (ed.) *Brexit Beckons: Thinking Ahead by Leading Economists*. A VoxEU.org Book (London, CEPR 2016).

Rodrik, Dani. *The Globalization Paradox: Why Global Markets, States and Democracy Can't Coexist* (Oxford, Oxford University Press 2011).

Shipman, Tim. *An All Out War: The Full Story of How Brexit Sank Britain's Political Class* (London, William Collins 2016).

Thompson, Helen. 'Inevitability and contingency: the political economy of Brexit', *The British Journal of Politics and International Relations* 19(3) (2017) pp. 434–49.

Tsoukalis, Loukas. *In Defence of Europe: Can the European Project Be Saved?* (Oxford, Oxford University Press 2016) pp. 135–45.

Wallace, Helen. 'Does Britain need the European Union? Does the European Union need Britain?' *Journal of the British Academy* 3 (2015) pp. 185–95.

Wallace, Helen. 'JCMS Annual Review Lecture: In the name of Europe', *The JCMS Annual Review of the European Union in 2016* (Oxford, Wiley 2017) pp. 8–18.

Young, Hugo. *The Blessed Plot: Britain and Europe from Churchill to Blair* (London, Macmillan 1998).

CHAPTER 7

# The EU in Crises: Brexit, Populism and the Future of the Union

Dimitris Tsarouhas

## Introduction

The UK referendum to exit the European Union (EU) is a watershed moment in EU history. The formal reason is that this constitutes the first exit from the EU club and is evidence membership need not be a one-way street. Importantly, and this goes beyond the formal, institutional processes of rearranging votes and seats in the EU institutions, the member state departing constitutes a major political, economic and cultural force within the EU and beyond. A permanent member of the United Nations' Security Council, a nuclear power, the EU's second largest economy and a major pole of attraction for the world's talent in finance, culture and the arts, the UK constitutes more than your average EU member (Matthjis 2017).

This chapter will focus on the repercussions of Brexit for the EU's cohesion and sustainability in the context of its crises and ongoing challenges. To analyse the issue, I will pay special attention to populism and its rise in the EU, inquiring on the extent to which the populist forces that propelled Brexit to the top of Britain's public policy agenda may be able to exert similarly successful pressures to other EU members. Nonetheless, it should be stressed that attributing Brexit solely to populist forces would be inaccurate; whether one endorses the thesis of Britain as an 'awkward partner' or not (George 1990), it remains true that Britain's EU trajectory had been different from that of Continental states from day one. Its historical ties to the Commonwealth and to a distinct aversion to political integration had often led Britain to strike a different tone in EU policy-making, despite the fact it has been at the heart of major EU initiatives, not least the Single Market and eastward enlargement.

The chapter's main argument is that the EU faces multiple crises at the same time, with Brexit occupying a large part of the EU agenda but by no means the core of its contemporary challenges. I focus on the economic crisis, and the migration and refugee crisis, as issues that place Europe's role in the world into question and the successful overcoming of which will alleviate populist pressures on the EU. In other words, the Union's sustainability will not be put into doubt following Brexit (at least directly) but may well be undermined if other parallel challenges are not handled in ways that enable the EU to move forward. Brexit is a symptom, not a cause, of the Union's current malaise. Victories by pro-European forces in some recent European elections, most notably in France with the election of Emmanuel Macron as president in 2017, do not and cannot suggest that populism as a political force has been defeated.

In what follows, I begin with a brief discussion of the Union's response to Brexit thus far, and argue that unity at this stage has been facilitated by Britain's largely incoherent stance on its departure. This is likely to change depending on the content of a possible agreement and the extent to which Britain will act in accordance with member states' core interests. The next two sections discuss the economic and migration crises respectively, pointing to the need for more and better policy on the EU's part to address current shortcomings and to safeguard cohesion in the wake of the ongoing populist challenge. The latter may be in retreat in the aftermath of Brexit yet its appeal has become deeper over time and is directly correlated to the EU's own behaviour. The concluding section will summarize the chapter and will outline a few practical policy suggestions that could aid the EU in facing up to the complex issues confronting the Union.

## The EU Response to Brexit: Unity with a Purpose

As UK Finance Minister, Gordon Brown would often talk of the need for 'prudence with a purpose'. The EU has so far sought to display unity in the face of the shock UK referendum result with an explicit, and easy to understand, purpose: deterrence. This is the first time that a member state is seeking to withdraw membership and is about to create a dangerous precedent. To obtain the best possible result from the Brexit negotiations, the EU has been unwilling to display, at least in public, flexibility towards the UK's negotiating position. In fact, the incoherence of the UK position, and the confusing discourse on the part of the UK government has to date greatly facilitated the EU's stance (Schrieberg 2017), and has allowed EU member states to close ranks and keep the British government guessing as to Brussels' 'real intentions'. This is especially true regarding the prospects for a future trade arrangement, a crucial issue for Britain, given the proportion of exports that it sends to members of the Single Market.

Attempts by Theresa May's government to suggest that future trade deals with non-EU trade blocs *could* be concluded prior to any final settlement with the EU have been repeatedly, and emphatically, rebuffed. Similar incoherence has characterized Britain's stance as to membership of a Customs Union and the Single Market, and regarding the jurisdiction of the European Court. All this plays into the hands of the EU's chief Brexit negotiator Michel and his team. Meanwhile, the improving economic outlook for eurozone countries and a pick-up in employment rates across the EU has led to an increasing sense of confidence on the part of Brussels that, ultimately, the UK will regret its decision to leave. This, however, is contingent on Britain feeling the 'pain' of Brexit. So far at least, the Remain camp arguments that warn of economic calamity have proven futile, with the UK economy performing well and riding on a wave of global economic recovery following the crisis. And then there is the heterogeneity of EU member states' positions vis-á-vis the UK, with different states wishing to focus on the different aspects of a possible deal that is of key concern to them. The Republic of Ireland is most concerned about the border with Northern Ireland. Poland wants guarantees on the considerable number of its citizens living in the UK, Spain is likely to try and make an issue out of the Gibraltar issue at a time of rising secessionist tendencies in Catalonia while France may prove hard to please given Emmanuel Macron's antipathy to the act of 'political vandalism' that the UK committed by opting to leave (Hammond 2017).

As Brexit talks continue, the price to pay for such a confusing stance is becoming increasingly clear. In December 2017, the two sides came to an agreement, in principle (though not yet in concrete detail) covering the three fundamental issues of the talks' first phase, namely a financial settlement, the rights of citizens and the Irish border issue (Joint Report 2017). The Council thus approved moving on to the second, and tougher, phase of Brexit talks. This is likely to be the start of a long series of clarifications that ardent Brexiteers are likely to interpret as a mistake at best, and treason at worst. The UK government stands on thin ice, not least due to domestic political realities that call into question the legitimacy and authority of Theresa May's government, and a unified EU bloc is unlikely to budge for the likes of David Davis or Boris Johnson. The controversy surrounding the post-Brexit settlement with Ireland in December 2015, and the possibility of the erection of a 'hard border', is indicative of the challenge that the UK administration, present and future, will face. The Labour Party, for its part, is now advocating staying in the Customs Union, contrary to the government's position, and is likely to ask for more if the government's double-speak on Brexit continues.

Though it may appear futile at present, not least given the urgent need of a settlement, it is worth remembering what brought Brexit to the forefront of Britain's, and the EU's, agenda. David Cameron's decision to put the membership issue to a public vote, above and beyond the inconsistencies that characterized the Leave campaign, was from day one a high-risk strategy. Cameron's governments had done little to portray the EU as a natural environment for Britain to operate in, given the current state of global interconnectedness and the need for Europe to speak with one voice on matters of transnational public policy. In fact, even ardent supporters of membership from years past, such as Tony Blair, had failed to directly challenge Britain's tabloid press in their unrelenting depiction of the EU as a monstrous bureaucracy determined to subvert national sovereignty and to undermine national governments through the back door. The Remain campaign was the cherry on the cake, continuing with helpless economic arguments regarding the benefits of membership in the face of a large populist challenge that led to several colourful alliances against 'Brussels' (Cassidy 2016). Finally, it is worth recalling that Cameron's negotiations with the EU had led to a deal that, had the referendum's outcome been different, would have undermined the four freedoms that are enshrined in the Treaties, by curbing the rights of EU citizens in the UK.

The populist challenge is, of course, nothing unique to Britain. The Continent is as affected by it as the United States under Trump, to name but one glaring example. A large, but by no means exclusive, set of reasons that account for the rise of populism relates to the EU's twin crises – sovereign debt and migration. Writing in 2018, both appear now to be increasingly under control, with economic growth picking up across the EU, and with the number of migrants and refugees arriving halved in 2017, compared to 2016. Yet the EU is not out of the woods just yet, and it is worth considering why.

## The European Union's Key Challenges

### The Economic and Social Crises

In recent months, positive economic data has been pouring in regarding the eurozone economy as well as that of EU member states. GDP levels are now back to pre-crisis levels in the Eurozone, productivity is on the increase and unemployment rates have now returned to pre-crisis levels (Khan 2017).

What is more, the economic boost is now widely shared, with countries in the Southern periphery of the eurozone appearing to be leaving the worst aspects of the crisis behind them. A return to business as usual is on the cards.

And yet that would be a fatal mistake. The economic and financial crisis had led to increasing Euroscepticism and many EU citizens, even in states that were not directly affected by austerity, thought that the EU was moving in the wrong direction. More importantly, economic and social dislocation has been experienced by most EU citizens and has hit citizens in the periphery of the eurozone especially hard (Owen and Tsarouhas 2018). The adoption of strict fiscal austerity has not only led to a rapid increase in unemployment and the proliferation of non-typical forms of employment; it has also resulted in the retreat of the sort of labour market policies favoured by labour representatives and trade unions in several countries (Heyes 2013). Further, the combination of austerity with weak social protection mechanisms and sharp economic shocks has resulted in the deterioration in health conditions as well (Karanikolos et al. 2013). The role of the EU in reforming welfare states by encouraging cuts to public expenditure, which undermines some prior achievements of European governments, has been very important in this regard. Moreover, what former US President Obama described as the defining issue of our time, namely inequality, is on the rise pretty much across the EU, which threatens the European Social Model.

## The Pillar of Social Rights

To its credit, the Commission has launched a timely initiative, the European Pillar of Social Rights. This consists of various documents and policy ideas, all of which boil down to three main headings forming the Pillar's basis. These are: a) equal opportunities and access to the labour market by means of stressing the employability of individuals; b) fair working conditions allowing for decent jobs whilst maximising flexibility for firms to respond to market needs; and c) adequate social protection to ensure citizens' full and unhindered participation in society (European Commission 2016: 7–8). The Commission now aims to integrate the Pillar into the European Semester cycle of economic and structural reforms, while the next Multiannual Financial Framework should make funding readily available for member states to reform along the lines of the Pillar's stated objectives (Kirk and Zalan 2017). Yet if the crisis has taught us anything it is that growing socio-economic divergence and non-respect for social rights undermines social and economic arrangements as well as the European

Social Model. Enshrining parts of the Pillar in the Treaties as an Annex and EU Directives pertaining to, for instance, the need to classify so-called self-employed people as employees (and thus not allowing unscrupulous employers to hide behind current legislation to exploit vulnerable workers further, through bogus self-employment and other ruses) would mean that EU citizens enjoy concrete benefits from the Pillar. The Union's discourse on bridging the gap with EU citizens will then be more than well-meaning rhetoric.

## Economic Governance: Greece, Italy, the Eurozone as a Whole

The social crisis of the Union is compounded by the challenges surrounding the future economic prospects of some of its Member States, and the eurozone's architecture itself. Greece and Italy are representative samples of cases that are far from being resolved. Greece remains the only country to remain in a financial bailout programme, and the participation or not of the IMF in the next phase of the country's supervision remains uncertain. This, in turn, relates to both the key issue of debt sustainability, as well as to the future architecture of the eurozone and its ability to emancipate itself from the Fund. Italy's better economic prospects allow for some optimism, but this is only half the story: youth unemployment remains comparable to the worst performers in the EU, and the forces of populism are blowing hard. The triumph of Beppe Grillo's 5-star populist movement in the March 2018 elections, the defeat of the governing centre-left Partito Democratico (PD), as well as the return of Silvio Berlusconi as junior partner to the national scene as part of the centre-right bloc raise serious concerns. Not only do they point to the fact that Euroscepticism is gaining a foothold in a traditionally Europhile state, but the result is likely to prolong political instability and thus remove Italy from the list of countries willing to press ahead with reforms of the sort being promoted by French President Macron.

And then there is the eurozone. It is uncertain to what extent the mistakes in handling the sovereign debt crisis have been learned and if the EU is now better prepared to handle a similar phenomenon in the future. Institutional innovations during the crisis have helped, but the project remains incomplete. The debate on the issue is ongoing, but a new institutional architecture is a *sine qua non* to guarantee stability. Enderlein et al. have rightly pointed out that such a design will require three key components: a) a reinforced European Stability Mechanism (ESM); b) the creation of a European Monetary Fund (EMF) that will be directly subject to political control and will entail a degree of supranational governance; and c) a combination of structural reforms that will dare to go beyond austerity and will be combined with meaningful, productive investment to boost growth and quality employment. It is a tall task and needs to be combined with 'Social Europe' – but it can be done so long as a sense of urgency governs the policies of Brussels and member states in the years ahead.

## The Migration Crisis

In 2015, Europe was hit by a major migration and refugee crisis, after countries in the Middle East were hit earlier as a consequence of the Syrian civil war. In the year 2015 alone, according to official data, 1.3 million people claimed asylum in Europe, which was more than double the equivalent figure of one year before (Angenendt et al. 2017). The EU has sought to deal with the problem in an *ad hoc* fashion, and has not hesitated to securitize the issue, both at member state level (Szalai 2016) and more widely. At the same time, the EU has sought to call member states to task to facilitate the process, but has had little success in terms of relocating refuges to even some of the member states least affected by the problem and convincing them of the need to display solidarity to their Southern neighbours (primarily, Italy, Greece, Malta). More importantly, the early outcome of the EU's handling of the crisis has been confusing and asymmetrical, with multiple refugee policies operating at member state level, thus diminishing the Union's coherence. This is significant, because the migration and refugee crisis has hit at a time when the EU seeks to make long-needed progress in forming a cohesive foreign and defence policy.

The most important measure undertaken by the EU to stem the flow of migrants and refugees was the agreement with Turkey in March 2016, the so-called EU-Turkey Refugee Deal. The very fact that 28 member states with very different positions and interests on the subject managed to sign such an agreement is noteworthy. The core of the agreement between the two sides was a transactional deal based on (short-term) mutual interests. Turkey committed to accept from Greece all 'irregular new migrants' and to work closely with EU authorities to implement that crucial part of the agreement. In return, the EU promised to accelerate the visa liberalization process for Turkish citizens, to open new negotiation chapters with Turkey and to offer substantial financial aid to Turkey to deal with the refugee and migration challenge, worth up to €6 billion (Collett 2016). This would come on top of cooperation with NATO through the European Border and Coast Guard

Agency (Frontex) and training from the European Asylum Support Office. When numbers entering the EU would drop substantially, a 'voluntary' relocation scheme designed to bring refugees from Turkey to EU member states would be enacted. Turkey, along with Jordan and Lebanon, has been at the high end of receiving Syrian refugees and it is estimated to date that more than 4 million Syrians currently reside in Turkey. Coping with this challenge on its own would have been difficult at the best of times, and the EU dependence on Turkey's goodwill gave Ankara a strong hand in negotiations.

As discussed previously, the deal has proved successful in achieving the EU's core objective of 'welcoming' fewer people to its member states. More than 10,000 people a day were crossing the Aegean in 2015, trying to move west. By the end of 2016 the equivalent number had been reduced to 80 or so. Despite occasional fluctuations, the number remains relatively low since then (European Commission 2017). Alternative routes to Italy have not proven successful for people smugglers and by end 2017, the peak of the crisis appears to have passed, to the great relief of Brussels as well as Italy and Greece. And yet the crisis has had several repercussions across the EU and its foreign relations, including enlargement. The crisis has helped consolidate Euroscepticism in many states, not least in Germany and Italy, and has drawn the ire of international humanitarian organizations in terms of its content. It has also, once again, exposed divisions between member states that were first highlighted during the peak of the eurozone crisis, with some members being reluctant to follow Commission guidelines to accept the resettlement of refugees (European Commission 2016).

To start with, the agreement with Turkey has met with heavy criticism from humanitarian NGOs and similar organizations, alleging that the EU has disregarded the fact that Turkey constitutes no safe harbour for refugees. Turkey has in turn transferred refugees to countries such as Pakistan and Afghanistan, which can also be unsafe. Further, both on the Greek islands and the Turkish mainland, conditions for refugees are described, and frequently documented, as squalid and inhumane (Gogou 2017). The criticism is serious but disregards a key point: if the EU was to adhere to all of its international legal obligations it would hardly ever be able to reduce the flow of people entering through Greece and Italy. When it does not do so, it justifiably draws the ire of outside observers and NGOs. It is an extremely difficult position for the EU to be in.

Then there is the key issue of Turkey. A candidate country since 2005, Turkey has been making no progress in converging with the EU *acquis* for at least seven years. When negotiations began, Ankara's reformist zeal was undermined by member state governments including in Austria (who promised a referendum on Turkey's membership once negotiations are concluded) and in France, where then-president Sarkozy repeatedly argued that Turkey does not belong to 'Europe' (Öktem 2007). Ankara accused the EU of 'double standards' and a self-fulfilling prophecy soon emerged, and the Commission's attempts to keep the process alive through initiatives such as the 'Positive Agenda' led nowhere (Demiral 2014). Stagnant relations between the two sides deteriorated sharply after the 15 July 2016 attempted *coup d'état* in Turkey, with Ankara cracking down hard on anyone remotely suspected of being involved, and Brussels has argued that Turkey is now sliding towards authoritarianism. President Erdogan's belligerent anti-Western rhetoric has made matters worse, as have repeated threats by Turkey to call off the deal with the EU, having exposed the bloc's feeble position on the matter (Wintour 2017). Those threats, in turn, result from the non-implementation of the visa liberalization programme and of the non-opening of new chapters, which the Union had mistakenly bundled together in 2016 to make the offer to Turkey more attractive.

Respect for human rights and the rule of law are meant to underpin EU external relations at all times but plans to replicate the deal with Turkey to incorporate states such as Egypt into similar programmes raise eyebrows. The trouble with Turkey is in fact indicative of the Union's larger failure to play any meaningful role in the Syrian civil war and therefore to be able to project influence over any post-conflict regime. The long-lasting conflict has had immediate effects on Europe but the EU has left centre-stage to Russia and the United States. Regional powers such as Turkey and Iran have also been actively involved throughout.

Perhaps the most troubling aspect of the migration and refugee crisis, at least on the part of the Commission and member states such as Germany, has been the fusion of unwillingness by some member states to carry a (relatively light) burden of hosting refugees from the likes of Greece and Italy, often espoused by hard-right populist policies, tactics and proclamations. On resettlement and relocation, the Commission set up a mechanism in 2015 to relieve Greece and Italy from some of the overt pressure, and the deal with Turkey has reduced the numbers of people needing resettlement within the EU. Such a need still exists, however, and countries such as the Czech Republic, Hungary and Poland have consistently refused to shoulder any burden, despite funding being allocated to member states by the Commission for each resettled refugee (Commission 2017). The inevitable result has been ongoing infringement procedures against these member states. What is more troubling is the set of arguments used by such states to justify refusing to display solidarity, which has focused on the raising of the fictitious spectre of a 'Muslim invasion' of Europe, an overtly aggressive rhetoric against Chancellor Merkel's policy to welcome migrants and refugees, and an assertion of state sovereignty over 'Brussels diktats' (*Euractiv* 2017). This discourse is by no means limited to those states, yet has acquired a degree of legitimacy among the political class that makes it increasingly difficult to keep a lid on such tactics.

Both sets of crises, the socio-economic and the migration/refugee one, are going nowhere, at least in the short term. The EU needs new policies and policy instruments to confront them, at least to avoid falling back on yet another round of introspection and self-doubt. But the populist challenge is harder still to confront, as it affects more and more states in the EU (and, of course, beyond). This undermines the very foundations of European unity and pits communities, and states, against each other in unforeseen ways. The next section examines the phenomenon in some detail.

## The Populist Challenge

Some argue that economic recovery will extinguish populism. This is a major fallacy and policy-makers ought to ignore it. Improved economic conditions for the more vulnerable will reduce some of the populist appeal but will not deal with it entirely. The phenomenon of populism in politics is by no means new. Europe has struggled to contain it for a very long time, including in the post-war era. The 'golden years' of welfare capitalism and homogenous societies arguably made this appear less urgent, but recent decades have led to an explosion of questions pertaining to issues such as identity politics, often framed along the lines of the immigration debate. These have been put to effective use by populists, who are often aware of the fears and insecurities that rapid change can cause in communities, especially among the most vulnerable. There are of course populists of different persuasions, on both the left and right. What matters for this study is evidence that shows how supporters of right-wing populist parties tend to reject both EU integration and globalization, while supporters of left-wing populists tend to see European cooperation as an antidote to globalization's destructive potential (De Vries and Hoffmann 2017).

## Western Europe: Austria, France, Germany

Austria and France are instructive case studies of how right-wing populist politics had gone mainstream in Western Europe before the migration and refugee crisis erupted. Austrian politics was transformed in the late 1980s, when the Freedom Party (FPÖ) was taken over by a charismatic populist, Jörg Haider. The party's links, at personnel and programmatic levels, to the country's Nazi past became a major focal point. Haider ruthlessly attacked the 'Proporz' system of job-sharing in the public sector between the Social Democrats (SPÖ) and Christian Democrats (ÖVP) as well as the 'waste' and 'corruption' that he saw as endemic in the 'Brussels system'. By the late 1990s, FPÖ became the country's second largest party and entered a coalition government with the ÖVP that lasted for eight years. The EU response to the FPÖ's participation in government proved counter-productive, with soft sanctions imposed on the country prior to any violation of EU principles concerning human rights and fundamental freedoms. Following a period of decline and an internal party split in the FPÖ instigated by Haider himself before his death in 2008, in 2017 the FPÖ re-joined a coalition government with the ÖVP, after attracting 26 per cent the all vote.

In France, Marine Le Pen's defeat in the second round of the 2017 presidential elections disguises the Front National's (FN) longevity in French politics. The party's founder, Marine Le Pen's father Jean-Marie, made a name for himself in the 1980s through his anti-immigrant rhetoric, combined with outbursts against globalization and France's multicultural society. In 2002, Le Pen shocked the political system by beating the centre-left candidate to enter the second round of the presidential elections. The incumbent Jacques Chirac was comfortably re-elected with more than 80 per cent of the vote in the second round, by uniting the 'democratic camp' and using Jean Marie Le Pen's extremism to his advantage. By 2017, however, and despite Macron's convincing victory, Marine Le Pen had rebranded the FN by dropping overt racism and by focusing on 'radical Islam' instead as the nation's main threat. Combined with a toning down of its anti-EU rhetoric, the party was able to broaden its appeal and emerge victorious in local elections.

Still, populism has been able to intrude into the domestic political arena more recently as well, not least due to the twin economic and migration crises identified above. A number of countries, including Spain and Greece, spring to mind, yet the most suitable example may be the EU's most powerful and influential state, Germany. The country had long appeared immune to populist pressures with the Christian Democrats (CDU) and Social Democrats (SPD) alternating in office since 1949, usually with the support of a smaller party, be it the Liberal Democrats or the Greens. The economic miracle of the post-war period had produced a consensus-seeking society, while the country had invested heavily in highlighting the failures that had led to the rise of Nazism, in educating the younger generation and in exorcising its past whenever necessary.

Increasingly embracing an image of Germany as open and tolerant, the German political elite's handling of the eurozone and migration and refugee crisis partly facilitated the growth of far-right populism. First came the eurozone crisis, which pitted Northern Europe against Southern Europe, and led to vicious anti-German sentiments in the Southern periphery. Importantly, the crisis led to the formation of a new populist party, the Alternative for Germany (AfD). Formed by Bernd Lucke, an Economics Professor at the University of Hamburg, the party argued against intra-EU solidarity and appealed to the basic instincts of the large swathes of the German population who were consistently told that they were bailing out the poorer South. When the migration and refugee crisis hit, the icing was put on the cake. Merkel's leadership on the issue was portrayed as betrayal, even treason, and the AfD capitalized on the insecurity that the crisis produced, particularly in the east of the country. The AfD has now entered the federal parliament for the first time and threatens to unravel the consensus that has underpinned German politics for decades, and to fundamentally change the role played by Germany within the EU. The clear defeat of both CDU and SPD in the 2017 election has squeezed the political centre, and the agonising decision by the two parties to form another grand coalition in March 2018 could prove just what the AfD needs to boost its electoral fortunes even further.

## Eastern Europe: 'Illiberal Democracies' and the Future of the EU

The challenge of populism is a threat to EU cohesion everywhere but has become especially acute in parts of Eastern Europe. In Hungary and Poland in particular, the combination of increasingly authoritarian tendencies on the part of large, governing parties and sustained criticism of 'Brussels' make for a toxic combination. Coupled with the weakness of civil society in these post-communist societies, developments in the said countries threaten to unravel EU foundations.

Hungary is an emblematic case. During the country's transition to democracy in the late 1980s, Viktor Orban played a protagonist's role in pushing for democracy and pluralism. Prime Minister in the 1990s, Orban has in the meantime undergone a radical political transformation. He is the most ardent supporter of the view that democracies need not be liberal in the Western sense (Rensmann et al. 2017) and has cultivated strong ties with Russia and Turkey. Popular at home and only really challenged domestically by the far-right Jobbik party, given the decline and fragmentation of the centre-left parties in the country (Veress and Veress 2018), Orban has used the migration and refugee crisis to securitize the problem (Szalai 2016) and to attack the EU's resettlement and reallocation scheme. Orban has consistently lamented the 'corruption' and 'failures' of the socialists to enlarge his voter base. Stealing the clothes of Jobbik when expedient, Orban warns of an alleged 'Muslim invasion' of Europe and declares that come what may, Hungary intends to remain 'loyal' to its Christian roots. Attempting to portray himself as a defender of Western civilization, Orban has repeatedly stirred controversy with legislative initiatives allegedly aimed at diminishing media freedoms, reducing the independence of the judiciary from the executive branch, and intruding into the Central Bank's independence. Opposition to his plans in Hungary remains muted while reactions in Brussels have not been particularly forceful either.

Poland constitutes an even greater challenge for the EU. Similar to Hungary and at an even higher level, the country's economic performance during the eurozone crisis has been stellar. The country continues to grow above the EU average, unemployment is falling and so are rates of social exclusion (Keuschnigg and Owczarek 2017). And yet its politics drift apart from EU norms at an accelerating pace. The Law and Justice (PiS) party has provoked civil society outcry recently when it attempted to fully ban abortion. The fact that this attempt was not successful is not to say that PiS is not going to try again. Moreover, the government has imitated Hungarian practice by interfering with media freedoms. Reeling against 'political correctness' is another common feature of populist forces demonstrated by both Polish and Hungarian populist parties. They claim to speak for the 'silent majority', expressing the sorts of views that people think but do not dare voice.

Populism in both Hungary and Poland is deep-rooted and both ruling parties are popular, and polling around 40 per cent of their respective electorates. Yet they constitute a threat to other member states by refusing to share a common burden on the migration and refugee issue, using a relentless Euroscepticist discourse at home and doubting EU usefulness in many policy areas, not least with respect to law and order. On the part of the EU and regarding Poland, what broke the camel's back was the government's sustained interference with the judiciary, which has not come to a halt despite repeated warnings from Brussels. In December 2017, the Commission triggered Article 7 of the EU Treaty, according to which, the EU is entitled to impose sanctions when there is a 'clear risk of a serious breach' of the EU's core principles (Cuddy 2017). The rule of law being at the core of the dispute, the EU has now issued a formal warning against Poland. The reaction by Warsaw has been predictable, with the government refuting that it puts EU democratic values at risk and counter-arguing that the EU's actions are politically motivated (Boffey and Davies 2017). Should the Polish government opt not to yield to pressure, the EU may find itself in an impossible position. The EU could opt to impose the harshest sanctions possible against Poland by suspending its voting rights in the Council and to cease the distribution the Structural Funds that the country is entitled to, but such a decision requires unanimity, and Warsaw's loyal ally, Viktor Orban's Hungary, has made it clear that his country would block such a move.

Developments in these countries will be followed with great interest across the EU and beyond. Triggering Article 7 indicates that leading EU officials now feel that EU values and principles are challenged from within the bloc. At this point, the question of whether countries like Poland have ever been truly democratic or not (Hanley and Dawson 2017) is not the most pressing issue for the EU. What is at stake is much bigger: does the EU constitute an assemblage of member states who share sovereignty on issues they choose and have the right to go their own way otherwise? Or does it, in the wake of major crises and at a time of global turbulence, seek to provide moral inspiration to those who pay due respect to fundamental democratic norms and values, and therefore seek to safeguard those, not least among its own member states? Which way the Union eventually develops will have huge repercussions. Allowing member states to get away with policies that disregard what the EU sees as fundamental values opens Pandora's Box for more violations in the future. It would also send a signal to candidate countries that respect for the rule of law and minorities' rights may be less of a stringent condition than has hitherto been claimed.

## Conclusion

Emmanuel Macron beat the FN's Marine Le Pen comfortably in the second round of France's presidential elections in 2017. In Austria, for the first time in the country's post-war history, a former leader of the Green Party was elected President of the Republic. In Germany, and despite the AfD's popularity, Christian and Social Democrats remain the largest parties and have formed a new coalition government. At EU level and according to the Pew Research Centre, the EU's popularity has bounced back after reaching record lows in recent years and trust towards EU institutions is moving upwards again (Stokes et al. 2017). In early 2018, such facts appear to suggest that the populist tide has reached its peak.

This chapter has suggested that such a conclusion is premature and dangerous. Brexit, the socio-economic crisis and the ongoing challenge of how to integrate migrants and refugees constitute inter-related challenges for the EU and for its member states. When faced with a large crisis in the past, the EU was able to close ranks and move forward by deepening integration. The pace and direction of integration has accelerated since the 1980s, while enlargement has made the EU less homogenous. More importantly, the rule ceases to apply at a time when crises are heading in the EU's direction thick and fast.

In that context, then, and despite positive signs, the future of the EU remains far from secure. The survey quoted above which points to a recovery of the EU's popularity also suggests that the EU's handling of the economic, refugee and migration crises are questioned by most EU citizens. The EU faces multiple crises simultaneously, and the way in which it will choose to handle them will determine its future. On the socio-economic crisis, maintaining a positive economic momentum is helpful to avoid an implosion, but is by itself inadequate to restore (or to build) cohesion in the EU. Structural reforms imposed during the crisis era and the politics of austerity pulled member states apart and undermined socio-economic convergence, which is the glue that keeps the eurozone states together in one cogent bloc. The Pillar of Social Rights is thus an opportunity not to be missed. The migration and refugee crises have no easy solutions but the challenge must be confronted. The EU needs to display solidarity both with the member states most seriously affected and with those that seek a better life among its states. This is even more pertinent at a time when the United States under President Trump appears unwilling to fulfil its traditional role in the world.

All in all, EU cohesion will be maintained, and the EU's future secured, only if the crises addressed here are met with bold political and economic reforms. Reinforcing social Europe, reforming the eurozone to make its institutions politically accountable, and using all available instruments to ensure member states continue to respect basic EU norms and values, are ways to resolve the impasse and to diminish the attractiveness of populist political forces.

## References

Angenendt, S., Kipp, D. and Meier, A. *Mixed Migration: challenges and options for the ongoing project of German and European asylum and migration policy* (Gütersloh, Bertelsmann Stiftung 2017).

Boffey, D. and Davies, C. 'Poland cries foul as EU triggers "nuclear option" over judicial independence', *The Guardian* (20 December 2017). Available at: https://www.theguardian.com/world/2017/dec/20/eu-process-poland-voting-rights (Accessed 16 July 2018).

Cassidy, J. 'Why the remain campaign lost the Brexit vote', *The New Yorker* (24 June 2016). Available at: https://www.newyorker.com/news/john-cassidy/why-the-remain-campaign-lost-the-brexit-vote (Accessed 16 July 2018).

Collett, E. 'The paradox of the EU-Turkey refugee deal', *Migration Policy Institute* (March 2016).

Cuddy, A. 'What is Article 7 and why was it triggered against Poland?' *Euronews* (20 December 2017). Available at: http://www.euronews.com/2017/12/20/what-is-article-7-and-why-was-it-triggered-against-poland- (Accessed 16 July 2018).

Demiral, N. 'Positive agenda for Turkey-European Union relations: what will it bring or what will it take?' *Procedia Social and Behavioural Sciences* (2014) pp. 143, 1011–14.

De Vries, Catherine and Hoffmann, I. *Globalization and European Integration: Threat or Opportunity?* (Gütersloh, Bertelsmann Stiftung 2017).

Enderlein, H., Letta, E. and De Geus, A. 'Seizing the Moment for Euro Area Reform' (Berlin and Jacques Delors Institut, Paris: Bertelsmann Stiftung and Jacques Delors Institut, May 2017).

*Euractiv* 'EU opens sanctions procedure against Hungary, Poland and Czech Republic over refugees' (13 June 2017). Available at: http://www.euractiv.com/section/justice-home-affairs/news/eu-opens-sanctions-procedure-against-hungary-poland-and-czech-republic-over-refugees/ (Accessed 16 July 2018).

European Commission. 'Relocation and Resettlement-State of Play' (6 December 2016). Available at https://ec.europa.eu/home-affairs/sites/homeaffairs/files/what-we-do/policies/european-agenda-migration/proposal-implementation-package/docs/20161208/update_of_the_factsheet_on_relocation_and_resettlement_en_0.pdf (Accessed 16 July 2018).

European Commission. '*Seventh Report on the Progress made in the implementation of the EU-Turkey Statement*', COM (2017) 470 final.

George, S. *An Awkward Partner: Britain in the European Community* (Oxford, Oxford University Press 1990).

Gogou, K. 'The EU-Turkey deal: Europe's year of shame', *Amnesty International* (March 2017).

Hammond, A. 'On Brexit negotiations, the European Union may not be that united', *South China Morning Post* (4 December 2017).

Hanley, S. and Dawson, J. 'Poland was never as democratic as it looked', *Foreign Policy* (3 January 2017). Available at: http://foreignpolicy.com/2017/01/03/poland-was-never-as-democratic-as-it-looked-law-and-justice-hungary-orban/ (Accessed 16 July 2018).

Heyes, J. 'Flexicurity in crisis: European labour market policies in a time of austerity', *European Journal of Industrial Relations* 19(1) (2013) pp. 71–86.

Joint Report. 'Joint report from the negotiators of the European Union and the United Kingdom Government on progress during phase 1 of negotiations under Article 50 TEU on the United Kingdom's orderly withdrawal from the European Union', TF50 (2017) 19 – Commission to EU 27.

Karanikolos, M., Mladovsky, P., Cylus, J. et al. 'Financial crisis, austerity and health in Europe', *Lancet* (2013) pp. 381, 1323–31.

Keuschnigg, C. and Owczarek, D. *Social Inclusion in Poland: catching up at an uneven speed* (Gütersloh, Bertelsmann Stiftung 2017).

Khan, M. 'Eurozone unemployment falls to lowest level in 8 years', *Financial Times* (31 July 2017).

Kirk, L. and Zalan, E. 'EU leaders make pledge on social issues after populist backlash', *Euobserver* (17 November 2017). Available at: https://euobserver.com/social/139922 (Accessed 16 July 2018).

Matthjis, M. 'Europe After Brexit', *Foreign Affairs* (January/February 2017) pp. 72–80.

Öktem, K. 'Harbingers of Turkey's Second Republic', *Middle East Report* (1 August 2007).

Parker, O. and Tsarouhas, D. (eds) *Crisis in the Eurozone Periphery: the Political Economies of Greece, Spain, Portugal and Ireland* (London, Palgrave MacMillan 2018).

Rensmann, L., de Lange, S. and Couperus, S. 'Populism and the remaking of (Il) liberal democracy in Europe', *Politics and Governance* 5(4) (2017) pp. 106–11.

Schrieberg, D. 'Pardon Me, Britain, Your Brexit Indecision Is Showing', *Forbes* (20 August 2017). Available at: https://www.forbes.com/sites/davidschrieberg1/2017/08/20/pardon-me-britain-your-brexit-schizophrenia-is-showing/#22d323d92569 (Accessed 16 July 2018).

Stokes, B., Wike, R. and Manevich, D. 'Post-Brexit, Europeans More Favourable Toward EU', *Pew Research Centre* (June 2017).

Szalai, A. 'Securitizing Migration in Contemporary Hungary: From Discourse to Practice', *CEEISA-ISA 2016 Joint International Conference* (Ljubljana, 23 June 2016).

Veress, J. and Veress, T. 'Could a united opposition knock Orbán off course?' *State of the Left* (18 March 2018). Available at http://www.stateoftheleft.org/could-united-opposition-knock-orban-off-course/ (Accessed 4 July 2018).

Wintour, P. 'Turkish PM warns EU over refugee deal ahead of Syrian peace talks', *The Guardian* (27 November 2017). Available at: https://www.theguardian.com/world/2017/nov/27/turkey-threatens-to-scrap-refugee-deal-over-syrian-peace-talks (Accessed 16 July 2018).

CHAPTER 8

# Brexit: A Consequence of Globalization or a Case of British Exceptionalism?

Roger Liddle

The vote to leave the European Union (EU) in the June 2016 referendum was a momentous event in British politics. But we are far from a full understanding of why the Brexit vote happened, what Brexit will actually mean, what new 'national strategy' for Britain in a world of globalization will emerge, and how Brexit may eventually reshape British politics.

How far can the Brexit vote be interpreted as a populist reaction against globalization? Was it, as many now see it, a protest revolt of the 'left behind', a signal of cultural alienation from multiculturalism and modernity, and 'two fingers' to a discredited elite? Can Brexit be viewed paradoxically as a very European (and also Trumpian) phenomenon of a growing populist reaction to mainstream politics? Or is it more a case of a peculiarly British exceptionalism?

The governing Conservatives are deeply divided on what Brexit means. The Brexiteers' distinctive interpretation is a reassertion of national sovereignty for at present hazily-defined ends, but not a protectionist 'taking back control'. Their vision of a Global Britain represents a different world view to the populism that magnified Vote Leave. What will be the reaction if the reality of Brexit both disappoints its 'Global Britain' champions and the quite different motivations of its many supporters? What will be the shape of post-Brexit politics and its impact on Britain's European policy? Of one thing one can be certain: Brexit will not abolish the European question in British politics, only change its nature in ways we as yet imperfectly understand.

The chapter first considers how globalization changed the European question; and then discusses how far structural change or contingency explains the Leave victory. The final section speculates about Britain's future national strategy and the shape of post-Brexit politics, given the likely economic prospects and the starting assumptions of the present political parties.

## How Globalization Changed the European Question in British Politics

Controversies over the European question in British politics well predate 'globalization'. The founding purpose of the Schuman Plan in 1950 was to make war between France and Germany unthinkable. Britain's Labour government fatefully rejected its proposed pooling of national sovereignty over the coal and steel industries. From a shaky start, the simple, noble goal of a United Europe triggered a hugely powerful integrationist dynamic, which Britain eventually saw no alternative but to join. Yet British opponents of EU membership always smelt a conspiracy to create a United States of Europe. While Margaret Thatcher was reluctantly persuaded that the single market was a Continental extension of her free enterprise vision, she put up such fierce resistance to the single currency as an unacceptable step towards a federal Europe that it brought her down.

From the 1990s, the EU began to think of itself as the answer to the challenges of globalization. Globalization and European integration were close relatives, in part a product of EU success. The Common Market had made itself the driving force in global trade liberalization in partnership with the United States: key political choices that created the necessary conditions for globalization. Secondly, 'social market' capitalism had proved a superior model to communism, contributing to the Soviet collapse. The British left once doubted that outcome, confident that, for all the Soviets' totalitarian deficiencies, state planning would ultimately emerge victorious as the superior economic model. That influence still lingers, and will become more influential if post-Brexit economic performance lags in line with expert forecasts.

In contrast, modern progressives hailed the rules-based order of the EU as an exemplar of how to manage globalization. The EU's 'step by step' pooling of national sovereignty could be replicated across the globe. Events have not turned out quite as both progressive globalizers and hubristic pro Europeans assumed: Vladimir Putin and Xi Jinping sustain their legitimacy with unabashed nationalism; Trade liberalization has stalled since the effective suspension of the Doha world trade round in 2008; Now with the Trump Presidency, Obama's TPP and TTIP trade initiatives have been abandoned. Trump's rhetorically aggressive, 'America First' protectionism is the biggest threat to free trade since the 1930s, though the Brexiteer champions of free trade appear not to have noticed. The 'global order' now looks frighteningly unordered.

Instead of becoming the confident exemplar of rules-based global governance, the EU has limped along. Why? Mainly because ambition has run well ahead of the practical possibilities of achievement. Three big EU projects contributed to public disillusion.

The **euro crisis** tested the EU's internal unity. Although sufficient was done to ensure the currency's survival, in spite of many British Eurosceptic predictions, the euro nevertheless became perceived as a mechanism of divergence, austerity and social stress, not an expression of European solidarity. In Britain, Gordon Brown's decision to oppose euro membership became the received wisdom and was hailed as one of his proudest achievements. The euro was 'for them, not for us', just as the Schuman Plan had been for Attlee and Bevin in 1950. Yet if Britain was to become the self-confident equal of France and Germany within the EU, it had at some stage to join the euro, as Tony Blair consistently argued. Had Britain joined, the cause of eurozone reform would have been strengthened. The City of London could have played a decisive role as the financial centre of Europe, whereas Brexit now imperils the City's position. Labour's decision to steer clear of the euro strengthened the semi-detached mentality that led to Brexit.

**Enlargement,** on the other hand, at first appeared a historic success for which Britain could take significant credit, integrating the liberated central and eastern European nations into an EU that upheld human rights, the rule of law and democracy. While rapid economic convergence has been sustained, nationalist governments in Hungary and Poland have dented that initial optimism, not just as a result of their challenges to media freedom and an independent judiciary, but also their fierce opposition to EU burden sharing in the refugee crisis, on the anti-liberal grounds that acceptance of Muslim refugees is a threat to their homogeneous Christian societies. This anti-immigration sentiment contrasted with the 'free movement' rights of EU citizenship that enabled new member state citizens to settle elsewhere in the EU. In Britain this proved hugely controversial, raising immigration – and the EU's role in it – to the top of electoral anxieties.

As for **common foreign policy and defence**, the EU struggled to become a credible global actor in its own right despite successes such as the global agreements on climate change, the Iran nuclear deal, the negotiation of a fragile truce in Ukraine, sanctions against Russia, and various EU peace-keeping missions without US participation. But the rupture over Iraq in 2003 highlighted EU ineffectiveness. EU common foreign and security policy will always be weak without consensus between the big member states. Bluntly, Europe's national leaders need to show the same level of loyalty to each other as had bound them together through the Cold War. In this context, Tony Blair's uncritical support for George Bush in Iraq in face of French and German opposition, must surely be judged a mistake. Britain should have prioritized hammering out a common policy with France and Germany which might have had greater leverage over the United States. Instead the defeats and sacrifices of Iraq and Afghanistan have strengthened isolationism. The use of military power for humanitarian ends has been discredited. As the Syria tragedy shows, Britain, in common with the EU, hates the world as it is, but lacks the moral confidence and military capacity to change course.

Where has the EU gone wrong? To simplify grossly, to be sustainable, globalization requires some combination of strengthened, rules-based global governance with fewer 'neo-liberal' domestic policies. Without the latter, domestic political support for economic openness inevitably erodes. Without the former, an inadequate supply of the public goods needed to manage the multiple, burgeoning challenges of interdependence persists. The EU is active on many fronts, but that hyperactivity has failed to demonstrate a 'Europe of results'. Eurosceptics ascribe these problems to integrationist overreach. Europe bit off more than it could chew. European integration has assigned itself tasks which it cannot fulfil for the simple reason that there is not the consent within the member states to pool the necessary sovereignty to make EU policies workable. The EU is caught in an awkward middle ground. EU integration has weakened the powers of individual member states to respond – however imperfectly – to their electorate's concerns: for example, to keep out unwanted migrants, to stop foreign takeovers, to defend local jobs. Yet there is not the popular consent for further centralization of power to enable the EU to respond more intelligently to such concerns. Hence the appeal of 'taking back control'.

This analysis defines the fundamental issue for the EU as over-ambitious political integration. A legitimate criticism of EU leaders has been their failure to prioritize: instead of European Council conclusions that promise far more than they can realistically deliver, Europe's leaders failed to identify a limited number of issues where political consent to a further radical pooling of sovereignty is essential in order to sustain public confidence in the European project. The most politically salient failure has been in developing capability to police the EU's external border effectively and to limit migration flows to sustainable levels.

This links to the EU's second major flaw in managing globalization: the neglect of the social. The EU's value system always made much of its commitment to 'social cohesion' and 'solidarity'. In the first decades there was real policy substance to this commitment. The Coal and Steel Community established a Social Fund to cushion industrial decline. The Common Market was balanced by a Common Agricultural Policy that slowed the movement of citizens off the land. British and Irish membership led directly to EU regional policy. The Mediterranean enlargement was accompanied by a doubling of EU Structural Funds.

The interaction of the single market, enlargement and globalization has had profound structural effects. The commitment to offer full EU membership to the new democracies of central and eastern Europe member states, where wages were a fraction of the EU 15s, resulted in investment shifting east, and citizens in search of work coming west. Chinese imports made large sections of European manufacturing uncompetitive, particularly the textile and footwear industries in Italy and Portugal. Help for the new member states was constrained within an EU budget restricted to roughly 1 per cent of EU GDP. Less EU funds became available to cushion the impact of economic change on the EU 15s 'left behind' regions. Nor was much practical commitment to social cohesion on display in the euro crisis: EU fiscal rules and the management of the crisis accentuated divergence, rather than promoting the convergence that had hitherto been the EU's principal mission and achievement. The very notion of a 'transfer union' became a toxic obstacle to balanced solutions. In Italy and Greece this was compounded by a not unjust perception that on migration, the EU let them down.

The root of the EU malaise is surely social – and that requires a social answer, not a crude attack on European integration. This is not an argument for a centralization of social policy at EU level. In limited areas 'more Europe' is needed – for example to control borders, to ensure transnational corporations pay their taxes, and to set social standards that prevent a race to the bottom. Fundamentally, a different concept of a more holistic political economy is required that all member states share, where fiscal responsibility goes hand in hand with more ambitious social and infrastructure investment to renew the social market economy; and conditional transfers from richer to poorer countries are made as 'money for reform', if a member state's ability to borrow is constrained by bond markets,.

Globalization's optimists were too 'laissez-faire'. They forgot that rapid economic change almost always has wrenching social consequences. In Western Europe as a whole, the dynamic of economic and social change shares many common characteristics: the disappearance of 'good' working class jobs; trade union decline; the emergence of a new 'knowledge and service' economy with plentiful opportunities for the educated, but less good news for those dependent on low paid, mostly non-unionized, private sector service jobs; demographic trends raising costs of health and pensions but squeezing resources for future-oriented public investments to spread life chances, widen educational opportunities and strengthen innovation; huge transformations in the role of women, yet with persistent gender pay gaps and patchy access to affordable child care; more diversity of lifestyles as well as ethnicity and religion; with migration a rising public concern and integration a huge cultural challenge.

Europe has witnessed a growing divide between those who embrace this pattern of change and those who feel alienated by it. In a paper I co-authored for the European Commission President in 2007, *The Social Reality of Europe* – before the 2008/9 banking crisis – we drew attention to the gulf in attitudes between 'cosmopolitans' and 'communitarians' and the risks of growing populism.[1] Populist parties on both right and left have surged in strength: with some exceptions, they share a deep Euroscepticism: in Southern Europe, Syriza in Greece and Podemos in Spain define themselves as pro-Europeans backing a 'different' Europe to the present neo-liberal model; in Italy, the Five Star Movement may be backing away from anti-European populism. Elsewhere, the populist right and the traditionalist left are strongly hostile to European integration.

Immigration has greatly extended electoral support for the populist right. In some cases, the motivation is economic: witness the role that the 'Polish plumber' played in the 2005 French referendum. But key sections of European electorates feel alienated at a deeper level from growing multiculturalism, particularly older white working class voters who left school at the first opportunity. Terrorism has heightened these cultural fears and strengthened Islamophobia. The EU's impotence in the 2015 refugee crisis joined together anti-EU and anti-immigration sentiments.

Here there has been no British exceptionalism. There may have been no alternative to the brutal deindustrialization that took place under the Thatcher governments of the 1980s: it overcame, at least partially, Britain's chronic post-war weaknesses of dysfunctional industrial relations, persistent inflation and declining competitiveness. But it led to severe and permanent social scarring in many old industrial regions, reviving memories of the 1930s Depression. In the medium term this provided a base for Labour recovery. When Labour returned to power in 1997, rebranded as 'New

Labour', it launched a massive programme to improve public services, extend life chances and tackle poverty. Labour also set aside resources for urban regeneration and regional development, but it failed to overcome the deep-seated problems at the economic base of once proud industrial communities that had seen their economic heart ripped out of them. Manufacturing decline continued apace. A political price was paid in the high Leave vote in many declining areas in the 2016 referendum.

UKIP capitalized on these discontents. Founded in the 1990s to take Britain out of the EU, in Nigel Farage it had a gifted populist leader. In a 2010 general election TV debate, he infamously linked the strains on Britain's NHS with African immigrants allegedly making their way to Britain to seek free NHS treatment for AIDS. With the impending Bulgarian and Romanian accession in 2014, Farage played successfully on the link between the EU, its free movement rules, unrestricted EU immigration, squeezed wages and public services creaking under austerity. In the 2016 referendum, he claimed five million Turks were about to settle in Britain as Turkey was about to join the EU! Because EU rules forced unwanted immigration on Britain, Islamic terrorists would be free to enter and do their worst.

While in Britain EU membership always aroused opposition for reasons with little direct bearing on globalization, since the 1990s a combination of EU weakness, disconcerting social and economic change and growing opposition to immigration magnified potential support for Brexit. There is, however, one key contrast between Britain and the rest of the EU. On the Continent, extreme populist parties have never broken through. In the 2016 referendum in Britain, potential support for Leave was translated into a narrow overall majority. But as the next section argues, there was no structural inevitability about this outcome.

## How Far does Globalization Explain the 2016 Referendum Outcome in Britain?

Analysis of the Leave referendum victory has tended to be simplistic: immigration trumped all else; a revolt of the 'left behind'; payback time from the 'losers' from globalization. Yet the golf clubs of comfortable England contained plenty of Leave voters. Cities that voted Remain – Glasgow, Liverpool and London – include the most deprived communities in Britain. There were significant age, class and level of education differences in the pattern of voting (Clarke et al. 2017: 154/155). Sixty-six per cent of over 65-year-olds, 64 per cent of social class DEs, and 60 per cent of those without degrees voted Leave: nonetheless so did 35 per cent of ABs and 37 per cent of university graduates – a corrective to those who see the result as representing an unbridgeable social polarization. A majority of Conservative voters backed Leave not Remain: the reverse was true for Labour.

Leave support was strongest in areas that have suffered sharp economic decline (the Black Country, the Potteries, the old coal fields from the North East to Nottinghamshire, the South Wales Valleys); market and coastal towns, particularly in Eastern England; and on London's Essex fringe. Ethnicity mattered too: 53 per cent of those identifying as 'White British' (and a much higher percentage of those who identify as 'English') voted Leave, whereas only 23 per cent of ethnic minorities did so.

Leave polled strongly in white working class and lower middle-class neighbourhoods, but won the support of relatively few graduates. These groups may perceive themselves as 'left behind', but socio-economic analysis would not identify them as amongst the most deprived: the Leave vote was highest among older voters who tend today to be better off. Why did they vote as they did? Might they have voted differently in different circumstances? The Leave victory can be described through the metaphor of the Russian doll. The outer layer consists of the failures of the Remain campaign itself: contingencies that might have been different, but in the end weren't.

Remain focused almost exclusively on economics, based on polling evidence that undecided voters were Eurosceptic at heart, but would not vote to make themselves poorer. This choice of strategy replicated Project Fear's success in the Scottish independence referendum two years before. Yet Remain's predictions of Brexit gloom did not shift sufficient voters into their camp. Exaggeration and over-precision may have lessened the message's credibility, as did public weariness of the messengers: the endless procession of politicians, bankers, industrialists, Bank of England governors, IMF managing directors and eminent economists. If ordinary people had had no pay rise for a decade, why listen to their words of wisdom? Hadn't the 2008 crisis demonstrated that the elite had been caught with their fingers in the till? Why not trust your own gut instincts, rather than this discredited 'expertocracy'?

Conservative backing for Remain was seriously compromised by the Johnson/Gove decision to lead the Leave campaign. Boris Johnson emerged as the most popular campaigner, with his perceived 'authenticity' crucial in boosting the Leave vote (Clarke et al. op cit: 173). Cameron was wrong-footed by this and unwilling to attack his colleagues directly in ways that would damage party unity. For example, while Farage was a strong motivator of large section of the electorate, it was a minority. But Cameron baulked at attacking Johnson and Gove for putting themselves in Farage's pocket.[2] The Johnson/ Gove camp showed no such restraint, with their claim that on Brexit, there would be an extra £350 million a week for the NHS, and their backing for the 5 million Turkish migrants scare. While Johnson's ratings soared, Cameron suffered a huge plunge in popularity. Having spent his political career mouthing Eurosceptic mantras, his sudden enthusiasm for EU membership did not ring true.

There was no proper cross party campaign and it mattered. Remain was far too dominated by Cameron and Osborne. As Labour leader, Jeremy Corbyn fought a lamentable campaign probably out of deliberate choice (Shipman and Collins 2016[3]). As a lifelong Eurosceptic, he showed a token loyalty to Labour's pro-Europeanism and the overwhelming views of Labour MPs, trade unions and party members, including many who had recently joined the party to support him. In another misjudged lesson of the Scottish referendum, Labour leaders refused to share platforms with Conservatives. Alan Johnson's Labour campaign for Remain was largely ignored. Given Labour's absence from the field, the referendum came across as an internal Conservative row, alienating Labour's traditional supporters. This posed a huge problem for Remain with the Labour base. An unexpectedly high turnout of mainly working class voters who had not voted for decades gave Leave its decisive edge. Two and half million abstainers in the 2015 general election voted in the referendum: some 80 per cent voted Leave. A stronger Labour effort for Remain campaign might have made all the difference.

No one really knows what motivated this howl of protest. Immigration dominated the polling, but was also a proxy for more complex social discontents. It proved crucial to the Leave surge. Britain needed to 'take back control': a message brilliantly driven by UKIP's Farage, but endorsed by Johnson and Gove, despite their posturing as 'global liberals'. The pro-Brexit media relentlessly focused on immigration. In the 1975 referendum, all the national press, with the single exception of the Morning Star, advocated 'Yes to Europe'. In 2016, the Express, Mail, Sun and Telegraph were stridently Leave. Press influence has declined since 1975, along with newspaper readership, but the press still has an agenda-setting capacity in the broadcast media. Uniquely in this referendum, the BBC interpreted the 'editorial balance' obligations of the BBC Charter, as awarding strictly equal time to Leave and Remain views, rather than subjecting the claims and counter-claims of both sides to their customary rigour. This served the purposes of unscrupulous advocates: remember the Goebbels principle that the 'larger the lie, the bigger its impact will be'. Undoubtedly the Remain side made absurdly exaggerated claims for which broadcasters should have held them to account, such as need for a post-Brexit emergency budget. The Leavers' 'extra £350 million a week for the NHS' was challenged, but much less so the alleged ease of establishing 'free trade' with Europe and the supposed certainty of five million Turkish migrants landing on British shores.

In a bad error, Remain chose to ignore immigration. Yet this was a huge dominating issue. The massive rise in EU migration following the 2004 enlargement occurred simultaneously with the squeeze on real wages. Then in 2015 the tens of thousands of refugees making their way to Germany added a new dimension of fear. There was little pushback against the assumption that migration was a wholly bad thing and that as an EU member, the nation state was powerless to act. Yet non-EU migration accounted for half the UK total and the failure to cut that number was no fault of the EU's. Studies of public opinion suggest that the majority of voters are not racist bigots. Their attitudes to migration are highly nuanced. But they want to feel their government has a plan.

Tony Blair in his heyday would never have made such a fundamental campaign error. He would have acknowledged legitimate public concerns, presented a coherent plan for what could and should be done to address them (both domestically and in terms of necessary EU reform), yet attacked extreme Leave claims as crossing the line into racism and xenophobia and argued that Islamophobia is morally wrong. The referendum campaign gave voters the false impression that the British state was powerless on migration and its abuses. In truth, British governments of all stripes had adopted too 'laissez-faire' an approach to migrant rights and labour market regulation, as well as doing little to relieve pressures on housing and public services. This admission should have been coupled with a defence of the benefits of migration and openness to genuine refugees.

The third layer of the referendum's Russian doll consisted of disillusioned 'valence' voters, supporters of EU membership in the past, put off by weak EU performance since: expensive bureaucracy, endless meetings, and little action. Plenty of voters repeated the refrain, 'we originally voted to join a free trade area, not what the EU has become...' to justify their change of heart. Remain was at fault in not explaining what the EU is, what the benefits of pooling sovereignty have been and most importantly, how a vote to Remain in the EU would be a vote for further EU Reform.

This was not what Cameron and Osborne had originally intended. In 2012, they assumed the euro crisis would require comprehensive treaty change, out of which Britain could position itself as comfortable members of a non-euro outer tier, thereby demonstrating that EU membership was not 'an escalator to a European superstate'. Cameron's January 2013 Bloomberg speech, in which he conceded an In-Out referendum, advocated a bold EU wide reform agenda. But there was to be no comprehensive Treaty revision within Cameron's arbitrary referendum timetable, designed to keep his anti-European backbenchers quiet. Only then did Cameron switch to a British specific set of 'renegotiation' demands. As a tactic this re-negotiation proved a flop. The Brexit media ridiculed its content. Any positive impact was completely overtaken by the Johnson/Gove decision to back Leave. Unwisely Cameron allowed future EU reform to disappear from the campaign debate. Gordon Brown seized on this mistake. In the Scottish referendum he instigated 'The Vow': a cross party declaration of how the devolution agenda would advance should Scots reject independence. Now Brown pushed hard for a vote to Remain to also become a vote for Reform. This never happened.

The inner core of the Brexit 'Russian doll' consists of long term opponents of European integration. The roots lie deep in national psychology. The post-war impulse to build a United Europe never touched Britain. Britain's peaceful development as a democracy, without suffering invasion or brutal territorial adjustment, (brilliantly described in David Cannadine's recent *Victorious Century*, 2017) reinforced faith in the sovereignty of Parliament, simply too precious and providential a gift to surrender. British exceptionalism overruled the very idea of pooling sovereignty and sharing the nation's destiny with Britain's Continental neighbours. More crudely, why debase ourselves in a putative union with unreliable foreigners with imperfect democracies whom we had seen off in the World War II!

The only reason an In/Out referendum was ever held in the first place was because of a failure to establish a national consensus among the political elite behind our EU membership. Public support for EU membership was weak, but generally positive, fluctuating over the decades with events. But it was not a highly salient issue with the electorate until Cameron made it one. As recently as the 2010 general election, only 10 per cent of voters put Europe among the top three issues they cared about. This emotional opposition to the EU became largely an elite Conservative obsession, latterly reinforced by UKIP 'noises off'.

Initially Labour was badly split: the party did not reconcile itself to European integration until the late 1980s, some 30 years after the German SPD. Around the same time as Labour became mildly pro-EU, the

Conservative elite – the party in Parliament and the country, and the 'party in the media', as Professor Tim Bale astutely describes it – became rancorously divided on matters European. Margaret Thatcher's ejection from the premiership in 1990, in which her increasingly strident objections to Europe and the single currency played a significant part, left lasting wounds. The ideological basis of this Conservative split has remained essentially the same through three decades. Leaving Europe was the necessary means to complete the Thatcher revolution. Many hoped and predicted the EU would break up. If not Brexit should be the goal. This position achieved huge traction among the ageing and dwindling 'selectorate' of the Conservative rank and file and was sustained by the virulently anti-European press.

Ever since 1990, supporters of Britain's EU membership have been dragged down a Eurosceptic path by a constant guerrilla war with hard core Conservative anti-Europeans. As a result, Britain's vision for Europe became generally narrow, too economistic and increasingly qualified and flawed. The bigger case for EU membership was never consistently made. Tony Blair was a partial exception: he wanted Britain to 'lead in Europe', but he chose to spend the political capital he had carefully built up on the US venture in Iraq. After 2003, the cause of Britain in Europe was on the defensive.

In the Conservative party division on Europe never went away despite Cameron's plea on becoming Leader that they should stop *banging on* about it. Whereas the wartime generation of Conservatives felt a Churchillian warmth for a United Europe, the Thatcher/Major generation were much cooler, and the Camerons cynical. As self-defined Eurosceptics, they accepted the reality of Britain's EU membership, adumbrated in William Hague's 1999 slogan: *In Europe, But Not Run by Europe.*

Osborne proved staunch in his support for Britain's EU membership, but for reasons few Continentals would empathize with. In his view, by reason of geography alone, Britain is bound to need a close working relationship with its immediate neighbours. Could anyone suggest a better arrangement than the semi-detached relationship offered by Britain's EU membership? The UK secured all the economic and security benefits of membership, but through the 'opt outs' successive British governments had negotiated, and the vetoes they had deployed, was protected against being sucked into a degree of integration it found uncomfortable, still less a federal United States of Europe. This may be cold realism, but in a referendum it proved difficult to turn into a convincing rallying cry. The Brexiteers had conviction in spades.

The contingency of the euro crisis convinced Cameron 'to lance the boil' by conceding a referendum. Contingency as much as any predetermined structural factors led to precisely the opposite outcome. But if there was no predetermined reason why the referendum was lost, does this suggest at some point in future a new pro-European case could be won?

## The European Question in British Politics Post-Brexit

The politics of the next decade may well be defined as follows: to bowdlerize Dean Acheson (1962),[5] 'Britain has lost its EU membership, and has not yet found a national strategy to replace it'. EU membership was not a perfect national strategy, but it helped Britain share the benefits of globalization – witness the success of the City, inward investment in the car industry, a booming service sector, and our internationalized universities. It kept Britain at the top table in world affairs, disguising the realities of post-Imperial decline. The downsides were the growing economic and social imbalances within Britain which European economic integration may have accentuated, though more activist domestic policies might have been able to correct. But Brexit has torpedoed that national strategy. The question facing Britain now is what, if anything, can replace it.

Brexit is legally set for 29 March 2019, but its precise shape will be far from determined by then. The Withdrawal Treaty that parliament must first approve will only contain a framework for treaty negotiations[6] that will take place after Brexit. The aspiration is to complete these treaty negotiations by December 2020 – the end of the transition period in which Britain will remain, in practice, an EU member while losing all formal say in EU decisions. This transition period may be extended,[7] raising the intriguing possibility that Britain will not fully have left the EU by the final date for the next general election in 2022.

In 2018, Labour hopes Cabinet divisions will lead to an early general election. This seems unlikely. In 2017 the Conservatives gambled on a Brexit general election, imagining they would sweep the country on a platform of strengthening Theresa May's negotiating hand. The gamble failed. Conservative strategists will be wary of fighting another election on Brexit. Even if they proved unable to muster a Commons majority for the Brexit the Cabinet majority favours, a general election would be high risk. Were divisions to reach the point of parliamentary crisis, say on the question of a Northern Irish hard border, a further referendum may suddenly seem more attractive. The hazier the outcome of the Brexit talks by the autumn of 2018, the less problematic will be parliamentary approval of Brexit. Brexit can still mean different things to different people. Even post-Brexit, maybe under a new prime minister, the party will be cautious about a general election that could turn into a referendum on Brexit or for that matter, expose acute Conservative divisions on the complex trade negotiations still ongoing. A general election looks much more realistic in 2021 or 2022.

Even then the eventual terms of these treaties will not finally settle the future British-EU relationship, for two big reasons: First, 'events' will constantly challenge the 'status quo' and require new interpretations of what is meant by such mushy concepts as 'mutual recognition', 'equivalence of outcomes' and 'managed divergence'.

Secondly, and more fundamentally, British politics is unlikely to cohere around the treaty settlement. The final outcome will almost certainly fall short of Brexiteer ambitions. Before Brexit, the Brexiteers will tolerate this, because for them 'any Brexit is better than no Brexit'. But once out, the Brexiteers will not let go, because their Brexit vision, incoherent though it may be, is fundamental to their ideological and political position. With Theresa May's impending demise, a personal and ideological battle for contested visions of Britain's future will open up within the Conservative party.

The Conservatives are fundamentally divided between pragmatists and ideologues. In the referendum, the majority of the party elite ended up as reluctant Remainers. Sceptical, half-hearted and opportunistic as was their backing for Britain's EU membership, they know Leaving is bad news, especially for the party of the wealth creators. Their basic motivation is to limit the damage. Many would prefer 'Norway' to 'Canada', but they have to stick with the mantra Theresa May unwisely established in her October 2016 party conference speech, that Brexit means Britain will be leaving the single market and customs union. Their strategic problem is twofold.

Firstly it will be extremely difficult to persuade the EU 27 to grant quasi-membership of the single market on the basis of continued 'regulatory alignment' while Britain claims theoretical sovereignty over its money, laws and borders. Why should the EU make a special case of Britain and relax their insistence that full access to the single market is indivisible and requires full compliance with the EU's four freedoms and its acquis? If Britain is allowed to be a special case, why not others?

Secondly while staying as close as possible to the EU is arguably the best means available to defend UK national interests, domestically it lacks political inspiration and vision: essentially its vision for post-Brexit Britain is 'making the best of a bad job'. The argument for continued EU alignment depends on the undoubted advantages of the 'status quo'. Being part of the EU and its related trading agreements, accounts presently for 60 per cent of all British trade. As Sir Martin Donnelly, former permanent secretary to the Department of International Trade put it, 'why give up a three course meal for the uncertain prospect of a bag of crisps?'[8]

Thirdly, this pessimistic realism is anathema to Brexit's true believers and their ambition to build a 'Global Britain'. That very phrase conveys a spirit of optimism and patriotism. Hard facts make little impression on the Brexiteers. Theirs is a religious faith that a sovereign Britain, free to set its own regulatory rules and negotiate its own trade agreements, would be able to seize global opportunities in a way Britain cannot, if we continue to tie ourselves to the EU. The proposition rests on an indisputable truth that the balance of economic power in the world is shifting away from Europe: while Remainers had a powerful argument that best way to open up these opportunities 'beyond the oceans' is through the collective power of the EU trading bloc, outside the EU, Britain loses that influence.

At present the Brexiteers disingenuously refuse to come clean on how they would use the regulatory sovereignty they crave. Of course all their past statements suggest a determination to enhance British competitiveness by eliminating the 'burdens' of EU regulation: in practice the social, worker, environmental and consumer protections that Britain's current membership of the single market offers. They are also naïve about the deregulatory implications of the free trade agreements they could realistically negotiate, which would in turn lead to further restriction of UK access to EU markets. As Thatcherites they may relish the growth stimulus they believe Britain would enjoy as a lightly regulated, free trading, mid-Atlantic tax haven. However, to suggest that this vision is in tune with the aspirations of people who voted Leave on the housing estates of the industrial Midlands and North is, to say the least, a bit of a stretch. The Brexiteers must be aware that they have not yet constructed a broad base of political support for their strategy. At present they are holding to the view that 'any Brexit is better than no Brexit' and that their opportunity to craft the Brexit they want will come later.

By 2022 it will have been five years since the Brexit vote. The Conservatives will boast by then that they have put a system of national immigration control in place, though it will be far too early to judge its effect. The British electorate will doubtless be offered some Brexit dividend in terms of additional funding for the NHS, even though if economic growth is less than it would have been without Brexit, the proposition is essentially bogus.

Although the economy will have been protected against a sudden cliff edge as a result of a (probably extendable) transition period, most economic forecasters predict that Brexit uncertainty will have had a dampening effect on business confidence and investment. Robust world economic growth may somewhat disguise this, but Britain will have become a global laggard – that is if the overwhelming weight of economic research on the impact of Brexit is right.

The interesting question then will be the nature of the Conservatives' 'future offer'. They are bound to assert that their national strategy is to make the best of Brexit for Britain. Their economic policy will attempt to offset the disincentives that Brexit has put in the way of business investment by promising lower corporate taxes, increased public money for research and innovation, visa schemes for high skilled workers, new freedoms for the City, and deregulation to cut business costs. Whatever trade deals can be cobbled together with the rest of the world will be trumpeted as examples of Britain's widening post-Brexit global influence. Noises off from the EU that this policy platform amounts to 'social dumping' or 'unfair regulatory competition' will be met with nationalistic bluster, though eventually it risks trade retaliation.

Will this work politically? The weakened state of public services and poor relative growth performance will be negatives for the Conservatives. The Brexit vision of a buccaneering Britain will be hard to reconcile with Theresa May's concerns to unite the country and help the 'just about managing'. Some sense a growing public mood that Britain needs less inequality, less emphasis on private gain, less tolerance of private sector excess, more public investment and more state intervention to make markets work in the public interest. Corbyn (or his Labour successor) will be standing a programme of 'state socialism-lite'. The hole in Labour's programme is explaining Labour's post-Brexit growth engine for the economy. If Brexit has knocked away the national strategy for attracting investment that successive governments pursued over 40 years, what replaces it? The Conservatives will have an answer, however imperfect, in 'Global Britain'. What will be Labour's? Maybe the sense of populist grievance will be enough. It will then have been a pretty dismal 15 years since the financial crisis, and maybe that will be enough to secure a change of government.

Of course Labour could argue that it wants to get back closer to Europe – to seek membership of the single market 'Norway' style, perhaps even to explore how Britain could re-join a reformed EU. Under the present leadership, this is unlikely. The state socialists now in control of the

Labour party fear the EU would get in their interventionist way. They see Europe is an issue that divides Labour's traditional support. Labour Leave voters back migration controls. Better therefore to concentrate Labour's pitch on the safer ground of attacking the rich and big business, and defending the NHS and other public services. However, without any direct appeal to the Remain support among progressive middle class and well educated under 45s that produced such rich and unexpected electoral dividends for Labour in 2017, Labour may find itself in tougher territory than it was then. The outcome in 2022 may be a further stalemate in which the old two-party blocs with around 40 per cent of the vote cancel each other out.

In time, the negative long-term consequences of Brexit will become clearer. Slower relative growth will induce a feeling of national decline. Disillusion will grow among Leave voters that Brexit – and migration controls – have not delivered a better life for them. This may be a danger moment for British politics. A new populism of the right could emerge: more likely the Tory Brexiteers will move more onto the ground of populist nationalism as the fallacies of Global Britain are exposed. But the inability of Brexit Britain to manage the challenges of globalization will have become all too apparent.

## Conclusion

Our conclusion is that conjuncture could provide the opportunity to remake the case for British re-engagement with the EU. The precise terms will be unclear and depend on developments within the EU itself. It may be a more confident pro-Europeanism than Labour demonstrated in the 1990s – less hung up on appeasing business and the City, less uncritical in its support for the United States, more willing to pool sovereignty to achieve progressive ends, for example on climate change or taxation of the global corporations and the rich.

This pro-European impulse may come from within the Labour party. Many of the new members who support Jeremy Corbyn are strongly anti-Brexit. Brexit has for the first time created a vibrant pro-European activism in British society. Europe could provide a key strand of a new generation progressive appeal once the older generation of state socialists have left the scene. Renewed British commitment to the single market would provide the growth and investment stimulus Britain will need, while offering at the same time higher standards of environmental and social protection that the Brexiteers will have unwound.

If Labour cannot make itself the vehicle for this new generation of progressive pro-European aspiration, surely the present two-party system will not survive. The 2017 General Election was seen as consolidating the two-party system. Brexit would still break it apart. As we have seen, Brexit was in part a consequence of globalization, but within a decade, reversing it may have become the only national strategy for Britain to manage globalization.

## Notes

1. (ec.europa.eu/citizens_agenda/social_reality_stocktaking/docs/background_doc). The paper drew heavily on Dutch experience and the work of the political scientist, Rene Cuperus.
2. The tactic Cameron had used so successfully in the general election the year before, when he had warned of the danger of an SNP-Labour Coalition and Conservative Central Office ran a poster campaign with a miniature of Ed Miliband peeping out of Alex Salmond's top pocket.
3. See particularly Chapter 19 'Labour Isn't Working'.
4. For many Conservative backbench MPs, worries about losing their seats as a result of the huge domestic unpopularity of the 'poll tax' probably counted as much.
5. 'Great Britain has lost an Empire and has not yet found a role'. Dean Acheson speech, US Military Academy, West Point, New York, 5 December 1962.
6. Apart from trade, the EU 27 anticipate treaties will need to be negotiated in three other areas: defence and foreign policy, internal security, and areas of common cooperation such as research and education.
7. The British Cabinet is presently pressing for what will almost certainly be classified as a so-called 'mixed agreement' because it would embrace all areas of economic activity and affect member state as well as EU competencies: any such treaty will require a full ratification process in accordance with each member state's constitutional requirements (e.g. ratification in Belgium by regional as well as the national parliaments and possible referendums in other member states such as Ireland). A free trade agreement in goods only would be simpler and quicker, but less beneficial to the UK.
8. Lecture to the King's Business School, 28 February 2018.

## References

Cannadine, David. *Victorious Century: The United Kingdom 1800–1906* (London, Allen Lane 2017).

Clarke, Harold C; Goodwin, Matthew and Whiteley, Paul. *Brexit: Why Britain Voted to Leave the European Union* (Cambridge, Cambridge University Press 2017).

Ford, Robert and Goodwin, Matthew. *Revolt on the Right* (Abingdon, Routledge 2014).

Goodwin, Matthew and Milazzo, Caitlin. *UKIP: Inside the Campaign to Re-draw the Map of British Politics* (Oxford, Oxford University Press 2015).

Liddle, Roger. *The Europe Dilemma: Britain and the Drama of European Integration* (London, I.B.Tauris 2014).

Liddle, Roger. *The Risk of Brexit: Britain and Europe in 2015* (London, Policy Network and Rowman and Littlefield International 2015).

Liddle, Roger. *The Risk of Brexit: The Politics of a Referendum (2nd edition)* (London, Policy Network and Rowman and Littlefield International 2016).

Liddle, Roger. *Seizing the Argument: How Labour can Save Britain from Brexit Disaster* (London, Policy Network December 2016).

Liddle, Roger and Lerais, Frederick. *The Social Reality of Europe*. Discussion Paper, Bureau of European Policy Advisers, European Commission (2007).

Shipman, Tim. *All Out War* (Glasgow, Harper Collins 2016).

# Part III

## What is to be Done? Domestic and International Policies to Deal with Globalization

CHAPTER 9

# Where Might the Next Generation of Progressive Ideas and Programmes Come From? Contemporary Discontents, Future Possibilities for Europe

Vivien A. Schmidt

In recent years, the European Union (EU) has suffered through a cascading set of crises, including the eurozone crisis, the refugee crisis, the security crisis, Brexit, and Trump. But rather than bringing the EU together, with concerted responses, these crises have revealed cross-cutting divisions among member states. What is more, they have been accompanied by major crises of politics and democracy for the EU as well as its member states.

At the EU level, questions are increasingly raised not only about the (lack of) effectiveness in solving the various crises but also democratic legitimacy. The causes are public perceptions of EU governance processes characterized by the predominance of closed-door political bargains by leaders in the Council and by a preponderance of technocratic decisions by EU officials in the Commission and the European Central Bank, without significant oversight by the European Parliament. At the national level, concerns focus on the ways in which the EU's very existence has diminished elected governments' authority and control over growing numbers of policies for which they had traditionally been alone responsible, often making it difficult for them to fulfil their electoral promises or respond to their voters' concerns and expectations.

The result has been increasing political disaffection and discontent across European countries, with a growing Euroscepticism that has fuelled the rise of populist parties on the political extremes. In a world in which citizens have become increasingly dissatisfied with current economics, politics, and society, populist politicians have been able to find the words to channel their anger. Using rhetorical strategies and 'uncivil' language in a 'post-truth' environment that rejects experts and the mainstream media, they have reshaped the political landscape by framing the debates in fresh ways while using new and old media to their advantage as they upend conventional politics.

The underlying causes of the malaise fuelling the rise of populists are known. These include the increase in inequality and those 'left behind', the growth of a socio-cultural politics of identity uncomfortable with the changing 'faces' of the nation, and the hollowing out of mainstream political institutions and party politics. But although these help explain the sources of citizens' underlying anger, they do not address the central puzzles: Why now, in this way, with this kind of populism? And where are the progressives? Where the progressive ideas?

In order to consider where the next generation of progressive ideas and programmes might come from that would be capable of reshaping the next phase of globalization (and regionalization with regard to the EU), we need to know first where we are, in terms of discontents with the current phase of globalization, and what problems result from such discontents. Having identified the problems, the question is then where do ideas about solutions come from? Who are the individuals, groups, coalitions or leaders? And how do they bring about progressive change – in a revolutionary moment or incrementally? Through the success of political leaders winning the electoral battles of mass party politics or of policy entrepreneurs winning the technical battles of administrative institutions? And how long might this all take, meaning how much worse might things get before we turn the corner? Finally, what about the substantive content of the progressive ideas meant to solve the problems? To illustrate this last issue, I focus mainly on the EU, with suggestions about how to think about a more progressive future.

## Contemporary Discontents and their Sources

We begin with problem definitions, which are a first and necessary step in addressing the question of where progressive ideas come from. Until we understand the sources of contemporary discontents, we won't come up with new ideas that address these discontents with discourses that resonate with citizens. Today, these sources are increasingly well understood. The root causes of citizens' discontents can be traced back to ideas – economic, political, and social. In the forefront are the neo-liberal economic ideas based on a philosophy focused on free markets, individualism, and a limited state. These ideas have promoted the liberalising and globalising policy programmes that have led to the current problems of inequality and insecurity. But the sources of discontent also come from the liberal sociopolitical ideas that promoted the cosmopolitan and multicultural political and social values that have led to cultural backlash. The rise in political distrust may also be a by-product of both sets of ideas, neo-liberal and social liberal, but it also has roots in how globalization and regionalization via the EU have undermined citizens' power and influence in national political processes.

## Political Economic Sources of Discontent

The sources of discontent are first of all political-economic, resulting from a globalization spurred by neo-liberal ideas that began with policy programmes focused on global free trade and market liberalization in the 1980s and ended with the triumph of financial capitalism and 'hyper-globalization' (Stiglitz 2002, 2016; Rodrik 2011; Mirowski 2013). Moreover, neo-liberal ideas promoting the opening of borders to trade through globalization have led to uneven development and significant economic disruptions, in particular the shift of manufacturing from advanced to developing countries that have left more and more people being and/or feeling 'left behind' (Gilpin 2000; Eberstadt 2016). These problems have arguably hit the United States and the UK harder than continental Europe, since the former introduced more radical, neo-liberal reforms earlier and have long had less generous welfare states (Scharpf and Schmidt 2000), with fewer and less effective labour market activation programmes in response (Martin and Swank 2012).

The discontents also come from the fact that the economic crisis that began in 2007/2008, far from changing the policy direction, also demonstrates the resilience of such neo-liberal ideas (Blyth 2013; Schmidt and Thatcher 2013a). Notably, the EU's 'ramp-up' of the (quasi) state in order to 'save the euro' at the onset of the sovereign debt crisis was based on 'ordo-liberal' ideas (Dullien and Guérot 2012; Blyth 2013) that promoted austerity along with neo-liberal ideas focused on 'structural reform' (Crespy and Verheuzin 2017) – which translated into 'smash the unions', deflate wages, lower job and social protections, and cut pensions for countries in trouble (in particular in the case of programme countries under supervision by the 'Troika' but also for non-programme countries in trouble in the context of the European Semester (Schmidt 2016a). These policies have had particularly deleterious consequences in eurozone countries, including low growth, high unemployment (in particular in Southern Europe), and rising poverty and inequality (Scharpf 2014; Matthijs and Blyth 2015).

## Socio-Economic and Socio-Cultural Sources of Discontent

The sources of discontent are naturally also socio-economic. These include the rise of inequality due to the accumulation of capital by the 'one per cent' (Piketty 2013), along with neo-liberal policies promoting such changes through regressive taxation plans and cost-cutting to redistributive social programmes and policies (Hacker 2006; Hemerijck 2013). Moreover, globalization has created a wide range of 'losers' or 'left-behinds' in de-industrialized areas, while generating a sense of insecurity for the middle classes, worried about losing jobs and status (Kalleberg 2009; Prosser 2016), or joining the 'precariat' (Standing 2011). Among specifically socio-economic issues, moreover, the 'race to the bottom' of lower skilled groups, especially of younger males, has become particularly salient (Eberstadt 2016).

The sources of political-economic and socio-economic discontent also link to the socio-cultural. These involve people uncomfortable with the changing 'faces' of the nation. Immigration is a key issue, as certain groups feel, not just their jobs, but also their national identity or sovereignty to be under siege in the face of increasing flows of immigrants (Berezin 2009; McClaren 2012), with rising nativist resentments tied to perceptions that other groups are 'cutting in line', and taking the benefits they alone deserve (Hochshild 2016). Nostalgia for a lost past together with fear of the 'other' have increased massively, along with the targeting of immigrant groups (Hochschild and Mollenkopt 2009). The question scholars raise here is whether the causes are solely because 'it's the economy, stupid' or also, if not mainly, the 'cultural backlash' of once-predominant sectors of the population – older, less educated, white, male – whose worldview is threatened by intergenerational shifts to post-materialist values such as cosmopolitanism and multiculturalism (Inglehart and Norris 2016).

The social discontent has not only been related to immigration, however. Also targeted has been social liberalism, which underpins ideas about individuals' rights to self-determination. These include the expectation of respect for differences not only involving race and ethnicity but also gender, accompanied by expectations of 'political correctness' in language (Lilla 2016). Particularly contentious have been questions of women's rights when related to abortion, LGBTQ rights when involving marriage and child adoption, and trans-gender issues, such as the 'bathroom' wars in US high schools (about which bathrooms may transsexuals and non-gender-identifying youths use). The discontented here are not only the economic left-behinds affected by neo-liberal economic ideas; they are also those unhappy with social-liberal political ideas. These are people who may be well off financially, but subscribe to socially conservative philosophies and/or oppose the socially liberal policy programme (Inglehart and Norris 2016).

## Political Sources of Discontent

Finally, the discontents are also political, as people feel their voices no longer matter in the political process. The problem is that citizens generally feel that they have lost control as a result of globalization and/or Europeanization – where powerful people at a distance make decisions that have effects over their everyday lives that they don't like or even understand (Schmidt 2006, 2017). These include not just global or regional decision-making bodies but also big businesses able to use the political system to their advantage, whether or not paying taxes (e.g. Apple) or to get the regulations they want, regardless of their effects on social and environmental policies (Hacker and Pierson 2010; Culpepper 2011). In the eurozone crisis, the problems were epitomized by the recourse to 'governing by rules and ruling by numbers,' as the Stability and Growth Pact was reinforced by 'pact' after 'pack,' including the Six-Pack, the Two-Pack, and the Fiscal Compact, all focused on forcing conformity to rules that, far from helping solve the problems of growth for countries in trouble, limited their ability to deal with them (Schmidt 2015, 2016a).

In this context, mainstream party politics has increasingly become hollowed out and delegitimized, as political leaders are forced to choose between 'responsiveness' to citizens and 'responsibility' for maintaining international and/or EU commitments (Mair 2013). Moreover, party government is under siege by opposing forces, with populists demanding responsiveness on the one hand while technocrats insist on 'responsibility' on the other (Caramani 2017). Additionally, the new electoral divides related to the increasing split between 'xenophobes' and 'cosmopolitans' only further complicate any kind of party politics (Kriesi et al. 2012). Finally, voters, instead of being the information-seeking issues-focused utility-maximizers expected by pollsters working with rational man models, tend to be deeply uninformed, lack meaningful preferences, or, when they do have preferences, base them on partisan loyalties, or norms and culture (Achen and Bartels 2016). This makes voters highly susceptible to the siren calls of populist leaders, who promise everything even though they are unlikely to deliver policies that will actually work to improve their lives.

All of the above manifests itself in the increasing discontent citizens have expressed in the ballot box as well as in the streets. Citizens generally have developed a growing distrust of governing elites and a loss of faith in their national democracies as well as in the EU (Pew and Eurobarometer polls, 2008–16). Votes for the political extremes, on the left as well as on the right, attest to strong desires to register protest against the sitting parties, the elites, and the establishment. Such votes – as well as higher and higher rates of abstention – are also citizens' protest against their growing sense of a loss of enfranchisement. Such disenfranchisement is a result of the removal of more and more decisions from the national to supranational level, whether to international institutions because of increasing globalization, or to the EU because of increasing Europeanization in the case of EU member-states. As I have written elsewhere, in the EU, the problem for member-state democracy is that it has increasingly become the domain of 'politics without policy', as more and more policies are removed to the EU level, where decisions take the form of 'policy without politics' (however political the policies are in reality), often with highly technocratic debates not recognisable to the citizens who expect more normative arguments based on the left/right divide (Schmidt 2006). It is therefore little surprise that 'take back control' became the slogan in the UK, or that populist parties across Europe advocate leaving the EU in order to take back national sovereignty. Indeed, we could even say that citizens everywhere have moved increasingly from politics *without* policy to 'politics *against* policy.'

Taken together, these sources of discontent – political economic, socio-economic and socio-cultural, and political – suggest that democratic legitimacy has increasingly come into question. The questions involve three aspects of legitimacy, including political (often known as 'input' legitimacy), meaning citizen representation and governing elites' responsiveness; performance-based ('output' legitimacy), linked to policies' effectiveness and outcomes; and procedural ('throughput' legitimacy), concerning the efficacy, accountability, transparency, inclusiveness and openness of the governance processes (Schmidt 2015, 2016). The problem with regard to legitimacy today is not only that citizens feel they have little political input into the decisions that most affect their lives. It is also that neo-liberal economic policies have increasingly failed to perform, in particular for those who feel 'left-behind,' and in light of the anaemic growth since the economic crisis, itself evidence of a neo-liberalism gone too far. Finally, the administration of the rules has been seen as lacking in accountability and transparency, while excluding citizens and dissenters alike from having any say over the decisions, given the multi-level nature of the EU's policy-making processes.

## Where Do Progressive Ideas Come From? And Who are the Agents of Change?

But once we know the sources of discontent, having identified the problems, there is no guarantee that progressive ideas will pop up to respond to those problems. So where do the new progressive ideas come from? And who develops them and/or brings them to public attention. Here, the question is about the circulation and dissemination of ideas. This is a question also, therefore, about the ideational agents – activists in social movements, advocacy coalitions of activists with policy-makers, epistemic communities of like-minded economic thinkers, bankers and financial reporters, policy entrepreneurs who coordinate the construction of policy ideas, and political entrepreneurs who translated policy ideas into language accessible to the general public, who campaign on platforms espousing such ideas, and win elections.

New ideas can come from social movements, as in the Occupy Movement and its idea of the 1 per cent that briefly electrified politics, such that everyone, including presidents and PMs on the left but also the right talked about it. But social movements don't necessarily always get it right in terms of the real sources of their own discontent, or the solutions. In the case of the British referendum on membership in the EU, for example, most remarkable was that although neo-liberal government policies were a major contributor to the causes for anger that lent support to the Brexit camp, it was largely absent from the campaign, which instead blamed the EU and immigration for all of Britain's ills (Schmidt 2016b, 2017). Only with the disastrous (for the Tories) snap election called by Theresa May did neo-liberalism become the target, with the 'dementia tax' symbolic of a new government that, despite a Manifesto discourse that suggested it was abandoning the radical neo-liberalism of the Thatcherite past, continued with specific austerity policies. The Grenfell Tower fire highlighted another deleterious effect of neo-liberalism, the move to deregulation, which has further galvanized opposition to the government.

Discursive coalitions are also important for the circulation of ideas, if not always the creation of new ones. Unions served this function in the past for workers. Today, discursive communities are also made up of virtual communities, through Facebook and other social media that bring together like-minded people across the globe. But, as we have seen, this has given tremendous strength to the forces of reaction – the white nationalists and the alt-right – even more than to progressives.

New ideas can come from a variety of places, including academic theorists in universities, policy analysts in thinktanks, as well as independent thinkers. Most notable on this score is Piketty's (2013) book *Capital* highlighting the rise of inequality linked to capital accumulation aggravated by regressive taxation, which graced the coffee tables of many of the very people it was about: the most unequal of all, the rich and powerful. Brain trusts, thinktanks, political philosophers, macro-sociologists, or economic theorists, in universities or in other venues, are most often the sources of progressive ideas. Thus, JFK had his 'Camelot' and the brain trust of Harvard academics; and Tony Blair had Anthony Giddens for the 'third way.'

Progressive ideas can naturally also come from a range of political entrepreneurs. These are political leaders, whose discourse ignites imaginations, persuading the people of the necessity and appropriateness of their ideas, as rhetorical leaders who usher in a new political economic order (Widmaier 2016). Here, I'm thinking of Teddy Roosevelt, the first 'progressive,' and of FDR, and even Macron.

A word of caution here: Non-progressive ideas also come through in this same way. In the United States, neo-liberal ideas were also explicitly under attack by Donald Trump, with his campaign discourse questioning how well the United States had actually done, and whether globalization was good for the economy, while promising to remedy the problems by bringing jobs back home, even if it meant imposing higher taxes and tariffs on US firms (Schmidt 2017a). Nigel Farage was also amazingly successful in the Brexit campaign, although admittedly helped by Conservative Party leaders such as Boris Johnson and Michael Gove. In continental Europe, moreover, populist leaders – such as Marine Le Pen or Geert Wilders – have also been successful in increasing their political presence and support, with anti-globalization, anti-EU as well as anti-euro memes having joined the long-standing anti-immigrant ones as central themes. And most such leaders also have their in-house organic intellectual, such as Beppe Grillo, helped on strategy by the internet expert Gianroberto Casaleggio (and now his son).

So what makes progressive ideas and political actors progressive – and different from extreme right wing populism? We have no room here to parse the differences between 'good' populism and 'bad,' and whether some progressives may be 'populists' or not. Suffice to say that progressives tend to adopt a certain kind of pragmatism that recognizes that one has to make promises that can be kept, more or less. Their goal is, for the most part, reform rather than revolution, even if such reform may appear revolutionary in terms of the reversal of past policies.

The challenge for progressive political actors in this context is how to regain control of both the agenda and the discourse, in ways that return to civil language and truth-based discussion while framing debates in ways that galvanize citizens just as much as the populists, but in a positive direction. The question is how to channel the anger in more positive directions, to get us beyond this possibly pivotal moment in history. Notably, Macron's discourse, with its positive take on the EU, and its straddling the centre ground with policies of what we could call the 'critical centre' – not centrist – seemed to have hit the mark.

The problems for progressives come not just from how to win against the populists with a more 'sensible' progressive message: It is also a question of how to combat neo-liberal ideas, given their embeddedness in the very rules of national, regional, and global institutions. Part of the problem is that the traditional social-democratic European alternatives such as greater public ownership and industrial policy, are not just marginalized, they are ruled out in advance as the target of EU action in the name of 'the single European market' and international competitiveness (Thatcher 2015; Jabko 2006). Moreover, the traditional domain of the social democrats involves deploying the state for the greater good, whereas nowadays the state always makes an easy target for neo-liberals, and campaigning against opponents in power – or even one's neo-liberal predecessors – is easy if the message is always that the state needs to be scaled back and reformed to meet the neo-liberal ideal. Similarly, portraying welfare spending as 'wasteful' or pointing to 'unsustainable' rising costs due to 'longevity risks' is easier to convey in political discourse than alternative ideas that such spending supports the competitive economy or reflects changing social preferences about collectively-provided benefits (Schmidt and Thatcher 2013b).

## How Do Progressive Ideas Bring About Change: Revolutionary or Incremental?

How do progressive political leaders put theory into practice? Is it in a 'revolutionary' moment of massive reforms? Or incrementally, through piecemeal reforms that slowly build momentum, guided by a set of ideas about the problems to tackle, but without any necessarily overall vision of what this would generate? And can we separate the two?

In some cases, a blueprint for reform may be in the minds of policy-makers – as when Thatcher came to power with a neo-liberal agenda nurtured by the works of Hayek and Friedman. With Macron, the policies announced in his campaign on reform of labour regulation were clearly laid out with regard to the sampling on the right (more flexibility in labour markets) and the left (more security for individual workers through universal unemployment insurance, better opportunities through training and education). Winning elections on the basis of such ideational platforms confer greater legitimacy, because the political leader promises, and then goes about keeping that promise. For Macron, this has been important for his ability to resist the strikes and protests in the streets, since it has meant that 'the people' did not join the strikes, but have given his progressive agenda a chance. Obama, in contrast, did not have as much of a chance because he was confronted by a hostile majority in Congress for most of his mandate.

But in most cases, including the seemingly revolutionary moments, the ideational innovations develop incrementally over time. It is only looking back from the vantage point of many years in the future, that they appear revolutionary, as a clear paradigm shift to a new political economic order. In the moment of change, the process appears much more incremental and experimental.

For example, FDR was elected as a result of a powerful discourse identifying the problems, but not many of the solutions. Indeed, his initial economic formula was some version of classical austerity, which he quickly dropped once in office. The full set of ideational solutions came to him only while in office – as Keynesianism *avant la lettre,* given that he was experimenting with his policy programme before Keynes had even written his *General Theory*. Thus, the coming to ideational solutions is not necessarily fully developed in advance but may involve a process of *bricolage* where new elements are added and exchanged for old elements and new ideas layered on top of old ones (Carstensen 2011).

This is the good news, then, since it means that progressives don't need a fully developed programme that is 'good to go.' But how long does such incremental change take, once problems are identified and new ideas about how to solve them developed? This can take a very long time – just think how long the neoliberals were out in the cold. If we date their beginning from the establishment of the Mont Pélerin Society in 1947, it took a very long time indeed for their ideas to take hold in the 1970s, and to become hegemonic beginning in the 1980s. For that matter, we could say the same about neo-Keynesianism in Europe, which may have begun in the

United States in the mid-1930s, but didn't get to Europe until much later, after fascism and Nazism were vanquished.

Lest people feel too optimistic, we should remember that Karl Polanyi (1944), in writing about the counter-movement of the people against classical liberalism that later was to produce the Keynesian revival of the post-war period, was all too aware that that counter-movement first brought fascism and Nazism. Let us hope that Marx building on Hegel in the *18th Brumaire of Louis Bonaparte* was correct, that 'the first time tragedy, the second time farce' holds true, with the farce of Trumpism and Mayism.

Moreover, our whole discussion here is focused on the national level, where elections can indeed produce sea changes through new political leaders with new ideas. But in the EU – let alone at the international level – the lack of elected governments ensures that change is slower. In the EU, one possibility for change would be for the election of progressives in country after country, to make up a new majority in the Council – although the more likely eventuality at the moment is a new majority developing on the other side, resulting from the election of increasing numbers of extreme right governments. Another possibility is that the ideas migrate to the supranational institutions, with a slow and incremental shift in policy ideas. We have already seen this with EU institutional leaders engaged first in doubling down on the ordo/neo-liberal rules and then, once they saw that these were producing poor economic outcomes and bad politics, shifted to 'reinterpreting the rules by stealth' beginning in 2013. This succeeded in improving economic performance, but left political legitimacy in question – as EU officials continued with the austerity discourse despite increasing flexibility in the interpretation of the rules. By 2015, however, stealth was replaced by the creation of rules for flexibility. This worked better in terms of political legitimacy, but the rules remain suboptimal and a constraint on better performance (Schmidt 2016a).

This, then, is about slow incremental change. Such cautious incrementalism ensures that we are unlikely to see any radical change in policies – let alone a paradigm shift in the Kuhnian sense. But, in a positive take on the future, this does not rule out the incremental reinterpretation of the rules and recalculation of the numbers over the medium term. Although one cannot expect a paradigm shift back to neo-Keynesian expansionism, we could see the emergence of a new set of ideas. For example, in place of today's 'expansionary fiscal contractionism' – the phrase sometimes used to describe the ideas behind austerity and structural reforms (Dellepiane-Avallaneda 2015) – why not a new paradigm of 'expansionary stability,' or 'stable expansionism,' in which the stability rules are made truly compatible with growth-enhancing policies?

If this were the outcome, then the euro crisis would have done what past crises have been touted to do: after an initial period of delayed or failed responses, the EU muddles through to a more positive set of results while deepening its own integration. If this were to be the case, 30 years hence, looking back, scholars could very well situate the beginning of the new political economic paradigm of 'expansionary stability' at the current moment of incremental rules reinterpretation.

## Toward a Next Generation of Progressive Ideas for Europe[1]

The resilience of neo-liberalism is not the only problem for progressives. Equally, if not more, problematic is the rise of populism, in particular on the extreme right, which constitutes a challenge to political stability and democracy not seen since the 1920s and 1930s (Mudde and Kaltwasser 2012; Müller 2016; Judis 2016). Progressives need to come up with new and better ideas that rally citizens around more positive messages that serve better ends than those of the populist extremes on the right. These need to be ideas that they can communicate effectively through the new social media as well as the old, and that resonate with a broad range of citizens. But which ideas, then?

With regard to economic and socio-economic ideas, progressives have some rethinking to do. Social democratic parties have yet to come to terms with their own complicity in the resilience of neo-liberalism, and the myriad policies focused on liberalising the financial markets, deregulating labour markets, and rationalising the welfare state that left large portions of the electorate open to the populist siren calls of the extreme right. Such policies, in many cases led by the social democrats in the name of a progressive agenda, benefited some people a lot: the top classes – not just the 1 per cent but the upper 20 per cent in particular since the financial crisis and eurozone crisis – but not the in-betweens, who neither benefited from the boom for the top nor the welfare for the bottom. These are the people who feel left behind, and are! They are increasingly frustrated, resentful, and insecure; they are looking for explanations and answers; and only the extreme right speaks to them! But what the extreme right proposes, involving increasing protectionism and an end to free trade, dismantling the EU and getting rid of the euro, closing borders to free movement and to immigration, are potentially disastrous for themselves, their countries, Europe, and the world.

At the same time, the populists' concerns ought not to be dismissed out of hand, in particular with regard to protecting the welfare state and jobs, nor should the populist desire for more national control over the decisions that affect people the most be ignored. The questions are: How to do this in the context not just of globalization but also of the eurozone crisis, with its austerity rules for countries in trouble, and its stability rules for all, which limit investment for growth; And what to do about the EU more generally, which appears to control what national leaders can do, thereby limiting their responsiveness to their own citizens?

For progressives, the way forward requires changing Eurozone governance as well as the way in which the EU works as a whole, in both cases to give more power back to the national level while at the same time enhancing the EU's coordinating ability.

## Progressive Ideas for the Eurozone

For countries in the euro, the EU needs to give back to the member-states the flexibility they have had in the past to devise policies that work for them. The eurozone has been 'reinterpreting the rules by stealth' for quite a while now, by introducing increasing flexibility in the rules and numbers while denying it in the public discourse (Schmidt 2015a, 2016a). As a result, the eurozone operates with suboptimal policies that, although revised to allow for improving performance, still haven't resolved the eurozone crisis once and for all. Countries in Southern Europe in particular suffer as a result. It is about time that political leaders – and in particular progressives – push harder for a rethinking of the rules, so that everyone can benefit from being in the euro and, indeed, in the EU.

One way of rethinking the rules would involve making the whole exercise of the European Semester more bottom up and flexible, rather than continuing with the top-down 'stability' policies of the European Semester – however flexibly interpreted through derogations of the rules (e.g. to France and Italy in 2013 and again in 2015) and recalibrations of the numbers (for Spain in 2013). The eurozone already has an amazing architecture of economic coordination, reaching into all the eurozone ministries of finance and country economic experts. Why not use that coordination to ensure that countries themselves determine what works for their very specific economic growth models and varieties of capitalism? And to have the new 'competitiveness councils' or the existing fiscal councils act more as industrial policy councils rather than structural adjustment hawks?

The countries' decisions on the yearly budgetary cycle could be debated with the other member-states in the Euro-group as well as the Commission, the EP, and the Council to enhance democratic legitimacy. They might additionally be coordinated with the ECB to allow for greater differentiation in euro-members' macroeconomic targets, to match their particular circumstances while fitting within the overall targets.

Such a bottom-up approach is likely not only to promote better economic performance but also much more democratic legitimacy at the national level. This is because it would put responsibility for the country's economics back in national governments' hands at the same time that it would encourage more legitimising deliberation at the EU level. All this in turn could help counter the populist drift in many countries, as political parties of the mainstream right and left could begin again to differentiate their policies from one another, with debates on and proposals for different pathways to economic health and the public good, that they then debate and legitimate at the EU level as well. This could help combat the populism that claims to be the only alternative to EU-led technocratic rule.

None of this will work, however, if member-states continue to have to contend with excessive debt loads that weigh on their economies (e.g. Greece and Italy), if they are left without significant investment funds provided by banks or the state (e.g. Portugal, Spain, Italy, and even France), as well as if some countries continue to have massive surpluses while failing to invest sufficiently (i.e. Germany and other smaller Northern European countries). Some extra form of solidarity is necessary, beyond the European Stability Mechanism. Innovative ideas for renewal, such as Eurobonds, Europe-wide unemployment insurance, EU investment resources that dwarf the Juncker Plan, a EU self-generated budget, and other mechanisms for other areas of concern – including solidarity funds on refugee or EU migration – would be necessary. Failing this, at the very least member-states should be allowed to invest their own resources in key areas needed to promote growth, like infrastructure, education and training, research and development, incurring long-term debt at low interest rates – without adding this to deficit and debt calculations, as under current deficit and debt rules.

## Progressive Ideas for (Re)Envisioning the Future of the EU

Finally, we need to re-envision the EU itself, neither as single speed nor two-speed, with a hard core around the eurozone. Rather, it should be seen as multi-speed with a *soft core* of members resulting from the overlap of different clusters of member-states in the EU's many different policy communities, with different duos or trios of member-states playing leadership roles. With this in mind, the EU could retain its appeal even for an exiting member-state like the UK, which could decide that it should reclaim a leadership role in Common Security and Defense Policy, as one of two European nuclear powers, while standing aside in other areas such as the eurozone. Seeing the future of EU integration as a differentiated process of member-state participation in different policy communities beyond the Single Market would thus also allow for each such community to further deepen by constituting its own special system of governance.

For such differentiated integration to work, however, with all member-states feeling part of this *soft core* EU, whatever their level of involvement, they need to be full members of the EU institutions. This means that all members should be able to exercise voice in all areas, but vote (in the Council and the EP) only in those areas in which they participate. Since all are members in the most significant policy community, the Single Market, this ensures that they will be voting a lot. For the eurozone, this would mean envisioning that where some members in the future, say, pledge their own resources to a EU budget, their representatives would be the only ones to vote on the budget and its use, although everyone could discuss it (no separate Eurozone Parliament, then, but separate voting for members of a deeper budgetary union).

The knotty problem remains the question of politics and democracy. Representative institutions need to be reinforced. At the moment, the EU serves the purpose of the populists, by hollowing out national representative institutions, allowing the populists to claim that they are the true representatives of the people. To change this, the EU needs to do more to reinforce citizen representation and participation. For the eurozone in particular, this at the very least demands more involvement of the European Parliament in decision-making, through a return to the 'Community Method'. Turning eurozone treaties into ordinary legislation, for example, would help break the stalemate that makes it impossible to change such legislation (given the unanimity rule), and make them subject to political debate. But the EP would also need to find more ways to bring national parliaments into EU level decision-making. And the EU as a whole must devise new means of encouraging citizen participation, from the ground up.

## Conclusion

The big question for progressives, in sum, is how to counter the populist upsurge with innovative ideas that go beyond neo-liberal economics while promoting a renewal of democracy and a more egalitarian society. But this requires more than just workable policy ideas developed by policy entrepreneurs that can provide real solutions to the wide range of problems confronting Europe today. It also demands political leaders with persuasive discourses that can resonate with an increasingly discontented electorate, more and more open to the siren call of populism. For the moment, we continue to wait not so much for the ideas – in many ways we know what they are – but for the discourse of new political leaders able to convey such progressive ideas in uplifting ways that offer new visions of the future able to heal the schisms on which the populists have long thrived.

## Note

1. Much of this section and the next extends my discussion in Schmidt (2017b).

## References

Achen, Christoper and Bartels, Larry M. *Democracy for Realists: Why Elections Do Not Produce Responsive Government* (Princeton, Princeton University Press 2016).

Berezin, Mabel. *Illiberal Politics in Neoliberal Times* (New York, Cambridge University Press 2009).

Blyth, Mark M. *Great Transformations: Economic Ideas and Institutional Change in the Twentieth Century* (New York, Cambridge University Press 2002).

Blyth, Mark. *Austerity: The History of a Dangerous Idea* (New York, Oxford University Press 2013).

Caramani, Daniele. 'Will vs. reason: Populist and technocratic challenges to representative democracy', *American Political Science Review* 111(1) (2017) pp. 54–6.

Carstensen, Martin B. 'Paradigm man vs. the bricoleur: An alternative vision of agency in ideational change', *European Political Science Review* 3(1) (2011) pp. 147–67.

Crespy, Amandine and Vanheuverzwijn, Pierre. 'What "Brussels" means by structural reforms: empty signifier or constructive ambiguity', *Comparative European Politics* (2017). Available at https://doi.org/10.1057/s41295-017-0111-0 (Accessed 7 July 2018).

Culpepper, Pepper. *Quiet Politics and Business Power* (Cambridge, Cambridge University Press 2011).

Dullien, Sebastian, and Guerot, Ulrike. 'The long shadow of ordoliberalism: Germany's approach to the Euro crisis', *European Council on Foreign Relations*, Policy Brief 49 (2012).
Eberstadt, Nicholas. *Men Without Work: America's Invisible Crisis* (West Conshohocken, Templeton Press 2016).
Esping-Andersen, Gøsta. *The Three Worlds of Welfare Capitalism* (Cambridge, Polity 1990).
Gilpin, Robert. *The Challenge of Global Capitalism: The World Economy in the 21$^{st}$ Century* (Princeton, Princeton University Press 2000).
Hacker, Jacob. *The Great Risk Shift: The Assault on American Jobs, Families, Health Care, and Retirement, and How You Can Fight Back* (New York, Oxford 2006).
Hacker, Jacob S. and Pierson, Paul. *Winner-Take-All Politics: How Washington made the Rich Richer – And Turned its Back on the Middle Class* (New York, Simon and Schuster 2010).
Hay, Colin and Smith, Nicola. 'The resilience of Anglo-liberalism in the absence of growth'. In V. A. Schmidt and M. Thatcher (eds) *Resilient Liberalism* (Cambridge, Cambridge University Press 2013).
Hemeriijck, Anton. *Changing Welfare States* (Oxford, Oxford University Press 2013).
Hochschild, Arlie Russell. *Strangers in Their Own Land* (New York, New Press 2016).
Hochschild, Jennifer and Mollenkopt, John H. *Bringing Outsiders In: TransAtlantic Perspectives on Immigrant Political Incorporation* (Ithaca, Cornell 2009).
Inglehart, Ronald and Norris, Pippa. 'Trump, Brexit and the Rise of Populism: Economic Have-Nots and Cultural Backlash.' Paper prepared for the annual meeting of the American Political Science Association (Philadelphia, 1–4 September 2016).
Judis, John B. *The Populist Explosion: How the Great Recession Transformed American and European Politics* (New York, Columbia Global Reports 2016).
Kalleberg, Arne L. 'Precarious work, insecure workers: Employment relations in transition', *American Sociological Review* 74(1) (2009) pp. 1–22.
Kriesi, Hanspeter, Grande, Edgar, Dolezal, Martin, Helbling, Marc, Höglinger, Dominic, Hutter, Swen and Wueest, Bruno. *Political Conflict in Western Europe* (Cambridge, Cambridge University Press 2012).
Lilla, Mark. 'The End of Identity Liberalism', *New York Times* (18 November 2016).
Mair, Peter. *Ruling the Void: The Hollowing of Western Democracy* (London, Verso 2013).
Martin, Cathie and Swank, Duane. *The Political Construction of Business Interests* (New York, Cambridge University Press 2012).
Matthijs, Matthias and Mark Blyth (eds) *The Future of the Euro* (New York, Oxford University Press 2015).
McClaren, Lauren. 'The cultural divide in Europe: Migration, multiculturalism, political trust', *World Politics* 64(2) (2012) pp. 199–241.
Mirowski, P. and Plehwe, D. *The Road from Mont Pèlerin: The Making of the Neoliberal Thought Collective* (Cambridge, MA, Harvard University Press 2009).

Mudde, Cas and Kaltwasser, Cristobal Rovira. *Populism in Europe and the Americas: Threat or Corrective to Democracy* (Cambridge, Cambridge University Press 2012).

Müller, Jan-Werner. *What is Populism?* (Philadelphia, University of Pennsylvania Press 2016).

Peck, J. *Constructions of Neo-Liberal Reason* (Oxford, Oxford University Press 2010).

Piketty, Thomas. *Capital in the Twenty-First Century* (Cambridge, MA, Belknap Press of Harvard University 2014).

Polanyi, Karl. *The Great Transformation: The Political and Economic Origins of Our Time* (Boston, Beacon Press 1944).

Prosser, Thomas. 'Insiders and outsiders on a European scale', *European Journal of Industrial Relations* (2016). Online doi: 10.1177/0959680116668026.

Ruggie, John. 'International regimes, transactions, and change: embedded liberalism in the postwar economic order', *International Organization,* 36(2) (1982) pp. 379–415.

Scharpf, Fritz W. 'Political legitimacy in a non-optimal currency area', in Olaf Cramme and Sara B. Hobolt (eds) *Democratic Politics in a European Union Under Stress* (Oxford, Oxford University Press 2014).

Scharpf, Fritz W. and Schmidt, Vivien A. (eds) *Welfare and Work in the Open Economy*, 2 vols (Oxford, Oxford University Press 2000).

Schmidt, Vivien A. *Democracy in Europe* (Oxford, Oxford University Press 2006).

Schmidt, Vivien A. 'Forgotten democratic legitimacy: "Governing by the rules and ruling by the numbers"', *The Future of the Euro*. In Matthias Matthijs and Mark Blyth (eds) (New York, Oxford University Press 2015).

Schmidt, Vivien A. 'Reinterpreting the rules "by stealth" in times of crisis: The European Central Bank and the European Commission.' *West European Politics* 39(5) (2016a) pp. 1032–52.

Schmidt, Vivien A. 'The Issue Remarkable for its Absence in the Brexit Debate: The Resilience of Neoliberalism in Europe.' Blog for Cambridge University Press (2016b). Available at http://www.cambridgeblog.org/2016/06/the-issue-remarkable-for-its-absence-the-resilience-of-neo-liberalism (Accessed 16 July 2018).

Schmidt, Vivien A. 'Britain-Out and Trump-In: A discursive institutionalist analysis of the British referendum on the EU and the US Presidential Election', *Review of International Political Economy* 24(2) (2017a) pp. 248–69.

Schmidt, Vivien A. 'How should progressives respond to the EU's many crises and challenges to democracy?' *Progressive Post* (Brussels, Foundation for European Progressive Studies 2017b).

Schmidt, Vivien A. and Thatcher, Mark. 'Introduction: The Resilience of Neo-Liberal Ideas' in *Resilient Liberalism in Europe's Political Economy* V. Schmidt and M. Thatcher (eds.) (Cambridge, Cambridge University Press 2013a).

Schmidt, Vivien A. and Thatcher, Mark 'Conclusion: Explaining the resilience of neo-liberal ideas and possible pathways out', *Resilient Liberalism in Europe's Political Economy*. In V. Schmidt and M. Thatcher (eds) (Cambridge, Cambridge University Press 2013b).

Schmidt, Vivien A. and Woll, Cornelia. 'The state: The bête noire of neo-liberalism or its greatest conquest?', *Resilient Liberalism in Europe's Political Economy*. In Vivien A Schmidt and Mark Thatcher (eds) (Cambridge, Cambridge University Press 2013).

Shapiro, Ian. 'What Challenges for Democracy.' Keynote speech at the conference *What Democracy?* Franciso Manuel dos Santos Foundation (Lisbon, 7 October 2016).

Standing, Guy. *The Precariat: The New Dangerous Class* (London, Bloomsbury 2011).

Stiglitz, Joseph. *Globalization and its Discontent* (New York, Norton 2002).

Stiglitz, Joseph. *How a Common Currency Threatens the Future of Europe* (New York, Norton 2016).

Streeck, Wolfgang. *Buying Time: The Delayed Crisis of Democratic Capitalism* (London, Verso 2014).

Thompson, Mark. *Enough Said: What's Gone Wrong with the Language of Politics?* (New York, St. Martin's Press 2016).

CHAPTER 10

# Globalization as a Losing Game? Reforming Social Policies to Address the Malaise of Globalization's Losers

Lorenza Antonucci

In the last two years European countries have been living through a 'Brexit moment', namely an 'eruption of new kinds of social forces, previously excluded, into the political arena in powerful, visceral and protean ways' (Dodds et al. 2017: 3). Such a process is often explained by examining the cultural roots of the new social forces, such as the proximity of 'globalization losers' to authoritarian and populist ideas (see Inglehart and Norris 2016). Cultural differences need, however to be understood as expressions of more profound socio-economic dynamics affecting European societies. European electorates seem to be expressing a social malaise due to their declining economic position and the inadequacy of the current support systems in protecting against the new forms of socio-economic insecurity. While that social malaise is channelled through cultural opposition, the aim of this article is to uncover the socio-economic roots.

The chapter critically examines the divide between globalization's winners and losers, questioning the very existence of the divide. The chapter argues that due to growing precarity and inequality, the game of globalization rather than dividing the population into two distinct groups ('winners' and 'losers') affects various groups across Western societies. The chapter goes on to discuss the failure of current social policies in addressing these processes by revising the assumptions of the social investment paradigm that dominates European social policy-making, encouraging individual investment in higher education and promoting outsiders in European labour markets. The final section of the chapter examines the possibility of reforming social policies to tackle the malaise of globalization by restoring universal principles, updating labour market protection systems and finding a new paradigm for European Union (EU) policy-making centred on addressing inequality. Overall, this contribution aims to encourage a critical revision of the happy marriage between social democracy and liberal principles post-neoliberalism, offering a re-evaluation of how public policy-making should address existing inequalities.

## Problematising the Globalization Winners-versus-Losers Debate

Several commentators refer to a 'working class revolt' that began with Brexit and spread across the European Continent and beyond. According to this proposition, Brexit is the manifestation of anti-establishment sentiment expressed by neglected working class communities through the referendum (Hobolt 2016; Goodwin and Heath 2016). This response is even more evident in the systems of proportional representations in Continental Europe where, as we have seen in the recent French, German and Dutch elections, voters have continued to abandon the two established political blocks that dominated European politics for decades (the Christian Democrats and the Social Democrats) to the benefit of other parties: populist left-wing and extreme right-wing parties, new formations, and anti-establishment movements. The motivations and underlying socio-economic rationale for their political choices are yet to be clarified, but the underlying dissatisfaction with 'the state of things' can hardly be denied.

The analyses of Brexit resuscitated Rodrik's division between globalization 'losers' and globalization 'winners' (1998). The current political events occurring across Europe, be they in the shape of Brexit or the rise of the National Front in France, are often explained using Rodrik's concept of 'globalization losers'. This term indicates the segment of the population which is affected by the increasing competition in global markets and has moved away from traditional politics as a result of its dissatisfaction. According to this idea, those who support anti-establishment parties and those who continue to support traditional parties reflect two sharply divided social constituencies: those who continue to support the 'established' political blocks are the globalization winners, while globalization losers are drifting towards more radical political proposals which aim to change the status quo.

This is certainly a convincing narrative; yet it is also a truism that does not really help us to answer the most compelling issues: understanding who are globalization's 'losers', and deciphering in which respect their differing ideological stances are motivated by their declining material position. Interestingly, liberal thinkers have placed much greater emphasis on the 'cultural' triggers of the social divide, namely the proposition that the move away from established politics is motivated by a distinct cultural identity. The most obvious example is Goodhart (2017), who finds cleavages in British society between ordinary British people who have rooted identities (the 'Somewheres'), and university-educated groups without cultural roots (the 'Anywheres'). Goodhart believes established parties have failed in the way they supported the agendas of Anywheres, instead of listening to the needs of Somewheres. The cultural cleavage stressed by Goodhart – the one between Somewheres and Anywheres – fails to identify the new lines of inequality emerging in society. Goodhart ignores the presence of increasingly precarious workers with high levels of cultural capital, but limited economic resources (Savage et al. 2014). Goodhart also overlooks the fact that the real globalization winners (the global super-rich) are 'Somewheres' and not 'Anywheres': they are bounded to specific localities that they super-gentrify with their presence (Hay and Muller 2010). The cultural hypothesis has some empirical grounding (see also Inglehart and Norris 2016), but as argued by Hopkin (2017) it is analytically misleading to present economics and identity as opposing forces. Voters might justify their political choice in terms of immigration and sovereignty, but 'wage stagnation, reductions in social expenditure, greater economic insecurity and high levels of migration' are, 'part of the same process of economic adjustment' (Hopkin 2017: 475). Gidron and Hall (2017), for example, found support for Brexit and right-wing populism among the white working class emerged as an effect of status anxiety rooted in broader processes of social marginalization, which is both material (due to declining living standards) and cultural (due to declining 'status').

When we move towards the material reasons behind the political drifts occurring in Europe, we realize that they do not concern a small group of globalization losers and the 'left-behind' (Hobolt 2016; Goodwin and Heath 2016), but are widespread and involve ordinary citizens. In our analysis of Brexit, for example, we pay attention to a category of British society that more closely represents the experiences of 'ordinary British people', namely the intermediate class (Antonucci et al. 2017). Rather than representing the voice of the 'left-out', we found that Brexit was the voice of the intermediate classes who had a declining financial position and felt left out rather than angry. This category of voters is a group of considerable sociological significance, labelled 'the squeezed middle': a cohort of ordinary workers with intermediate incomes whose position is rapidly declining. We found this to be true in respect to different areas: education, perceived change in personal finances, emotional feelings, income and class identification.

The corollary of our findings is that 'globalization losers' are not only those at the bottom of the social scale. Our finding mirrors Williams' description of the Trump vote (Williams 2017): many people have conflated 'working class' with 'poor', while the American working class represents, in fact, the elusive disappearing middle class (or ordinary citizens). The sources of socio-economic insecurity to explore are, therefore, those that concern the majority of the population and go beyond explanations centred on identity or culture. Importantly, such a general malaise, which is not limited to the white working class, takes the shape not only of right-wing populism, but of other forms of left-leaning political radicalism and resistance that are too often dismissed as populism in social-democratic circles, even though they express demands in line with classical redistribution.

Even though it is not always articulated in these terms, the existence of populism questions the inequality in the distribution of resources in Western societies after globalization. There are two main processes behind the rise of inequality: a macro historical process and a micro dynamic mediated by welfare state intervention. The historical long-term process is the result of the struggle between capital accumulation and labour in global capitalism described by Wallerstein (2000). The latest evidence is a confirmation that global capitalism is resulting in progressive capital accumulation from the richest parts of society (the progressive rise of wealth inequality described by Piketty [2014]), and is shifting labour gains away from Western countries (the changing global income distribution analysed by Milanovic [2016]). Milanovic's description of the global changes in inequality finds that the progressive rise of the emerging world middle class and the global plutocracy is accompanied by the hollowing out of the Western middle class and the declining position of those at the bottom. In this new dynamic of the world economy, therefore, globalization losers in the Western world are not just the poorest parts of the population, but also the lower middle classes, affected by a change in economic dynamics and a shift in welfare state interventions. This second element (i.e. the change in welfare state interventions), although mentioned by both Piketty and Milanovic, rarely receives in-depth consideration, despite its profound effect in shaping the internal dynamics of redistribution within Western democracies. The rise of the middle classes in Asia should not be interpreted as the inevitable consequence of a shift of wealth from the West to new countries: attention should be focused on the politics of taxation and spending within Europe and their effects on the rise of inequality.

The sense of dissatisfaction with the system found in very different groups could well reflect their increasingly similar material conditions. One of the elements that Gidron and Hall (2017) propose is that behind the lower subjective social status of those who vote for right-wing populism are the declining conditions of work. This calls into question the wave of reforms since the 1990s that have been centred on job creation at the cost of wage negotiation, redistribution and improving working conditions, thus affecting 'ordinary' citizens who are increasingly subject to precarity (Standing 2013). While not all those belonging to the 'squeezed middle' are in irregular and casual contracts, an increasing number of workers are affected by precarity in the broad sense. For example, indicators of precarity that affect the squeezed middle are: the stability of employment income; the ability to find a similar job in the labour market; the benefits paid in case of illness; and the effects of precarity on health and mental well-being. The hidden face of precarity is, according to Gallie et al. (2017), more than the fear of losing a job (which affects the so-called left-out), and involves a perceived threat to valued features of job insecurity such as personal treatment by superiors, and the loss of job characteristics such as skills, task discretion, task interest and pay. Crucially, the authors find such growing job insecurity partially overcomes class differences, in the sense that they affect more than the usual working class groups.

From a political point of view, the general diffusion of precarity demands solutions that speak to the majority and create new coalitions between ordinary citizens and the left-out (be that globalization 'losers' or 'outsiders' in the labour market). New political actors are mobilising widespread frustration experienced by insiders and outsiders in the labour market focusing on the common experience of dissatisfaction, which often involves labour market conditions. Before discussing solutions, we need to review the principles of the current social investment paradigm and identify its limitations.

## The Limitations of Social Investment

The social policy paradigm that has dominated European social policy-making is social investment, which achieved ascendency in the 1990s and became the latest justification for social policy in Europe in times of public cuts and austerity after the crisis. It is also a paradigm that has helped to shape the 'progressive' response to how social policy evolved in times of globalization (Morel et al. 2012). The diagnosis of the current crisis therefore has to include an understanding of the limitations of this paradigm in addressing the roots of the current social malaise described above.

One of the most fascinating aspects of social investment is its continued popularity in European policy circles after austerity. Social policy scholarship has interpreted social policy developments post-2008 as a new unprecedented reconfiguration of the welfare state defined by austerity (Farnsworth and Irving 2015). This period has indeed been characterized by visible welfare cuts in several social policy areas, including health and social security, in particular in the UK (Taylor-Gooby 2013). Empirical studies have also shown that even post-2008 (therefore during austerity times), social investment policies have remained popular in European welfare states (Kvist 2013). The diffusion of social investment during the crisis has been cited as testament to the fact alternatives to austerity are still in place (van Kersbergen et al. 2014). An unanswered question remains how and why the use of social investment has been insufficient in limiting the rise of inequality in Europe.

As rightly suggested by Hopkin, the new 'anti-system' politics in Western democracies 'Shak[es] the existing consensus around economic integration, free markets and liberal values' (2017: 476). Crucially, one of the central purposes of social investment has been precisely to overcome the purely Keynesian paradigm, by mixing redistributive concerns with liberal market principles. While mixing insurance, redistribution and markets has been a longstanding feature of European welfare states (in particular in the Beveridge system) social investment attempted to strike a balance between these elements. The influence of post-neo-liberal ideas can be traced to several places: the idea of investing in human capital, and in reference to equality of opportunity, the relevance to choice and the important role of the market in delivering social provision (Jenson 2012). Some have found problematic ambiguity and have argued that the choice of justifying social expenditure through economic investment would have undermined the very existence of social policy (Barbier 2012). The defenders of social investment stress, instead, that alongside a liberal version of social investment, there is a Scandinavian version that places more emphasis on public investment for education and training – as well as activation measures and investments in getting workers back into the labour market; and childcare (Bonoli 2009). While this distinction might be relevant when looking at the empirical applications of social investment, in this instance, I am interested in discussing the principles underlying social investment and their effects on European social policy-making.

## Encouraging Private Investment in Higher Education

A core limitation of social investment policies is the nexus between higher education and labour market policies, which has affected young people in particular. Since the early 2000s European youth policies have been designed around the strategy of investing in higher education (HE) from a human capital approach (e.g. for the EU Youth Strategy 2008–12) (see Bessant and Watts 2014). Participation in HE reached its peak before the crisis and has remained stable since, but has not contributed to reducing inequalities (Antonucci 2016).

Social investment policies have wrongly assumed that a supply-side focus would automatically smooth youth transitions to the labour market, in particular for young graduates (Keep and Mayhew 2010). In reality, with the development of higher qualifications, the value of lower qualifications has declined. Despite having the most educated labour force in its history, the EU is increasingly affected by the issue of graduate unemployment and underemployment, with graduates taking up jobs that do not require a degree. Social investment has used the expansion of higher education as an economic panacea, but this expansion has resulted in a decline in the economic value of qualifications in the labour market (Keep 2012). This reality does not deprive higher education of its social value, but, rather, highlights that the policy assumptions made about the automatic smoothing effects of degrees in the labour market need to be revisited. Crucially, the social investment paradigm has placed an emphasis on higher education as a form of investment in human capital (see Nelson and Stephens 2012), not as a path with a social value per se, therefore undermining its social function.

Social investment policies also cannot begin to address another problem that is becoming increasingly visible in the public domain: making young people and their families take on (privately) the costs of this expensive investment, thereby increasing inequalities among young people *through* higher education. Social investment policies in HE have indeed focused on macro HE spending (Nelson and Stephens 2012), neglecting the stratification effects of shifting towards individual funding (Antonucci 2016). As shown by Piketty (2014), student funding is a crucial mechanism to reinforce existing wealth inequalities and reproduce them across generations. During their mass expansion, HE policies have progressively shifted the focus to private forms of welfare support for young people under the principle that the previous system of student support reserved for the elite would have been economically unsustainable in a higher education system for the masses (Trow 2006). So, paradoxically, with the move of HE from the elite to the masses, which has meant access for young people from lower socio-economic backgrounds, the systems of student support have become less generous in their public investment and increasingly based on private investment.

Several strategies have been developed in Europe to sustain the mass expansion and maintain a financially sustainable system, such as providing loans and asking students to pay fees (Salmi and Haptman 2006). This is in line with the idea in the new social investment state that it is not just the responsibility of the state to provide welfare, but the family and the market also need to contribute. The discussion of HE policies by the social investment literature reflects the focus on private investment by employing a human capital approach, which seeks to encourage the state to invest in institutions offering HE, but neglects the function of public spending on individuals in the form of student support (Nelson and Stephens 2012). As my cross-national research on inequality in higher education demonstrates, the privatization of student funding results in several issues affecting young people at university and their families (even in the Scandinavian version of social investment that is Sweden): use of private loans via the bank while in HE, mental well-being issues due to the difficulty of facing everyday costs, student housing issues, and a divide between those who can afford a comfortable student experience and those who struggle while in HE (Antonucci et al. 2016). In the United States, the burden of students on their parents affects the majority, 'except in the case of children of the rich, who gain a huge head start' (Hacker 2011: 34). Similarly, the increasing private contributions demanded of students in Europe affect young people from low and intermediate socio-economic backgrounds, leaving a minority of young people from upper socio-economic backgrounds benefiting from the system – which serves to contribute to increasing inequalities via higher education (Antonucci 2016).

## Overcoming the Insider–Outsider Divide

The social investment literature has identified an inevitable division between insiders and outsiders in the labour market – a division which has shaped the subsequent reforms of labour market protection systems. According to this idea the tertiarization of the employment structure, the education revolution and the feminization of the workforce created a division between those who access standard jobs, and those who can access non-standard jobs (Emmenegger et al. 2012: 28–9). Emmenegger et al. (2012) identify a division between the low-skilled, who are in precarious jobs, and are therefore excluded from labour market participation, and high-skilled people who are labour market insiders and whose labour market needs are fully protected. This division fails to account for many current experiences of young graduates who remain outside labour market protection systems, despite having a high level of skills (see Murgia and Poggio 2014). It also neglects the existence of 'mid-siders', who are in precarious jobs and have features in common with the outsiders: they are in (very) low-paid jobs, have no job protection, and experience sporadic periods of unemployment (Jessoula et al. 2010).

More profoundly, social policy reforms have been developed in an attempt to limit the insider–outsider division by reducing the forms of social protection for insiders; however, these reforms have, in reality increased rather than tackled the existence of precarious jobs (ibid.). Clegg (2008) described a series of reforms that have reduced protection in the labour market with the idea of reducing insider protection: cost containment (consisting of cutting the level and duration of benefits and making eligibility criteria stricter); recalibration, with more focus on those with atypical work histories, accompanied by declining protection for those with a long work history; and activation, which has focused on increasing investment in training, as well as implementing stricter job-search procedures, including sanctions. As labour market conditions have sharply deteriorated in recent years, scholars have started to overcome the dichotomy between labour market insiders and outsiders. As correctly indicated by Keune, this division is analytically unhelpful: it does not capture the fact that 'differences between groups of workers are more a matter of degree' and is based on a, 'mistaken belief that the interests of insiders and outsiders necessarily differ' (2015: 51). The diffusion of precarity might create common experiences across different social groups. Marx and Starke (2017) have shown the new politics of inequality surpass the insider–outsider division, as demonstrated by the recent support of the German Social-democratic party to 'outsider-friendly' policies. As stated by Keune: 'The fate of the two groups is interrelated and employers use precarious workers to put pressure on the wages and conditions of standard employees' (2015b: 396). Recent evidence (see also Gallie et al. 2017) shows the widespread diffusion of precarity asks for shared policy solutions that also speak to previously considered outsiders in the labour market and overcome this division altogether.

Finally, another important effect of social investment on social protection has been to shift resources from cash transfers to provision of services, resulting in negative effects on poverty (Cantillon 2012; Nolan 2013). Due to the idea that outsiders had to become insiders with more training, social policy has devoted fewer resources to sustaining the living standards of the poorest parts of the population. Since the crisis, even in the EU's most developed welfare states, minimum income protection systems for work-poor households with children have fallen short compared to the poverty threshold (defined as 60 per cent of the equalized median household income) (Cantillon et al. 2015). Social protection systems have focused on job growth since the 1990s, and have neglected the importance of direct cash redistribution (Marx 2013). As an effect of those changes in protection systems, precarity is now widely diffused among those in work, touching larger segments of the population than only the 'left-behind'.

## The Way Forward for Social Democracy

Social policies are crucial instruments for social democracy, both in their capacity for triggering political support and for the transformative effects they potentially have in European societies. In this section I will review three areas of reform that could overcome the limitations of the current progressive paradigm: the popularity of universal principles in social policy-making; the necessity of updating labour market protection systems; and the need to have a new paradigm for social policy interventions that overcomes both austerity and the limitations of social investment, able to tackle the new inequalities.

### Restoring Universal Principles

Looking at the growing mismatch between European lives and European policies described above, it is not hard to understand why a basic income strategy, as a universal and unconditional form of support, is becoming so appealing. A basic income policy would offer direct cash and its unconditionality would break the costly (and often counterproductive) orientation in our social protection systems towards means-testing. A basic income policy would partially address the gaps of the current system of social protection by offering support for 'the precariat', namely providing a safety net for those who experience frequent spells of unemployment in current precarious labour markets (Standing 2011).

Basic income activists tend to portray the basic income as an inherently positive policy strategy (Standing 2017). This is not always the case. For example, the Silicon Valley version of a basic income, which has gained momentum in venture-capital circles, promotes an idea of welfare without the welfare state that risks reinforcing existing inequalities. The venture-capitalist initiative 'Y Combinator' is working to create a market-based basic income measure. This private version of a basic income without a welfare state, however, does not allow the exploitation of a key feature of a basic income strategy: its capacity to de-commodify people's lives, namely to make people able to survive without having to rely on the market.

Furthermore, a basic income policy will not directly address one of the main drivers of social exclusion: in-work poverty generated by the declining level of wages. One of its major caveats is that it does not deal with labour market failures, such as the presence of low wages. A basic income policy which is not combined with a strategy to 'make work pay' would end up using public resources to absorb social externalities created by the market, such as falling wages. A basic income strategy cannot be considered an all-embracing strategy for issues of inequality and poverty as Standing (2017) assumes, and other ad hoc measures should be implemented to address the declining condition of people in the labour force.

Despite the many weaknesses of this instrument (see the persuasive Sage and Diamond 2017), the basic income has some merits. First of all, it is indicative that, as reported by recent European-wide (Neopolis 2017) and British (Ipsos Mori 2017) surveys, the majority of individuals have at least some familiarity with the concept of basic income, and the majority of them also state that they would vote in favour of its implementation. The motivation behind the support for a basic income challenges one of the most persistent mantras in social policy and political circles to have emerged in recent years: the idea that, after New Labour, Europeans have abandoned support for universal provision in favour of means-tested provisions, in particular in the area of unemployment benefits (see Deeming 2015; van Oorschot 2002). According to the respondents of the European study (Neopolis 2017), the top three effects of basic income would be the possibility of reducing anxiety about basic financing needs, the creation of more equality of opportunity, and the encouragement of independence and self-responsibility. Individuals remain in favour of some forms of conditionality: when asked about their strongest fears in relation to basic income, the majority of respondents agree with the possibility that it could encourage people to stop working, while two popular reasons to be against are the idea that foreigners might take advantage, and the belief that the system would be impossible to finance. The financing issue comes up in the research on basic income by Ipsos Mori (2017) showing widespread support that decreases substantially if it is to be financed by raising taxes. For these reasons, we could think about basic income as a proposal that could be implemented for categories of people that society recognizes should not have to work, such as students. Considering the issues of higher education costs I presented above, the idea of a basic student income (Antonucci 2016) could be considered appealing. Overall, the idea of basic income challenges dogmas that pervade European social policy, not least the popularity of means-testing, and the assumption that public support favours means-testing (Taylor-Gooby 2012).

## Updating Labour Market Protection

Alongside basic income, another relevant policy discussion concerns the reforms of labour market protection systems, under the assumption that current systems are rigid and unable to cope with the flexible nature of contemporary labour markets.

An appealing proposal in European social policy has been creating Individual Activity Accounts (IAAs) for each new entrant into the labour market, where points are earned on the basis of the type of job and are fully portable across sectors and jobs (Pisany-Ferri 2015). According to this scheme, rights and benefits would be attached to individuals, not to companies or employment status. The points accumulated could be 'spent' across various areas of welfare provision, for example in receiving training or for pension benefits. The flexibility and freedom to choose are certainly appealing features of this proposal. Such individual-based systems would not exploit the benefits of a collective social protection system which offer 'risk pooling' across generations and groups of workers. The current limitations of labour market protection systems lie not only in their rigid organization, but in how the collectivist principle has not created new lines of solidarity relevant to our contemporary societies based on gender, age and other dimensions.

A reformed system could instead take the shape of a contemporary version of Bismarck's *kasse*, namely a scheme aimed at pooling resources from employers and workers. These modern versions of *kasse* should be dedicated to precarious workers, and able to cover short-term spells of unemployment and transitions from education to work. These forms of labour market protection are intended for those in work and in temporary contracts who face spells of unemployment and irregular patterns of income. Employers and those with more regular working patterns should contribute to the funding of those systems in order to ensure 'risk-pooling'. The mechanism of funding such systems is crucial in order to redefine the respective contributions of work and capital in contemporary global capitalism.

Many commentators see the current informatization and digitization of the economy and the passage to the fourth industrial revolution as roots of very profound changes in work (Mason 2015). The ineluctability of the fourth industrial revolution, and its implications for work, is taken for granted even among left-wing figures, who are now proposing measures to manage (rather than to oppose) such labour market evolutions.[1] Initiatives regarding the 'revenues' of the new labour market protection systems are already starting to be proposed across Europe. For example, there is a discussion of a so-called 'tax on robots' involving taxes that are designed to obtain a societal revenue from companies which are IT-intensive and rely heavily on automation. These ideas have been put forward in a recent recommendation by the European Parliament (European Parliament 2016), and are spreading across Austria and France, though they are in an embryonic stage.[2] The modern *kasse* systems could be funded by putting a tax on automation which socializes the benefits made by companies that use automated production systems.

## A New Paradigm for EU Social Policy

The reforms discussed involve not only nation-states, but also the complex governance of EU social policy in its powerful instruments (i.e. the European Semester) and competing policy paradigms (austerity and social investment). This does not mean that these reforms should occur at the European level – and setting up European-wide policies in this realm is unattainable at the moment – but that national social policies carry an inevitable European dimension.

Regarding the instruments, it is important to stress that during the crisis, the EU developed powerful policy tools to reform national social policies, such as the European Semester. The European Semester can be defined as a cycle of economic, fiscal and policy co-ordination that has been reinforced following the economic crisis. The European Semester has strengthened the process of tightening and subsuming social policy to economic objectives focused on competitiveness by transferring areas previously under 'social policy' into 'economic governance' (Crespy and Meinz 2015: 200). This is evident when looking at the example of labour market policies, and specifically wage-setting, which, even if formally excluded, is covered in the European Semester because of its competence in economic governance. As Bekker and Klosse point out, although the EU has no direct competence in matters related to pay, nominal unit labour costs are used as indicators to measure country performance. Through specific recommendations on economic issues, the EU can greatly influence countries' social policies, in particular regarding wage-setting systems (Bekker and Klosse 2013).

The current debate on the effects of the European Semester on European social policy is open-ended. Regarding competing policy paradigms, some authors argue that the social policy targets (reduction of poverty and social exclusion) and the social investment agenda are inevitably affected by the strict fiscal discipline and budget rules (De la Porte and Heins 2015), while others find that recently the European Semester has become more social (Zeitlein and Vanherke 2018). For some scholars the national reforms pushed through the European Semester are promoting austerity and neo-liberalism (Crespy and Vanheuverzwijn 2017), while others find that the Semester embodies and puts forward the social investment paradigm (Bekker 2017). The influence on the EU is never considered to go beyond the social investment paradigm (when diverging from the neo-liberal and austerity paradigms). If the EU approach is influenced by the social investment paradigm, it is deeply affected by the limitations of social investment discussed above, in particular the neglect of inequality. This is evident when analysing the most recent attempts at reforming the European Semester and socialising it through a new Pillar of Social Rights (European Commission 2016, 2017). The language used in this Pillar is not new and reproduces the social investment paradigm, referring to equal opportunities and access to the labour market, dynamic labour market and fair working conditions, and social protection and inclusion. In other words, social inequalities are excluded by the EU policy-making infrastructure, despite the effects of economic policies on social inequalities.

## Conclusion

If globalization is a 'losing game', the losers are not just a small group of the 'left-behind'. Even those who were supposed to win from globalization – the educated and intermediate classes – are affected by growing inequality and precarity. Separated by the so-called cultural divide, old and young, insiders and outsiders, and the high- and low-skilled in reality meet in their increasingly challenging material conditions; for this reason both groups are moving away from the established political blocks of European policies (Christian democracy and social democracy). In this sense the focus on the cultural divide behind the Brexit effect, which is the subject of most public debates on this issue, hinders the potential of creating cross-societal coalitions to address the declining material conditions of vast segments of European populations.

Public policies, which are crucial in shaping the material conditions of individuals, seem unable to respond in their current form despite the potential window of opportunity that 2008 opened up to recalibrate economic and social policy. Some core flagships of the social investment paradigm have consisted in enhanced social mobility, upskilling and increasing the participation of younger generations in education. The limitations (if not contradictions) of these policies are visible to all: graduate unemployment and underemployment, growing inequalities through higher education, and the most educated generation in Europe at risk of becoming the 'lost generation'. The turn towards means-testing, the disappearing role of cash transfers, and the lack of policies addressing the realities at work of both outsiders and insiders have weakened social bonds in European societies.

The current realities of the so-called European lost generation and the angry working class pose an important dilemma for social democracy; if austerity cannot deliver any long-term solution, social investment does not seem well equipped to address entrenched inequalities either. The appeal of the basic income across Europe tells us there is a profound need to restore the universal principle of creating bonds among different social groups. In its imperfect (and in all probably unrealistic) nature, basic income helps to challenge the dogma of the spread of 'means-testing' in contemporary social policy. The most pivotal area of reform for social democracy is beyond the basic income; it concerns updating labour market protection systems which, paraphrasing Esping-Andersen (1999), are increasingly ineffective as they mirror a society that no longer exists. Finally, national policy reforms would be limited in scope if they were not accompanied by profound reform of EU social policies, in the procedures of social policy-making (European Semester), as well as redefinition of the dominant policy paradigms (austerity and social investment).

Several years ago, Taylor-Gooby (2012) identified a Left Trilemma affecting European social democracy: the difficulty of finding plausible responses to the economic crisis, developing generous and inclusive social policies, and addressing issues relevant to public opinion in order to be elected. If the current social malaise was channelled and articulated through support for reformed welfare state intervention, as appears increasingly possible, the 'Left Trilemma' (Taylor-Gooby 2012) would become the usual European social democracy dilemma: finding a way to address social inequalities while taking into account major budgetary constraints.

## Notes

1. See, for example, the current work on these topics inside the British Labour Party (e.g. Labour List (2016) http://labourlist.org/2016/11/corbyn-tell-business-well-use-the-state-to-power-new-industrial-revolution/).
2. For example, the Machine Tax, or *Maschinensteuer*, is currently discussed in Austria and a tax on robot to fund Universal Basic Income was included in the agenda of Benoit Hamon, the candidate of the Socialist Party at the latest French presidential elections.

## References

Antonucci L, Horvath L, Kutyski Y. and A Krouwel. 'The malaise of the squeezed middle: Challenging the narrative of the left behind Brexiter', *Competition and Change, Special Issue: Brexit: a year later*, 21(3) (2017) pp. 211–29.

Antonucci, L. *Student Lives in Crisis. Deepening Inequality in times of Austerity* (Bristol, Policy Press 2016).

Barbier, J. C. 'Social investment, a problematic concept with an ambiguous past: A comment on Anton Hemerijck', *Sociologica* 1(2012) (2012) 1–11.

Bekker, S. 'Flexicurity in the European Semester: still a relevant policy concept?' *Journal of European Public Policy* 25(2) (2017).

Bekker, S. and Klosse, S. 'EU governance of economic and social policies: chances and challenges for social Europe', *European Journal of Social Law* 2 (2013) pp. 103–20.

Bessant, J. and Watts, R.W. '"Cruel optimism": a southern theory perspective on the European Union's Youth Strategy, 2008–12', *International Journal of Adolescence and Youth* 19(Suppl. 1) (2014) pp. 125–40.

Bonoli G. 'Varieties of social investment in labour market policy', in Morel N., Palier B. and Palme J. (eds) *What Future for Social Investment?* (Stockholm, Institute for Futures Studies 2009) pp. 55–66.

Cantillon B. and Van Lancker W. 'Three shortcomings of the social investment perspective', *Social Policy and Society* Vol. 12(4) (2013) pp. 553–64.

Cantillon, B, Collado, D. and Van Mechelen, N. 'The end of decent social protection for the poor? The dynamics of low wages, minimum income packages and median household incomes'. Discussion Paper No. 15/03, Herman Deleeck Centre for Social Policy, University of Antwerp (2015).

Clegg, D. 'Continental drift: On unemployment policy change in Bismarckian welfare states', in Palier, B. and M. Claude (eds) *Reforming the Bismarckian Welfare Systems* (Oxford, Wiley 2009) pp. 62–81.

Crespy, A. and Menz, G. (eds) *Social Policy and the Euro Crisis: Quo Vadis Social Europe* (Houndmills, Palgrave Macmillan 2015).

Crespy, A. and Vanheuverzwijn, P. What 'Brussels' means by structural reforms: empty signifier or constructive ambiguity? *Comparative European Politics* (1) (2017) pp. 1–20.

de la Porte, C. and Heins, E. 'A new era of European integration? governance of labour market and social policy since the sovereign debt crisis', *Comparative European Politics* 13(1) (2015) pp. 8–28.

Deeming, Christopher. 'Foundations of the workfare state: reflections on the political transformation of the welfare state in Britain', *Social Policy and Administration* 49(7) (2015) pp. 862–86.

Dodd, N., Lamont, M. and Savage, M. Introduction to BJS special issue. *The British Journal of Sociology* 68(1) (2017) pp. 3–10.

Emmenegger, P., Häusermann, S., Palier, B. and Seeleib-Kaiser, S. (eds) *The Age of Dualization: the changing face of inequality in deindustrializing societies* (Oxford, Oxford University Press 2012).

Esping-Andersen, Gøsta. *Social Foundations of Post-industrial Economies* (Oxford New York, Oxford University Press 1999).

European Commission. 'Communication from the Commission to the European Parliament, the Council, the European Economic and Social Committee and the Committee of the Regions: Launching a Consultation on a European Pillar of Social Rights', COM (2016) 127 final.

European Commission. 'Commission recommendation of 26.4.2017 on the European Pillar of Social Rights', COM (2017) 2600 final.

European Parliament. 'Draft report with recommendations to the Commission on Civil Law Rules on Robotics' (2015/2103(INL) (2016).

Farnsworth, K. and Z. Irving (eds) *Social Policy in Times of Austerity: Global Economic Crisis and the Politics of Welfare* (Bristol, Policy Press 2015).

Gallie, D., Felstead, A., Green, F. Inanc, H. 'The hidden face of job insecurity', *Work, Employment and Society* 31(1) (2017) pp. 36–53.

Gidron, N. and Hall, P. A. 'The politics of social status: economic and cultural roots of the populist right', *The British Journal of Sociology* 68(1) (2017) p. 557.

Goodhart D. *The Road to Somewhere: The Populist Revolt and the Future of Politics* (London, C. Hurst & Co. 2017).

Goodwin M. J. and Heath O. 'The 2016 Referendum, Brexit and the left behind: an aggregate level analysis of the result', *The Political Quarterly* 87(3) (2016) pp. 323–32.

Hacker, J. S. 'The institutional foundations of middle-class democracy' (London, Policy Network 2011). Available at http://www.policy-network.net/pno_detail.aspx?ID=3998&title=The+institutional+foundations+of+middle-class+democracy (Accessed 16 July 2018).

Hay, I. and Muller, S. '"That tiny, stratospheric apex that owns most of the world"- Exploring geographies of the super-rich', *Geographical Research* 50(1) (2012) pp. 75-88.

Hobolt, S. B. 'The Brexit vote: A divided nation, a divided continent', *Journal of European Public Policy* 23(9) (2016) pp. 1259-77.

Hopkin, J. 'When Polanyi met Farage: Market fundamentalism, economic nationalism, and Britain's exit from the European Union', *British Journal of Politics and International Relations* 19(3) (2017) pp. 465-78.

Inglehart, Ronald and Norris, Pippa. 'Trump, Brexit, and the Rise of Populism: Economic Have-Nots and Cultural Backlash (29 July 2016). HKS Working Paper No. RWP16-026. Available at: https://ssrn.com/abstract=2818659 (Accessed 16 July 2018).

Ipsos Mori. 'Half of UK adults would support universal basic income in principle' (2017). Available at https://www.ipsos.com/ipsos-mori/en-uk/half-uk-adults-would-support-universal-basic-income-principle (Accessed 16 July 2018).

Jenson, J. 'Redesigning citizenship regimes after neoliberalism: moving towards social investment', in N. Morel, B. Palier and J. Palme (eds) *Towards a Social Investment Welfare State? Ideas, Policies and Challenges* (Bristol, Policy Press 2012) pp. 61-87.

Jessoula, M., Graziano, P. and Madama, I. '"Selective flexicurity" in segmented labour markets: the case of Italian "mid-siders"', *Journal of Social Policy* 39(4) (2010) pp. 561-83.

Keep, E. *Youth Transitions, the Labour Market and Entry into Employment: Some Reflections and Questions* (Cardiff, Skope 2012).

Keep, E. and Mayhew, K. 'Moving beyond skills as a social and economic panacea', *Work, Employment and Society* 24(3) (2010) pp. 565-77.

Keune, M. 'Shaping the future of industrial relations in the EU: Ideas, paradoxes and drivers of change', *International Labour Review* 154(1) (2015a) pp. 55.

Keune, M. 'Trade unions, precarious work and dualization in Europe', in Eichhorst, W. and Marx, P. (eds) *Non-Standard Employment in Post-Industrial Labour Markets: An Occupational Perspective* (Cheltenham, Edward Elgar 2015b) pp. 378, 396.

Kvist, J. 'The post-crisis European social model: developing or dismantling social investments?', *Journal of International and Comparative Social Policy* 29(1) (2013) pp. 91-107.

Marx, I. 'Why direct income redistribution matters if we are really concerned with reducing poverty', *Intereconomics: Review of European Economic Policy*, 48(6) (2013) pp. 350-6.

Marx, P. and P. Starke. 'Dualiziation as destiny? The political economy of the German minimum wage reform', *Politics & Society* 45(4) (2017) pp. 559-84.

Mason, P. *Post-capitalism. A Guide to Our Future* (London, Allen Lane 2015).
Milanovic, B. *Global Inequality: a new approach for the age of globalization* (Cambridge, MA, Harvard University Press 2016).
Morel, N., Palier, B. and Palme, J. (eds) *Towards a Social Investment Welfare State? Ideas, Policies and Challenges* (Bristol, Policy Press 2012).
Murgia, A. and Poggio, B. 'At risk of deskilling and trapped by passion: a picture of pre-carious highly-educated young workers in Italy, Spain and the United Kingdom', in. Antonucci, L., Hamilton, M. and Roberts, S. (eds) *Young People and Social Policy in Europe. Dealing with Risk, Inequality and Precarity in Times of Crisis* (Basingstoke, Palgrave Macmillan 2014) pp. 62–86.
Nelson, M. and Stephens, J. D. 'Do social investment policies produce more and better jobs?', in Morel, N., Palier, B. and Palme, J. (eds) *Towards a Social Investment Welfare State? Ideas, Policies and Challenges* (Bristol, Policy Press 2012) pp. 205–34.
Neopolis. 'What do Europeans Think About Basic Income?' (2017). Available at https://www.neopolis.network/wp-content/uploads/basic_income_survey_2017.pdf (Accessed 16 July 2018).
Nolan, B. 'What use is "social investment"?' *Journal of European Social Policy* 23(5) (2013) pp. 459–68.
Piketty, T. *Capital in the Twenty-First Century* (Oxford, Oxford University Press 2014).
Pisany-Ferri, J. 'Social Benefits In The Age of Uber' (2015). Available at http://www.socialeurope.eu/2015/11/social-benefits-in-the-age-of-uber/ (Accessed 16 July 2018).
Rodrik, D. 'Globalization, social conflict and economic growth', *World Economy* 21(2) (1998) pp. 143–58.
Sage, D. and Diamond, P. *Europe's New Social Reality: The Case Against Universal Basic Income* (London, Policy Network 2017).
Salmi, J. and Hauptman, A. M. 'Innovations in tertiary education financing: A comparative evaluation of allocation mechanisms'. Education Working Paper: forms and phases of higher education in modern societies since WWII, Washington, DC: The World Bank (2006).
Savage, M., Devine, F., Cunningham, N., Taylor, M., Li, Y., Hjellbrekke, J., Le Roux, B., Friedman, S. and Miles, A. 'A new model of social class? Findings from the BBC's Great British Class Survey experiment', *Sociology* 47(2) (2013) pp. 219–50.
Standing, G. *The Precariat. The New Dangerous Class* (New York, Bloomsbury 2011).
Standing, G. *Basic Income: And how we can make it happen* (London, Penguin Random House 2017).
Taylor-Gooby, P. *A Left Trilemma: Progressive public policy in the age of austerity* (London, Policy Network 2012).
Trow, M. 'Reflections on the transition from elite to mass to universal', in J. F. Forest and P. Altbach (eds) *International Handbook of Higher Education* (New York, Springer 2006) pp. 243–80.

van Kersbergen, K., Vis, B. and Hemerijck, A. 'The great recession and welfare state reform: Is retrenchment really the only game left in town?' *Social Policy and Administration* 48(4) (2014) pp. 883–904.

van Oorschot, W. J. H. 'Targeting welfare: on the functions and dysfunctions of means-testing in social policy', in Townsend, P. and Gorden, D. (eds) *World Poverty: new policies to defeat an old enemy* (New York, Springer 2002) pp. 171–93.

Wallerstein, I. 'Globalization or the age of transition? A long-term view of the trajectory of the world system', *International Sociology* 15(2) (2000) pp. 251–67.

Williams, J. *White Working Class* (Cambridge, Harvard Business Review Press 2017).

Zeitlein, J. and Vanherke, B. (2018) 'Socializing the European Semester: EU social and economic policy co-ordination in crisis and beyond', *Journal of European Public Policy* 25(2) Online First.

CHAPTER 11

# Social Investment Beyond Lip-Service

Anton Hemerijck and Robin Huguenot-Noel

## Introduction

Ten years after the first economic crisis of twenty-first century capitalism, Europe seems to have passed the nadir of the Great Recession, unleashed by the 2008 global downturn. Time to count our blessings: a rerun of the Great Depression has been avoided and recovery is under way. The jury is still out on whether economic and employment growth will return to pre-crisis levels. Unemployment remains very high, especially in the economies most heavily scarred by the euro crisis, such as Greece, Spain and Italy. The political aftershocks of the Great Recession, from the rise of populism and Brexit to the nationalist authoritarian turns in Hungary and Poland, may still blur the horizon of nascent growth. Moreover, given that the European Union (EU) has failed to effectively uphold its commitment, anchored in the treaties, to foster economic prosperity and social protection in unison both within and between the member states, anti-globalization and national welfare chauvinist sentiments have risen significantly.

Deep economic crises are moments of political truth. They expose the strengths and weaknesses of extant policy repertoires and their underlying causal beliefs and normative mind-sets. In a Popperian fashion, crises and failures encourage fresh thinking about policy and governance. In the aftermath of both the Great Depression of the 1930s and the Great Stagflation of the 1970s, policy paradigms were transformed in fundamental ways. The Great Depression that spilled out into World War II gave rise to the establishment of the Keynesian-Beveridge welfare state after 1945. A quarter century later, the Great Stagflation crisis inspired the neoliberal critique of the welfare state of the 1970s and 1980s. After 2007, practically overnight, a number of widely cherished laissez-faire dogmas were taken off the shelf. Initially, immediate crisis management focused on the financial sector by bailing out overly-indebted banks. Central banks were pressed to amass new functions, including liquidity and credit enhancing interventions while at the same time becoming lenders of last resort. In the process, they also gained public responsibilities in maintaining general financial stability far beyond the narrow remit of inflation targeting so as to maintain price stability.

For decades, growth strategies were pursued on the assumption of the 'efficient-markets hypothesis', the inference that deviations from equilibrium values cannot last for long. With the onslaught of the crisis, the efficient-market hypothesis' fall from grace inspired new thinking and policy action in relation to the financial system. Surprisingly, financial and monetary policy learning has had little to no effect on the still hegemonic neoliberal critique of the welfare state, in spite of a crisis of mass (youth) unemployment not seen since the Great Depression. Whilst the economic teachings of John Maynard Keynes on volatile open capital markets have been re-habilitated, his ideas, and those of William Beveridge, on full employment and the need for inclusive social security 'buffers' for economic stabilization and household-income consumption-smoothing and poverty alleviation in times of recession, have yet to be rekindled. To wit, the neoliberal critique of the welfare state, revolving around social insurance moral hazard, unemployment hysteresis, and employment policy deadweight loss, experienced a strong comeback with the Eurozone fallout of the global financial crisis. Being interviewed by the *Wall Street Journal* at the height of the euro crisis in early 2012, Mario Draghi, President of the European Central Bank (ECB), declared the 'European social model' as 'long gone'. A year later, speaking at the World Economic Forum in Davos on 5 January 2013, German Chancellor Angela Merkel likewise dramatized the European predicament, by underscoring that the crisis-prone continent, covering '7 per cent of the world population', while making up for 'almost 25 per cent of global GDP (...) 'accounts for nearly 50 per cent of global social spending', thus intimating that Europe's generous welfare state commitment inescapably undermines competitiveness (Merkel 2013).

The Great Recession has brought Europe and the EU to a new crossroads. In shadow of high unemployment and rising inequality, more than ever the social dimension will assume pride of place in political debates. What kind of welfare state is effective and legitimate in the aftermath of the crisis under the radically altered economic, social, demographic conditions of the twenty-first century? Has globalization gone too far? Can an assertive social investment agenda counter the protectionist-populist backlash? Will the austerity reflex continue to be jeopardized by international joint-decision traps, intensifying downward welfare competition between 'socio-economic' models? These urgent questions we address in this chapter. We proceed in three steps. Firstly, Section 2 subjects the hypotheses of 'trade-offs' between equity and efficiency, social spending and competitiveness, to the empirical scrutiny of key macroeconomic indicators. After having disproved these intuitively appealing axiomatic propositions, Section 3 seeks out the micro-economic logic and the meso-level institutional mechanisms behind the well-being returns of social investment reform. By so doing, we also confront the academic critique of social investment, suggesting 'capacitating' social services, a term coined by Charles Sabel (2012), in early childhood education and care (ECEC) and active labour market policy (ALMP) are plagued by so-called 'Matthew Effects' with the upper and middle classes disproportionately benefiting from social investment reform. The conclusion, Section 4, reflects on the ambiguous politics of social investment that lay behind the Third Way between the mid-1990s and mid-2000s. While Wim Kok, Tony Blair, Poul Nyrup Rasmussen, Gerhard Schroeder, Antonio Guterres, and Jose Luis Zapatero prepared the ground for social investment welfare recalibration, they never really challenged, in the name of social investment, the pro-cyclical 'default' policy theory of balanced budgets, fixed exchange rates, (labour) market liberalization and welfare retrenchment inherited from the neoliberal era since this would go against the governance design of the Single Market and EMU. Very often, concerns about inequality, poverty and mass (youth-)unemployment, as well as their scarring effects on future employment opportunities for youngsters and labour market outsiders, aggregate productivity gains and real economic growth, were subordinated to pro-cyclical austerity welfare reform. The Third-Way discrepancy between the primacy of budgetary equilibrium in hard times and social investment when the economy expands, we conclude, urgently needs to be resolved in favour of the latter growing to its full potential for both economic and political reasons, including the very survival of modern social democracy in the EU.

## Beyond Trade-Offs and Trilemmas

Over the past 40 years, essentially since the 1970's oil shocks, the relationship between economic prosperity and social protection has predominantly been couched in terms of tough trade-offs and deep trilemmas, indicating intuitively appealing common-sense limits to welfare provision in advanced market economies. In the mid-1970s, the American economist Arthur Okun came to formulate a 'big trade-off' between equality and efficiency (Okun 1975). Okun argued that generous welfare states, employed as a political instrument to reduce inequality and relative poverty, harm economic growth by producing all kinds of income and labour market distortions (e.g. through the impact of progressive taxation). In the early 1990s, the OECD received a mandate to examine the labour market performance of its member countries. The *OECD Jobs Study*, published in 1994, exposed the 'dark side' of double-digit unemployment of many of its West European members at the time. Hovering around 10 per cent with few signs of improvement, unemployment rates in France, Germany, and Italy were twice as high as in the United States while their employment rates were about 12 points below that of the United States. In a similar vein to Okun, the OECD economists singled out downward wage rigidity (linked, e.g. to minimum wage legislation) as the main obstacle to full employment. They also pointed out strong 'insider–outsider' cleavages curtailing employment opportunities for the young, women, the old, and the low-skilled. The central policy recommendations that followed naturally for the *OECD Jobs Study* included wage bargaining decentralization, lowering minimum wages, reducing non-wage labour costs, restricting the duration of unemployment insurance, privatising pensions, lowering taxes, and loosening employment protection, so as to help Western European economies to achieve US-level's of employment. The inevitable price to pay to improve labour market allocation and 'make work pay' was to attenuate the generosity of the welfare state and thus allow for greater wage and income inequality (OECD 1994, 1997).

By the late 1990s, the political economists, Torben Iversen and Ann Wren, moving away from a logic of trade-offs, figured that advanced European welfare states were increasingly faced with a tragic predicament, which they coined the 'trilemma of the social service economy' (Iversen and Wren 1998; Wren 2017). The gist of their trilemma is that, with the shift from an industrial to a service economy against a background of accelerating economic internationalization, it was becoming inherently more difficult for welfare states to simultaneously attain the triple aspiration of earnings equality, employment growth, and budgetary prudence. Any government may pursue any two of these goals, but no longer all three at the same time. Within a tight budgetary framework, private employment growth can only be accomplished at the expense of higher wage inequality. If wage equality remains a primary objective, employment growth can be generated only through the public sector, at a cost of higher taxes, public borrowing, debt or deficits. And as international competition and technological innovation restricted job creation in the exposed (mainly manufacturing) sector, employment growth in advanced economies was to be achieved mainly through well-paid public service sector jobs, with the consequence of undercutting budgetary restraint, or through an expansion of low-paid private services, whereby earnings equality was to be sacrificed. The service economy trilemma is strongly rooted in the so-called 'Baumol cost disease', named after the American economist and Nobel Laureate William Baumol (1967), who conjectured that productivity improvement in labour-intensive welfare services – health, education and family care services – would consistently lag behind productivity gains in competitive industries. To the extent that public service pay increases follow wage developments in the more dynamic capital-intensive private sectors, low productivity services, as a consequence, would become ever more expensive. In other words, any expansion of welfare services would incur a competitiveness deficit.

What is the relevance today of Arthur Okun's equity-efficiency trade-off, the OECD Job Study's equity-employment dilemma, Torben Iversen and Ann Wren's service sector trilemma, the Baumol cost disease, and Chancellor Angela Merkel's social-spending and economic-competitiveness trade-off? Has the crisis sharpened these predicaments? Or, should we, in the light of the available evidence, judge these dilemmas as misleading? Let us consider the postulated welfare disincentive problems in reverse order, beginning with Merkel's welfare spending and competitiveness predicament. On close inspection, the EU's share of global welfare spending is a little less than 40 per cent and broadly in sync with the United States and Japan in the OECD area. Moreover, the emerging economies are catching-up in taking up global social spending, but these are moot points (Begg et al. 2015). If we simply plot social protection spending, as measured by the OECD in its Social Expenditure Database (SOCX), to the World Economic Forum competitiveness league for 2015–16, as represented in Figure 11.1, we reveal that social protection spending does not hurt competitiveness: If anything, the relationship is positive. Some of the most competitive EU economies, including Finland, Germany, the Netherlands and Sweden, preside over high spending welfare states, devoting between 20 and 30 per cent of GDP to social protection.

Although the statistical relationship between competitiveness and social spending is positive, it has to be acknowledged at the same time that the spread is nevertheless wide, especially for the eurozone. Among the high spending but less competitive EU welfare states (countries below the blue line) we find Greece, Spain and Italy. These countries, all badly affected by

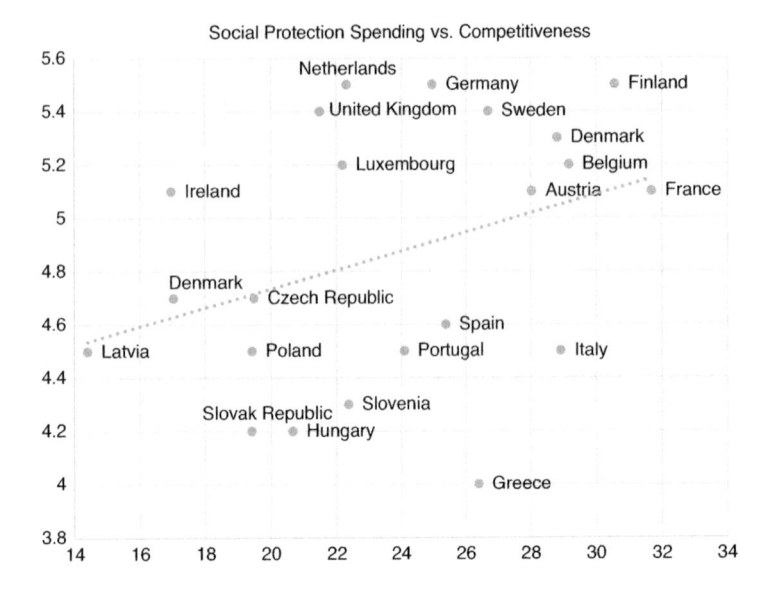

**FIGURE 11.1** Social protection spending vs. competitiveness.

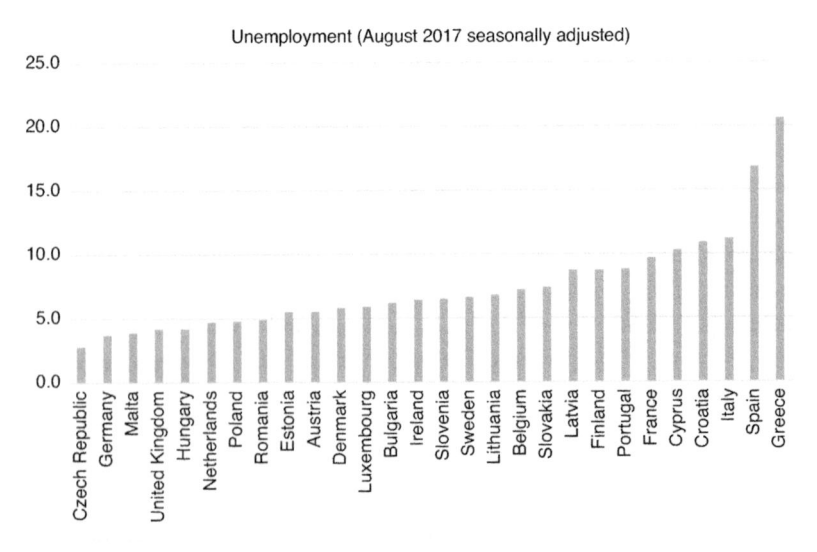

**FIGURE 11.2** Unemployment 2017.

Participation rate

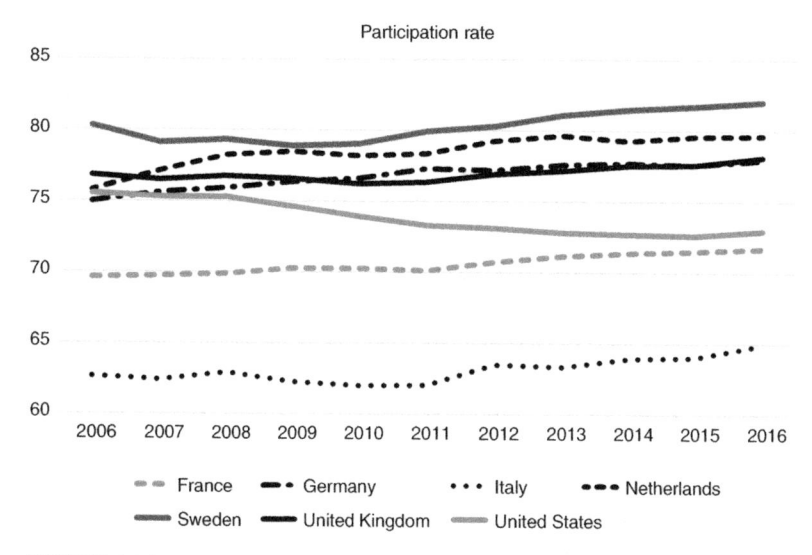

[Figure: line chart showing participation rates from 2006 to 2016 for France, Germany, Italy, Netherlands, Sweden, United Kingdom, and United States]

**FIGURE 11.3** Participation rate.

the crisis, experienced rising social protection spending due to dramatic levels of unemployment (see Figure 11.2).

The more conspicuous long-term trend relates to employment participation for different groups. When we bring the case of the United States back into the analysis, one can easily see that the model which the Paris-based thinktank hailed back in the 1990s, has seemingly exhausted itself. The US job 'miracle' – based on a less protective welfare state – is no more. Today, the highest levels of employment in the OECD area are in effect achieved by the high social spending competitive economies of Northern European Scandinavian countries, such as Sweden, joined by the Netherlands, Germany and the UK (see Figure 11.3).

Among US economists, there is a heated debate about America's mediocre employment record levels in the early twenty-first century. In hindsight, America's aggressive fiscal stimulus and quantitative easing measures, right after the 2008 global credit crunch, do not appear to have saved many jobs. Some economists suggest that the sluggish decline in employment participation is the long-term consequence of demographic ageing; others relate the decline to automation and digitalization as the prime cause of stagnation; still others believe that globalization lies behind US employment decline. However, in terms of demography, the US populace is younger than most EU countries. In addition, most high-employment EU countries preside over small open economies, except for Germany. In other words, they are far more exposed to globalization than the relatively closed US economy. Finally, in terms of ICT coverage, the better performing European economies are at the vanguard of digitalization. In short, more adverse demography, more intense economic internationalization, and more intrusive technological change, do not seem to have adversely affected employment performance in the most competitive EU economies. Should the design of their expensive welfare state be – counter intuitively – reconsidered as a 'productive factor'?

By taking a closer look into the gender and age dimension of employment growth, two developments stand out. Sweden, Germany, Denmark, the Netherlands and Great Britain employ more older workers (55–64 years) than the United States. A starker divergence appears when we compare female employment. Ever since the late 1990s, female employment in the United States declined from a relatively high level of just under 70 per cent. Today, Sweden, Denmark, Germany, the Netherlands, and the UK, employ 5–10 per cent more women than in the United States (OECD 2017).

Admittedly, the overall European picture is not all rosy. Some of the high spending EU welfare states still employ fewer people than the United States. France, today the biggest social protection spender in the OECD area, has employment at a level of about 70 per cent of the working age population. Italy, second in EU social protection spending, is employing less than 65 per cent of the working age population. These figures are reflected in below par

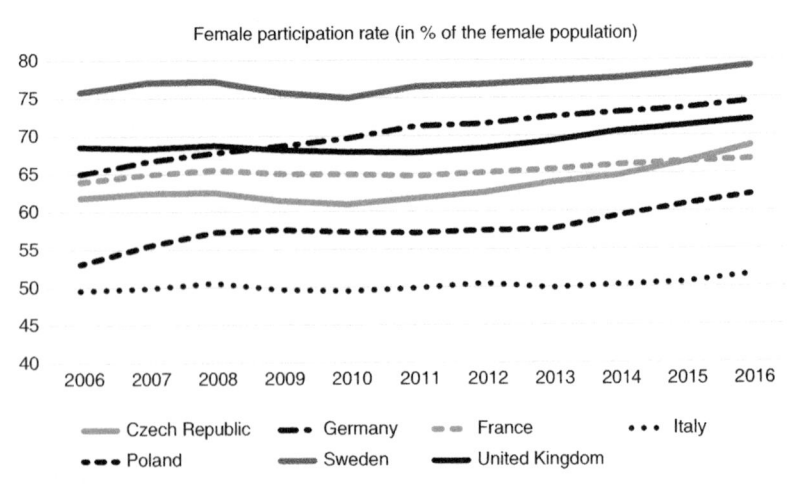

**FIGURE 11.4** Female participation rate.

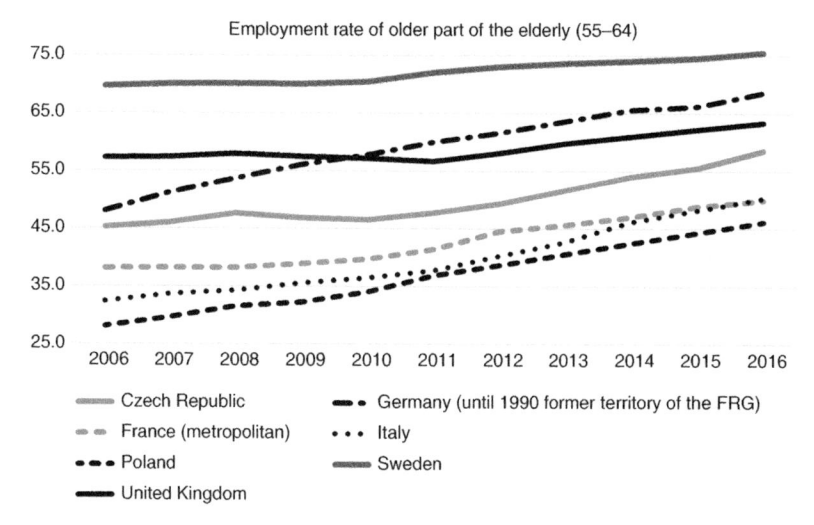

Employment rate of older part of the elderly (55–64)

**FIGURE 11.5** Elderly participation rate.

old age and female employment in these two countries. By contrast, among the member states that joined the EU in 2004, Czech Republic and Poland show rising levels of employment of both female and elderly workers (see Figures 11.4 and 11.5).

Active labour market policies (ALMP) that help unemployed workers to return to employment as swiftly as possible, in order to avoid unemployment persistence and to secure adequate job and skill matches, clearly play an important role in the employment successes of Finland, Sweden, Germany, Austria and the Netherlands. These welfare states stand out as high ALMP spending countries, especially when calculated in terms of ALMP-spending per unemployed (see Figure 11.6), with Luxembourg leading the pack. By contrast, we find a rather poor job-skill match performance in Greece, Italy and Spain, where ALMP spending is at low levels.

Another surprising relationship concerns the service sector, with its potential for female employment creation, in relation to the growing importance of child care for working parents. Female employment is highest in the countries where participation in formal childcare and pre-school services is equally high, as in Denmark, the Netherlands, France and Sweden. *Ex negativo*, enrolment in pre-primary education is lowest, among the OECD economies, in the United States. This, in combination with extremely high rates of child poverty can partly explain declining American levels of female employment. Recent research has robustly established that early

**216** The Crisis of Globalization

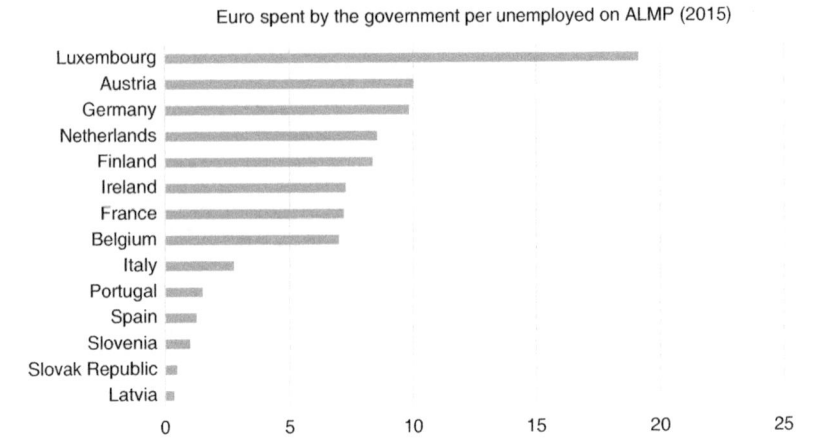

Euro spent by the government per unemployed on ALMP (2015)

|  |  |
|---|---|
| Luxembourg | ~19 |
| Austria | ~10 |
| Germany | ~10 |
| Netherlands | ~8.5 |
| Finland | ~8 |
| Ireland | ~7 |
| France | ~7 |
| Belgium | ~7 |
| Italy | ~3 |
| Portugal | ~2 |
| Spain | ~1.5 |
| Slovenia | ~1 |
| Slovak Republic | <1 |
| Latvia | <1 |

**FIGURE 11.6** ALMP spending per unemployed.
Data for the UK is not available. The selection below also reflects the limited availability of data.

Employment rate by educational level (Eurostat, 2016 data)

Legend:
- TOTAL
- Lower secondary education or below
- Upper secondary and post-secondary non-tertiary education
- Tertiary education

Countries: Greece, Italy, France, Poland, United Kingdom, Germany, Netherlands, Sweden

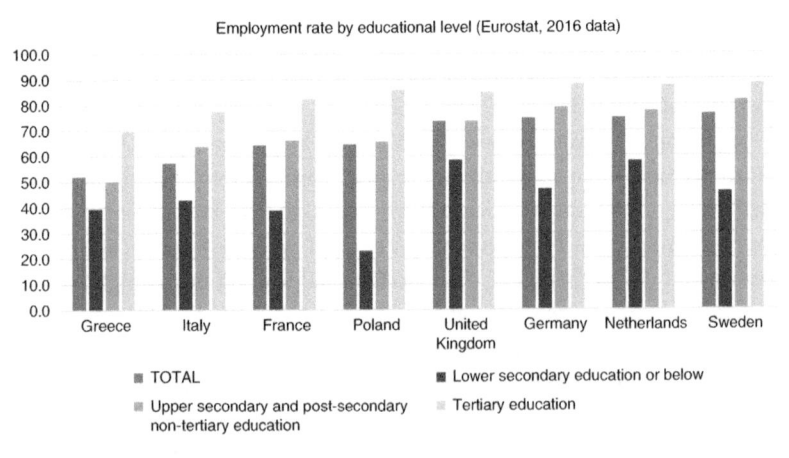

**FIGURE 11.7** Employment rate by educational level.

childhood education and care (ECEC), beyond its supporting role for female employment, is also instrumental to prevent large achievement gaps between children of socio-economically advantaged and more disadvantaged families (OECD 2011) Universal and subsidized high-quality ECEC helps to mitigate child poverty by allowing for dual earner families, and especially mothers, to seek employment, while at the same time reducing inequality in

Population at risk of poverty or social exclusion
(pre-and after redistribution, 2016, Eurostat data)

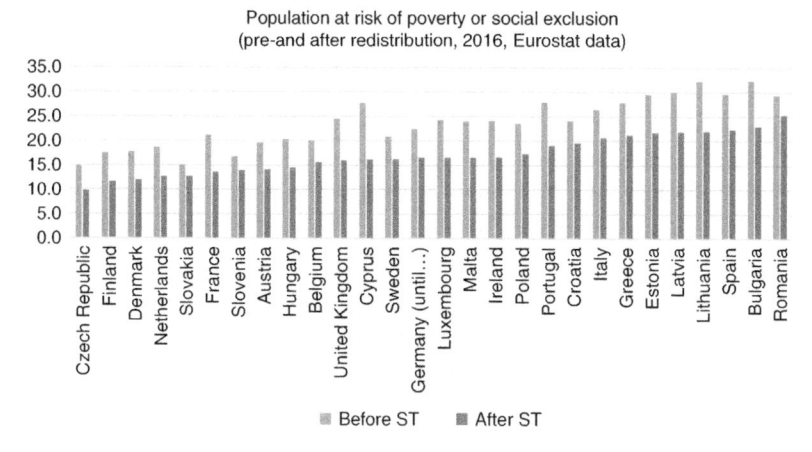

■ Before ST   ■ After ST

**FIGURE 11.8** At-risk-of-poverty before and after taxes.

educational opportunity. These factors are, in turn, good for more long-term educational attainment, occupational opportunity, employability and growth. As a high-level of educational attainment remains the best route into employment (see Figure 11.7), ensuring that all children are granted similar access to school and university is not only a matter of fairness, but it also increases long-term growth prospects.

After having surveyed comparative labour market performance and their policy support structures from different angles, we look at the distributive performance of EU welfare states and their fiscal sustainability. The first point to notice is that income inequality, as measured by the Gini coefficient, has increased in most OECD economies since the 1980s. Indeed inequality increased strongly in Finland and Sweden from very low levels, but also in Germany, among the mid-range inequality countries. Inequality spiralled most dramatically in the UK and the United States among the high inequality countries in the OECD. As result of the crisis, inequality has gone up again in already highly unequal Greece and Spain. Intergenerational inequality further increased, in part because of massive cuts in education and family spending in the Mediterranean countries. This trend is visible in Ireland, where old age pension spending remained constant, but also in Italy and Spain, where pension spending actually increased.

As the Gini coefficient is a relative inequality index, a better indicator is the population at risk of poverty, especially after taxes (see Figure 11.8).

The best performing countries in terms of low levels of relative poverty and high rates of employment include the Czech Republic and Slovenia, among the Central and Eastern European member states, together with Austria, Denmark, Finland, the Netherlands and Sweden. Germany combines high employment with medium levels of relative poverty, while France and Belgium match medium rates of employment with low at-risk-of-poverty levels. Overall, the European experience suggests, against received wisdom, that high levels of income inequality actually frustrate employment growth and, as a feedback consequence, inter-generational social mobility and economic dynamism. These findings are again consistent with recent research on the United States with high income inequality resulting in stagnant employment via interrupted (upward) social mobility, the very basis of the American Dream.

The 2015 OECD report on inequality, *In It Together: Why Less Inequality Benefits All*, represents a sea change in perspective from the 1994 *Jobs Study*, in arguing that one of the main transmission mechanisms between inequality and growth is human capital development. While there is always a gap in education outcomes across individuals with different socioeconomic backgrounds, this divergence is particularly wide in high inequality countries with disadvantaged households struggling to gain access to quality education, especially in the early childhood years, for their offspring (OECD 2008, 2011, 2015). In other words, today high inequality is associated with low social mobility. We know from extensive research that children growing up in poverty are at greater risk than non-poor peers to do worse in education later in life, which in turn is likely to spill over in adverse employment opportunities and dampen growth prospects. Today the lowest levels of child poverty are to be found in Denmark and Finland, at respectively 3 and 4 per cent. Germany and France are respectively at 9 per cent and 12 per cent. The advanced economy record is set by the United States, at a rate of 20 per cent (see Figure 11.9).

In the final analysis, taking a cue from the service economy trilemma, we look at the public finances to gain a perspective on the budgetary sustainability of country-specific distributive efforts and employment successes and failures (see Figure 11.10).

Stable public finances in support of high levels of employment and subdued poverty can be found in Denmark, Finland, the Netherlands and Sweden, which also happen to be countries that have among the most progressive taxation systems. Among the late entrants to the EU, fiscal positions are particularly healthy in Estonia, Latvia, Lithuania, Poland and Slovakia. Low employment Eurozone countries, including France, Greece, Italy, Portugal and Spain, face troubled public finances at low levels of

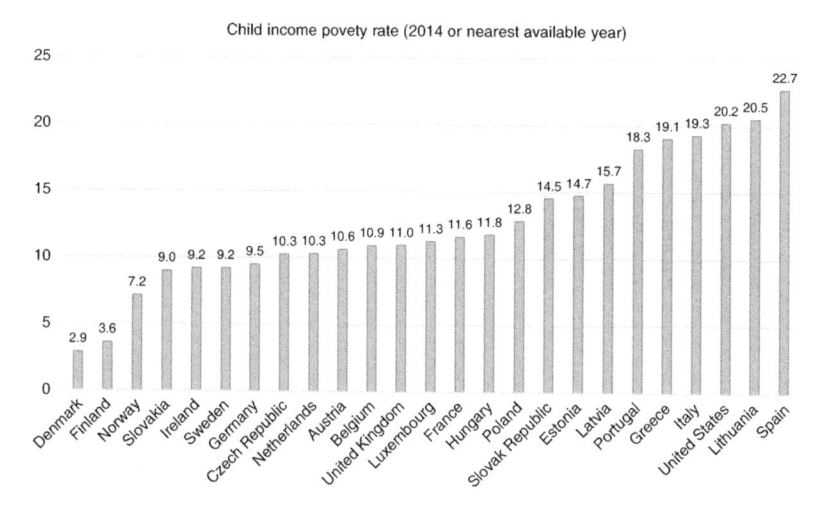

**FIGURE 11.9** Child income poverty rate.
*Data:* OECD. Measured as a share (per cent) of the total population and of children (0–17) with an equivalized post-tax-and-transfer income of less than 50 per cent of the national annual median equivalized post-tax and transfer income

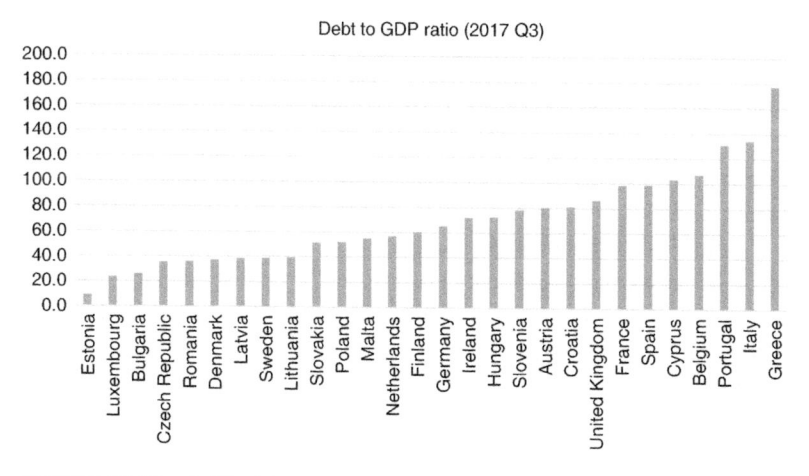

**FIGURE 11.10** Public debt to GDP ratio 2017.

employment. Germany also remains a twilight zone of above average levels of debt relative to GDP (see Figure 11.11).

The main take-away from our 'snap-shot' overview of the recent macro-economic evidence is that strong and competitive European welfare states, with levels of social spending hovering between 25 and 30 per cent of GDP

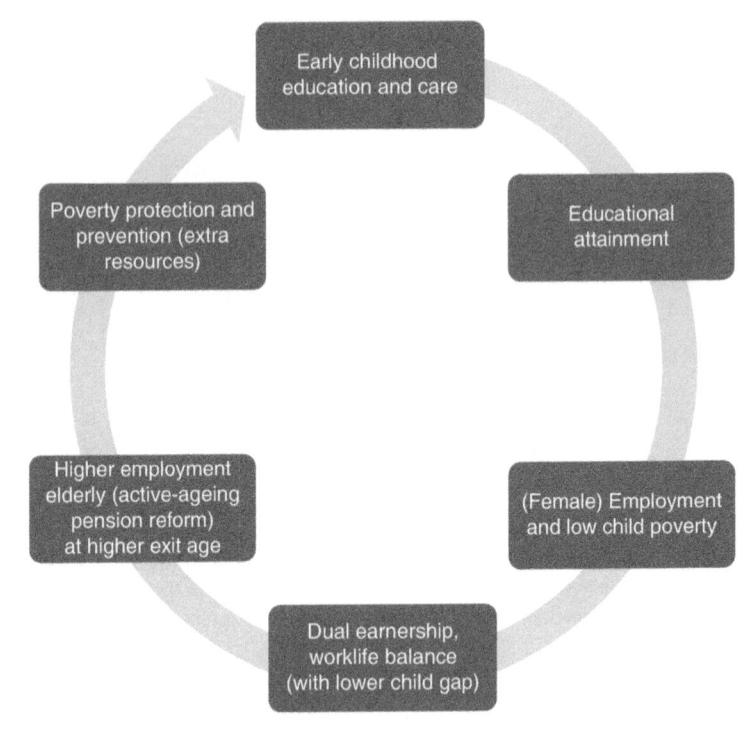

**FIGURE 11.11** Social investment life-course multiplier effect.

are best at achieving high employment, subdued poverty, and healthy public finances. *Ex negativo*, the battered, weak and fragmented US welfare state, confronted with stagnant levels of employment, high levels of debt, and very high levels of inequality and child poverty, and low social mobility certainly no longer appeals as a 'model' worth emulating. This suggests that the axiomatic disincentive predicaments associated with generous welfare provision, originally derived from neo-liberal economic doctrine of the 1980s and 1990s, are false beliefs and dangerous myths. To be sure, there are many interacting factors at play. Furthermore, the observed variation in socioeconomic performance behind various levels of welfare spending presses us to consider the *quality* rather than the *quantity* of social spending in trying to better understand the relationship between economic prosperity and social well-being in rich democracies.

The empirics of wholesome combinations of economic growth, inclusive labour markets and fair redistribution, but also adverse problems of high social protection spending, low employment and unequal redistribution, requires a more institutionally sensitive, multi-factor policy analysis than simplified trade-offs and trilemmas allow for. It is to this novel kind of 'sometimes true' mid-range theorising that we turn in the next section.

## Social Investment Synergies and the Matthew-Effect Fallacy

Over the past two decades, academic experts from various disciplines have started to rethink, in a rather understated fashion, the interaction between economic progress and social policy: from equity-efficiency 'trade-offs' and associated 'trilemmas' to Pareto-optimal 'social investment synergies', even in Rawlsean terms of benefiting the worst off (Esping-Andersen et al. 2002; Esping-Andersen 2009; Morel et al. 2012; Hemerijck 2013, 2017; Hemerijck et al. 2016). Social investment is today understood as welfare provision that helps 'prepare' individuals, families and societies *ex ante* to respond to the changing nature of social risks in advanced economies, by investing in, upkeeping and protecting human capabilities from early childhood through old-age, rather than pursuing policies that only 'repair' social misfortune *ex post*, after moments of economic and personal crisis.

The policy theory behind the social investment paradigm was given explicit impetus with the publication of the book, edited by Gøsta Esping-Andersen, *Why We Need a New Welfare State* (Esping-Andersen et al. 2002), commissioned by the Belgian Presidency of the European Union in 2001. The core diagnosis of this book is that economic internationalization, technological innovation, demographic ageing, and changing family structures in the post-industrial age, increasingly foster suboptimal life chances for large parts of the population. Esping-Andersen et al. not only took issue with the neo-liberal axioms that generous welfare provision inevitably implies a loss of economic efficiency, but were equally critical about the staying power of male-breadwinner, pension-heavy and insider-biased welfare provision in many European countries, reinforcing stagnant employment and long-term unemployment, in-work poverty, labour market exclusion, family instability, high dependency ratios and below-replacement fertility rates.

The work-family life course is the lynchpin of the social investment policy paradigm (Kuitto 2016). More flexible labour markets and skill-biased technological change, but also higher divorce rates and lone-parenthood, make female economic independence an important prerequisite for curbing child poverty. Gendered employment opportunities are key to effective poverty mitigation. Absent possibilities of externalising child and elderly care, a rising number of female workers face 'broken careers' and postponed motherhood, with low fertility intensifying the ageing burden in pensions and healthcare in the medium term (Esping-Andersen 2009). Particularly worrying is the rise of marital homogamy in the new era of high female employment where indiviudals with similar social backgrounds and levels of education are more likely to marry. The likelihood is that highly-educated and dual-earning households, with easy access to high quality childcare, will race ahead while low-skill and low-work intensity households fall behind (Cantillon and Van Lancker 2013). For a better work-life balance, *Why We Need a New Welfare State* urged social investment policies that could secure improved resilience over the family life course, with special attention placed on avoiding career interruptions for women with small children; and promoting dual earner families with a gender-equal parental leave. The orientation towards the life course is crucial. Lengthier, more diverse and volatile working lives harbour important implications for social policy. People are most vulnerable over critical transitions in the life course: (1) when they move from education into their first job; (2) when they aspire to have children; (3) when they – almost inevitably – experience spells of labour market inactivity; and finally, (4) when they move to retirement. To the extent that policy-makers are able to identify how economic well-being and social problems at such transitions in the life course impinge on subsequent well-being, preventive policies should be advanced to forestall cumulative social risk and poverty reproduction. Here, the eradication of child poverty should take pride of place together with more continuous female careers. Targeted support for the most vulnerable families, especially lone parents, single mothers and low-income families with children, should therefore be prioritized

Like any notion of 'investment', the concept of social investment begs the question of measurable welfare 'returns' (De Deken 2017; Verbist 2017; Begg 2017; Burgoon 2017). Well-being returns on social investment hinge fundamentally on the synergy effects across complementary – capacitating and compensatory – policy interventions. In recent years, the lead author of this chapter developed an operational taxonomy of three interdependent and complementary social investment policy functions: (1) easing and improving the 'flow' of contemporary labour market and (gendered) life-course transitions; (2) raising and up-keeping the quality of the 'stock' of human capital and capabilities; and (3) maintaining strong minimum-income universal safety net 'buffers' for micro-level income protection and macro-economic stabilization in support of high employment levels in aging societies, for further empirical analysis and assessment (Hemerijck 2015, 2017). In this taxonomy, the 'buffer' function is about securing adequate and universal minimum income protection, thereby further stabilising the business cycle and buffering economic shocks. Next, the 'stock' function, including cognitive and non-cognitive and physical and apprenticeship training and on-the-job professional skills. The 'stock' function of social investment has wider bearings, relating to the provision of 'capacitating social services', bringing under one roof adjustable bundles of professional assistance from child- to elderly care, including skill enhancement and training services in case of unemployment, health, family and housing support (Sabel et al. 2017). The 'flow' function, finally, is about efficient and optimal allocation of labour and employment over the lifespan, making sure that unemployed workers can return to work as fast as possible through active labour market policies and job matching. In this context, Guenther Schmid (2015) aptly speaks of a shift from 'making work pay' to 'making transitions pay'.

In everyday policy-practice, there is ample overlap between the policy functions of 'stocks', 'flows' and 'buffers'. They can run as 'institutional complementarities' with the operation of one social investment function being enhanced by one of the others or both in a mutually reinforcing fashion (Hall and Soskice 2001). Policy provisions that seemingly focus on one of the three functions often back up the others in an interconnected fashion and need to do so (Dräbing and Nelson 2017). For example, poverty alleviation is principally a 'buffering' policy, but adequate financial security can facilitate smoother labour market 'flow' as a consequence of mitigated pressure to accept any job on offer, with the potential overall benefit of better job matching and less skill erosion. It is also important to highlight with respect to 'buffers' that insurance provision induces two kinds of behavioural response: opportunism and trust (Schmid 2017). In the opportunistic case, people exploit the insurance contract deal through overly careless behaviour or even fraud; this is the well know *moral hazard* predicament. The alternative behavioural response concerns an increased willingness to take calculated risks under the assumption of fair redistribution in case of failure. If people can rely on security through insurance or solidarity, they are more willing to take risks, to invest in human capital (with uncertain returns) and to voluntarily change jobs (with unknown career and pay opportunities). The second kind of behavioural response can be understood as stimulating innovation and change by securing important material background conditions. In the area of social security 'buffers', narrowly understood, it is fair to say that in the past two decades, the moral hazard predicament has been reined in by activation requirements and more effective employment services.

The rise of the knowledge economy has already pressed policy-makers to ring-fence human capital 'stock' spending against austerity pressures and, if public budgets allow, to adapt education and training systems to rapid technological change in order to raise the productivity of the workforce. The experience of the crisis has revealed that countries with more encompassing and generous 'buffers' have done a better job in macro-economic stabilization than countries with more fragmented and lower benefit 'buffers'. The incipient rise of precarious employment, which certainly should not be seen as a positive contribution to labour market 'flow', has more recently entered the policy purview. Precarious work entails not only low wages, low upward mobility, but also low investment in human capital 'stock' and low benefit 'buffers' over inactive transition and old age. Moreover, given that precarious work is highly feminized, its vulnerabilities are carried disproportionately by women. The added value of part-time work lies in its contribution to better reconciliation of family and working life. However, in the absence of fair regulation and easy access to social security and high quality childcare, part-time employment can also be suboptimal. For example, the under-utilization of the quantity and quality of female 'human capital' supply and low levels of aspirational fertility have a negative long-term knock-on effect on pension system sustainability. There is therefore a strategic need to transform passive social insurance systems, targeting the working-age population, into a life-course security system that is able to handle risks related to all the critical transitions over the life course.

As Europe's workforce is shrinking, measures to improve labour market 'flow' must be accompanied with effective 'stock' and 'buffer' policies to make sure that more mobile workers receive the training, skills and a measure of income protection through effective support, empowering them to make successful transitions. In the recent reports of inequality cited above, OECD experts argue that any reduction of inequality between rich and poor citizens today requires the mobilization of a whole range of policies, from turning female employment into good quality careers ('flow'), to proactive early childhood development, youth and adult training policies ('stock'), and the expansion of effective and efficient activating tax-and-transfer systems ('buffers') in times of dire need.

The mid-range theoretical argument about institutional complementarities can be understood in negative terms, in the sense that a 'missing' policy complementarity can cause policy failure to incur high costs. Looking at the example of labour markets, upgrading human capital 'stock' without protecting human capital through social security 'buffers' and promoting activating 'flows' is wasteful, as peoples' skills continuously deteriorate when faced with unemployment or job mismatches. Having fragmented benefit systems undermines the automatic stabilization capacity of safety net 'buffers' in bad times. Not extending social security entitlements to zero-hour contracts and other employment arrangements is bound to lead to problems of social security coverage in a manner that undermines the effectiveness of safety nets in the future. By the same token, overgenerous family benefits with unnecessarily long leave periods will create undesirable incentives for working mothers to leave the labour market for longer than necessary, resulting in suboptimal (female) employment growth. The 'sometimes true' nature of institutional complementarity implies careful and well-balanced policy design that allows a range of interventions to work together to achieve higher aggregate well-being returns. The identification of institutional complementarities cannot be dealt with by a causal inference on single functions or mechanisms with the highest explanatory leverage, as favourable dynamics come in pairs or triads of matching 'stock', 'flow' and 'buffer' policy packages over the life course. By reframing the welfare conundrum through probing variegated theoretical insights on changing and sometimes puzzling empirics, social investment experts, mostly coming from sociology and political science, have transcended the political frame of distributive bargains that juxtapose hard-working 'contributors' and rent-seeking 'beneficiaries' in the 'here and now'. In the process, a solid social investment policy paradigm has emerged, befitting the knowledge economy in times of adverse family demography.

The growing evidence on how effective 'stock', 'flow' and 'buffer' policies reinforce the proficiency of each other, has allowed Anton Hemerijck (2015, 2016, 2017) to conjecture the operation of a social investment 'life-course multiplier' effect, whereby high quality early childhood care over time contributes to higher levels of educational attainment, which in turn, together with more tailor-made vocational training, can spill over into higher and more productive employment in the medium term. To the extent that employment participation is furthermore supported by effective work-life balance policies, including adequately funded and publicly available childcare, higher levels of (female) employment with lower gender pay and employment gaps can be foreseen. More opportunities for women – and men – to combine parenting with paid labour is, in addition, likely to have a dampening effect on the so-called 'child gap', the difference between the desired number of children per couple (aspirational fertility) and the actual number of children (realized fertility) (Bernardi 2005). A final knock-on effect is a higher effective retirement age, provided the availability of active ageing policies, including portable and flexible pensions, for older cohorts.

Social investment is not without its critics. In the much-cited article 'What use is social investment', Brian Nolan (2013) cast doubts on the positive employment effects associated with social investment. The most empirically pernicious critique of social investment policies is that they are plagued by 'Matthew Effects' of middle-class groups disproportionately benefiting from capacitating services at the expense of vulnerable groups in society (Cantillon 2011; Cantillon and Van Lancker 2013). It is worth putting the two trenchant criticisms about the doubtful employment effect and regressive distributive effects of social investment policies to the empirical test of the available evidence. In a unique interdisciplinary methodological study, Hemerijck et al. (2016) produced an in-depth analysis of two prime examples of social investment policy provision, active labour market policy (ALMP) and early childhood education and care (ECEC) in relation to their direct, indirect, and interactive – that is institutionally complementary – impact on employment and poverty (Hemerijck et al. 2016). The most prominent finding is that social investment, in terms of ALMP and ECEC effort, strongly supports high employment and productivity growth. These findings falsify Nolan's scepticism about the employment and employability potential of social investment policies. With respect to the Matthew Effect predicament, the picture is more ambiguous, but still largely positive. ECEC spending, while supporting female employment, sometimes does enhance relative poverty, suggesting a Mathew Effect. By contrast, ALMP efforts, using both micro- and macro-data, is associated with significantly lower poverty for vulnerable groups. The qualitative institutional analysis on this score is more revealing, showing far lower Matthew Effects in Denmark and more so in the Italian case of a singular pension 'buffer' welfare state. The overall conclusion is that Matthew Effects are not predetermined by social investment reform, as Cantillon and colleagues would have it.

## The Ambivalent Politics of Social Investment and the Crisis of Social Democracy

Over the span of two decades, the notion of social investment matured from a benign concept of 'social policy as a productive factor' to nothing less than a paradigmatic rethink of the welfare states for twenty-first century knowledge economies in times of adverse demography. Relying now on context-dependent mixes of 'stock', 'flow' and 'buffer' policies to obtain well-being returns over the family life span, the social investment paradigm departs in important ways from the Keynesian-Beveridge welfare compromise of the post-war era and the neo-liberal critique of the interventionist welfare state from the 1970s and 1980s.

In terms of policy diffusion, the social investment turn has, however incomplete, gathered significant steam. It is striking to see that where social investment reform took root, it did so without a formidable economic or political crisis as a precursor (Van Kersbergen and Hemerijck 2012; Hemerijck 2013; Van Kersbergen et al. 2014; Bouget 2015; Hemerijck 2017). It is also remarkable that the high-spending European welfare states championed upward social investment recalibration, including Germany, in spite of Merkel's ordo-liberal preference for a small German welfare state. By contrast, the less generous, low-tax, fragmented, private and corporatized US welfare state went further down the path of social policy exhaustion (Hacker and Pierson 2010). How to explain the progressive, gradual but transformative diffusion of social investment across the high-spending welfare states of the EU, where even incremental reforms do not pass by unnoticed? The mainstream 'new politics of the welfare state' literature, contending that austerity leaves little leeway for proactive welfare recalibration (Pierson 2001, 2011) cannot explain Europe's changing welfare states. With levels of social spending edging up today to about quarter and a third of GDP, concerns about welfare state sustainability are indeed intense, but this predicament has not pre-empted social investment innovation.

In this context, high social spending commitments that are indeed difficult to retrench may counter intuitively have acted as a 'productive constraint', spurring political authorities, supported by administrative elites, to pursue social investment reform. The political-administrative logic at play is one of welfare-oriented political parties, which after having promised to resist retrenchment reform are, once in office, confronted with fiscal sustainability constraints. This then presses them to mastermind reform coalitions, including societal stakeholders, of layering novel 'stock' and 'flow' policies on top of streamlined, more universal but perhaps less generous, social security 'buffers'. These new coalitions are often based on the overarching aim of raising effective employment rates, especially of women and older workers, precisely to put the 'carrying capacity' of the welfare state on a safer financial footing. With this logic in mind, it is no surprise that social investment reform never seriously reached the political agenda of the low-tax, low-spend, and fragmented US welfare state, precisely because the American political economy lacks a formidable 'beneficial' budgetary constraint for upward recalibration. Caught in between the Scylla of widely popular welfare provision and the Charybdis of intrusive fiscal constraints, the European social investment 'turn' is a joint-product of coalition governments pressed to honour outstanding welfare commitments. Such coalitions have to understand they can only uphold their welfare commitments if they raise employment levels through improved human capital 'stock' development and maintenance, and better 'flow' labour market regulation to ease life course transitions that foster longer and more robust working careers. Once social investment policies are in place, a bandwagon effect ensues, as their expanding clienteles – working families in the first place – step up demands for better childcare and parental leave, gender equity in work and family life, and long-term care expansion. This dynamic effect has the consequence of anchoring a social investment layer as an integral part of the new welfare state, alongside its core social security 'buffers'. To the extent that the social investment reform in effect contributes to higher lifetime employment participation and productivity gains, this in turn will ease fiscal pressures on pensions and health care, as more productive workers pay taxes and contributions over longer careers. As such, there is little conflict between 'old' compensating social insurance provision and 'new' capacitating social investments, as is sometimes suggested in the recent literature (Busemeyer 2017; Häuserman and Palier 2007). Finally, social investment reform, pursued by governments facing taxing sustainability constraints, easily engages social democrats, social liberals, Christian democrats, and the Greens. This is good news for social investment, but not per se for its principle architect: modern social democracy.

In hindsight, it is fair to say that social democracy, in particular the Third Way project in Austria, Belgium, Great Britain, Denmark, Finland, Germany, the Netherlands, Portugal and Spain round the turn of the millennium, has been a major driving force behind the social investment turn since the mid-1990s (Giddens 1998). But while Third Way policy innovation in active labour market policy, family support, early childhood development and work-life balance reconciliation policies contributed to employment growth and possibly improved poverty mitigation, these policy successes have not brought long-term electoral gains to social democratic parties across increasingly fragmented electorates. We consider that three reasons may explain this tragic paradox. First and foremost, Third Way reformers have, by and large, remained 'handmaidens' to the default neo-liberal policy paradigm, allowing social investment progress when the economy grew, but falling back onto pro-cyclical austerity when the chips were down. Tony Blair, Gerhard Schroeder, and Wim Kok never really dared to pursue a more counter-cyclical social investment strategy in the face of a deep recession. In the exemplary case of Blairite Britain, social spending as a share of national income rose fairly dramatically, with the lasting effect of lowering child poverty. When he had left office by the time the crisis struck in 2007-8, Gordon Brown could at first avoid fiscal austerity and resort to quantitative easing. Eurozone economies, irrespective of being run from the centre-right or -left, were condemned to pursue retrenchment. National policy market could not fathom that assertive investments in the social infrastructure of their advanced economies would create new jobs, not only public ones but also private jobs as a knock-on effect. The consequence of this intellectual inhibition effectively boiled down to sacrificing employment opportunities and family aspirations, to the primacy of budgetary equilibrium and monetary stability, enshrined in the EU treaties and now also in some national constitutions. This brings us to the second, more ideological, reason for the lukewarm political embrace of social investment on the European centre-left. After the Beveridge report of 1942 brought the eradication of the 'five great evils of want, disease, idleness, ignorance and squalor' to the top of post-war policy agenda, social democracy and the trade union movement, as a cohesive social class, compromised to support a mixed market economy, committed to full employment, while leaving private economic actors free to make for-profit investment decisions (Beveridge 1994). Ideologically, the social democratic politics of socially embedding – rather than socialising – markets to redress Beveridge's 'great evils' brought about path-breaking reforms in the areas of minimum income and job protection, comprehensive unemployment insurance, old age pensions, national health care, equal access to education and progressive taxation.

All of these public goods can, in hindsight, be defended in terms of the fairness principle of John Rawls (1971), prescribing that any change in relative position should also be to the benefit of the least well off. The conception of justice from a social investment perspective is altogether different. In comparison to Beveridge, the negative logic of eradicating *freedom from want* is replaced by a more positive logic of *freedom to act*, privileging 'redistribution of opportunities' as a fundamental precondition to the 'redistribution of outcomes'. Any *freedom to act* in post-industrial economies inescapably touches on far wider, dynamic, inter-generational and contextualized life-course conditions and orientations, including childhood development, employment opportunities, fertility aspirations and independent living in old age, to mention but a few. These variegated life-cycle dependent aspirations cannot be benchmarked around a singular transcendental principle of (distributive) fairness, as in Rawls. In this respect, the normative scope of the social investment perspective is more in line with the 'capability approach' of Amartya Sen (2001, 2009) and Martha Nussbaum (2013). Economic growth, employment and fair distribution, from this perspective, cannot be assessed as ends but should be judged as means for human development and the liberty of individuals and families to live the kind of lives they value. Public goods like social security and active labour market policies have to be understood in terms of their contribution to enable citizens and families to live 'flourishing lives' (Morel and Palme 2007) nurtured by mutual recognition and care (Honneth 1995).

There are many reasons for anchoring the social investment approach in terms of multidimensional, inter-generational and gendered capabilities. This would rest on the objective of increasing the *freedom of individuals and families*, and no longer in terms of *freedom from want* in the positive terms of life-course agency. The emphasis on context-specific capabilities and resources, required for individual development, sits somewhat uneasily with the more collectivist social democratic legacy of protecting citizens from market adversities through the redistributive instruments of the Keynesian-Beveridge welfare compromise. This may explain why social democracy, while venturing social investment reform to sustain the welfare state, never really invested much ideological energy into articulating the changing nature of social risks and the provision of differentiated services and benefits across the life-course into a more encompassing notion of the good life, relating to the kind of society that most people want to live in. This, finally, touches on the third reason for the current crisis in European social democracy in relation to social investment. After Third Way parties put social investment innovation, without articulate normative support, on the policy agenda, social investment policies have been taken over by the greens, social liberals, and even Christian Democracy (Gingrich and Häusermann 2015). Christian Democracy at first faced considerable difficulties in bidding farewell to male-breadwinner social insurance provision and female-homemaker subsidiarity. Yet, after it too came to accept dual-earner family life-course aspirations, often after electoral defeat, a more secularized centrist Christian Democracy took over from social democracy in championing early childhood, work life balance and gender equity policies (Fleckenstein 2011; Seeleib-Kaiser 2017). More on the left, especially since the crisis, social democracy has come under fire by populist left parties, such as *Die Linke* in Germany, who always opposed pro-cyclical concession bargaining in the name of monetary stability and budgetary equilibrium, and condemned mainstream social democracy's lack of a strategy to counter growing inequality. Meanwhile on the far-right, anti-establishment populist parties have transformed themselves into prominent defenders of the post-1945 Keynesian-Beveridge social contract, albeit with one exception: that social contract should be defended for 'native' citizens only. Against all existing evidence, these parties argue that policies, such as retirement at 65, could be sustained through a ban on migration, protectionism, and by bidding farewell to European integration and globalization. Right and left populists may not enter political office. However, to the extent that they successfully portray a nostalgic image of a national welfare paradise lost, resulting from economic globalization or mass migration, they nevertheless reduce the political space for European social democracy to prosper. Because of the myths propagated by these populists, modern social democrats – both within and out of government coalitions – have faced an uphill battle in claiming credit for universal childcare and active labour market policies.

Paradoxically, these reforms have now been embraced by Christian democracy, the green and social liberals, as side-payments for a higher pension age to ensure more inclusive and resilient welfare state futures. In other words, social democracy is losing blue collar votes to the far right, low-skill service sectors workers to the far left, and the centre to modern Christian democracy. A striking example of post-crisis social democratic pro-cyclical self-harm can found in the Netherlands. The social-investment-oriented Dutch Social Democrats participated in two austerity coalitions between 2010 and 2012 and again between 2013 and 2017. While in terms of governability and economic recovery, the latter coalition of liberals and the labour party in the Netherlands has been a resounding success, its principal architect, Dutch social democracy, effectively died in the operation. In the 2017 elections, the Dutch Labour Party, losing more than two-thirds of its support, imploded from being the second largest party in the Netherlands to outright political insignificance, with just 6 per cent of the popular vote. Dutch youngsters stopped voting for social democracy altogether.

Here, in conclusion, lies the fundamental *political* reason why social investment can no longer be dismissed. Modern social democracy must bid farewell to its inhibition, based on a deficient diagnosis, to relegate social investment to 'fair weather' politics. As long as the European centre left remains 'by default', through ignorance and fear, bound by the disproven conjectures of deep trade-offs and intrusive trilemmas, it risks sacrificing income security, skill enhancement, and family support for those very citizens social democracy was invented to support. Social investment is not a strategy that is good to pursue only when the economy is expanding, it also has a key role to play during periods of adversity. A more assertive – that is anti-cyclical – social investment strategy should prioritize first and foremost citizenship and well-being aspirations, especially in times of economic setbacks where social needs are most acute. Linking bundles of human capital 'stock', labour market and life-course 'flow', and incomes security 'buffer' policies, to a *positive* ideology of *capacitating social justice* in a pro-active manner, we believe, is quintessential to the survival of European social democracy.

## References

Baumol, W. J. 'The macroeconomics of unbalanced growth', *American Economic Review* 57(3) (1967) pp. 415–26.

Begg, I. 'Social investment and its discount rate', in A. Hemerijck (ed.) *The Uses of Social Investment* (Oxford, Oxford University Press 2017).

Bernardi, F. 'Public policies and low fertility: rationales for public intervention and a diagnoses for the Spanish case', *Journal of European Social Policy* 15(1) (2005) pp. 27–42.

Beveridge, W. H. *Full Employment in a Free Society: A Report* (London, Allen & Unwin 1944).

Bouget, D., H. Frazer, E. Marlier, S. Sabato and B. Vanhercke. 'Social Investment in Europe: A Study of National Policies', European Social Policy Network (ESPN), Brussels: European Commission (2015).

Burgoon, B. 'Practical pluralism in the empirical study of social investment: Examples from active labour market policy', in Hemerijck, A. (ed.) *The Uses of Social Investment* (Oxford, Oxford University Press 2017).

Busemeyer, M. R. 'Public opinion and the politics of social investment', in Hemerijck, A. (ed.) *The Uses of Social Investment* (Oxford, Oxford University Press 2017).

Cantillon, B. 'The paradox of the social investment state: growth, employment and poverty in the Lisbon era', *Journal of European Social Policy* 21(5) (2011) pp. 432–49.

Cantillon, B. and Van Lancker. 'Three shortcomings of the social investment perspective', *Acta Sociologica* 55(2) (2013) pp. 125–42.

De Deken, J. 'Conceptualizing and measuring social investment', in Hemerijck, A. (ed.) *The Uses of Social Investment* (Oxford, Oxford University Press 2017).

Dräbing, V., Nelson, M. 'Addressing human capital risks and the role of institutional complementarities', in Hemerijck, A. (ed.) *The Uses of Social Investment* (Oxford, Oxford University Press 2017).

Esping-Andersen, G. *The Incomplete Revolution: Adapting to Women's New Roles* (Cambridge, Polity 2009).

Esping-Andersen, G., Gallie, D. Hemerijck, A. and Myles, J. *Why We Need a New Welfare State* (Oxford, Oxford University Press 2002).

Fleckenstein, T. 'The politics of ideas in welfare state transformation: Christian democracy and the reform of family policy in Germany', *Social Politics International Studies in Gender, State and Society* 18(4) (2011) pp. 543–71.

Giddens, A. *The Third Way: The Renewal of Social Democracy* (Cambridge, Polity Press 1998).

Gingrich, J. and S. Häusermann. 'The decline of the working-class vote, the reconfiguration of the welfare state support coalition and consequences for the welfare state', *Journal of European Social Policy* 25(1) (2015) pp. 50–75.

Hacker, J. S. and Pierson, P. *Winner-Take-All Politics: How Washington Made the Rich Richer – and Abandoned the Middle Class* (New York, Simon Schuster 2010).

Häusermann, S. and Palier, B. 'The politics of social investment: Policy legacies and class coalitions', in Hemerijck, A. (ed.) *The Uses of Social Investment* (Oxford, Oxford University Press 2017).

Hemerijck, A. *Changing Welfare States* (Oxford, Oxford University Press 2013).

Hemerijck, A. 'The quiet paradigm revolution of social investment', in *Social Politics: International Studies in Gender, State and Society* (2015) doi: 10.1093/sp/jxv009.

Hemerijck, A. (ed.) *The Uses of Social Investment* (Oxford, Oxford University Press 2017).

Hemerijck, A., Burgoon, B., Dipietro, A. and Vydra S. *Assessing Social Investment Synergies (ASIS), A Project to Measure the Returns of Social Policies*, Report for DG EMPL (European Commission Brussels 2016).

Iversen, T. and Wren, A. 'Equality, employment, and budgetary constraint: the trilemma of the service economy', *World Politics* 50(4) (1998) pp. 507–74.

Honneth, A. *The Struggle for Recognition: The Moral Grammar of Social Conflicts* (Cambridge, Polity Press 1995).

Kuitto, K. 'From social security to social investment? Compensating and social investment welfare policies in a life-course perspective', in *Journal of European Social Policy* 26(5) (2016) pp. 442–59.

Merkel, A. Speech by Federal Chancellor Merkel at the World Economic Forum Annual Meeting 2013, Davos (24 January 2013).

Morel, N., Palier, B. and Palme, J. (eds) *Towards a Social Investment Welfare State? Ideas, Policies, Challenges* (Bristol, Policy Press 2012).

Morel N. and Palme, J. *Social Investment and Capabilities: a Normative Foundation* (2017).

Nolan, B. 'What use is "social investment"?' *Journal of European Social Policy* 23 (2013) pp. 459–68.
OECD. *The Jobs Study: Facts, Analysis, Strategies* (Paris, OECD 1994).
OECD. *The OECD Jobs Strategy: Making Work Pay: Taxation, Benefits, Employment and Unemployment* (Paris, OECD 1997).
OECD. *Growing Unequal* (Paris, OECD 2008).
OECD. *Doing Better for Families* (Paris, OECD 2011).
OECD. *In It Together; Why Less Inequality Benefits All* (Paris, OECD 2015).
OECD. *Employment Outlook* (Paris, OECD 2017).
Okun, A. M. *Equality and Efficiency: The Big Trade Off* (Washington, DC, The Brookings Institution 1975).
Pierson (ed.) *The New Politics of the Welfare State* (Oxford, Oxford University Press 2001).
Pierson. 'The Welfare State Over the Very Long Run', ZeS-Working Paper (02/2011).
Rawls, J. *A Theory of Justice* (Cambridge MA, Harvard University Press 1971).
Sabel, C. 'Individualized service provision and the new welfare state: Are there lessons from Northern Europe for developing countries?' In C. Luiz de Mello and M. A. Dutz (eds) *Promoting Inclusive Growth, Challenges and Policies* (Paris, OECD 2012) pp. 75–111.
Sabel, C., Zeitlin, J. and Quack, S. 'Capacitating services and the bottom-up approach to social investment', in A. Hemerijck (ed.) *The Uses of Social Investment* (Oxford, Oxford University Press 2017).
Schmid, G. 'Sharing risks of labour market transitions: Towards a system of employment insurance', *British Journal of Industrial Relations* 63(1) (2015) pp. 70–93.
Schmid, G. 'Towards life course insurance', in A. Hemerijck (ed.) *The Uses of Social Investment* (Oxford, Oxford University Press 2017).
Seeleib-Kaiser, M. 'The truncated German social investment, 2017' in A. Hemerijck (ed.) *The Uses of Social Investment* (Oxford, Oxford University Press 2017).
Sen, A. *Development as Freedom* (Oxford, Oxford University Press 2001).
Sen, A. *The Idea of Justice* (Cambridge, MA, Harvard University Press 2009).
Van Kersbergen, K. and Hemerijck, A. 'Two decades of change in Europe: The emergence of the social investment state', *Journal of Social Policy* (2012) pp. 1–18.
Van Kersbergen K., Hemerijck, A. and Vis, B. 'The great recession and welfare state reform. Is retrenchment really the only game left in town?' *Social Policy and Administration* (London, Blackwell 2014) pp. 24–66.
Verbist, G. 'Measuring social investment returns: Do publicly provided services enhance social inclusion?' in Hemerijck, A. (ed.) *The Uses of Social Investment* (Oxford, Oxford University Press 2017).
Wren, A. 'Social investment and the service economy trilemma', in Hemerijck, A. (ed.) *The Uses of Social Investment* (Oxford, Oxford University Press 2017).

CHAPTER 12

# Addressing Global Inequality: Is the EU Part of the Equation?

Frank Vandenbroucke[1]

## 'The Force of Globalization': An Unsatisfactory Account

If globalization leads to increasing inequality in the economically most advanced nation states, and if we want to reverse this trend, is the European Union (EU) then part of the solution? Or, is the EU part of the problem? I argue that our discussion of these questions is impaired by intellectual amalgamation and determinism in influential accounts of globalization and Europeanization. The debate on the legacy and potential role of the EU should move beyond such accounts, however thought-provoking they are.

Are we doomed to live with steadily increasing inequalities, because our national welfare states are under siege by the 'force of globalization'? The ceaseless recurrence of the 'winners and losers of globalization' mantra in our debates certainly feeds into that pessimistic idea. Readers of Branko Milanovic's *Global Inequality* – an outstanding academic bestseller often quoted in these debates – may come to the same depressing conclusion, even if Milanovic's analysis is multifaceted and his conclusion relatively open. Why is that? The problem with Milanovic's influential book is that it lumps together a complex set of developments, related to technology, international openness, changes in the balance of power and ideational changes, into one notion: 'globalization'. Milanovic explicitly defends this amalgamation, by arguing that technological change and globalization are 'wrapped around each other' and that 'trying to disentangle their individual effects is futile', whilst policy changes are 'endogenous to globalization'. Hence, 'technology, openness and policy are mutually dependent and cannot be separated in any meaningful sense' (Milanovic 2016: 110).

The mutual interdependence of these drivers of change should not be denied, but conflating them into one single 'force' is analytically unsatisfactory and politically unhelpful. If all mature welfare states are under siege of 'the force of globalization' and policy changes are 'endogenous' to globalization, the considerable national differences in levels and trends of inequality are hard to explain. Yet, these national differences are so important that they should be centre stage for anyone who is interested in policies and politics. Moreover, even if we accept that common trends affect all nation states on the backdrop of 'globalization', we need policies that identify and tackle specific issues, such as trade and its distributive impact, financial regulation, technology, migration, tax-and-benefit systems and collective bargaining – at least if our aim is to formulate practical solutions. We should not deny globalization as an overarching background condition, nor should we deny that 'openness' can have adverse distributional consequences through tax competition, trade and migration, but we have to disentangle the different forces at play.[2] This complexity probably explains why empirical studies that assess the impact of 'globalization' on welfare states with a limited set of explanatory variables (such as trade), do not find much evidence. A study that tested a large variety of econometric models in that vein concludes that we should be 'skeptical of bold claims about globalization's effect on the welfare state': 'Globalization may exert a very modest influence on policy-makers and welfare states. But policy-makers and welfare states are and always have been influenced by a diverse mix of pressures. The aging of the population, for instance, exerts far greater pressure than globalization. Moreover, economic or demographic pressures are always mediated and channeled by domestic political actors, and how or if they choose to address those pressures is always a political process' (Brady et al. 2005: pp, 945–6). A recent empirical study that avoids amalgamation by focusing on the sole impact of manufacturing imports from the global South on income inequality in the global North, finds a clear 'inequality effect' of such imports, but that effect decreases significantly with the degree of wage coordination through collective bargaining and welfare state generosity across countries. It concludes that we need to 'move beyond debates about the *relative* importance of domestic and global drivers of inequality'; we need 'theories of inequality at the *intersection* of the global and the national.' (Mahutga et al. 2017: 183).

A new major report on global income inequality, the *World Inequality Report 2018*, provides a useful antidote to deterministic accounts of the 'force of globalization'. The report shows that income inequality has increased in nearly all world regions in recent decades, but at different speeds. The fact that inequality levels are so different among countries, even when countries share similar levels of development, highlights the importance of national policies and institutions. The divergence in inequality levels has been particularly extreme between Western Europe and the United States, which had similar levels of inequality in 1980 but today are in radically different situations. The *World Inequality Report 2018* projects income and wealth inequality up to 2050 under different scenarios. In a future in which 'business as usual' continues, global inequality will further increase. Alternatively, 'if in the coming decades all countries follow the moderate inequality trajectory of Europe over the past decades, global income inequality can be reduced – in which case there can also be substantial progress in eradicating global poverty' (Alvaredo et al. 2017: 17). In other words, within-country inequality dynamics have a tremendous impact on the eradication of global poverty, and Europe can serve as a beacon for the rest of the world. For sure, European welfare states face many challenges, and we see cracks in our welfare systems. But the European experience signals that we are not doomed to live with ever increasing inequalities.

The authors of the *World Inequality Report 2018* do not refer to 'Europe' as an institution: 'Europe' stands for a region in which inequality – on the regional level – is estimated to have increased only mildly, compared to other regions in the world. National welfare state institutions are an important explanatory factor in the account of the *World Inequality Report*; whether or not the existence of the EU is part of the equation, is not discussed. Milanovic does not refer to the EU either. This lacunae has to be addressed.

## The EU and Social Cohesion: An Optimistic and a Pessimistic View

In order to discuss the role the EU can play in the future, we should first understand its role in the past: did European integration contribute to increasing inequalities in the European region, or was it a mitigating factor? Whilst empirical social scientists have difficulty in establishing a simple and significant relationship between 'the force of globalization' and inequality, some researchers do find a simple and significant relationship between, on the one hand, *European* economic and political integration, and, on the other hand, two simultaneous trends: decreasing inequality *between* EU member states and *increasing* inequality within EU member states. But this research also underscores that the perceived inequality-enhancing impact within EU member states, was dampened at the very high levels of economic integration exhibited by small, open economies that are stabilized by strong welfare states and corporatist institutions, such as Belgium and the Netherlands. According to Beckfield, who studied the impact of regional integration on 13 EU member states, the net effect was a decrease in *total inequality* (i.e. inequality measured from a pan-European perspective, as if these 13 member states would constitute one country) between circa 1980 and circa 2000 (Beckfield 2009: 501). Beckfield concludes that scholars of EU welfare states and inequality may be looking in the wrong place when they focus on globalization: 'It may be regional integration, not globalization that structures the welfare state in the advanced capitalist societies of Western Europe' (Beckfield 2006: 980).[3] In addition he emphasizes, correctly in my view, that globalization and Europeanization are *not* the same type of process on a different scale.

However useful such empirical research is in refocusing our attention on the impact of European integration, its difficulty is that it establishes *correlation* rather than *causation*. The UK's trade integration into the EU correlates with the drastic increase of inequality in the 1980s in Beckfield's data; but was it Europeanization, or rather Margaret Thatcher? The honest answer, so it seems to me, is that it is hard to say what would have happened to inequalities in Europe without the EU: we cannot compare Europe's trajectory since 1958 with a counterfactual scenario without Common Market and European Union. Interestingly, two opposite *narratives* on the social impact of the EU were present in past debates: an optimistic one and a pessimistic one. Let me briefly elaborate on this.

The optimistic narrative transpires, sometimes explicitly and often implicitly, in the documents and policies accompanying the preparation and early years of the European project. The *founding fathers* of European integration – the signatories of the Treaty of Rome – were convinced that economic integration would contribute to the development of prosperous and inclusive national welfare states. In retrospect, we can summarize this optimistic belief as follows:

- Economic integration would not only stimulate growth in all participating countries but would also allow for less developed countries to catch up, thanks to access to the common market and, in addition, targeted support by so-called 'cohesion policies': integration was a convergence machine.
- Social policy could safely be left to the national level, where trade unions and political parties would develop sufficient pressure to redistribute the economic benefits of integration fairly. There was no need to agree on pan-European social standards. Countries that were ahead economically and socially would not be hindered in their social policy: the convergence machine would not affect their internal social cohesion.

In short, the *founding fathers' credo* was based on two articles of faith, which should be clearly distinguished: convergence-through-integration between the member states and cohesion-in-convergence within the member states. I should immediately add that the second article of faith (cohesion-in-convergence) was not undisputed. In the fifties, there was no consensus on whether economic integration was possible without social harmonization. This question was at the heart of the 1956 Ohlin report, which, together with the Spaak report, prepared the launching of the European Economic Community (International Labour Organization 1956). Bertil Ohlin believed that differences in wages and related social expenditures between the countries involved were mainly related to differences in productivity; hence, one would not have to fear downward pressure on wages when allowing free trade. However, Ohlin added that, if any divergence in wages would diminish some member states' competitiveness in the common market, such an adverse development would be corrected by adapting exchange rates. Thus, Ohlin was not describing a monetary union, which is not an insignificant caveat. The founding fathers followed suit to a large degree.[4]

Hence, formulated with hindsight in the terms of today's debates and with a slightly benign interpretation of their motives, we may say that the founding fathers of European integration were deeply convinced that European economic integration would be a force for decreasing inequalities at the regional European level. Thus, their view was exactly opposite to today's dominant doom-mongering about the consequences of economic openness. Their view – as I reconstruct it here – was optimistic, in that they did not think the EU was in need of a European-level social policy, except for the coordination of social security entitlements (granted by national welfare states) for mobile citizens (citizens who would move from one welfare state to another, and who would always be included in a national solidarity circle). They had a neat division of labour in mind: economic policy had to become, in part, supranational; social policy could be left safely to national welfare states.

Consequently, for many years EU-level social initiatives were seen as – at most – politically attractive, but not at all necessary to sustain social objectives in the member states. Below, I will argue that this neat division of labour is no longer sustainable today: while it worked relatively well in the EU of the twentieth century, in the EU of the twenty-first century, the underlying optimism is naïve.

*Prima facie*, history has not proven Ohlin and the founding fathers wrong, at least not until halfway through the first decade of the twenty-first century: integration and catching-up went hand in hand, and the spectre of a social 'race to the bottom' did not materialize. The *World Inequality Report* concludes that inequality increased only moderately in the European region between 1980 and 2016. That assessment may even underrate the positive side of what happened with the successive enlargements of the EU: depending on the indicators and the time span under review, there may have been episodes in which total inequality in the European region actually diminished, as already mentioned above with reference to Beckfield.[5] Over the last decade, however, the model started to show cracks, the first one predating the 2008 crisis. The convergence machine was spinning, but inequality was increasing in several mature European welfare states: 'cohesion-in-convergence' no longer applied. The second crack, or, rather, a spectacular fissure, emerged with the crisis: the convergence machine stopped, with the north and the south of the Monetary Union tearing apart. Since 2008, inequality has not only been increasing within (a number of) member states but also between member states, particularly in the eurozone. The optimistic view on European integration as a self-sustaining force for upward convergence and cohesion, which I attribute somewhat benignly to the founding fathers, is certainly naïve in today's world. The advent of the Monetary Union is one reason why the initial division of labour between the economic and the social is no longer sustainable; the increased heterogeneity of today's enlarged EU constitutes a second reason why the EU needs a social policy concept.

The pessimistic account of the EU's role can be found in an impressive stream of scholarly work on the EU, in which Fritz Scharpf stands out as one of the main authors: his thesis is that the EU *cannot* be a social market economy, and that European welfare states are doomed to become gradually but steadily more 'market liberal', because of the asymmetric way in which European institutions are bound to function. Given the constellation of the European treaties, negative integration and market-making policies prevail over positive integration and market-correcting policies; European institutions, notably the European Court of Justice, prefer liberalization over domestic social cohesion (Scharpf 2009). Scharpf is also pessimistic about the eurozone, which combines incompatible national socio-economic models (Scharpf 2016).

Whilst the optimistic view is naïve in today's Europe, the pessimistic view is too schematic and deterministic in its understanding of the EU.[6] It offers important critical insights and it may find comfort in the statistical correlation between European political integration and increasing inequalities. But it does not provide a real explanation for the longer-term trend in inequality in some of the most advanced EU welfare states, which was to a large extent mediated by domestic politics and socio-demographic change. This is not to say that the EU did not play a role in shaping domestic politics and policies, notably on an ideational level before the eurozone crisis and with austerity policies after the eurozone crisis. However, I concur with Maurizio Ferrera in his contribution to a volume on the EU's social dimension; Ferrera calls for:

> a reframing of some classical issues that in the last two decades have dominated debates on the social deficit of the EU as an institutional and political construct, such as the asymmetry between negative and positive integration, market-making and market-correcting (...) If Social Europe is a composite construct that cannot be reduced to a single component and thus has to live with inherent tensions, there is no single asymmetry or deficit to which weaknesses can be imputed. Likewise, there is no single instrument or solution that can remedy such weaknesses (Ferrera 2017: 50).

Dani Rodrik represents a related but different strand of pessimism with regard to the EU. He considers the drive towards the Single Market and Monetary Union as an instance of 'hyperglobalization', which exacerbates the democratic problem of the EU: either political integration catches up with economic integration – which he deems increasingly difficult – or economic integration needs to be scaled back.[7] Rodrik's work contains healthy warnings: I agree with him that one should not jump too readily to the conclusion that the interdependence of nation states *imposes* supranational solutions upon them in all kinds of policy domains. Elsewhere, I argue that one should not overstretch functionalist arguments in support of an active social dimension to the EU: the problem at hand is political and the challenge is to identify common standards and policy rules that are functionally relevant (for the Monetary Union and the Single Market) and legitimate in view of shared aspirations across the member states. What is 'needed' and what is 'imposed' by monetary unification in Europe, depends on the fundamental aspirations that drive the European project at large (Vandenbroucke 2017a). On the other hand, Rodrik's recent pessimism about the EU is premised on an analytical framework – the famous 'trilemma' between globalization, sovereignty and democracy – that is too rigid to capture both the EU's record and its future potential.[8] Undoing the Single Market and the Monetary Union seems the worst of all options, whilst there is no compelling argument – other than an *a priori* judgment – that no *intermediary* solutions can exist for the EU's 'trilemma', in which the political contract is extended sufficiently to allow common goal-setting and risk-sharing in some key domains with respect for subsidiarity and without sacrificing any national prerogatives in many other domains. Admittedly, this requires a basic consensus on some key features of welfare states in selective policy domains, informed by shared values and aspirations. But that perspective is not bound to end in the demise of national democracies.

In the face of globalization, the EU can mobilize a variety of policy instruments to sustain national welfare states, more than it has done in the past. Politically, that is an uphill battle, but there is no deep, deterministic reason why it cannot be successful. In yet other words, if Europe is to be a beacon of equality for the rest of the world, as the authors of the *World Inequality Report 2018* would have it, the EU, qua political institution, should and can be part of the equation. To rise to this challenge, EU-level initiatives are needed in three domains: the completion of the Monetary Union, the organization of fair mobility, and fair taxation; the EU is also well-placed to promote investment in human capital, or, more generally, social investment policies. The upshot is that the EU, for it to remain a beacon for the rest of the world, must become a 'Social Union', that is, a true Union of Welfare States. To set the scene, I first emphasize the complex social nature of trends towards increasing inequality at the bottom end of the income distribution.

## The Erosion of Mature Welfare States

Much attention is given nowadays to the increasing share of top incomes. One should not overlook developments at the bottom end of the income distribution: in many European welfare states poverty has been increasing, signalling a gradual erosion of the redistributive capacity of mature welfare states, such as Germany, Sweden or Denmark. This erosion had already started before the financial crisis of 2008. Crucial factors explaining increases in inequality at the bottom end of the income distribution are homespun, and there is no single, silver bullet to address them. However, migration, cross-border mobility and increased competition in the enlarged EU also play a role, in interaction with shifts in labour market policies. The EU cannot be blamed as the main culprit, but it cannot be completely absent from the analysis either.

Individual poverty refers to the situation of households, since its metric is 'household income'. A key determinant of the poverty risk of individuals is the labour market participation of the members of the household in which the individual lives. We measure this by an indicator called 'household work intensity'. Around the middle of last decade, people living in households with very low work intensity were confronted with a poverty risk of 54 per cent, whereas people living in households with a very high work intensity were confronted with a poverty risk of only 5 per cent. This sizable divide has further heightened. By 2015, the poverty risk of individuals living in households with low and very low work intensity had increased considerably; conversely, the poverty risk of individuals living in households with very high work intensity remained the same. Hence, what we see is a polarization in poverty risks, starting already before the crisis. Simultaneously, we witnessed a polarization of employment across households in Europe: today, if we take all EU member states together, the share of individuals living in households with very high work intensity is higher than before the crisis of 2008. The share of people living in 'work-poor' households (by which we mean households with low and very low work intensity) increased and is – as yet – not returning to its pre-crisis level. Thus, there was a hollowing out of the middle: the share of people living in households with medium and high (but not very high) work intensity is lower than before the crisis. Compared to 2007, more people live in a household that is 'very rich' in terms of work intensity, and more people live in households that are 'very poor' in terms of work intensity.

Thus, two mutually reinforcing factors are at play: more people live in work-poor households; these households experience higher poverty risks than before the crisis. The combination of these two types of polarization goes a long way in explaining why non-elderly poverty increased in Europe. For sure, the pattern of change was far from homogeneous across Europe. Since 2004, some countries have combined increasing employment with decreasing non-elderly poverty, notably Poland. In other countries, poverty increased despite increasing employment. These diverse trajectories cannot be explained by one single driver; rather, a set of drivers is at play and their impact differs from country to country. In principle, three sets of factors can explain why the poverty-risk of work-poor households increased in so many countries:

i. tax-and-transfer systems may have become less generous for people without work, compared to people in employment;
ii. changes in household structures can also play a role: a lone-parent household with a medium or low work intensity (say, a lone mother

who holds a part-time job), is confronted with a higher financial poverty risk than a couple with children with the same medium or low work intensity (say, a couple where both partners work part-time or where one partner works full-time and the other is not employed);

iii. if households with lower work intensity (but not *zero* work intensity) are dependent on a segment of the job market where the quality of jobs is lower, both in terms of contractual security and earnings, they lose out in terms of earned income compared to other households.

The first factor, tax-and-transfer systems, may be associated with the 'activation turn' in public policies, which emphasized that financial incentives to take up employment had to be increased: if enhanced financial incentives are not accompanied by success in activation in the segment of work-poor households, relative poverty can increase because the income gap between employed and unemployed people grows. This does not imply that activation and concern about financial incentives to take up jobs should be abandoned. However, activation must be based on a 'high road' to quality jobs and real investment in human capital. In other words, both the quantity and the quality of jobs count; the quality of employment should actually be seen as a condition for a full valorization of human capital. Also, Europe needs a combination of adequate social investment and adequate social protection; they cannot be substitutes for each other. The emphasis on 'investment' in human capital should not ignore the need for protection of human capital, that is, the traditional 'protective' functions of welfare states.

Observations with regard to the decreased generosity of welfare states also point to the role of minimum wages, but we should understand that role correctly. It is not the case that increasing minimum wages would immediately have a significant impact on poverty; however, to a certain extent (and with considerable heterogeneity across countries) minimum wages function as a 'glass ceiling' for the generosity of benefit systems. In countries where minimum wages are under pressure, the generosity of social benefits will in the end also be under pressure.[9] Minimum wages are indeed seen as under pressure because of cross-border mobility: part of the fears of social dumping may be unwarranted, but in specific sectors competitive pressure from 'low-wage' employers within the EU cannot be denied. In addition, there are problems with enforcement of minimum wage standards, in the context of posting of workers. The result is grey areas, and sometimes blatant cases of exploitation. All these considerations support the idea that the EU would be well advised to develop a policy on minimum wages; I return to this below.

## A True Insurance Union

In contrast to the developments sketched in the previous section, the sharply increasing inequalities between southern and northern Eurozone member states since 2008 are clearly related to design flaws in the EU, notably in the European Monetary Union (EMU). In the wake of the crisis, a number of scholars have issued pessimistic statements about the viability of the eurozone, as they consider the diversity of the member states too large to be accommodated; Scharpf, referred to above, is an example. Schelkle (2017) proposes a contrasting, positive perspective: by organizing monetary solidarity, a monetary union enhances international risk sharing and thus allows diversity across its members.[10] However, to be an effective risk-sharing device, the monetary union must be complete. What does 'completing the monetary union' mean? A basic insight, that has gained prominence in the European Commission's thinking on the completion of EMU, is that nearly all existing monetary unions are true 'insurance unions'. They not only centralize risk management with regard to banks, they also centralize unemployment insurance. EMU is the one exception, but it is gradually developing policies driven by the need for mutual insurance, notably in its progress towards a banking union. Next to a banking union, the European Commission now argues that EMU also needs fiscal stabilizers; to achieve this, one options would be the re-insurance of national unemployment benefit schemes at the eurozone level. Another option, which the Commission seems to prefer at the time of writing this contribution, would be a scheme that supports member states' public investment capacity when they are hit by a crisis and have to cope with reduced revenue and increased spending on unemployment benefits.[11] In fact, both options share a common insight, to wit, that it is important that member states' automatic stabilizers can play their role in times of crisis whilst simultaneously their public investment capacity remains protected.

The reference to unemployment insurance in these policy scenarios is not happenstance: unemployment insurance supports purchasing power of citizens in an economic downturn, and is therefore an 'automatic stabilizer' *par excellence*. Existing monetary unions either opt for a downright centralization of unemployment insurance (like in Canada or in Germany), or they demand some convergence in the organization of unemployment insurance and provide a degree of reinsurance and centralization when the need is really high (like in the United States, which combine centralization and decentralization in unemployment insurance). This is rational behaviour for two reasons. First, risk pooling enhances resilience against asymmetric shocks. The second reason also applies when shocks are symmetric across the whole Union and risk *pooling* across member states has no added value *per se*. National insurance systems create an externality; a country that properly insures itself, also helps its neighbours. Therefore, the concern with the stability of the eurozone entails a cluster of policy principles to sustain an effective stabilization capacity in *each* member state: sufficiently generous unemployment benefits; sufficient coverage rates of unemployment benefit schemes; no labour market segmentation that leaves part of the labour force poorly insured against unemployment; no proliferation of employment relations that are not integrated into systems of social insurance; effective activation of unemployed individuals; and the constitution of budgetary buffers in good times, so that the automatic stabilizers can do their work in bad times. These principles become *a fortiori* imperative, as *quid pro quo*, if the eurozone were equipped with reinsurance of national unemployment insurance systems; but even without that perspective, the implementation of such 'stability-related' principles would benefit the eurozone as a whole.

The upshot of this argument is that monetary unification implies a degree of convergence in some key features of the participating member states' social and employment policies. This is not necessarily a flat denial of Schelkle's argument that a monetary union allows and even valorizes diversity; my emphasis is on 'convergence' (not uniformity) and on 'some' (in some policy domains, not in all domains). Admittedly, the idea that there is a social policy corollary to monetary unification is not new. Already in the 1990s, reform in labour markets was justified by the advent of the monetary union. The 1997 European Employment Strategy emphasized supply-side flexibility: an agenda for flexible labour markets was interwoven with an agenda of investment in individual labour market opportunities and the development of 'enabling' policies; together, this would create 'flexicurity'. In a nutshell, my argument adds 'stability' as a desideratum to 'flexibility': stability both in terms of the avoidance of large financial and economic shocks, and of a stable development of the wage share in national income, thanks to coordinated collective bargaining (space forbids to develop the latter point here; see Vandenbroucke 2017a). Whilst the 'enabling' dimension of flexibility focuses on equipping individual people with adequate skills, in order to achieve stability, one needs collective action: collective bargaining, but also the organization of collective insurance devices. Stability requires instruments that typically protect vulnerable individuals: unemployment insurance stabilizes the economy, because it protects the purchasing power of the unemployed. In other words, stability is intrinsically associated with collective action and 'protective' policies. Enabling and protective policies can be mutually reinforcing in creating *resilient* social systems. In the debate about tackling inequalities, a monetary union that is an insurance union for resilient social systems becomes – positively – part of the equation.

## Investment in Human Capital

Both Milanovic and the *World Inequality Report 2018* emphasize the importance of education in fighting inequalities. It is not sufficient to expand (higher) education in order to make the number of years of education the same for all, as Milanovic rightly argues, in tune with the authors of the *World Inequality Report*:

> [If] access to Harvard remains for all practical purposes limited to the children of the rich and the returns to four years of education at Harvard exceed manifold the returns to four years of education at a state college, nothing fundamental will have changed. There would be an apparent but not fundamental equality of education endowments. To attain fundamental equality, we need to equalize access to the schools that produce better returns to education and/or to equalize returns across schools. To equalize the returns by fiat is impossible in a market economy, since no one can dictate to firms that they must give equal pay to people who studied at different schools, regardless of the quality of those schools. The only remaining sensible way to equalize educational endowments is to make access to the best schools more or less equal regardless of parental income and, more importantly, to equalize the quality of education across schools. The latter can only be done by state investment and financial support (Milanovic 2016: 222).

This argument fits well into the education policy tradition of many European countries, where public quality assurance of education institutions aims at putting the bar sufficiently high for *all* educational institutions, and equal access to educational opportunity is a generally accepted policy goal. However, there is no reason for European complacency: the EU is deeply affected by a human capital divide, both between and within the member states (Vandenbroucke and Rinaldi 2015). European countries are therefore faced with a double challenge: they should consider how to boost skills and competence levels whilst also addressing the issue of how to bring high levels of competences to a broader share of the population.

For it to be effective, investment in education requires sufficiently egalitarian background conditions in the society at large. The OECD illustrates this convincingly in its work on the relationship between inequality and growth. The main transmission mechanism between inequality and growth, according to a recent OECD report, is human-capital investment (OECD 2015). While there is always a gap in education outcomes across individuals with different socio-economic backgrounds, the gap widens in high-inequality countries as people in disadvantaged households struggle to access quality education. Also, investment in education should be part of an overall policy of investing in human capital that starts early in the life cycle. Hence, reducing background inequalities between families with children and investing in child care and education support both *national cohesion* and *long-term EU-wide convergence*. Obviously, creating greater access to success in education for all children is not just a question of money; it also requires reforms in the education system in many member states.

The European institutions certainly recognize the huge education challenge and the European Commission has developed a comprehensive agenda on education, training and skills, and issued excellent recommendations on the modernization of education systems. However, this educational agenda does not carry much weight at the highest levels of European political decision-making and in the setting of budget priorities. During the years of austerity, social investment policies suffered from budgetary pressures in member states where they were highly needed (Bouget et al. 2015; Hemerijck 2017).

To counter such negative developments, the priority afforded to investment in human capital must be perceptible and tangible in the Commission's own initiatives, in its Country-Specific Recommendations (CSRs, issued in the context of the so-called 'European Semester') and in its fiscal surveillance procedure. With regard to its own initiatives, the Commission can reinforce the 'human capital' strand of the Juncker Plan, as explained by Fernandes (2017). The financial instruments of the Juncker Plan currently suffer from insufficient promotion and visibility amongst social actors; social actors do not yet consider this instrument as useful for financing loans for social projects. For the post-2020 period, a third pillar could be added to the European Fund for Strategic Investments (EFSI), devoted to investment in human capital, in addition to the two pillars devoted to infrastructures, innovation and SMEs. Also, a new evaluation framework is needed to better take into account the projects' social returns (using social indicators like the acquisition of skills or social inclusion).

The Commission must use the CSRs to insist on measures to promote the development of human capital. And to ensure that Europe's action is consistent and offers incentives to national governments, the Commission's fiscal surveillance should accommodate the measures adopted by each country to respond to such European recommendations, just as it has done with other structural reforms (particularly in consideration of the fact that the countries with the most progress to make in developing their human capital are often those with the least margin in their budgets for doing so). Finally, the EU should be ready to offer tangible support to member states that commit themselves to social investment strategies but face tight budgetary constraints: the idea of 'reform commitment packages' (as proposed in European Commission 2017b) can be a starting point.

## Fair Mobility

Milanovic argues that the immigration practices of the Gulf countries (welcoming foreign workers *en masse* but discriminating against them, in some respects rather harshly) actually contribute to the reduction in world poverty. He does not say that these practices should be generalized, but nevertheless defends a policy shift that goes some way in that direction by differentiating between different types of citizen status: 'Allow for a limited but higher level of migration than what currently exists, with legally defined relatively mild differences in treatment of local and foreign labour' (Milanovic 2016: 154).

This view on migration constitutes a significant departure from the way migration and cross-border mobility have been organized in the EU over the last 60 years, notably with regard to intra-EU migration. European citizens have a right to free movement within the EU; moreover, with the exception of non-active citizens (in specific conditions, to which I return below), mobile citizens have non-discriminatory access to social benefits in the European member state where they reside. The EU applies congenial principles to migration from outside the EU to European member states, in so far as it regulates it (which is the case when those non-Europeans move from one EU member state to another, or when they become long-term residents). Since those principles have become controversial – witness the British debate that finally triggered Brexit – I think one should pause and think whether one indeed wants to maintain and defend them. I, for one, believe that these principles merit support, *contra* Milanovic; however, there is an important, albeit complex distinction to be drawn between active and non-active citizens; and reform is needed to guarantee *fair mobility*.

The principles of free movement and non-discriminatory access to social benefits for active European citizens can not only be justified on the basis of an ideal of European citizenship, but also on the basis of more contingent arguments (see Vandenbroucke 2017b, 2017c for a more elaborate argument). First, freedom of movement for workers is a logical corollary of a single market, as we have it in the EU: allowing capital, goods and services to move freely across borders, whilst restricting the movement of workers, would create an asymmetry that can be questioned on grounds of fairness. Second, non-discriminatory access to social benefits for mobile active citizens supports the idea that the EU should be union of welfare states. The fact that a Polish worker enjoys the same social rights as Belgian workers when working and living in Belgium justifies that his employment generates the same social security contributions and tax revenue for the Belgian government as the employment of a Belgian national in Belgium. In other words, non-discrimination in terms of social rights justifies and so sustains the principle that we do not tolerate unbridled competition between the Polish and the Belgian social and taxation system on Belgian territory. Such competition exists in the form of 'posting' of workers, which creates an exception to the principle sketched here (since the employer of the posted workers does not have to pay social security contributions in the country where his employee is actually working); for this reason, 'posting' should be well delineated. Thus, the non-discrimination principle establishes a notion of reciprocity across EU member states, in the following sense: all member states guarantee that all economically active mobile citizens will have equal access to social policies in each of the member states; simultaneously, all member states understand that including economically active mobile citizens in the solidarity circle of their host country protects these solidarity circles against practices of social dumping within their own territory.

This justification of free movement and non-discriminatory access to social benefits for active citizens is not premised on the idea that there are no social risks attached to cross-border mobility as it has developed in the EU. This is one of the reasons why the system of posting – which allowed the development of a grey area, with blatant cases of exploitation and abuse – needs thorough reform. Moreover, there should be no denying that intra-EU migration, even if not in the form of posting, can have an undesirable impact on labour markets in host countries (notably in poorly regulated labour markets) and/or can create pressure on social services (notably when they are in short supply). Next to reforming posting, the best way to tackle the distributive risks associated with mobility is to be more demanding *vis-à-vis* member states with regard to the quality of their welfare states, notably in the realm of labour market regulation and the provision of social services; more demanding than the EU is today. The regulation of minimum wages is a prime example. Different traditions exist with regard to the regulation of minimum wages: in some member states public authorities set minimum wage levels, in other member states this is the exclusive domain of social partners. But, however minimum wages are determined, a common European principle should be that *all* workers are covered by minimum wage regulation: decent minimum wages should apply universally in the EU's member states, without exceptions for certain sectors, or types of jobs, or types of workers. A related example is access to social protection: there should be no jobs that do not create access to social protection.

In short, if we don't want immigration to boost a precarious, hyper-flexible segment of labour markets, there should be limits to precariousness and flexibility *across the board*. Or, think about access to social services, which can be under pressure in municipalities or regions with significant immigration: member states should guarantee sufficient provision of social services to safeguard universal access, for non-mobile citizens as much as for mobile citizens. The *European Pillar of Social Rights* can be the starting point to develop such common principles. Admittedly, turning such principles into tangible realities is an uphill battle in today's Europe; but there is no alternative if free movement is to be reconciled with domestic social cohesion.

There is, however, one important *caveat* in this debate. The coexistence of national welfare states and free movement in the EU is made possible by a principle of 'earned social citizenship'. Historically, the tension between free movement and the bounded welfare state was reconciled by granting the right to move only to the economically active (and their dependents) to the exclusion of the economically inactive and by establishing a coordination regime for social security systems to the exclusion of social assistance. This simple dichotomy was not tenable, but, when the right to free movement became open to economically non-active citizens, EU citizens were granted a right of residence throughout Europe 'as long as they do not become an unreasonable burden on the social assistance system of the host member state'. Dion Kramer sketches the combination of continuity and change in the evolution of the EU's principle of 'earned social citizenship' and situates that evolution in a broader notion of 'neo-liberal communitarianism', which 'combines a communitarian care of the national welfare state with a neo-liberal emphasis on the individual's responsibility to achieve membership of that welfare community'. He labels it 'neo-liberal' since 'it becomes the individual's own responsibility, expressed in the form of "earning" citizenship, to convert to a bounded community of economic, cultural and social values' (Kramer 2016: 272 and 277). Kramer sees dangers in the current evolution, as an expanding notion of individual responsibility risks to be pushed further and further within the confines of the national welfare state itself. However, taking on board these cautionary notes, there is also a more positive reading of the notion of 'earned social citizenship' for mobile Europeans, at least *if the EU would oblige its member states to develop comprehensive and adequate systems of minimum income protection* and if an increasingly restrictive interpretation of what 'earned social citizenship' means can be avoided. In this more positive reading, a carefully delineated possibility for member states to exclude non-nationals from domains of social policy in which principles of compassion rather than principles of responsibility dominate (such as social assistance) would be a corollary of a *duty* for each welfare state to protect its own citizens against vulnerability on the basis of compassion.

I would indeed argue that in a 'European Social Union' – a true union of welfare states – two complementary logics can apply legitimately with regard to social citizenship if they are applied conjointly:

1) Economically active citizens have the right to take up employment opportunities across borders, and on the basis of employment they – and those who depend on them – 'earn' non-discriminatory access to all social benefits in the member state where they work, including protection against the consequences of involuntary inactivity (unemployment, illness). National regulations that guarantee fairness in labour markets apply fully to them.
2) A non-active citizen who needs protection cannot simply rely on any member state of his (or her) choice: his nationality determines the member state which is first and foremost responsible for his protection. Under carefully delineated conditions, another member state to which he has no bond of nationality is allowed to say that the non-active citizen's social protection would create an 'unreasonable burden' on its welfare state. In contrast, it would be 'unreasonable' for any member state not to provide adequate social protection for its national citizens, whatever the causes of their vulnerability and dependence.

I don't say that, today, the EU and its member states apply these complimentary logics carefully and consistently: both with regard to 'fair mobility' and minimum income protection for the non-mobile citizens there is an agenda to be taken up.

My argument concerns migration and mobility within the EU. It provides support for the principle of non-discriminatory access to social benefits that regulates intra-EU migration. However, congenial EU regulation applies to non-EU ('third country') nationals who move from one country to another in the EU and to third country nationals who become long-term residents.[12] Milanovic's view on migration sits uneasily – to put it mildly – with the traditional European aspiration to develop and maintain inclusive welfare states, in which there are no 'second-class' citizens, and children of migrants can enjoy all opportunities open to children of natives, whilst migration into the EU is limited for non-EU citizens. Admittedly, my discussion of intra-European migration does not exhaust arguments on how one should organize external migration into the EU. However, I think it is not happenstance that European welfare states generally entertain an inclusive perspective on migration – by not subjecting migrants to a second-class social citizenship – and are, despite all the difficulties with the integration of migrants, relatively successful in the realm of equality compared to other regions in the world.

## Conclusion: A European Social Union is Part of the Equation

We are not doomed to undergo increasing inequalities. For sure, international competition, technological and demographic changes and sociological and ideational shifts all put pressure on welfare states; but the difference between the trajectory of most continental European welfare states on one hand, and the United States and the UK on the other hand shows that, so far, national institutions and policies played a crucial role in mitigating the impact of these changes. What the exact role of European integration was in this respect is a moot question. Sixty years ago, European integration was premised on a neat division of labour: important aspects of economic policy would become supranational, social policy could be safely left in national hands. *Prima facie*, that neat division of labour seemed to work tolerably well for many years, notwithstanding a number of early, critical observations about the EU's impact on the social fabric of member states, mentioned in this chapter. But, in today's EU, this division of labour is without doubt no longer sustainable: one reason is monetary unification, another reason is the economic heterogeneity after enlargement. Revising that division of labour requires a political contract at the European level that sustains risk-sharing and common social objectives; agreeing on such a political contract raises issues of sovereignty, solidarity and shared values, but is possible without getting trapped in and paralysed by Rodrik's 'trilemma' of democracy, sovereignty and integrated markets. However, to indicate the way forward, we need a coherent conception of a 'European Social Union' (Vandenbroucke et al. 2017d).

My emphasis on a social *union* is no coincidence. A European Social Union is not a European Welfare State: it is a union of national welfare states, with different historical legacies and institutions. A union of national welfare states requires more tangible solidarity between those welfare states as collective entities. But its primary purpose is not to organize interpersonal redistribution between individual European citizens across national borders; the main mechanisms of solidarity which the EU now needs to develop are between member states; they should refer to insurance logics rather than to redistribution, and to support for social investment strategies. Solidarity between member states necessitates shared values and a degree of convergence, but convergence is not the same as harmonization. More generally, the practice of a social union should be far removed from a top-down, one-size-fits-all approach to social policy-making in the member states.

The core idea can be summarized as follows: a social union would support national welfare states *on a systemic level* in some of their key functions and guide the *substantive development* of national welfare states – via general social standards and objectives, leaving ways and means of social policy to the member states – on the basis of an operational definition of 'the European Social Model'.[13] If we want to resist the negative impact of the complex set of challenges that is often captured in the notion of 'globalization', a European Social Union is definitely a crucial part of the equation. Sweeping analyses about the impact of globalization and deterministic accounts of either globalization or Europeanization are not helpful in this respect: rather than mobilising our intellectual and political creativity, they paralyse our thinking.

## Notes

1. I thank Jonathan Zeitlin for comments on an earlier version.
2. Milanovic would not deny the need to develop specific policies. However, to see the extent to which his approach relies on an amalgamation of various explanatory factors into one single concept, it is useful to compare it with

Bourgignon's account of 'the globalization of inequality': there is no denying that globalization contributes to inequality within advanced welfare states, but Bourguignon (2015) carefully distinguishes different mechanisms at play.
3. Beckfield's results should be contrasted with Tober and Busemeyer (2015), who find a positive association between political integration and inequality in 14 EU member states for the time period 1999–2000, but no association between economic integration and inequality on the other hand.
4. I write 'to a large degree' since the developing European Economic Community did link market integration to social harmonization in specific areas, notably safety and health at work since the 1980s. It would be incorrect to argue that there was no social dimension to the European project; the EU became also an important player in anti-discrimination policies.
5. Research such as published by Lefebvre and Pestieau (2012), Goedemé et al. (2017) and Eurofound (2015, 2017) also suggests that there have been significant time spans during which European inequality, measured on a pan-European level, actually diminished. Goedemé et al. show this for net disposable household incomes, for the second half of the 2000s, that is, the period following the enlargement to Eastern and Central European member states. An implicit conclusion from Lefebvre and Pestieau is that between 1995 and 2010, pan-European social inequalities, measured for the whole EU15 with a variety of indicators, must have diminished. Eurofound's work on wage inequality in the EU shows that wage inequality across Europe diminished between 2005 and 2014, which was the net effect of increasing wage inequality within countries and decreasing wage inequality between countries.
6. Martinsen (2015) challenges the assumption that a strong causal link exists between legal and political integration in the EU, in which Court rulings progress and shape European integration in important dimensions of social policy and health care. She underscores the role of politics, *contra* Scharpf's determinist view on the role of the Court of Justice. For references supporting my contention that Scharpf's and likeminded authors' understanding of the eurozone crisis is too schematic and deterministic, see Vandenbroucke 2017a, note 4 on pp. 6–7.
7. Rodrik's recent writing on the EU is more pessimistic than his earlier work; compare his assessment of the EU in *The Globalization Paradox* ('For all its teething problems, Europe should be viewed as a great success considering its progress down the path of institution building. For the rest of the world, however, it remains a cautionary tale' (Rodrik 201: 220) and his assessment in *Straight Talk on Trade: Ideas for a Sane World Economy*: 'Macron notwithstanding, today it may be too late to entertain fiscal and political integration within the EU' (Rodrik 2017: 78).
8. Sabel (2018) challenges Rodrik's trilemma as a poor account of the actual functioning of the EU (and even of the WTO).
9. The idea of a 'glass ceiling on poverty reduction', associated with minimum wages, is developed by Cantillon and colleagues in several publications of the Herman Deleeck Centre of Social Policy.

10. I do not want to suggest that Schelkle would agree with the remainder of this section, as I conclude that a degree of convergence in some, key features of member states' labour markets is useful for the well-functioning of the monetary union.
11. See European Commission (2017a), notably on pp. 25-6 and European Commission (2017b), notably pp. 13-16.
12. In other words, it does not apply to the situation of a non-EU third country national who has links only with a third country and a single member state: therefore, in principle, member states can pursue their own policies with regard to the integration of third country nationals, in so far as they are not regulated by specific agreements between the EU and other countries or regions in the world. The UK and Denmark have also opted out of the extension of the EU's social security coordination to third-country nationals who move from one member state to another.
13. The development of a fiscal stabilization capacity in the eurozone, to support national automatic stabilizers in one way or another, is a prime example of *systemic support* for national welfare states. Coordination of corporate tax policy is another example. I did not discuss the challenge of fair taxation, which features prominently in the agenda set out by the *World Inequality Report 2018*. Milanovic is sceptic about the potential of tax and benefit measures to redress inequalities: according to him, during the second Kuznets wave, states should work more on endowments and less on taxes and transfers. Here, I would concur with the authors of the *World Inequality Report 2018*, who argue, on the basis of solid empirical evidence, that regressive changes in taxation systems are a key explanatory factor for the surge in inequality in countries such as the United States and the UK. Given the mobility of capital, fair taxation requires supranational coordination, notably in the realm of corporate taxation. The EU is well placed to take up this challenge.

## References

Alvaredo, F., Chancel, L., Piketty, Th., Saez, E. and G. Zucman (coordinators). *World Inequality Report 2018* (World Inequality Lab 2017).

Beckfield, J. 'European integration and income inequality', *American Sociological Review* 71(6) (December 2006) pp. 964-85.

Beckfield, J. 'Remapping inequality in Europe. The net effect of regional integration on total income inequality in the European Union', *International Journal of Comparative Sociology* 50(5-6) (2009) pp. 486-509.

Bouget, D., Frazer, H., Marlier, E., Sabato S. and Vanhercke, B. *Social Investment in Europe: A Study of National Policies* (European Social Policy Network [ESPN], Brussels: European Commission 2015).

Bourguignon, F. *The Globalization of Inequality* (Princeton and Oxford, Princeton University Press 2015).

Brady, D., Beckfield, J. and Seeleib-Kaiser, M. 'Economic globalization and the welfare state in affluent democracies, 1975–2001', *American Sociological Review* 70 (December 2005) pp. 921–48.

Busemeyer, M. R, Tober, T. 'European integration and the political economy of inequality', *European Union Politics* 16(4) (2015) pp. 536–57.

Eurofound. *Converging Economies, Diverging Societies? Upward Convergence in the EU* (Eurofound, Dublin 2017).

Eurofound. *Recent Developments in the Distribution of Wages in Europe* (Publications Office of the European Union, Luxembourg 2015).

European Commission. *Reflection Paper on the Deepening of the Economic and Monetary Union*, 31 May 2017 (2017a) (COM(2017) 291).

European Commission. *New Budgetary Instruments for a Stable Euro Area Within the Union Framework*, Communication from the Commission to the European Parliament, the European Council, the Council and the European Central Bank of 6 December 2017 (2017b) (COM(2017) 822 final).

Fernandes, S. *Social Investment and the Juncker Plan* (Jacques Delors Institute, July 2017).

Ferrera, M. 'The European Social Union: A missing but necessary "political good"', in Vandenbroucke, F., Barnard, C. and De Baere, G. (eds) *A European Social Union after the Crisis* (Cambridge, Cambridge University Press 2017) pp. 47–67.

Goedemé, T., Zardo Trindade, L. and Vandenbroucke, F. 'A pan-European perspective on low-income dynamics in the EU', CSB Working Paper 17/03, Antwerp: Herman Deleeck Centre for Social Policy (University of Antwerp 2017).

Hemerijck, A. (ed.) *The Uses of Social Investment* (Oxford, Oxford University Press 2017).

International Labour Organization. 'Social aspects of European economic co-operation: Report by a group of experts (summary)', *International Labour Review* 74(2) (1956) pp. 99–123.

Kramer, D. 'Earning social citizenship in the European Union: Free movement and access to social assistance benefits reconstructed', *Cambridge Yearbook of European Legal Studies* 18 (2016) pp. 270–301.

Lefebvre, M. and Pestieau P. *L'Etat-Providence en Europe. Performance et Dumping Social*, Editions Rue d'Ulm, Collection CEPREMAP (2012).

Mahutga, M.C., Roberts, A., Kwon, R. 'The globalization of production and income inequality in rich democracies', *Social Forces* 96(1) (September 2017) pp. 181–214.

Martinsen, D. S. *An Ever More Powerful Court? The Political Constraints of Legal Integration in the European Union* (Oxford, Oxford University Press 2015).

Milanovic, B. *Global Inequality. A New Approach for the Age of Globalization* (Cambridge MA, Harvard University Press 2016).

OECD. *In It Together: Why Less Inequality Benefits All* (OECD, Paris 2015).

Rodrik, D. *The Globalization Paradox. Why Global Markets, States and Democracy Can't Coexist* (Oxford, Oxford University Press 2011).

Rodrik, D. *Straight Talk on Trade. Ideas for a Sane World Economy* (Princeton and Oxford, Oxford University Press 2017).

Sabel, Ch. 'Sovereignty and complex interdependence: Some surprising indications of their compatibility', in Lever, A. and Satz, D. (eds) *Ideas that Matter: Democracy, Justice,* Rights (Oxford, Oxford University Press, forthcoming 2018).

Scharpf, F. 'The Asymmetry of European Integration, or Why the EU Cannot be a Social Market Economy', KFG Working Paper, No 6 (September 2009).

Scharpf, F. W. 'The costs of non-disintegration: The case of the European Monetary Union', in Chalmers, D., Jachtenfuchs, M. and Joerges, C. *The End of the Eurocrats' Dream: Adjusting to European Diversity* (Cambridge, Cambridge University Press 2016) pp. 29–49.

Schelkle, W. *The Political Economy of Monetary Solidarity: Understanding the Euro Experiment* (Oxford, Oxford University Press 2017).

Vandenbroucke, F. and Rinaldi, D. 'Social inequalities in Europe – The challenge of convergence and cohesion', in Vision Europe Summit Consortium (eds): *Redesigning European Welfare States – Ways Forward* (Gütersloh 2015) pp. 38–77.

Vandenbroucke, F. 'Structural convergence versus systems competition: limits to the diversity of labour market policies in the European Economic and Monetary Union', ECFIN discussion paper 065, *European Commission Directorate-General for Economic and Financial Affairs* (Brussels, 20 July 2017a).

Vandenbroucke, F. 'EU citizenship should speak both to the mobile and the non-mobile European', in Maurizio Ferrera and Rainer Bauböck (eds) 'Should EU citizenship be Duty Free?' EUI Working Papers, RSCAS 2017/60 (2017b) pp. 9–12.

Vandenbroucke, F. 'Basic income in the European Union: a conundrum rather than a solution', ACCESS EUROPE Research Paper 2017/02, (1 August 2017c).

Vandenbroucke, F., Barnard, C. and De Baere, G. (eds) (2017d) *A European Social Union After the Crisis* (Cambridge, Cambridge University Press 2017).

CHAPTER 13

# Social Democracy in an Era of Automation and Globalization

Jane Gingrich

The last years have not been kind to social democratic parties. The political earthquake election of Donald Trump in the United States, the British Brexit vote, and rising populism across Europe are the most recent manifestations of a longer-term unsettling of traditional political alignments, an unsettling that has cost social democratic parties almost everywhere. In the European national elections of 2017, only in Norway did the Social Democrats maintain power (with a smaller vote share); in the French presidential election, the first-round vote share of the Socialist Party candidate fell from 29.4 per cent in 2012 to 7.4 per cent; the German Social Democrats fell from an already depleted 25.7 per cent to 20.5 per cent of votes; while the Dutch Labour party sunk from 24.8 per cent in 2012 to 5.7 per cent. British Labour, which increased its vote share in 2017, forms a notable exception, albeit not a victorious one.

This electoral decline of social democratic parties comes at a time when many of their core values remain both economically and politically viable, and indeed, are in ascendency in some contexts. Employers and mainstream economists have, in some cases, called for more (not less) investment in skills and infrastructure (e.g. Heckman 2011), and recent work by the OECD and International Monetary Fund (Cingano 2014; Ostry 2014) has pointed to the deleterious consequences of inequality on long-run growth. Voters, too, support an active state. Figure 13.1 displays public opinion data from five European nations taken from the European Social Survey (2016), and shows that in all cases, a majority of citizens report to support income redistribution, and in most cases, average support has risen over the last decade. Why has the mainstream left not captured more of this basic support for left-wing economic policy? Can it reverse this changing tide?

This paper follows much work in political science to argue that the left's woes are in part due to structural changes in the economy that have both created economic challenges and altered the social bases of the left's electoral support. The following pages focus on these economic policy changes,

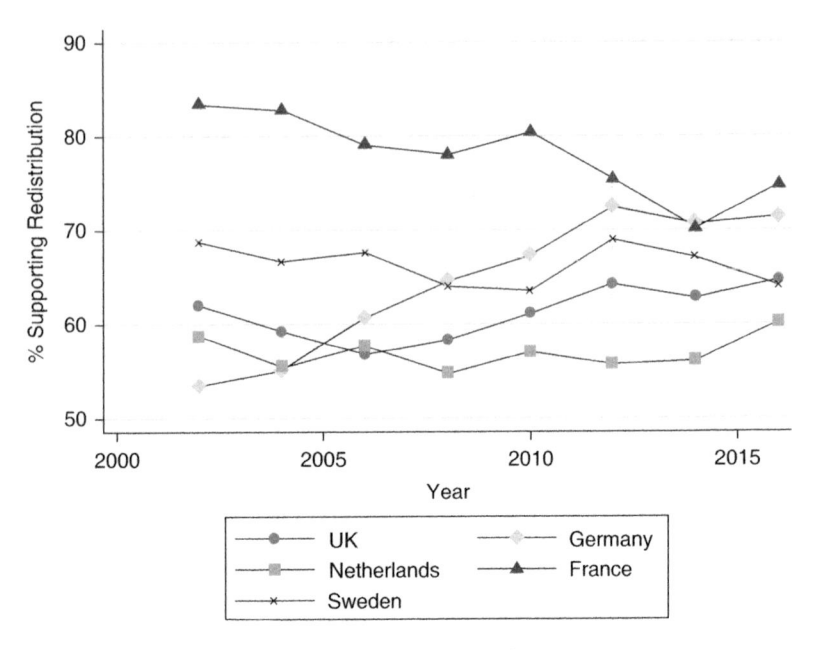

**FIGURE 13.1** Public support for redistribution in five EU countries.

although other policy dilemmas, such as those around immigration, cultural liberalism, and nationalism are also relevant.

In focusing on economic change, this paper argues that structural pressures manifest through a series of policy challenges that individually the mainstream left is well placed to address, but that collectively, it has faced more difficulty in reconciling. The changing structure of labour markets has meant that left parties concerned with inequality and poverty have faced the simultaneous policy challenge of expanding skills among workers and attracting 'good' jobs to changing local labour markets while also continuing to address the needs of their traditional constituencies, many of whom have been displaced (directly or indirectly) by economic change. At the same, social democratic parties have faced a very different electoral environment, as the class structure has radically changed (Oesch 2016).

The challenge of addressing individual and geographic vulnerability in post-industrial labour markets and maintaining traditional vote share have often pulled in different directions, with left parties either prioritising policies that create more economically competitive citizens and regions, without the political visibility or stability of past appeals, or maintaining traditional class and community support without longer term policies able to address economic change.

The paper outlines these challenges, and then suggests some lessons for moving forward.

## The Post-Industrial Challenge: Skills and Communities

In examining the turbulent fortunes of left parties in the post-financial crisis era, scholars and pundits alike have pointed to the deeper economic and political roots of social democratic decline (e.g. Beramendi et al. 2015). Both global economic integration and the automation of many manufacturing jobs have altered the economic structure of advanced industrial economies, radically reshaping the types of skills demanded in many labour markets. Through the 1980s and 1990s, many labour economists pointed to the growing compatibility between new technologies and higher levels of general skills (e.g. university degrees), meaning that the economic returns to higher-skilled work have grown (Goldin and Katz 2009; Berman and Machin 2000). This shift hit those in mid-skilled 'routinisable' jobs particularly hard, with declining employment in traditional industrial jobs as well as many types of clerical work (Autor et al. 2003; Goos and Manning 2007). As industrial jobs disappeared, newly created jobs often required either higher levels of skills or lower levels of pay.

These structural changes in the labour market have created new policy challenges in addressing individual level risk and vulnerability. While scholars debate the relative contribution of technology, globalization and other factors to growing inequality, there is no doubt that across most advanced industrial economies income inequality has risen since the 1980s, and low-skilled individuals are bearing the brunt of these shifts. In many contexts, relative increases in the wages of low-skilled citizens have lagged behind their higher-skilled counterparts – even as the size of the high-skilled workforce has expanded – and in the post-financial crisis period low-skilled citizens have been hit particularly hard (OECD 2014). Some workers have lost jobs, but perhaps more importantly, new cohorts of low- and mid-skilled workers have faced difficulty finding work, or finding high quality work.

The disappearance of industrial jobs and rise of new service sector work has not only created new categories of vulnerable workers but also vulnerable geographic regions. Post-industrial labour markets have often privileged more concentrated urban areas (Moretti 2012), placing pressure on declining

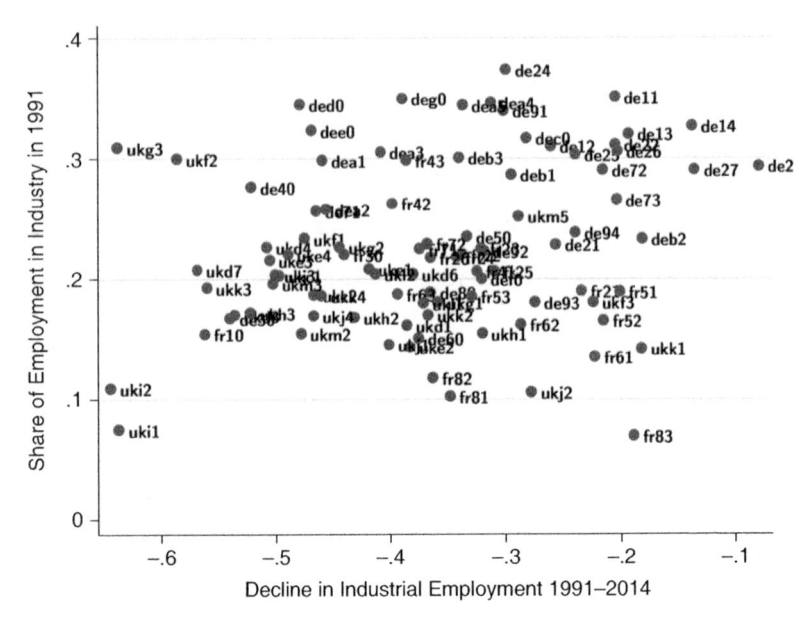

**FIGURE 13.2** EU relative employment loss in manufacturing 1991–2014.

industrial regions. These geographic shifts have meant that entire places, as well as workers with particular types of skills, have faced tough economic adjustment.

Since 1991, all 15 European Union (EU) countries have lost employment in manufacturing, but this loss affected some regions more than others. Figure 13.2 shows a scatter plot of relative employment loss in manufacturing between 1991 and 2014, and the percentage of local employment in manufacturing in 1991 in UK, France and Germany.[1] Figure 13.2 illustrates substantial variation in regional experiences. Some regions have been harder hit by industrial decline than others, with the industrial regions of the UK, for instance, losing more jobs than their counterparts in Germany. Equally, the adjustment path has varied even in regions with similar levels of decline; some have faced higher rates of unemployment than others; French regions, for instance, face higher long-run levels of unemployment than their similarly affected British counterparts (Eurostat 2016).[2]

Maintaining living standards in regions where upwards of half of industrial jobs have disappeared, or where there is persistently high unemployment, can be challenging. Even those regions that have avoided high levels of unemployment, such as the industrial regions of the UK,

**Gross Value Added Per Capita 2014, 1000s Euros**

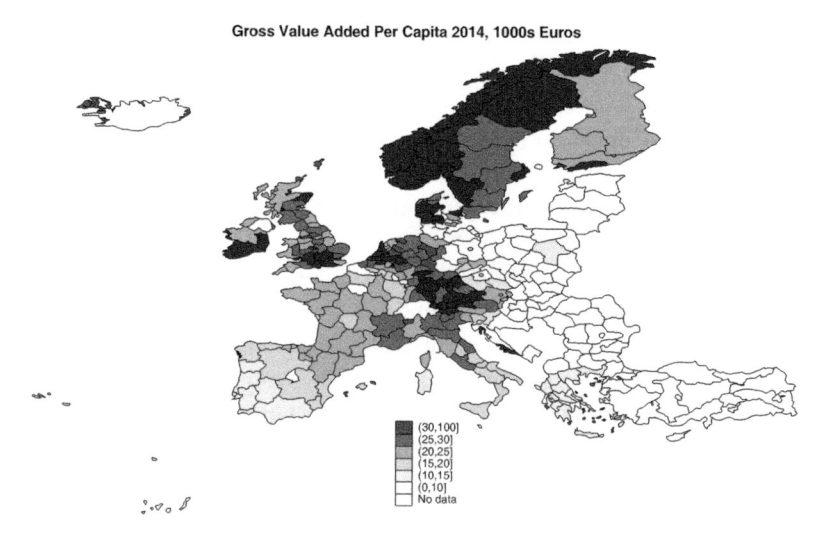

Legend:
- (30,100]
- (25,30]
- (20,25]
- (15,20]
- (10,15]
- (0,10]
- No data

**FIGURE 13.3** GVA per capita across Europe's regions in 2014.

have faced difficult economic adjustment. Figure 13.3 shows the tremendous variation within and across European countries in productivity levels, as demonstrated by the map of gross value added per capita across European regions in 2014. This regional variation matters for policy-makers concerned with equity in living standards within a country.

Why do these changes matter for the left? At first glance, new post-industrial pressures offer opportunities for left parties, as economically left policies are often compatible with improved economic performance. In the long-run, many argue that public investment in skills is likely to be growth producing (Krueger and Lindahl 2001). Moreover, as job creation in declining regions is often anaemic, with labour mobility not offsetting the decline, some argue that public investment in the infrastructure of deindustrialising regions can improve productivity. For instance, a recent working paper by economists Anna Valero and John van Reenan (2016) suggests that the expansion of universities in an area can enhance regional growth. Put differently, public investment in both skills and local job creation can boost long-run growth above and beyond a laissez-faire minimalist approach. There is a seeming economic and equity 'win-win' to certain kinds of public spending, as investment in both skills, and physical infrastructure that diffuses skills and technologies to a broader set of citizens and communities, promises to be growth- and equity-producing.

This congruence between economic adjustment and left policy goals has not gone unnoticed in either policy or academic circles. Indeed, work on the political economy of post-industrial transition has pointed to the potential complementarity between economic growth and expanded equity by investing in the supply side of the economy (Boix 1998). However, this shift to the supply side and the 'win-win' scenario for the left has faced two major challenges in practice.

First, while expanding education and skills, and regional infrastructure is potentially equity creating in the long-run, in the short-run, maintaining equity still requires some conventional income security programmes to address economic dislocation. Addressing the vulnerabilities of lower-skilled workers, or mid-skilled workers employed in newly created lower-skilled jobs, and of local labour markets facing decline, often requires both new types of policies – investments in skills, training, education and active labour market policy – while also maintaining many traditional policies (e.g. pensions, unemployment insurance) and public service investment to compensate individuals and communities hit by economic change.

Spending on education and skills, while also investing in public infrastructure, and providing security to those hardest hit by economic changes, proved, in many cases to be beyond the capacity (or some might argue, the political will) of many left-wing governments, leading some to prioritize new spending over income security, while others attempted to slow the pace of economic adjustment while maintaining compensatory spending. I will argue below that these choices created tough trade-offs.

Second, next to these economic challenges, the voting base of the left has changed, and the new 'win-win' economic and equity creating policies often did not create durable 'wins' at the ballot box.[3] Early work by Herbert Kitschelt (1994) and others, pointed to the growing gap between more culturally-oriented left voters and more traditional economic constituencies. As the manual working class has declined in numbers, and new urban service-oriented workers (both low and high skilled) have increased, the electoral base of left support has radically changed (Gingrich and Hausermann 2015; Gingrich 2017). However, for left parties, swapping industrial workers for the new urban service sector workers often meant moving from relatively developed organizational structures linked to trade-unions and local party affiliates to both less developed structures of mobilization and less attached voters.

These changes have, in many countries, meant that traditional left voters have shrunk in number, while newer voters are more willing to switch among left and centrist parties. With weaker links to organized labour, social democratic parties have increasingly relied on policy appeals and issues of competence to attract voters. However, as mentioned above, their policies have often been constrained, and policies alone have often not been enough to create secure centre-left voting blocs.

Social democrats then have faced a triple challenge: to address the real vulnerabilities and fallout created by structural economic change; to support dynamic and inclusive labour market adjustment both for individuals and regions; and to maintain vote share. The following sections suggest that parties often favoured one or two of these goals over others, struggling to combine all three. The final section returns to the possibilities inherent in the current moment, suggesting that aspects of left policy remain popular, are often economically efficient, and more equitable than the alternatives.

## Social Democracy Constrained

In an early study of the challenge of addressing post-industrial economic adjustment, political scientists Torben Iversen and Anne Wren (1998) pointed to what they called the 'trilemma' of the transition to the service economy. Iversen and Wren argued that as productivity growth was slower in services than in manufacturing, the transition to a service based economy threatened to create new income equality by driving a wedge between the returns to those in productive industrial jobs and lower productivity service jobs. Governments could address this inequality by employing service workers in the public sector, a strategy that came at a cost of budgetary restraint, or by limiting service job growth, a strategy that threatened higher levels of unemployment. For Iversen and Wren, there was an inherent three-way trade-off among budgetary control, lower unemployment, and inequality, of which, at most two were achievable. Iversen and Wren argued that the Anglo-American countries were largely accepting higher levels of inequality, while the Continental European countries opted for higher unemployment, whereas the Scandinavian countries opted for greater public spending.

The development of the service sector has proven complex, as have national responses to it, but nonetheless, Iversen and Wren's initial insight that trade-offs exist in how national political economies approached deindustrialization remains crucial. These differences have had important implications for the way social democratic parties have adjusted.

## The Anglo-Approach – Visible Skills and Technocratic Redistribution

For both the United States and the UK, the experience of the 1980s and 1990s was of a more direct market-oriented approach to changing industrial structures, which produced, particularly in the case of the UK under the Conservative Thatcher governments, a sharp and prolonged shock to the manufacturing sector with rising income inequality through the 1980s. Similar patterns, albeit to differing extents, occurred through the Anglo world.

While the nature of political control varied across the Anglo countries, by the mid-1990s, many left parties were looking to reorient their appeal in the face of both electoral decline and the changing economic structure. Social democrats (or their mainstream left equivalents) in these countries faced the challenge of attracting new middle-class voters while also addressing the needs of traditional constituents in the face of rising inequality and stagnating wages.

In response, both in the United States and UK, and to a lesser extent elsewhere, mainstream left parties adopted a 'third way' mantra, ostensibly promising to make the market work better for all. The solution to squaring middle-class votes with more equity in the economy lay in supporting the development of individual skills, access to the labour market, and greater individual responsibility (Giddens 2013).

This approach generally accepted the inevitability of structural economic change – both globalization and automation – and eschewed policies to limit or blunt the pace of change. Moreover, instead of emphasising more traditional welfare programmes and public management to compensate for economic changes, Third Way left parties promised to achieve more equity by supporting the development of better jobs for a wider group of citizens. In so doing, Third Way politicians focused in particular on labour markets, promising to 'make work pay', while limiting – rhetorically – more traditional passive forms of redistribution such as cash transfers to the unemployed.

The key to do doing so involved investment in skills and the expansion of work opportunities. Most prominently, this approach involved the expansion of more general skills. In the UK, New Labour staked much effort on expanding the quality of schooling and the number of pupils leaving school with basic qualifications, while also expanding access to universities and higher education. Between 2000 and 2015, the percentage of the 25–64-year population with tertiary (university) education, expanded from 25 per cent to 45 per cent in UK, 22 per cent to 44 per cent in Ireland, 27 per cent to 44 per cent in Australia, and 40 per cent to 56 per cent in Canada. The United States, which started with a higher baseline expanded less, from 36 per cent to 45 per cent (OECD 2016).[4]

While much has been written on the 'neo-liberal' turn in the left, it is worth pointing out that third way policies did have a strong statist element to them. In the UK, the Blair and Brown governments substantially increased spending and central managerialism (Chote et al. 2010), while American Democrats pushed hard for both new health programmes and expanded regulation around education.

However, even as third-way left parties through the 1990s and 2000s called for, to quote New Labour, 'education, education, education', left parties recognized that a long-run investment in skills alone was not sufficient: addressing poverty, inequality, and vulnerability also required current spending on workers and other vulnerable groups such as children and the elderly. The result was that the left tended to combine an emphasis on skills and public services with a more technocratic approach to redistribution.

Technocratic redistribution, here, refers to the use of lower visibility and less overt forms of government spending, such as tax credits to support work or benefits targeted to families with children, rather than traditional spending programmes such as unemployment benefits. Through the 1990s and 2000s, both under left and non-left governments, in many Anglo countries, the real value of unemployment benefits fell. At the same time, however, most of these countries, often under left control, expanded alternative forms of income support. In the United States, alongside the welfare reforms of the 1990s (supported by both Democratic President Clinton and the Republican Congress), the expansion of tax credits for low income families with a worker became a central tranche of income support. In the UK, New Labour also expanded tax credits to families, as well as child benefits, cutting child poverty. Combined, these shifts meant a move towards less income support for the childless adults (pensioners have fared better), but more income support for families, particularly low-income families.

Figure 13.4 combines data on unemployment and pension replacement rates – the amount of income the average worker might anticipate during a spell of unemployment/during retirement as a percentage of the wages of a 'standard' worker in manufacturing – and child benefits as a percentage of average wages and low-earners' (half of average) wages. What Figure 13.4

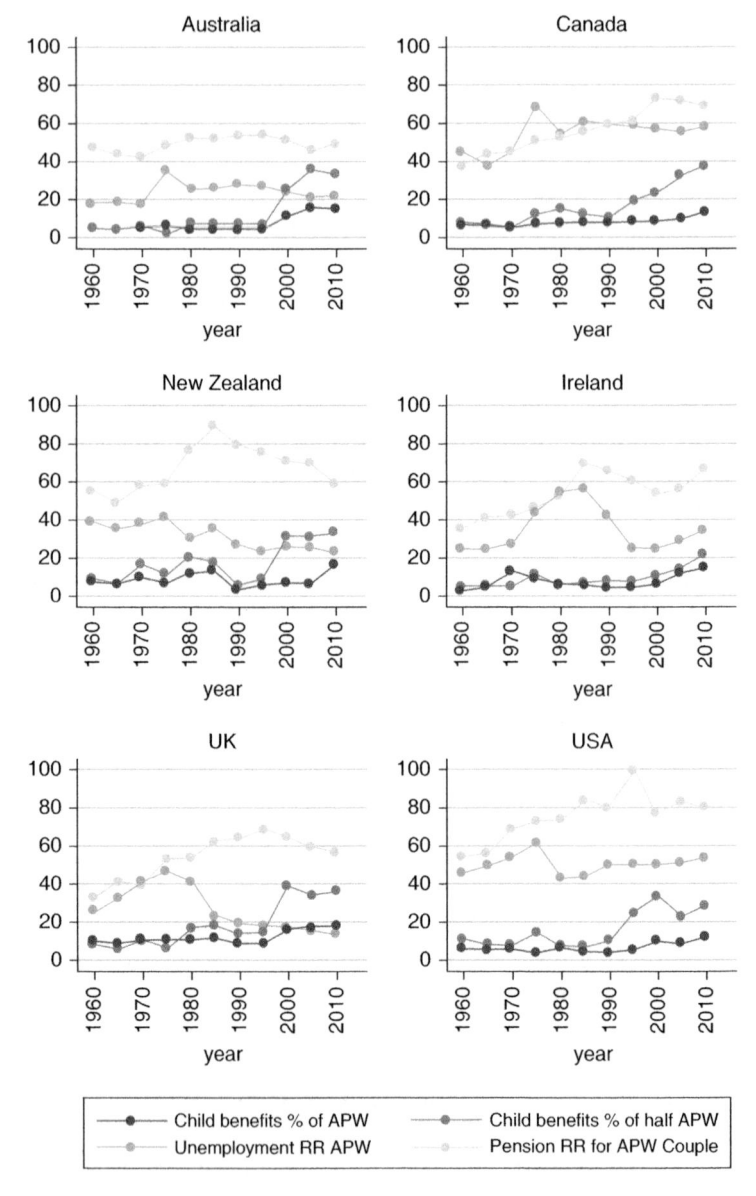

**FIGURE 13.4** Income support programmes in major industrialized countries.

shows is that across the Anglo countries, child benefits, particularly for low-income working age adults, became increasingly important, even as unemployment benefit rates fell.[5] Traditional income support programmes did indeed change, but the state continued to play a crucial role in redistributing resources and reducing poverty.

Technocratic approaches were often a reaction to a political moment in which many voters were less sympathetic to redistribution, and in particular, more passive redistribution (Cavaille and Trump 2015). However, technocratic redistribution often meant the individuals and communities who received it felt less vested in the system, and often more beleaguered, than past voters linked to organized labour or more visible benefits. As Geoff Evans and James Tilley (2012) show in the UK, working class voters (and other groups) increasingly saw little difference among political parties, despite the large increase in spending and reduction in poverty under Labour. By contrast, middle class urban voters supporting education and skills are increasingly quite securely linked to left policies, but not necessarily a given party.

In sum, while the expansion of educational access and the shift in the distributive structure of benefits had important effects, these policies in the short-run left much of the underlying market structure in place – low wage and low-productivity jobs remained a key part of the political economy, as did uneven geographic patterns of growth. At the same time, unlike earlier policies, such as building the NHS in the UK, or the New Deal in the United States, third way policies created fewer direct vested interests or mobilized voters linked to left parties themselves. The result was a less durable coalition around parts of the welfare state than the past, making parts of it more vulnerable, and political support more ephemeral.

## Continental Path – Compensation and Liberalization

Social democratic parties in many Continental European countries were initially more reticent about cuts to traditional welfare programmes and less supportive of expanding higher general skills than their Anglo counterparts. However, as the costs of this approach – both politically and economically grew – many of these parties did move to a more reformist position, often with serious electoral consequences.

The extent of de-industrialization has varied substantially across the European continent, with some regions, particularly in Germany, retaining a strong industrial base. However, as elsewhere, both automation and globalization have put pressure on these labour markets.

During the 1980s and the 1990s, unlike in Britain, many Continental countries moved to slow the pace of change, and ease the burdens on workers. Oftentimes, this approach involved the expansion of benefits, particularly early retirement and disability benefits, to would-be displaced workers. Through the 1990s, labour force participation of older men fell, in 1995, across the EU-15 countries, only 39 per cent of men aged 55–64 were still active in the labour force, ranging from a high of 68 per cent in Sweden, to a low of 24 per cent in Belgium (European Commission 1996).

The expansion of access to early retirement often drew on cross-party policy, or collectively bargained benefits, and was not specific to social democratic parties (e.g. see Hemerijk and Visser 1997 on the Netherlands), yet these moves put social democratic parties in a particular bind. David Rueda (2005) has characterized this bind in terms of a conflict between social democratic constituents with secure jobs and benefits and younger cohorts of workers outside of this system. Initially, many social democratic parties found it hard to take the Anglo path. Their constituents in the manufacturing sector and unions resisted moves to liberalize labour markets or cut traditional unemployment and pension benefits, and for fiscal and political reasons new expenditure on active labour market policy in addition to existing benefits was seen as infeasible. The result was through the 1990s, in both Continental and Southern Europe, older industrial workers, and to a lesser extent the communities they inhabited, maintained both greater protection from structural change and compensation for it, but younger workers often faced new insecurities in finding permanent high-quality employment.

In response, in some contexts, social democrats began to reconsider their compensatory approach. In the Netherlands, the Dutch Labour party in the early to mid-1990s, moved towards supporting more labour market flexibility, with support for skills and active labour market policy. In Germany, the SPD-led Schroeder government also adopted a 'third way' rhetoric, which preceded a fairly substantial liberalization of the labour market for temporary employment, and cuts to some traditional benefits like unemployment insurance.

It is outside the bounds of this paper to evaluate the economic efficacy of these changes, but politically, they put social democrats in a difficult position, as these policies were not well received by the traditional voting base, and at the same time, did not create stable support elsewhere.

Hanna Schwander and Philip Manow (2017), writing about the cuts and liberalization introduced by the SPD in Germany through the Hartz reforms, argue that while the direct consequences of the reforms on social democratic voters were more limited than is often assumed by the popular press, indirectly, they were highly consequential. Schwander and Mannow argue that the reforms played a crucial role in expanding the popularity and stability of left-wing competitors to the SPD, namely the Linke party, by mobilising voters that lost out from change. At the same time, those that benefitted from the changes in terms of job creation, often continued to face income insecurity, and offered less clear allegiance to the social democrats.

Again, we see the challenge of combining a more technocratic set of policies aimed at accomplishing a goal – here job creation – with electoral imperatives.

## The Scandinavian Path – a Model for Social Democracy?

Throughout the post-war era, left parties in the Nordic countries were famously electorally successfully, and today, social democratic parties across the Nordic countries continue to command sizeable vote shares. These parties have also changed, however, in the face of changing industrial and electoral conditions.

While the small, open Nordic economies had long had high levels of trade and exposure to global economic currents, as elsewhere, the combination of increased financial globalization and technological shifts put pressure on domestic manufacturing industries, and spurred a growth of services. As Iversen and Wren (1998) argue, the Scandinavian countries responded to early pressures of de-industrialization by both expanding the public sector and largely maintaining the institutions of wage compression through extensive union bargaining. Structural shifts, combined with an early push to expand female labour force participation, created both a supply and demand for public sector jobs.

The basic contours of this early strategy are in place today. Close to a third of employees in Sweden, Denmark and Norway work in the public sector (compared to an OECD average 21.3 per cent) (OECD 2015). Equally, while unionization rates have fallen in the Nordic countries, a half to two thirds of workers in these countries are still union members, membership levels that dwarf all other European countries, with the exception of Belgium.

This combination of high levels of unionization and the development of high quality service sector work in the public sector, has led political scientist Kathleen Thelen to influentially characterize the Nordic path as one of 'embedded flexibilization'. Thelen argues that the long-standing investment in skills, combined with explicit bargains between service and manufacturing unions, meant that the Nordic countries were able to transition to more flexible labour market structures without the surge in inequality experienced in the Anglo-world.

Social democrats in the Nordic countries maintain a strong base, and while inequality has substantially increased, these countries continue to have a more egalitarian labour market and electoral success. But differently, this combination appears to square the circle for social democrats, providing them with an economically viable and equitable strategy for growth, which continues to maintain strong links to traditional mobilising agents in unions.

This path, while a long-run model in many ways for social democrats elsewhere, has also faced some challenges. As elsewhere, the combination of traditional working-class voters and newer middle classes within the social democratic base has caused some tensions – notably over migration – but also over the management of public services and greater competition and choice within the public sector (Gingrich 2011). However, in contrast to elsewhere, the ongoing structure of unionization, and in particular the growth of unionized public-sector jobs, has given social democratic parties a continuing base for mobilising around equity issues.

## The Post-Industrial Responses: Effective, Visible and Cross-Class?

The above analysis is meant to show that social democratic parties have faced significant challenges, and there is no one-size fits all, off the shelf, approach to economic, social and political success. However, these structural challenges equally do not mean that the mainstream left is doomed. There is appetite for left policies, and in post-industrial economies where skills matter greatly and private employers alone are often not investing sufficiently in skills and infrastructure, there are many areas in which left policies offer both the possibility to expand growth and to improve social equity. Even where spending is less pro-growth, the public often supports spending to help those facing challenges.

The task then for the left is to build and mobilize stable networks around these policies. General investment in skills and more technocratic redistribution alone may not build allegiances to the mainstream left that are as stable as more traditional policies and links to organized labour previously provided. Supporting traditional policies and organized labour, however, has often led to a shrinking base and long-term concerns about growth and employment. The Scandinavian approach of maintaining unionization and expanding the public sector offers some lessons for elsewhere, but may not be fully replicable.

A few potential lessons however, come out of the above experience. First, policies alone may not be enough to build support bases, policies need to be visible to voters and their intermediaries. While third way left parties emphasized efficient solutions, and through the 2000s, often defined the best policy as the one that was least noticeable policy – tax credits, behavioural incentives, 'nudges', and so on – efficiency is only one desideratum of good policy. As argued through this paper, efficiency and equity can be highly compatible in the post-industrial economy, but micro-policy efficiency does not guarantee long-run allegiance by voters. Policy-makers on the left may need to consider policies that allow voters to understand the role of the state, by making clear and visible appeals.

Second, in the long-run, skills are absolutely crucial to any successful left strategy. Raising the skills and capacities of citizens is both normatively and economically desirable. But, in the short-run, skills alone are not enough, and mainstream left parties need to support individuals and communities affected by structural economic change. While most left parties clearly recognize this, and electoral support for redistribution and labour market regulation varies, these policies and skill-based investments should not be substitutes. Education can only be one tranche of left policy towards labour markets.

Finally, mobilising public sector workers is likely to be a vital part of any economic and political strategy for social democratic parties, but it alone is not enough. While expanding the public sector workforce has been an important part of the long-run Nordic strategy both economically and politically, elsewhere, conservative parties have often mobilized against public sector workers. This mobilization is particularly virulent in the United States, with a number of states taking more restrictive positions towards public sector workers.

Mobilization of the young, private sector workers, and other groups outside the labour force will be important to the long-run success of social democratic parties. In an era of declining unionization, other forms of mobilization have emerged, such as Organizing for America around the Obama campaign. These organizational strategies have often successfully brought voters to the polls, but struggled to create networks outside of electoral cycles (something that contrasts to quite successful grassroots mobilization through the Tea Party and churches for the Republican party). Investing in greater mobilization is crucial to the long-run success of social democrats.

The above paragraphs are not meant to advocate a return to inefficient policies or machine politics, but rather, to suggest that connecting the efficient and popular policies to durable electoral support requires some attention to the way policies are perceived by voters and the organizational structures on the ground that sustains them.

## Notes

1. These data are compiled from the European Regional database (Cambridge Econometrics 2014) and exclude one Scottish region (UKM6) for presentational ease.
2. The average unemployment rate between 1991 and 2014 in French regions with greater than 20 per cent industrial employment in 1991 was 9.5 per cent, whereas in similar British regions it was 6.3 per cent over this period (author's calculation, from European regional yearbooks and Eurostat).
3. In addition, in some context, growing income inequality has led to concerns of disproportionate policy influence by higher income voters or interest groups (Gilens 2012).
4. The rate of increase in higher education has been slower in some Continental countries. The Nordic countries, see below, have similar levels of education, but began expansion somewhat earlier. The Southern European countries also dramatically expanded higher education during this time, but from a lower baseline.
5. The data on pension and unemployment replacement rates come from the CWED-2 dataset (Scruggs 2014). The data on child benefits are from the Child Benefit Dataset (SOFI 2015).

## References

Ansell, Ben W. 'University challenges: Explaining institutional change in higher education', *World Politics* 60(02) (2008) pp. 189–230.

Autor, David H., Levy, Frank and Murnane, Richard J. 'The skill content of recent technological change: An empirical exploration', *The Quarterly Journal of Economics* (2003) pp. 1279–333.

Beramendi, Pablo, Häusermann, Silja, Kitschelt, Herbert and Kriesi, Hanspeter. *The Politics of Advanced Capitalism* (Cambridge, Cambridge University Press 2015).

Berman, Eli and Machin, Stephen. 'Skill-biased technology transfer around the world', *Oxford Review of Economic Policy* 16(3) (2000) pp. 12–22.

Boix, Carles. *Political Parties, Growth and Equality: Conservative and Social Democratic Economic Strategies in the World Economy* (Cambridge, Cambridge University Press 1998).

Chote, Robert, Crawford, Rowena, Emmerson, Carl and Tetlow, Gemma. 'Public spending under Labour', *Institute for Fiscal Studies* (2010).

Cingano, Federico. *Trends in Income Inequality and its Impact on Economic Growth* (OECD, Paris 2014).

Cambridge Econometrics. *European Regional Database* (Cambridge, Cambridge Econometrics 2014).

European Commission. *European Regional Yearbook* (multiple years).

European Social Survey Cumulative File, ESS 1–7 (2016). Data file edition 1.0. NSD – Norwegian Centre for Research Data, Norway – Data Archive and distributor of ESS data for ESS ERIC.

Gilens, Martin. *Affluence and Influence: Economic inequality and political power in America* (Princeton, Princeton University Press 2012).

Gingrich, Jane. 'A new progressive coalition? The European left in a time of change', *The Political Quarterly* 88(1) (2017) pp. 39–51.

Gingrich, Jane and Häusermann, Silja. 'The decline of the working-class vote, the reconfiguration of the welfare support coalition and consequences for the welfare state', *Journal of European Social Policy* 25(1) (2015) pp. 50–75.

Goldin, Claudia and Katz, Lawrence F. *The Race between Education and Technology* (Cambridge MA, Harvard University Press 2009).

Heckman, James J. 'The economics of inequality: The value of early childhood education', *American Educator* 35(1) (2011) p. 31.

Iversen, Torben and Wren, Anne. 'Equality, employment, and budgetary restraint: the trilemma of the service economy', *World Politics* 50(04) (1998) pp. 507–46.

Kitschelt, Herbert. *The Transformation of European Social Democracy* (Cambridge, Cambridge University Press 1994).

Moretti, Enrico. *The New Geography of Jobs* (New York, Houghton Miin Harcourt 2012).

OECD. *Government at a Glance* (Paris, OECD 2015).

OECD. *Education at a Glance* (Paris, OECD 2016).

Oesch, Daniel. *Redrawing the Class Map: Stratification and Institutions in Britain, Germany, Sweden and Switzerland* (New York, Springer 2016).

Ostry, Jonathan David, Berg, Andrew and Tsangarides, Charalambos G. *Redistribution, Inequality, and Growth* (International Monetary Fund 2014).

Rueda, David. 'Insider–outsider politics in industrialized democracies: the challenge to social democratic parties', *American Political Science Review* 99(01) (2005) pp. 61–74.

Schwander, Hanna and Philip Manow. '"Modernize and Die"? German social democracy and the electoral consequences of the Agenda 2010', *Socio-Economic Review* 15(1) (2017) pp. 117–34.

Scruggs, Lyle, Jahn, Detlef and Kuitto, Kati. 'Comparative Welfare Entitlements Dataset 2. Version 2014–03', University of Connecticut and University of Greifswald (8 July 2014). Available at http://cwed2.org (Accessed 16 July 2017).

SOFI, Social Policy Indicators SPIN, The Child Benefit Database. Technical report, Stockholm University (2015).

Thelen, Kathleen. *Varieties of Liberalization and the New Politics of Social Solidarity* (Cambridge, Cambridge University Press 2015).

Valero, Anna, Van Reenen, John et al. 'How universities boost economic growth', Technical report, Centre for Economic Performance, LSE (2016).

Visser, Jelle and Hemerijck, Anton. *A Dutch Miracle: Job growth, welfare reform and corporatism in the Netherlands* (Amsterdam, Amsterdam University Press 1997).

# Postscript

Patrick Diamond

## Introduction

This book's central claim is that the inability of nation-states to protect citizens from the effects of the 'great globalization disruption' and resulting economic turmoil is imperilling the legitimacy of global capitalism and representative democracy. Since the 2008 crisis which led to the most protracted downturn in the history of Western capitalism, global economic performance stagnated as the eurozone countries struggled to cope with an unprecedented sovereign and banking debt crisis. Globalization is perceived to be responsible for rapidly rising inequality, as well as declining living standards for those on middle or low incomes (OECD 2017). Despite the pessimistic mood, it is important to remember globalization has led to impressive levels of growth and productivity across the world economy in recent decades. Millions of people in developing countries have been lifted out of poverty. Yet across the industrialized societies, too few citizens perceive themselves to be beneficiaries of globalization's great promise.

The political conundrum is that throughout the West, the domestic consent for trade liberalization and economic openness is eroding; anger at the consequences of the free movement of capital and labour across borders has rarely been more explosive, underlying Donald Trump's rise to the presidency of the United States, Britain's exit from the European Union (EU), the defeat of Matteo Renzi's referendum on constitutional reform in Italy, and the emergence of 'authoritarian populist' parties in the established democracies of Europe. The growing strength of political populism is *both* a material reaction against economic distress, as well as a cultural revolt against the politics of identity associated with a rootless, liberal cosmopolitanism (Hall, 2015). The next era of globalization is likely to be more destabilising; digitization and technological change are provoking a further shift in the balance of economic power from west to east. The restructuring of markets leads to the exponential rise of inequality, as incomes are redistributed to the most highly educated. What emerges is the apocalyptic nightmare of a meritocratic society where global elites believe they have earned their extraordinary wealth and good fortune, but that they have few moral obligations to citizens who inhabit particular national communities.

The consequence is the atrophy of Western liberal democracy. The most visceral opponent of liberal democracy is populism. The political scientist Cas Mudde defines the populist appeal as a 'thin-centred ideology' that treats society as if it is, 'ultimately separated into two homogenous and antagonistic groups, "the pure people" versus "the corrupt elite" [arguing] that politics should be an expression of the general will of the people' (cited in Rodi 2018). The claim of populists on left and right is that globalization is indefensible; the best way to protect citizens is to raise the economic drawbridge, restoring the authority and efficacy of the nation-state.

On the face of it, the populist argument is hardly difficult to refute. Countries that unilaterally retreat from the world economy are likely to experience prolonged and painful stagnation that erodes the material living standards of citizens. The challenge for those political forces committed to liberal democracy is to regain the explicit consent of citizens for economic openness by strengthening the political institutions that help to guarantee security and opportunity. That will only be achieved if economic elites recognize their material and social obligations to the rest of society, as they were compelled to do in the aftermath of World War II when the Beveridge-Keynes settlement was forged. There are a multitude of proposals discussed in this volume that seek to entrench liberal social democracy, notably the reform of labour market institutions to deal more effectively with today's challenges such as reconciling 'work' and 'care' across the life-cycle; increasing the bargaining power of workers in insecure employment markets; targeted basic income strategies to alleviate precarity, particularly for younger generations; human capital investment that helps workers through structural economic change; more controversially, the case is presented for a further crackdown on tax avoidance which has insidiously undermined the tax state and the social contract, alongside new wealth and inheritance taxes.

It is clear that the progressive strategies of the 1990s that sought to redistribute the gains of economic growth while improving the distribution of human capital through investment in education and training have run their course. In many industrialized countries, support for fiscal redistribution has fallen, as the financial crisis led to a hardening of attitudes towards the less fortunate. While mainstream economists recommend a response to globalization that is centred on 'compensating losers', most workers do not want more social benefits; they aspire to decent jobs through which social standing and respect in their community can be earned (Hall

2015). Communitarians legitimately criticize the liberal egalitarian left for abstracting human relationships while reducing matters of inequality to technocratic calculations and Gini co-efficients. In a 'moral' political economy, social ties and mutual obligations matter at least as much as the utilitarian calculus of profit and loss (Rogan 2017). Communitarianism invests hope in the institutions of civil society in affirming the common good. Yet there is still a decisive role for the state in ensuring the plentiful supply of public goods.

## Universal Basic Services

The big idea in the next phase of 'knowledge-driven' globalization ought to be the construction of an infrastructure of Universal Basic Services (UBS) that provide the 'essentials of modern life' – food, shelter, housing, transport, digital access – to every citizen alongside the core services of health and education. Basic services do not replace jobs but are intended to support citizens in navigating the labour market and finding decent work. These community-based institutions can be a source of high-skilled, fulfilling employment. They need not be provided directly by the state but through a variety of employee and community-owned mutual associations. Services do not only meet material needs but enable citizens to participate more fully in the life of their community. The proposal for Universal Basic Services pioneered by Professor Henrietta Moore at University College, London is compatible with an era of fiscal and budgetary restraint. The infrastructure is funded by fair progressive taxation including a Financial Transactions Tax operating at the European level. Taxation of financial markets is but one example of where the pooling of sovereignty can create more powerful *national* governments. Property taxes and levies on large inheritances are well suited to an era in which capital flows easily across national jurisdictions. Across the Organization for Economic Co-operation and Development (OECD) countries, wealth taxes account for less than 1 per cent of total tax revenues, yet wealth taxes are critical for reducing inequalities, and for encouraging assets to be used more productively (CHASM 2013).

The Universal Basic Services strategy addresses the vulnerabilities of the 'social investment' paradigm that dominated the debate about social policy in the EU from the late 1990s. Social investment was an influential approach in European social policy. But social investment overemphasizes human capital at the expense of services that guarantee dignity to all citizens, especially those vulnerable to economic dislocation in an era of rapid digitization and global economic integration. The EU should promote a pan-European approach to Universal Basic Services. There would be discernible political gains from, 'blunting the image of the EU as an institution focused mainly on market competition by taking action to address contemporary concerns about social cohesion' (Hall 2013: 437). The most pernicious feature of the politics of globalization over the last 20 years has been the claim that in the face of structural transformation, governments can do little to protect citizens from the forces of change; lower taxes, a race to the bottom, deindustrialization, rising inequality are all accepted as inevitable, a fact of life and a force of nature. Progressive parties must first and foremost revive the basic ideal that there *are* choices to be made, and that states have the power to act where they have democratic legitimacy. A European infrastructure of Universal Basic Services would serve to underpin the claim of political and social citizenship.

Embedding social and political citizenship requires progressive egalitarians to abandon the 'growth first, distribute later' strategy of the last three decades of economic and social policy in the advanced capitalist states. It will be necessary to actively intervene in markets to promote more equal outcomes while strengthening the bargaining power and agency of workers. So-called 'predistributive' policies focus on regulatory interventions that are designed to transform the rules of the game in which markets operate. It is as Jacob Hacker (2015: xxi) maintains, 'A focus on market outcomes that encourage a more equal distribution of economic power and rewards even before government collects taxes or pays out benefits'. Measures are required to raise and enforce national minimum wages, to encourage flexibility for workers not only firms, to design public sector procurement to ensure fair employment, and to promote moral norms that outlaw excessive pay and promote fair wages. Workers should have a voice in the management of firms through reformed corporate governance structures. Progressives must confront unequal labour, product and capital markets to attack the root causes of social injustice in post-industrial societies.

## Conclusion

Ensuring that each citizen can access the services necessary to lead a flourishing life is consistent with Amartya Sen's view of 'capabilities', where the role of the state is not merely to distribute resources, but to ensure a wide distribution of opportunities, enabling all citizens to participate in their societies regardless of their access to wealth or power. To respond credibly to globalization, progressives need a political approach that does not jettison the individualism that is integral to post-industrial societies, but seeks to cultivate strong forms of solidarity and collectivism. An open, liberal world economy has to be counter-balanced by a vigorous nation-state and national communities that retain the capacity for domestic action to reassure anxious voters. Sen's work has been crucial in emphasising the central importance of personal freedom and need for intervention by the state to ensure that citizens have the 'capabilities' to lead rich and meaningful lives. Progressive liberal egalitarians need a moral vision of social justice that can counter the resentments and insecurities stirred up by populist forces, grounded not only in the essential belief that everyone is entitled to the opportunities of a fair society, but that there must be a 'civic minimum' of basic decency in living standards and well-being beneath which no citizen should be allowed to fall.

## References

CHASM briefing paper (2013). Available at https://www.birmingham.ac.uk/Documents/college-social-sciences/social-policy/CHASM/briefing-papers/2013/wealth-taxes-problems-and-practices-around-the-world.pdf (Accessed 4 February 2018).

Hacker, J. 'The Promise of Predistribution' in Diamond, P. and Chwalisz, C. *The Predistribution Agenda: Tackling Inequality and Supporting Sustainable Growth* (London: I.B.Tauris 2015) pp. xxi–1.

Hall, P. 'The Future of the Welfare State' in Diamond, P. and Chwalisz, C. *The Predistribution Agenda: Tackling Inequality and Supporting Sustainable Growth* (London: I.B.Tauris 2015) pp. 241–53.

Hall, P. 'Democracy in the European Union: The Problem of Political Capacity' on Armingeon, K. (ed.). *Staatstatigkeiten, Parteien und Demokratie* (Berlin, Verlag fur Sozialwissenschaften 2013) pp. 429–41.

OECD, Minutes (Paris June 2017). Available athttps://www.oecd.org/mcm/documents/C-MIN-2017-2-EN.pdf (Accessed 21 February 2018).

https://www.google.co.uk/?client=safari&channel=ipad_bm&gws_rd=cr&dcr=0&ei=4CqPWo38IOzNgAaJmp-4Bg (Accessed 17th February 2018).

https://www.google.co.uk/?client=safari&channel=ipad_bm&gws_rd=cr&dcr=0&ei=4CqPWo38IOzNgAaJmp-4Bg (Accessed 17th February 2018).

https://www.google.co.uk/?client=safari&channel=ipad_bm&gws_rd=cr&dcr=0&ei=4CqPWo38IOzNgAaJmp-4Bg (Accessed 17 February 2018).

# Index

*f* = figure; *n* = endnote.

Acheson, Dean 157, 162*n5*
active labour market policies (ALMPs) 215, 216*f*, 226, 264
AfD (Alternative for Germany) 11, 30, 96, 138, 141
age
   and employment prospects 214, 215*f*, 222–3
   relationship with political views/voting patterns 76–7, 151–2
   of retirement 231
Alliance Party (Sweden) 68*n4*
'America First' slogan/policies 3, 32, 46
   roots 46–7
'anti-system' parties 11
Antoniades, Andreas 74
Atkinson, Anthony 124*n7*
Attlee, Clement 7, 147
austerity, programmes of 28–9, 192
   backlash 231, 248
   impact on populism 32–3
Australia
   educational levels 267
   social/living conditions 11
Austria
   domestic politics 30, 137, 140–1
   employment/poverty levels 218
   labour market policies 215
   projected taxation schemes 199, 202*n2*
'authoritarian populism' 5, 29

Bale, Tim 156
Balestrini, Pierre P. 79
Bank of England 118
Bank of International Settlements (BIS) 28

Bannon, Steve 31, 32, 38
Barnier, Michel 129
basic income strategy 196–8, 201
   advantages 196, 197–8
   funding projects 202*n2*
   limitations/risks 197
Batsaikhan, Uuriintuya 78
Baumol, William 211
Beckfield, Jason 237–8, 240, 255*n3*
Begg, Iain 124*n19*
Bekker, Sonja 200
Belgium, employment/poverty levels 218, 270
Bell, Daniel 10
Benn, Tony 37–8
Berlin Wall, fall of 3, 91
Berlusconi, Silvio 132
Bernstein, Eduard 21
Beveridge, William 95, 100, 192, 207, 208, 227, 229–30, 231, 278
Bevin, Ernest 147
bilateral trade agreements 48
Bini Smaghi, Lorenzo 74
birth rates 40
Bismarck, Otto von 198
Blair, Tony 55, 56, 154, 229, 267
   pro-European stance/policies 15, 112–13, 130, 147
   promotion of 'third way' 7, 14, 92, 174, 209
   support for Iraq War 148, 156
BNP (British National Party) 62
Bogdanor, Vernon 123*n4*
Bouguignon, François 254–5*n2*
Bretton Woods Agreement (1944) 12, 36, 43
   objectives 44

'Brexit' 1, 14–16, 45, 109–23, 127–42, 145–62, 167, 201, 249, 277
   arguments against 158–9
   demographics of support/opposition 120, 151–2
   EU responses to 128–30
   flaws in Remain campaign 153, 154–6
   hardcore support 155–6, 159
   impact on two-party system 162
   intra-party divides 110–11, 152–3
   mainland European attitudes to 30
   misinformation on both sides 153–4
   presentation of case for/against 118–19, 151, 152–4
   press support/opposition 153–4, 155
   projected date 157
   range of procedures 157–8
   reasons for support 39–40, 119–21, 151–7, 189–90
   referendum (2016) 5, 7, 14–15, 30–1, 57, 60, 109, 116–17, 119, 122, 127, 145, 173
Brown, Gordon 61–2, 67, 128, 147, 155, 229, 267
'buffers', policy functions of 223–5, 227
Busemeyer, Marius R. 255n3
Bush, George W. 148
Buti, Marco 73, 79–80

Cameron, David 57, 63, 114–17, 119, 130, 152–3, 154–5, 156–7, 162n2
Canada
   social/living conditions 11
   trade agreements 48, 49
   unemployment insurance 245
Cannadine, David 155
Cantillon, Bea 226, 255n9
Casaleggio, Davide 174
Casaleggio, Gianroberto 174
central banks, handling of financial situations 2–3, 28, 207–8
centre-left 53–68
   challenges to 55–6, 263–5
   domination of European politics 54
   economic policies 14
   history 54–7
   immigration policies 40
   loss of support 54
   national variations 20–1
   relationship with populism 12–13, 39, 40, 67–8
   relationship with social investment 229
   selection of candidates/party leaders 104
   strategic errors 19–20, 39
   voter base 39, 98, 104
   see also social democracy; names of parties
child benefit 267–9, 268f
'child gap' 225–6
childcare 215–16, 222
   see also early childhood education and care
children see child benefit; 'child gap'; childcare; education; poverty
China
   economic growth 2, 33–4, 51n2
   exports to EU 149
   participation in global economy 45, 47
Chirac, Jacques 137
Christian Democrats 137–8, 141, 230–1
Churchill, Winston 15, 110, 123n2, 156
City of London 111, 116, 147
Claeys, Grégory 80, 82, 87
class (social)
   blurring of boundaries 54–5
   relationship with political views/voting patterns 152
Clegg, Daniel 195
climate change 101
Clinton, Bill 7, 267
Clinton, Hillary 31
coalitions
   discursive 173–4
   governmental 30, 65, 137, 138, 141, 231
   reform 227–8

Cold War
  ending/aftermath 33
  security issues 36
Conservative Party (UK)
  convergence with Labour 118
  divisions over 'Brexit' 129–30, 145, 152–3, 155–7, 158, 159–60
  immigration policies 116–17
  industry policy 150
  Labour attacks on 63–4, 67
  pro-/anti-Europe factions 110–11, 114
  shift to right 114
Corbyn, Jeremy 64, 104, 114, 153, 160, 161
  'populist' image 53, 57, 67
cultural identity, divisions in 188–9
Cuperus, Rene 162*n1*
Czech Republic
  employment/poverty levels 215, 217–18
  refusal to accept refugees 135–6

Dahrendorf, Ralf 73, 75, 87*n1*
Darvas, Zsolt 78
Davis, David 129
deflation 2–3
deindustrialization 2, 7–8, 261–5
  geographic impact 261–2
  impact on voting patterns 264–5
  national variations 263*f*, 269–70
'dementia tax' 173
democracy
  deepening, need for 101
  differing forms of 57
  erosion 4–5, 9
  *see also* legitimacy; 'trilemma'(s)
Democratic Party (US) 47–8, 267
Denmark
  employment rates 214, 215, 218
  poverty levels 218
  public finances 218
  welfare system 102
Devine, Fiona 10
Di Blasio, Bill 104
*Die Linke* (Germany) 231

discursive communities *see* social media
Donnelly, Sir Martin 159
Draghi, Mario 208
dummy variables 88*nn6-7*

early childhood education and care (ECEC) 215–17, 226
'earned social citizenship', principle of 251–2
education
  and employment prospects 216–17, 216*f*
  as focus of policies 247–8, 266–7
  investment in 247–9, 264
  relationship with political views/voting patterns 77–8, 77*f*, 151–2
  *see also* early childhood education and care; higher education
elite negativity 59–60, 61, 63–4, 67
elites
  calls for limitation on power 60
  contrasted with 'the people' 59, 96–7, 278
  hostility to 30, 45–6, 58–60 (*see also* elite negativity)
  reluctance to share 277–8
Emmenegger, Patrick 195
employment 211–21, 212–217*ff*
  female 214–17, 221–2, 224, 225, 271
  national variations 213–14
  public sector 265, 271, 273
  service sector 215–16, 265, 271–2
  *see also* unemployment
energy policies 101
Erdogan, Recep Tayyip 135
Ernst and Young 80–2
Esping-Andersen, Gosta 19, 201, 221–2
ethnicity, relationship with political views/voting patterns 152
euro (currency)/eurozone 113, 116
  crisis 7, 122–3, 130–1, 138, 154–5, 157, 178, 207
  mismanagement 178

projected reforms 178–9
UK refusal to join 147
Eurobarometer 75–9, 87n4
European Central Bank (ECB) 7, 29, 167, 180, 208
European Commission 113, 115–16, 167
  economic initiatives 80, 131–2, 245
  education/training initiatives 248–9
  handling of refugee crisis 135–6
  opinion surveys 75–9
  political orientation 101
  proceedings against member states 136, 140
European Court of Auditors 86
European Employment Strategy (1997) 246
European Fund for Strategic Investments (EFSI) 80–2, 248
  allocation of funds 81t
  financing by country/sector 83f
  number of projects by country/sector 84f
European Globalization Adjustment Fund (EGF) 80, 87
European Investment Advisory Hub 80
European Investment Bank (EIB) 80
European Investment Project Portal 80
European Monetary Fund (EMF) 132–3
European Monetary Union 240, 242, 245–7
European Parliamentary elections (2014) 60
European perceptions of globalization 13, 73–9
  demographic factors 75–7
  economic factors 78–9, 78f
  educational factors 77–8, 77f
  gender/age factors 76–7
  national variations 77
  relationship with domestic economy 78–9
  studies 73–5
European Semester 178–9, 199–200, 248

European Social Model 131–2
European Social Survey 259
'European Social Union' 20, 242, 252–3, 254
European Stability Mechanism (ESM) 132–3
European Union 73–87
  citizens' perceptions of 79–80, 86–7
  common agricultural policy 149
  common defence/security policy 147–8, 181
  common foreign policy 147–8
  discontent with 7, 86–7, 154, 155–6, 159, 168–73; political sources 171–3; politico-economic sources 169; socio-economic sources 170–1
  economic crises 7, 121–2, 127–8, 130–3, 167
  economic differences 13–14
  economic initiatives 79–86, 81t, 83–4ff, 85t
  economic integration, principle of 238–9
  enlargement 112–13, 141, 147
  EU-Turkey Refugee Deal 133–4
  founding principles 39, 238–9
  future prospects 141–2, 279–80
  governmental structure 35–6
  immigration policies/figures 39
  import/export balance 149
  inequality between member states 7, 178
  inequality within/across member states 7, 217–18, 235, 237–8, 239–42
  internal divisions 13–14, 15–16, 200–1
  legitimacy, questioning of 7, 167, 172–3
  mismanagement of globalization 148–50
  monetary union 112, 147
  need for reform 101, 199–202
  optimistic vs. pessimistic assessments 240–2

populist opposition to  30, 167–8, 172
poverty levels/risks  242–5
re-envisioning  180–1
refugee crisis  121–2, 127–8, 133–6, 167
regained popularity  140–1
social policy governance  199–200, 238–9
trade agreements/relationships  48, 49
UBS approach, proposed  279–80
undemocratic institutions  7, 167, 172
voters' disillusion with  154, 172
Youth Guarantee  80, 82–6, 85*t*
*see also* 'Brexit'; European perceptions of globalization; UK relationship with EU
Exchange Rate Mechanism  112
exchange rates  36

Facebook  173–4
fairness principle  229–30
Farage, Nigel  53, 56, 57, 113–14, 121, 151, 152–3, 174
Fernandes, Sofia  248
Ferrera, Maurizio  241
Finland
  economic crisis/reforms  102
  employment/poverty levels  218
  income inequality  217
  labour market policies  215
  public finances  218
Five Star Movement (Italy)  11, 30, 96, 132, 150
'flexicurity'  102, 246
'flows', labour market  223–5, 227
  measures to improve  224–5
France
  derogations from rules  179
  election results  188
  employment rates  210, 214, 215, 218, 274*n*2
  issues with 'Brexit'  129
  issues with Turkish accession  135

(perceived) domination of EU  111
populist movements  57, 96, 113–14, 137, 140, 174
poverty levels  218
projected taxation schemes  199, 202*n*2
public finances  218–19
referendum on EU  119
La France Insoumise (political party)  96
free movement (of goods/people), principle of  16, 39, 112–13, 147, 249–53
  justification  250
  pitfalls  250–1
  restrictions on  251–2
freedom of action, principle of  229–30
Freedom Party (FPÖ, Austria)  137
Friedman, Milton  36, 176
Front National (France)  30, 137, 188
Fukuyama, Francis  10

Gallie, Duncan  191, 195
Gardner, Anthony  125*n*22
Garton Ash, Timothy  123*n*5
gender
  and employment prospects  214–17, 214*f*, 221–2, 224, 225
  relationship with political views/voting patterns  76–7
general elections (UK)
  2010  62, 151
  2015  62–3, 115, 152
  2017  63–4, 162, 173
  future, potential date/issues  157–8
Germany
  election results  188
  employment rates  210, 213, 214, 218
  labour market policies  215
  (perceived) domination of EU  111
  populist movements  11, 30, 96, 137–8, 141, 231
  public finances  219
  social policies/reforms  21, 227, 245
  *see also* AfD; Christian Democrats; Social Democrats

Germany
  income inequality  217
Gibraltar  129
Giddens, Anthony  174
Gidron, Noam  189, 191
Gini coefficient  217
global economy  43–51
  expansion  2, 44–5
  future prospects  3–4, 28–9, 39, 43–4, 49–51
  history  44–5
  integration  8, 11, 33–4
  moves towards integration  44–5
  non-US based  48–9
  (projected) recovery  28
  (projected) reforms  43
  relationship with national sovereignty/democratic legitimacy  35–6 (*see also* 'trilemma')
  relationship with trends in US  48–50
  *see also* global financial crisis (2008)
global financial crisis (2008)  3, 5–6, 13, 27, 45, 93, 150
  aftermath  45, 93–5, 97, 160, 196, 201, 207, 208–9, 261, 278
global governance, instability of  3–4
globalization  1
  backlash against  45–6
  diminishing legitimacy  6
  future challenges  280–1
  'globalization euphoria'  45
  'great disruption'  1–2
  'knowledge-driven'  5, 12
  'managed'  13
  policy package  36–7
  (problems of) definition  2
  relationship with 'Brexit'  151–7, 162
  relationship with populism  27, 32–40
  rise of  10, 33–4, 146
  'winners' *vs.* 'losers'  18–19, 34–5, 94, 118, 151, 187–8, 200–1, 278
  *see also* European perceptions of globalization; global economy; 'trilemma'(s)

Goebbels, Josef  153–4
Goedemé, Tim  255*n*5
Goodhart, David  189
Gove, Michael  152–3, 155, 174
Gramsci, Antonio  99
Great Depression (1930s)  207–8
Great Recession *see* global financial crisis: aftermath
Great Stagflation (1970s)  207–8
Greece
  differences with EU  149
  domestic politics  14, 30, 96, 137, 150
  economic situation  82, 132, 180, 207
  refugees entering EU via  133, 134, 135
Greece
  income inequality  217
  labour market policies  215
  public finances  218–19
Grenfell Tower fire  173
Grillo, Beppe  132, 174
gross value added (GVA), regional variation  262–3, 263f
Gulf states, immigration policies  249
Guterres, Antonio  209

Hacker, Jacob  280
Hague, William  156
Haider, Jörg  137
Hall, Peter A.  189, 191
Hamon, Benoit  202*n*2
Hayek, F.A.  176
Heath, Edward  112
Hegel, Friedrich  177
higher education
  basic student income  198
  employment prospects  217, 261
  levels of participation  193, 266–7
  national variations  274*n*4
  private investment in  193–4
  and socio-cultural divides  189
  state investment in  266–7
Hitler, Adolf  32
Hobhouse, Leonard  21
Hopkin, Jonathan  189, 192

human capital
  investment in 247–9
  'stocks'/'flows'/'buffers' 227
Hungary
  nationalist politics 138–9, 147, 207
  refusal to accept refugees 135–6, 139–40, 147
  support for Poland 140

immigration 39–40, 58, 150, 170, 249–53
  centrality to 'Brexit' debates 113, 116–18, 147, 151, 154, 249
  misrepresentation of statistics 118
  *see also* free movement; refugees
India, economic growth 33–4
Individual Activity Accounts (IAAs) 198
inequality 3, 6, 20, 39, 94, 190, 235–54, 277
  generational 99
  moves to counter 101, 195–6
  national variations 217–18, 235–7
  and policy influence 274*n*3
  role of globalization 34–5, 46, 86, 235–6
  studies 124*n*7
  in UK 114
  *World Inequality Report 2018* 236–7, 240, 242, 247
Information and Communication Technology (ICT) 9
  and employment 214
  (proposals for) taxation 199, 202*n*2
instability 2–3
international economy *see* global economy
International Monetary Fund (IMF) 6, 28, 36, 58, 118, 132, 152, 259
  adjustment programmes 76–7, 82, 88*n*7
Iraq War (2003– ) 147–8, 156
Ireland
  educational levels 267
Ireland, border concerns 129
Islamophobia 137, 150, 154 (*see also* 'Muslim invasion')

Italy
  derogations from rules 179
  differences with EU 149
  domestic politics 14, 30, 96, 132, 277
  economic situation 132, 180, 207
  employment rates 132, 210, 214
  industrial decline 149
  labour market policies 215
  public finances 218–19
  refugees entering EU via 133, 134, 135
Iversen, Torben 210–11, 265, 271

Jacoby, Wade 74
Jennings, Will 13
Jobbik (political party, Hungary) 139
Johnson, Alan 153
Johnson, Boris 129, 152–3, 155, 174
Juncker, Jean-Claude 53, 86, 113
  investment plan 80–2, 87, 180, 248

Kennedy, John F. 174
Keune, Maarten 195
Keynes, John Maynard 8, 17, 21, 95, 100, 176–7, 192, 207, 208, 227, 230, 231, 278
Khan, Sadiq 104
King, Stephen D. 2
Kitschelt, Herbert 264
Klosse, Saskia 200
'knowledge economy' 150, 224–5
Kok, Wim 209, 229
Kołakowski, Leszek 22
Kramer, Dion 251–2
Kuhn, Thomas 177

labour market(s)
  active labour market policies (ALMPs) 215, 216*f*, 226, 264
  and higher education 193
  Individual Activity Accounts (IAAs) 198
  insider/outsider divisions 194–5, 210
  protection systems 195–6, 198–9
  structural changes 242, 260, 261–5
  urban focus 261–2

Labour Party (Netherlands) 231
Labour Party (UK) 60–4
  compared with Swedish SDP 57, 66–7
  divisions over 'Brexit' 110–11, 152, 155–6, 160–2
  education policies 266–7
  immigration policies 112–13
  (perceived) convergence with Conservatives 118, 269 (*see also* Blair)
  policies on 'Brexit' 129–30
  populist rhetoric 13, 54, 61–4, 66–7
  postwar government (1945–51) 146, 147
  pro-European segment 110, 161
  social policies 150–1, 202n1, 266–7
Laclau, Ernesto 99
Laffer, Arthur 36
Law and Justice (PiS) party (Poland) 139
Le Pen, Jean-Marie 137
Le Pen, Marine 57, 96, 113–14, 137, 140, 174
Leandro, Alvaro 82
Lefebvre, Mathieu 255n5
'left behind' social groupings 151, 152, 168, 189–90, 200–1
left wing
  attacks on social democracy 231
  impact of deindustrialization 263–4
  loss of traditional support 264–5
  *see also* centre left; social democracy; *names of parties*
legitimacy
  democratic, and 'trilemma' 35–6
  of EU 167, 172–3
  of globalization 6, 17
  sources 37, 38
Lehman Brothers 93
Liberal Democrats (UK) 110
liberalism (economic) 14–15, 17–18, 36–7
liberalism (social) 10–11, 18, 170–1
Liddle, Roger 123n3, 124n6
Löfven, Stefan 66, 104

Lucke, Bernd 138
Luxembourg, active labour market policies 215

'Machine Tax' 202n2
Macron, Emmanuel 15, 57, 98, 128, 129, 132, 137, 140, 174, 175, 176
Major, John 156
Manow, Philip 270–1
manufacturing industries, job losses 262, 262f
Martinsen, D. Sindbjerg 255n6
Marx, Karl 177
Marx, Paul 195
'Matthew Effect' 209, 226
May, Theresa 129, 157–8, 160, 177
  calling of 2017 election 63, 173
McGrew, Anthony 2
Mead, Margaret 1
Meade, James 100
Mélenchon, Jean-Luc 96
MERCOSUR (Southern Common Market) 48
Merkel, Angela 136, 138, 208, 211, 227
Meunier, Sophie 74
Milanovic, Branko 190, 235, 237, 247, 249–50, 253, 254–5n2, 256n13
Miliband, Ed 62–3, 67, 162n2
minimum wages 244–5, 251
Mont Pélerin Society 176
Moore, Henrietta 279
Mudde, Cas 12–13, 278
Murdoch, Rupert 63
'Muslim invasion,' fears of 136, 139, 147, 151

national insurance 245–6
neoliberalism 3–4, 13–14, 91, 173, 178, 267
  attacks on 174
  excesses/failure 18, 172
Netherlands
  election results 188, 231
  employment rates 213, 214, 218
  labour market policies 215

poverty levels  218
public finances  218
referendum on EU  119
Nolan, Brian  226
non-governmental organizations (NGOs)
  humanitarian  134
  increase in numbers  37
Nordic countries
  employment rates  213
  responses to deindustrialization  271–2, 273
  welfare systems  102–4
  *see also names of countries*
North Atlantic Treaty Organization (NATO)  12, 31, 37, 133–4
Norway
  national elections  259
  relationship with EU, as post-Brexit model  158, 160
  welfare system  103
Nussbaum, Martha  230

Obama, Barack  118, 131, 146, 176, 273
Occupy Movement  173
Ohlin, Bertil  239–40
Okun, Arthur  209–10, 211
Orban, Viktor  139, 140
Organization for Economic Cooperation and Development (OECD)  6, 224, 248, 259, 279
  employment levels, by country  213
  *In It Together* (inequality report, 2015)  218
  *Jobs Study* (1994)  210, 211, 218
Osborne, George  153, 154–5, 156

Paris Agreement on Climate Change  31
PASOK (Panhellenic Socialist Alliance, Greece)  95
pensions, national systems  103, 267–9, 268f
'the people'  58–60
  (alleged) homogeneity  59
  (alleged) virtues  59
  claims to represent  59
  contrasted with elites  59–60
People's Party (Denmark)  11
Pestieau, Pierre  255n5
Pichelmann, Karl  73, 79–80
Piketty, Thomas  94, 174, 190, 193
Pillar of Social Rights  131–2, 141, 200, 251
Podemus (political party, Spain)  55, 96, 150
Poland
  concerns over 'Brexit'  129
  employment rates  215, 243
  government interference with judiciary  140
  nationalist politics  139–40, 147, 207
  refusal to accept refugees  135–6, 139–40, 147
Polanyi, Karl  91, 177
populism  11–14, 27–40, 53–68
  across EU  136–40, 172
  arguments against  278
  'backlash'  11–12, 53–4
  dangers of  57
  defining characteristics  58–60
  electoral successes  30, 32, 174, 188
  immigration and  39–40, 170
  impact on mainstream parties  12–13, 56–7, 105
  'openness-nationalism axis'  97
  predicted decline  136, 141
  problems of definition  29, 59, 67
  reasons for rise  14, 27, 39–40, 54, 55–6, 96, 130, 150, 168, 231, 278
  relationship with globalization *see under* globalization
  right *vs.* left competition  55–6
  right-wing  11, 30, 45, 55–6, 58, 96, 113–14, 138, 150, 178, 189, 231
  role in UK politics  13, 60
  'up-down axis'  96–7
  'zeitgeist'  53
  *see also* 'authoritarian populism'; *names of parties*

Portugal
　industrial decline  149
　public finances  218–19
　'post-truth' environment  167–8
　posting  250–1
　poverty
　　child  215, 218, 219*f*
　　determinants  242–3
　　relative levels  217–20
　　rise in  196, 242–4
　predistribution  100–1, 280
　progressive thought
　　challenges to  175, 182
　　distinguished from populism  174–5, 178–9
　　future possibilities  178–82
　　potential for EU  180–1
　　potential for eurozone  179–80
　　(problems of) implementation  175–8
　　sources of  173–4
　PSOE (Partido Socialista Obrero Español/Spanish Socialist Workers' Party)  95
　public finances, national comparison  218–19, 219*f*
　public sector, employment in  265, 271, 273
　Putin, Vladimir  146

'quantitative easing'  2–3, 11

Rasmussen, Poul Nyrup  209
Rawls, John  22, 221, 229–30
redistribution policies  100–1, 278–9
　public support levels  259, 260*f*, 269
refugees
　flow into EU  122, 133–6, 167
　living conditions  134
　refusal to accept  135–6, 139–40
Renzi, Matteo  5, 277
Republican Party (US)
　internal dissensions  45–6
　(lack of) response to 2016 election  47–8
　(projected)  45–6

Rodrik, Dani  4, 7, 27, 35, 37–8, 124*n13*, 188, 241, 255*n7*
Rome, Treaty of (1957)  238
Romney, Mitt  45
Roosevelt, Franklin D.  7, 18, 174, 176
Roosevelt, Theodore  174
Rueda, David  270
Ruggie, John G.  51*n1*

Sabel, Charles  209, 255*n8*
Salmond, Alex  162*n2*
Sánchez, Pedro  104
Sandel, Michael  22
Sanders, Bernie  46, 53
Sapir, André  80, 87
Sarkozy, Nicolas  135
Savage, Mike  10
Scharpf, Fritz  240, 245, 255*n6*
Schelkle, Waltraud  245, 256*n10*
Schmid, Guenther  223
Schroeder, Gerhard  14, 92, 209, 229, 270
Schulz, Martin  53
Schuman Plan (1950)  146, 147
Schwander, Hanna  270–1
Scotland
　independence movement  114, 162*n2*
　independence referendum (2014)  152
Scottish National Party (SNP)  162*n2*
Sen, Amartya  22, 230, 280
service sector, employment in  215–16, 265, 271–2
Slovenia, employment/poverty rates  217–18
social contract  8–9
social democracy  91–105, 259–74, 278
　attitudes to globalization  94
　electoral decline  95–7, 188, 201, 228–9, 231, 259
　emergence/precepts  91, 105
　failings  94–5
　impact of deindustrialization  263–5
　internal structures  104
　new agenda/future directions  99–102, 105, 196–200

in Nordic countries 271–2
present/future challenges 97–9, 105, 201–2, 231–2, 265, 266
promotion of social investment 228–9
responses to deindustrialization 269–71
shift in focus 55, 91–2, 94
*see also* Social Democratic Party (Germany); Social Democratic Party (Sweden)
Social Democratic Party (Sweden) 13, 60–1, 64–7
compared with UK Labour Party 54, 57, 66–7
populist rhetoric 54
Social Democrats (Netherlands) 231
Social Democrats (SPD, Germany) 137–8, 141, 155–6
electoral decline 95, 259
social policies 270–1
Social Democrats (SPÖ, Austria) 137
social investment 19–20, 191–6, 221–32
arguments for retention 232
continuing popularity 192
criticisms 226
evolution of concept 226–7
and higher education 193–4
and labour market 194–6
limitations 191–2, 193, 279–80
objectives 192
policy functions 227 (*see also* 'buffers'; 'flows'; 'stocks')
preferred strategy 232
'returns' on 222–3
'turn' towards (in Europe) 228–9
*see also* human capital
social media 173–4
social protection *see* labour market; welfare states
Socialist Party (Denmark) 259
Soros, George 112
South America, trade agreements (internal/external) 49
*see also* MERCOSUR

South Korea 45
sovereignty, national
problems of implementation 159
relationship with economic interdependence/democracy 35–6 (*see also* 'trilemma')
sovereignty, popular 59–60
Soviet Union, collapse/division of 33, 45, 146
Spain
concerns over 'Brexit' 129
domestic politics 14, 30, 96, 137, 150
economic situation 82, 179, 207
income inequality 217
labour market policies 215
public finances 218–19
'squeezed middle' 189–90
Starke, Peter 195
'stocks' (of human capital) 223–5, 227
ring-fencing 224
Stoker, Gerry 13
Streeck, Wolfgang 93
sustainability 101
Sweden
economic crisis/reforms 102
electoral system 54, 57
employment rates 213, 214, 215, 218, 270
general elections 64–6
income inequality 217
labour market policies 215
party conferences 68n3
public finances 218
welfare system/social policies 103, 194, 213
*see also* Alliance Party; Social Democratic Party
Syria
civil war 133, 135
refugees from 134
Syriza (political party, Greece) 96, 150

Taiwan 45
taxation 98, 279
ICT (proposed) 199, 202n2

Taylor-Gooby, Peter  202
Tea Party movement  45, 274
Thatcher, Margaret  112, 146, 150, 156, 173, 176, 238, 266
Thelen, Kathleen  271–2
'third way'  7, 14, 92, 209, 228–9, 267, 270–1
   problems of  92
Tober, Tobias  255*n3*
trades unions, membership levels  271–2
transnational institutions, relationship with national democracies  37
TransPacific Partnership (TPP)  31, 49–50
'trilemma'(s)  7–8, 35–9, 124*n13*, 232, 241, 254
   difficulty of resolution  37–8
   'Left Trilemma'  202
   'of the social service economy'  210–11, 265
Trump, Donald  1, 3, 5, 53, 123, 130, 167
   anti-internationalist stance  31–2, 43, 46, 49–50, 141, 146
   economic policies/rhetoric  12, 28, 46, 174
   election to Presidency  8, 11, 12, 31, 43, 46, 110, 120, 122, 259, 277; reasons for  40, 47
   relationship with EU  121
   support base  40, 190
Turkey  133–6
   debates on accession to EU  118, 134–5
   refugees from/passing through  133–4
   UKIP focus on  151

UK relationship with EU  14–15, 109–23, 181
   exceptional nature  121, 123
   lack of warmth  110–11
   levels of influence  111
   long-term mistrust  155–6, 159
   loss of confidence  154
   peripheral nature  110–11, 116–17, 119
   prospects post-'Brexit'  157–61, 162*nn6–7*
   renegotiation, calls/plans for  114–17, 154–5
   'special case' status, objections to  158
   strategic errors  148
   variations between member states  129
UKIP (UK Independence Party)  13, 30–1, 113–14, 156
   2015 election predictions/performance  30, 62, 66–7
   electoral successes  60, 62
   influence on UK politics  57
   populist rhetoric  151
unemployment  208, 210
   increases in  44, 131, 262, 264, 270
   insurance  210, 229, 245–6
   temporary  198–9
   youth  18, 82–6, 132
   *see also* employment
United Kingdom
   deindustrialization  150
   educational levels  266–7
   electoral system  54, 57, 67, 162
   employment rates  213, 214, 261–3, 274*n2*
   immigration policies/figures  39
   income inequality  114, 217
   national debt  29
   social/cultural divisions  114, 188–91
   social reforms  21, 150–1
   *see also* UK relationship with EU; *names of political parties*
United Nations  101
United States
   anti-globalization backlash  45–6, 48
   educational levels  267
   employment rates  210, 213–14, 215–16, 218
   global hegemony  3, 38, 43; withdrawal from  32, 43
   higher education  194
   income inequality  34, 46, 217, 218, 220, 236–7

industrial regions 46–7
national debt 28, 29
potential political developments 47–8, 50
poverty levels 218, 220
social reforms 21, 267, 269
trade deficit 28
trends on public opinion 46
welfare system/policies 220, 227–8, 246, 267
*see also names of parties/leaders especially* Trump, Donald
Universal Basic Services (UBS) strategy 279–80

Valero, Anna 263
van Reenan, John 263
Van Rompuy, Herman 114
Vietnam 45

Wallace, Helen 73–4, 123*n1*
Wallerstein, Immanuel 33, 35, 190
welfare states 18–19, 195–6, 209–10, 221–6
 calls for reform 19, 221–2
 comparative spending levels 214–15, 219–20
 correlation with competitiveness 211, 212*f*
 emergence 21–2, 91
 erosion 242–5

modernization 102–4, 105
national variations 169, 253
Nordic 102–4
support at EU level 242
UK system 266–9
unification 252–3, 254
*see also* social investment
Wilders, Geert 174
Williams, Joan C. 190
Wilson, Harold 115
Wolf, Martin 2, 17, 38
women *see* employment; gender
World Bank 36
*World Inequality Report 2018* 236–7, 240, 242, 247
World Trade Organization (WTO) 2, 31, 49–50, 255*n8*
World War Two, aftermath 21–2, 44
Wren, Anne 210–11, 265, 271

Xi Jinping 146

'Y Combinator' 197
Young, Hugo 123*n3*
young people 82–6
 voting patterns 98–9
 *see also* unemployment; Youth Guarantee
Youth Guarantee (EU) 80, 82–6, 85*t*

Zapatero, Jose Luis 209